Linguistics and Literature

Blackwell Textbooks in Linguistics

Linguistics and Literature
Language in the Verbal Arts of the World

Nigel Fabb

BLACKWELL
Publishers

First published 1997
2 4 6 8 10 9 7 5 3 1

Blackwell Publishers Ltd
108 Cowley Road
Oxford OX4 1JF
UK

Blackwell Publishers Inc.
350 Main Street
Malden, Massachusetts 02148
USA

British Library Cataloguing in Publication Data

A CIP catalogue record for this book is available from the
British Library.

Library of Congress Cataloging-in-Publication Data

Fabb, Nigel.
    Linguistics and literature / Nigel Fabb.
        p.   cm. — (Blackwell textbooks in linguistics; 12)
    Includes bibliographical references (p.   ) and index.
        ISBN 0–631–19242–5 (hc: alk. paper).—ISBN 0–631–19243–3 (pbk.:
alk. paper)
        1. Philology. I. Title. II. Series.
    P121.F25   1997
    410—dc21   97–9054
                                                                CIP

This book is printed on acid-free paper

For my parents
Alan and Margaret Fabb

Contents

Acknowledgements

This book could not have been written without the help of others. I am particularly grateful to the following people for their advice, for reading part or all of the manuscript, and for giving permissions to use material which they recorded from the original authors: Daniel Abondolo, Kristján Árnason, Richard Bauman, Marie Berg, Mairi Blackings, Victoria R. Bricker, Jill Brody, Deborah Cameron, Susan Clack, Bernard Comrie, Ellen L. Contini-Morava, Peter Cooke, Susanna Cumming, Gordon Dangerfield, Chaumont Devin, R. M. W. Dixon, Janet Fabb, Margaret Fabb, Jacek Fabisjak, Joe Farrell, Gregory Forth, James Fox, Donald Fraser, Judit Friedrich, Ives Goddard, Chris Golston, Ken Hale, Morris Halle, Kristin Hanson, Beatrice Hartzband, Bruce Hayes, Susan Herring, Astrid Holtman, Dell Hymes, Virginia Hymes, Sam Kasule, Susan Kiguli, Alex King, Abasi Kiyimba, William Labov, Anne Lorne Gillies, Barbara Macmahon, Aonghas Macneacail, Joseph Malone, Shakila Manam, Stephanie Marriott, Richard Moyle, Gordana Nesterovic, Martin Orwin, Sheena Phillips, Sudha Rai, Charles Randriamasimanana, Helen Reid-Thomas, Alan J. K. Sanders, Ronald P. Schaefer, Russell G. Schuh, Peter Sells, Mahmood Shamsher, John D. Smith, Andrew Spencer, Alan Thomas, Bertil Tikkanen, Maura Velázquez-Castillo, Zoe Wicomb, Anthony Woodbury, Moira Yip.

It has not been possible, for the most part, to consult the original authors of most of the verbal art quoted in this book. I hope to have their permission to use these materials, and regret any inappropriate recontextualization or discussion.

I am also grateful to the following for granting permission to reproduce copyright material: Cambridge University Press, Mouton de Gruyter, Oxford University Press, *Pacific Linguistics* (Australian National University), Routledge, and the School of Oriental and African Studies, London.

The Department of English Studies and Programme in Literary Linguistics at the University of Strathclyde gave me a semester's leave to enable me to begin writing this book; thanks to my colleagues who covered for me.

At Blackwell, Philip Carpenter first suggested I write this book, and Steve Smith encouraged me through to its completion; thanks to them, and to Margaret Aherne for her careful reading of the manuscript.

A Note on Texts

Texts have been drawn from a variety of sources, most having been published before. On the whole, I have copied the transcription and translation of the text unchanged. However, in some cases I have chosen to add or alter translations and word-for-word glosses, and to retranscribe certain texts (e.g. for the Greek texts, from Greek into Roman script). I am grateful to the native speakers and specialists who did most of this for me, and apologize for any of my errors which may have crept in. There is no attempt at overall consistency between different texts, either in how texts are translated, or in transcription systems. The meanings of symbols in transcription can usually be found by consulting the original sources; Pullum and Ladusaw (1986) covers many of the variations.

Special symbols used in metrical transcriptions

The representations of metrical structure in chapters 2–5 use a consistent system of symbols wherever possible.

:	colon (a word boundary falls here)
=	bridge (there must not be a word boundary here)
ˉ	macron (symbolizes a heavy syllable)
˘	breve (symbolizes a light syllable)
( )	a bracketed constituent is optional
X	anceps position (e.g. matches a syllable of any weight, or a mora etc.)
S, s	strong position in a metrical template
W, w	weak position in a metrical template
σ	syllable
σ̆	stressed syllable
•	musical pulse
φ	phonological foot

μ   mora
F   metrical foot
M   metron
| constituent boundary (used both for metrical constituents and musical
         constituents; in the latter case it corresponds to a bar line)

1 Literary Linguistics and Verbal Art

This book looks at how language is used in the written and oral literatures of the world, and hence engages in what we might call literary linguistics. The central hypothesis of the book is that it is possible to generalize about the use of language in literature. This is a development of the claim central to many linguistic theories that it is possible to generalize across languages to produce a unified account of linguistic form. Following the same trajectory, this book seeks to generalize across languages to produce a unified account of how linguistic form is exploited in the many different kinds of literature found in human cultures. Thus a discussion of parallelism in a poem by John Dryden, a seventeenth-century English poet, can be put next to a discussion of parallelism in a ritual song by Simni, a chief of the Asmat of New Guinea, and there are things to be learned from the comparison.

The first chapter introduces some of the basic notions and puts the study of language and literature into its broader context. Chapters 2–4 look at how metrical texts are built from the sound-structure of language, and chapter 5 looks at how individual sounds are organized into patterns of rhyme and alliteration. Chapter 6 examines how the underlying similarities between utterances in their syntactic and lexical structures are exploited to build the parallel structures which are characteristic of many of the world's literatures. Chapters 7 and 8 focus on narratives, looking specifically at those aspects of narrative form which depend on linguistic form. Chapter 9 looks at the verbal performance of literature to an audience. Chapter 10 takes communication – one of the basic functions of language – and looks at how it is adapted to the functions of literature. Chapter 11 summarizes the book and speculates on some future directions for literary linguistics.

1.1   Linguistic form and literary form

Verbal behaviour is the production of texts, products which have verbal form in the media of writing or speech. Some of those texts are verbal art, also called 'literature': they are literary texts. Literary texts have linguistic form because they are texts (the product of verbal behaviour), and they also have literary form. This book looks at those aspects of literary form which are an adaptation of linguistic form to literary purposes.

Consider for example the following fragment of a literary text by Shakespeare. It has both linguistic form and literary form, and certain aspects of the literary form are adaptations of the linguistic form.

> *So long as men can breathe and eyes can see,*
> *So long lives this, and this gives life to thee.*

Among this text's elements of linguistic form are the words which it uses, and the ways in which those words are combined into the complex linguistic structures called 'sentences'. These elements of linguistic form are not specific to literature. In contrast, it also has specifically literary form, which includes the organization of the words into constituents called 'lines' and the matching of sounds to create a rhyme between the final parts of each line. Both of these elements of literary form are adaptations of elements of the linguistic form of the text. Thus the division of the text into lines depends on the organization of the text into distinct words, which is an aspect of linguistic form: the literary line-division coincides with the linguistic word-division. And the possibility of rhyme depends on the linguistic formal organization of sounds into syllables: rhyme always involves a specified sub-part of a syllable and must therefore be defined in terms of aspects of linguistic form. The division of a text into lines and the creation of rhyme are both characteristic of literary texts, and are not found in all kinds of verbal text: this is why we classify them as specifically literary form and not linguistic form more generally. However, though these are specifically literary form they depend on linguistic form for their existence: they are adaptations of linguistic form to literary form. I will use the term 'literary linguistics' to describe the sub-kind of linguistics which is the study of the adaptation of linguistic form to literary form.

Not all kinds of literary form exploit linguistic form. For example, as Vladimir Propp (1968) and others have shown, some genres of verbal narrative are built from constituent units each of which is a type of event and in terms of which types of character are defined; event-type and character-type are kinds of literary form which do not exploit linguistic form. This can be seen for example in the fact that, as narrative form more generally, event-type and character-type can be used in a non-linguistic medium, such as a silent film. Similarly, not all kinds of linguistic form are the basis of literary form: no tradition has yet been described in which the complex systems by which noun phrases co-refer within a clause are systematically exploited to create a kind of literary form. One of the interesting questions for literary linguistics is which kinds of linguistic form can be adapted to which kinds of literary form, and why.

1.1.1 Linguistics and the study of form

In the twentieth century, linguistics has been prominent in the study of form, partly because linguistic form is particularly rich and complex. The prominence of linguistics has enabled it to have a significant influence on the development of other disciplines which study form in areas other than language: anthropology, psychoanalysis, sociology, musicology, film theory and literary study, for example. This influence has come about for basically two reasons. First, one of the most influential early works on linguistics, Ferdinand de Saussure's *Course in General Linguistics* (1913), suggested that the methods of linguistics might be extended to all communicative systems whether or not they use language, to become the basis of a general semiotics. Second, contact between two Europeans who met in New York in the 1940s, the linguist Roman Jakobson and the anthropologist Claude Lévi-Strauss, left the latter convinced that phonology (the study of linguistic sounds) could provide a methodological basis for all the human sciences, and thus laid the path towards the French structuralism of the 1950s and 1960s, in which linguistics inspired a range of disciplines.

The influence of linguistics on other disciplines, including the study of literature, has been fruitful, but has also had the effect of de-emphasizing the specificity of linguistics and the distinctive status of linguistic form. Thus it has become common to describe various kinds of non-linguistic form by using the terminology of linguistics: writers refer to 'the syntax of film' or 'the language of clothing', for example. And literary form is sometimes analysed as though it was like linguistic form: thus narratives are sometimes seen as analogous to sentences. These kinds of approach see 'form' as something very general which exists similarly in many different media. In opposition to these tendencies, most kinds of modern linguistics emphasize the distinctive characteristics of language, and the fact that when linguistic form is brought into proper focus, it does not resemble any other kind of form. This has been a fundamental principle of generative linguistics from its inception with Noam Chomsky's *Syntactic Structures* (1957). It has also been the basis for a claim about the human mind: if linguistic form is different from any other kind of form then the human child's ability to acquire a language so rapidly and efficiently (and therefore learn how to speak and understand a language) might be based on some propensity towards the learning of specifically linguistic form. Thus it is possible that linguistic form emerges from mental structures which are specialized for language, and with which humans are born. This has a further implication for literary linguistics. If linguistic form depends on specific mental structures, and certain aspects of linguistic form are adapted to literary use in ways which conform to general principles across languages, then it is possible that by studying the adaptation of linguistic form in literary form we can therefore study the mind. Literary scholars have sometimes been content to borrow the terminology of linguistics while being resistant to the psychological implications of linguistic theory; both tendencies can be traced to the same underestimation of the distinctiveness of linguistic form.

1.1.2   Linguistic form

As an illustration of some of the special characteristics of linguistic form, consider the sequence of sounds [n] and [s]. This sequence is found at the end of the word 'pence' (and 'hence', and 'dense' etc.). We can represent the sound of the word 'pence', using symbols for each of the four sounds in the word, as [p ɛ n s]. While there are plenty of English words which end with the sequence [n s], there are none which begin with it. Thus there is no word [n s ɛ p] ('nsep') in English, and never will be: it is not a possible word in the English language (though it might be possible in other languages). In order to explain why this word is not possible in English, we must appeal to an aspect of the linguistic form of this word which involves more than just the linear order of sounds. Instead we must recognize that the sounds are grouped together into a higher-level unit called the syllable. A syllable has a certain typical internal structure: it begins with a part called the onset, then has a nucleus, and then ends with a part called the coda. These would be the syllable structures of the two words discussed:

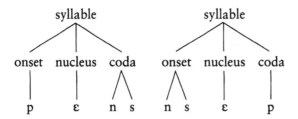

The reason that [nsɛp] is not a word is that it contains a syllable which contains an onset which comprises the sequence [ns], which is not a permitted onset in English. This is the generalization, the basic principle, which is violated by the word [nsɛp] – a prohibition on the organization of sounds within the syllable rather than a prohibition on the sequence of sounds as such. The organization of sounds into structured syllables, and prohibitions on possible sequences within the parts of the syllable, is a kind of form which is specific to language, and which in fact is found in all human languages. Syllables are themselves grouped into higher-level units of sound-structure including phonological words and phonological phrases. The name for this collection of layers of constituents of sound is 'prosodic phonological structure', which is potentially the basis of a kind of literary form called metrical form.

Remaining with the word [p ε n s] 'pence', we can now see another aspect of linguistic form when we compare it with the word 'pens', the plural form of the word 'pen'. This word is a sequence of sounds [p ε n z], and thus differs from 'pence' by having a voiced sound [z] at the end instead of the voiceless sound [s]. (Voiced and voiceless sounds differ in whether the vocal cords are tight or slack respectively.) The word 'pens' ends with the plural suffix -s, and sometimes this plural suffix is in fact pronounced as voiceless [s]: it is pronounced like this in 'pets' [p ε t s] for example. So why isn't the word 'pens' pronounced as [p ε n s] with the same voiceless form of the suffix? The answer is that the sound which makes up the suffix assimilates in part of its internal structure to the sound [n], becoming a voiced sound because [n] is a voiced sound. In contrast, in 'pets', the same suffix assimilates to the sound [t] and becomes a voiceless sound because [t] is a voiceless sound. Thus the identities of sounds can depend on the identities of other sounds, and can be changed: this is the basis of another of the kinds of phonological form, which involves the structure of individual sounds and alterations in structure. Issues regarding the identity of a sound and its internal composition arise in some cases of systematic variation in meter and sound-patterning, as we will see; thus again an aspect of linguistic form is adapted for use in literary form.

Note next that the assimilation of the final sound to the preceding [n], to make it into [z], happens in 'pens' but not in 'pence'. This is because of the presence of another kind of linguistic form and the organization of sounds into higher-level units, not syllables this time but morphemes. A morpheme is a re-combinable component (such as a suffix) of a word, and the process which assimilates the two sounds is sensitive to the fact that the 's' in 'pens' has a specific morphological identity as the plural affix, and thus undergoes the assimilation process which does not apply to the identical sound with a different morphological structure in 'pence'.

Here we have seen illustrations of three of the most fundamental aspects of linguistic form. First, linguistic form is typified by constituent structure: units are grouped together into larger units, which are themselves grouped together into larger units. The organization of sounds into syllables or into morphemes is an example of this. Second, there can be several simultaneous and different organizations of the same units into distinct kinds of constituents: in both 'pens' and 'pence' the sequence of four sounds is part of a single syllable, but in the former word and not the latter the four sounds are grouped into two morphemes. Third, the identity of a linguistic unit is best understood as a series of identities spread out over levels of representation: the final [z] sound in 'pens' and the final [s] sound in 'pets' differ at the level of speech but at some other level they must be the same because they are the same plural morpheme, with the differences arising from what happens to that plural morpheme when it is attached to a word. All three aspects of linguistic form are exploited in literary form, as we will see.

1.2   Functions of verbal behaviour

Verbal behaviour has various functions, and any instance of verbal behaviour may serve several functions at the same time. One of the most important functions of verbal behaviour is to communicate, but not all verbal behaviour is communicative or has communication as its primary function. The production of verbal art or literature can in principle serve any of a wide range of functions, including but not restricted to communication. Here are some of the other functions which can be served by verbal behaviour and which are sometimes served specifically by verbal art:

- entertainment
- the display of skill
- praise of a good patron, or censure of an enemy
- the promotion of cultural values and morality
- the expression of mutual experience, thus bonding together an audience
- recording of historical events, or laws, or tenets of religion
- communication with supernatural beings
- the control of the physical world by magical means
- healing

Any of these functions can also be served by non-verbal behaviour: for example, while communication is one of the possible functions of verbal behaviour, it is also possible to communicate non-verbally. In some cases the same text might have different functions in different contexts. Thus Toelken (1987) describes the use of stories about Coyote in Navajo culture: in one context the stories entertain and teach moral values, while in another context allusion to these same stories is part of ritual healing, and in yet another context witches use the stories in their pursuit of personal gain and harm to others.

1.2.1   *Obscurity, and other functions of verbal art: some examples*

To illustrate the varieties of function which can be performed by verbal art, we now consider several cases of verbal art where the texts are made deliberately difficult to understand. Here, the function of communication is significantly demoted or dispensed with altogether in favour of other functions.

We begin with Iatmul song cycles from Papua New Guinea, discussed by Wassmann (1991: 60). These songs tell stories, but in some cases the full meaning of the stories is obscured in various ways relating to the language of the text. The vocabulary may include unfamiliar words; sentences are clipped, omitting pronouns and so obscuring who is acting or acted upon in any particular action; and the verbs may have very general meanings and are placed in contexts where their more specific meanings are obscured, thus in turn obscuring the nature of the situations described. Thus the texts are shaped such that the function of communication is hindered rather than enabled. Instead, the texts have another primary function which is to act as repositories of hidden meaning. The ability possessed by older men to interpret the hidden meanings of the texts is a source of social power in several ways, first because it underlies claims to land ownership (the texts are about places and the people who are associated with them), and second because those meanings can be used in magic as a means of causing harm to others. Thus the primary function of the verbal art is as a source of law and power, and this function is promoted in part through the demoting of communication as a possible function.

As a second example we consider the sacred languages used by the medicine men of the Oglala Lakota (USA: South Dakota), as outlined by Powers (1986). One kind of sacred language is called *wakan iye*. This language consists of words which are altered versions of ordinary Lakota words, or ordinary Lakota words with new meanings, put together by rules which are systematically different from the rules of Lakota syntax. Texts in *wakan iye* are considered to be incomprehensible by their Lakota audience, although they are usually able to say what the meanings of the words are (Powers 1986: 11). The performance of these texts is a part of ritual healing, which thus constitutes the dominant function of the verbal behaviour, and the deliberate obscurity of the text might be taken to serve this dominant function by demonstrating the specialized skills of the speaker (the medicine man) who is skilled both in speech and in healing. Lakota sacred texts also present another kind of obscurity. One of the strategies for making language incomprehensible is to make it perceptually difficult, and this is particularly true for the way of speaking called *hanbloglaka*, a conversation between a medicine man and his spirit which involves invented words. Here there is also a performance obscurity, because the text is spoken in the dark thus obscuring any meaning which might be supplied by gesture, in a subdued or muffled voice, and with final words in a line of prayer sometimes being almost inaudible. Furthermore, the fact that the discourse is one half of a conversation with a spirit (whose replies are not audible at all to other hearers) adds to the difficulty of making any sense of it. Thus again we see that the demoting of the communicative function of the texts is in the service of other functions played by the texts.

As a third example of the function of deliberate obscurity we consider a discussion by Hale (1984) of the songs of the Warlpiri (Australia: Northern Territory). Hale focuses specifically on the problem of learning the texts of the songs, a problem which faces each new generation, and which is central to the culture since the songs must be transmitted unchanged between generations: the culture or religion holds that these songs have been unchanged since they were created by the ancestors at the beginning of time. The young are not explicitly taught the songs, but as listeners must decipher the text for themselves. Two problems face the listeners/learners, one arising from the text and one arising from the performance. In the text of the song, some of the words are invented and specific to the song, while others may have their sound-structure altered. In the performance of the song, the words are blurred by what Hale calls 'muffled' choral performance. Why create these difficulties for a learner? Hale suggests several possibilities. One is to assert the authority of the performers, in particular their privileged access to cultural knowledge. But another possibility is that the learning of the songs is understood as a creative act: the learner must recreate the song on the basis of relatively degenerate and fragmentary information. (In this, learning a song is a bit like learning a language: again, something which a learner typically does without explicit instruction.) Thus in this culture, obscurity can be related to aesthetic pleasure, which is associated not with the composition of something new, but with the re-composition of something anew. Another kind of creativity emerges from the attempt to reconstruct the text exactly, which inevitably leads to various changes which are the result of creative decisions which must be made by the performer. Here, the communicative function of the text is pushed aside in favour of other functions, relating to creativity and aesthetics.

1.2.2 Form, function, and approaches to language and literature

Linguistics does not have a universally agreed role in the analysis of literature among either linguists or literary theorists. Disagreements about the use of linguistics can often be traced to views about function, and the relation between form and function.

One view is that form cannot be finally determined:

> Formalisation *is* a fruitful, useful activity. . . . But there is nothing fortuitous in the fact that these codifications, this formalisation of the codes, can never be completed. . . . Science and linguistics must never give up . . . the necessity, the desire to formalise, to exhaust, the analysis of codes and invariants; and of course the opening of closures, the contact situations, are a continual challenge which is not a contradiction of the search for invariants, but on the contrary a way of provoking it and enriching it. (Derrida, 'Some questions and responses', in Fabb et al. 1987)

In this view, linguistics is a practice which seeks to find a final analysis of the forms of language, but which cannot do so because it is unable to escape its own disciplinary presuppositions. Thus in the end it can never escape itself to become a theory of how the world actually is. This view is associated in particular with poststructuralist theorists, who as a general principle feel that any kind of form can never finally be determined, but always shifts away from the gaze of the analyst.

Another view is that literary texts exceed their form. Thus the text as a whole may be seen as having holistic qualities such that as a whole it is more than the sum of its parts, and has qualities as a whole which cannot be understood by the analysis of the parts. Or the text may be seen as having transcendent qualities, aspects which hold of it but which cannot be discovered by formal analysis. Both views are associated in particular with Romantic and post-Romantic theorists; these views remain quite influential, and are often invoked in the suggestion that linguistics cannot ultimately cope with literature. This is tied to another view about the function of literary texts, which sees literature as functioning primarily to express personal experience, and that personal experience escapes formal limits.

Most linguists reject these first two positions, by suggesting for example that poststructuralists or post-Romantics base their knowledge of linguistics on a reading of a few secondary sources, lack any detailed understanding of the practices of linguistics, and derive their claims about linguistics from philosophical presuppositions rather than from observation of linguistic theory and practice. However, linguists themselves are not agreed on the application of linguistics to literary studies, and we can divide linguists into two broad camps which we can call formalists and functionalists. Functionalists focus on possible connections between form and function, such that a formal analysis should be able to reveal functions for a text: in particular, they are interested in the connection between linguistic/literary form and the communicative function of this form. Thus functionalists may do a formal analysis of the text, and on the basis of the formal analysis make claims about the meanings which that text communicates. The functionalist tradition in literary linguistics is particularly associated with Michael Halliday and others, and is the foundation of the practice of stylistics. Stylistics can be seen as a use of linguistics in the analysis of particular literary texts, to reveal functions (including the communication of particular meanings) for those particular texts.

The other type of linguistics is formalist linguistics. Formalists separate the study of form from the study of function and reject any of the more radical functionalist claims about the relation between the two. Instead, formalists are interested in determining the general characteristics of linguistic form, and in literary linguistics formalists are interested in determining the general ways in which linguistic form is exploited in literary form. Thus formalists are less interested than functionalists in individual texts, and more interested in whole traditions; less interested in individual literatures and more interested in cross-linguistic/literary comparison. This book is guided primarily by the concerns of formalist linguistics.

1.3   Linguistic form in communication

Linguistic form serves a variety of functions, but one of its primary functions is to enable communication. Communication involves a communicator and a communicatee. Verbal communication is one of the kinds of communication (others include gestural, visual, etc.), and involves language. The two primary media for verbal communication are speech and writing; for clarity here (and to avoid terms like 'communicatee') we'll refer just to speech but all claims apply equally to writing or other media of verbal communication. Thus we will refer for convenience of exposition to the communicator as the speaker (and as 'she'), the communicatee as the hearer (and as 'he'), and the act of communication as an utterance. The approach to communication outlined in this section and assumed throughout the book is based on a very loose version of the insights of Relevance Theory (Sperber and Wilson 1986, 1995).

A speaker produces an utterance and thus communicates to the hearer. Communication is successful when the hearer attributes a set of thoughts to the speaker as her informative intention: when the hearer recognizes what the speaker intends to tell him. These thoughts can have any content whatsoever. Thus for example if the speaker tells the hearer a story, among the thoughts which she communicates are thoughts about the narrated world and its characters and what happens, but she also communicates thoughts about the structure and function of the story itself – communicating that the story is about to reach its peak, or that there is a shift from one episode to another, for example. We will see in chapters 7 and 8 that linguistic form has a major role in communicating the structure of narratives.

Communication can be vague. For example the speaker may say 'my love is a red red rose' . The hearer may use this as evidence that the speaker intends to tell him that the loved person is beautiful, precious, will not live for ever, and so on: the analogy with a flower means that various characteristics of the flower will be carried over to the loved person. Successful communication involves the hearer reconstructing some of these thoughts and attributing them to the speaker: the communication is equally successful with different sets of thoughts. There is no single tightly constrained set of meanings intended, just some set of meanings which can be inferred from the utterance. Sperber and Wilson suggest that this effect of deriving a loosely defined set of meanings, often quite a large set, is experienced by the hearer as a variety of aesthetic experience.

How does the speaker's utterance enable the hearer to construct a set of thoughts which he attributes to the speaker? This is the fundamental problem for the type of linguistics called pragmatics (and more generally involves semantics, the study of meaning). In the tradition initiated by H. P. Grice, Sperber and Wilson suggest that linguistic communication involves two kinds of process whereby thoughts are derived from utterances. One kind of process is decoding and involves the use of a number of linguistic codes; another kind of process is inference and involves general reasoning, taking the utterance as partial evidence for the thoughts which it communicates.

The decoding processes are part of the basic and automatic processing of linguistic form, part of the phonology, syntax and lexicon which make up the language. For example, the process by which a sequence of sounds is identified as a particular word, or the process by which a sequence of words is provided with a syntactic structure: these are decoding processes, involving the codes of phonology, lexicon and syntax. A sequence of sounds can be said to code (or encode) a particular word. Decoding processes can usually identify for an utterance what kind of situation is being described, and some information about the participants in that event. Thus for example an utterance which consists of the words 'He ate the fish yesterday' can be decoded as a representation of a situation of eating, involving a male eater, a fish which is eaten, taking place the day before some specified day (such as the day on which the utterance is produced). By itself, this is not a fully specified thought. A fully specified thought, or proposition, is a description which provides enough information to count as a true or false statement about the world: this one does not because we do not yet know, for example, who 'he' refers to.

Decoding an utterance will clarify certain aspects of the thoughts communicated but is rarely enough on its own. For the rest, the hearer must use what he has decoded as evidence, add more evidence to it, and by combining evidence must decide on the set of thoughts which is being communicated. This process is called inferencing; the utterance is said to imply the thoughts which can be inferred from it. The additional evidence can come from other utterances, from general knowledge, from knowledge of the situation of the speaker, and so on. It need not be linguistic evidence. In most cases of verbal communication, the utterance underdetermines the thoughts which it communicates: it constitutes partial evidence for those thoughts but not complete evidence. This has several interesting consequences. First, it means that communication is risky: because meanings are not encoded into the linguistic form, meanings cannot be guaranteed. Second, it means that a single utterance can communicate a large number of thoughts, simply by providing crucial evidence for a large number of thoughts. Third, it means that communication need not be literal: we can communicate what we mean perfectly adequately by being 'loose' in our utterances. Since the utterance only constitutes partial evidence for its interpretation, I can in principle say anything and mean anything by it. Fourth, I can communicate the opposite of what I say: thus for example I can say 'I really like being in a noisy environment', and communicate that I do not like being in a noisy environment. The utterance is only partial evidence for the thoughts which I wish to communicate, and the decoded (literal) meaning might be reinterpreted in the light, for example, of the tone of voice (e.g. sarcastic) which I use in uttering the words.

1.3.1 *Stylistic alternatives*

One of the characteristics of verbal communication is that the utterance can be reshaped in ways which do not affect how it is decoded, but which do affect how it might be used as evidence for thoughts. These reshapings are 'stylistic variations' in an utterance. In chapter 6 we will be looking at parallelism, which is a kind of repetition; here we look at how repetition can provide evidence of the communicator's intended thoughts, in a presentation based on Sperber and Wilson (1986: 219–22).

Consider first the texts (1a) and (1b):

(1a)   Here's a red sock, here's a blue sock.
(1b)   Here's a red sock, here's a red sock, here's a blue sock.

(1a) provides evidence to suggest that the speaker has discovered one red sock and one blue sock, while (1b) provides evidence that she has discovered two red socks and one blue sock. Thus the literal meaning of the two utterances is affected by the repetition, but this is derived not by decoding the utterance but by taking the repetition as evidence for meaning. (1b) thus has a similar interpretation to (1c):

(1c)   Here's two red socks, here's a blue sock.

While the interpretations of (1b) and (1c) are similar, at least to the extent that they describe the same number of socks discovered, nevertheless they are not identical. The stylistic feature of repetition in (1b) implies that the two red socks are found one after another; (1c) provides no evidence to this effect. To summarize: stylistic differences often affect the evidence presented by a text for its interpretation; any stylistic difference may alter the evidence.

Repetition in (1b) does not encode number and sequence, even though these are likely to be the interpretations of the repetition. We can see that repetition does not encode number and sequence by looking at a text where repetition has a different effect on interpretation.

(2a) I went for a long walk.
(2b) I went for a long, long walk.

In (2b) the repetition of *long* provides evidence that the walk was very long, an interpretation which is not evidenced by (2a) (though it still might be true for (2a)). An example of repetition with a different function again can be seen in (3b):

(3a) I shall never smoke again.
(3b) I shall never, never smoke again.

Here, the repetition in the text constitutes evidence that the speaker is particularly determined not to smoke again. In this section we have seen that stylistic choices can contribute evidence towards an interpretation but do not determine it.

1.3.2 *Markedness*

Form can be unmarked or marked. Marked form (also called 'foregrounded form') is form which is distinctive, standing out from its surroundings, and drawing attention to itself. Unmarked form (also called 'backgrounded form') is the form of the surroundings, relatively unnoticed. In a prose text, a metrical section of the text is marked because it is unusual in its context. In a metrical text such as a sonnet, an unmetrical line would be marked because it is unusual in its context. Parallelism is marked in non-parallelistic texts but unmarked in canonically parallel texts where the whole text involves parallelism. Marked form is often communicatively significant: for example, it indicates to an audience that the text is of particular importance at that point, particularly worth paying attention to.

1.4 Distinguishing 'literature'

1.4.1 *'Literature' and 'verbal art'*

The English term 'literature' calls up various associations. These are some of them:

- Literary texts have literary form.
- Literary texts require skill for their production and can be evaluated.

- Literary texts are written.
- Literary texts exist in authoritative versions which are preserved relatively unchanged.

If we look at other cultures and their understanding of their own kinds of verbal behaviour, we might find a kind of verbal behaviour which results in texts with exactly these characteristics. On the other hand we might find that some characteristics are missing. Thus some cultures have no written texts, but we might still want to argue that the songs and stories of that culture are analogous in essential ways to the literary texts of a written culture. In some cultures, literary texts are constantly transformed with each new performance: thus a song or an epic might in some sense be 'the same' across a range of different performers or performances but at the same time certain aspects of the text will constantly be changing. (The possibility of change is more likely in an oral culture, but it occurs also in written cultures, and there are plenty of oral traditions in which texts are preserved precisely over the generations by word of mouth.)

There are several reasons for grouping these kinds of oral practice with a written literary tradition. The first reason is that if we look at these kinds of verbal behaviour in their cultural context, we can see that songs in an oral culture can perform functions very similar to poems in a literate culture. Second, when we consider the exploitation of linguistic form by literary form we find that similar practices and strategies emerge in all cultures, whether they have written 'literature' or its oral equivalent, and whether texts are preserved unchanged or are constantly changing. There are undoubtedly some differences which relate to differences in medium: thus writing has its own form which can be exploited in literature (for example in visual pattern poems), but these seem relatively minor when compared with the major similarities between literary uses of linguistic form in literate and oral cultures. In this book I will have very little to say about writing as a medium and its use in literature.

I will be using 'literature' and 'verbal art' interchangeably in this book, assuming that they have the same meaning (i.e. they both can apply to oral texts). However, it can be argued that the term 'literature' is in the end weaker as a descriptive term than 'verbal art'. The term 'verbal art' expresses the first two characteristics of the list above: verbal art has its own formal characteristics (and each genre has its own formal characteristics), and it requires skill for its production and is evaluated. We now consider these two primary characteristics of verbal art, and their relationship.

Roman Jakobson suggested that one of the primary characteristics of verbal art is that it draws attention to its own formal structure. Using the notion of 'markedness' introduced earlier, we might say that the language of verbal art is more marked than the language of other kinds of verbal behaviour. Jakobson suggested that there are six basic functions of verbal behaviour, and that in verbal art the 'poetic function' is dominant. The poetic function of language is the use of language to create 'a focus on the message for its own sake', with 'message' here meaning the material substance and linguistic form of the utterance rather than its meaning. The poetic function of language is the use of language to draw attention to itself as material and as linguistic form; this function might be found in any kind of use of language, but is the dominant function, the most important and central function, of verbal art. Rhyme is a simple example of the use of language to perform the poetic function: a rhyme holds between two words because some part of each word (the end of the final syllable) is identical. Thus rhyme draws attention to a specific component of linguistic form – the syllable – and hence draws attention to the linguistic form of the text, thus focusing on 'the message'. This poetic function is achieved as follows (in a formulation sometimes known as the 'projection principle', from Jakobson (1987a: 71)): 'the poetic function projects the principle of equivalence from the axis of selection into the axis of combination.' Jakobson views the production of language as involving two processes, selection and combination. Selection ('the axis of selection') is the selection of a linguistic item. The item might be a sound, syllable, morpheme, word, or phrase, from a range of possible items any of which in principle could be inserted in that place and hence all the items in that range are equivalent. For example, in constructing the onset of an English syllable, once the first and second consonants have been chosen as [s] and [k], there is a restricted range of four consonants from which one can be chosen as the third consonant in the onset: [w], [y], [r] and [l]. Thus these four consonants are equivalent for this purpose. Combination is the placement of one linguistic item after another, in a sequence. Thus [s] and [k] and [r] are combined in a sequence [skr]. Items which are combined are not normally equivalent in the sense in which we have characterized it here: 'the principle of equivalence' normally applies only to the axis of selection rather than to the axis of combination. Thus there is no equivalence between [s], [k] and [r] in [skr]. However, in verbal art it can commonly be shown that the units which are in sequence are also units which are equivalent. For example in a metrical poem, one line comes after another but is equivalent to the previous line; they are the same metrically and so in principle either could be chosen to fill a particular metrical position. Thus the principle of equivalence now applies to the axis of combination, in poetry. Why does this equivalence of items in combination perform the poetic function? The poetic function requires that attention be drawn to linguistic form, and it is precisely linguistic form which is the basis of the equivalence; if we recognize the equivalence we can only do so by paying attention to linguistic form – the fact that the text is made from syllables, for example.

Jakobson's view of verbal art is oriented to the text, the linguistic material itself. However, texts always exist in a context, generally a context in which they are presented by the author or performer to an audience. That is, the text is always contextualized as part of verbal behaviour in a particular situation with particular participants. Richard Bauman (1975, 1984) proposes that to understand fully why verbal art 'focuses on the message for its own sake' we must understand verbal art not just as text but as the exploitation of a text in verbal behaviour. Bauman's proposal is based on his definition of a particular kind of verbal behaviour which he calls 'performance'. Verbal behaviour is never random; like any kind of social behaviour, it is governed by rules, though the rules may not be explicitly recognized by the participants. When verbal behaviour breaks its rules, it is likely to be recognized as deviant by the members of the culture (even if they might have difficulty explaining what exactly is wrong). Verbal art is thus like any kind of verbal behaviour in being rule-bound; what makes verbal art distinctive, in Bauman's view, is that the rules of acceptability are particularly prominent. This prominence is the basis of performance. When verbal behaviour is performed, the performer thereby explicitly takes responsibility for adequate adherence to the rules of that type of verbal behaviour, and will be judged by the audience in terms of her success in doing do. Thus if a particular way of speaking is characterized by perfect adherence to a particular rhyme scheme, its performer will commit herself to that adherence and will be judged by the audience in terms of whether she has achieved adequacy. Bauman defines verbal art as verbal behaviour which is performed. Bauman's definition of verbal art is clearly linked to Jakobson's and furthermore motivates Jakobson's definition. Verbal art must draw attention to itself because performance must draw attention to itself: performance must be explicitly signalled as performance by a performer and must be recognizable as performance to an audience.

1.4.2 *Looking at someone else's culture*

Many linguists study languages spoken in cultures other than their own. One reason for doing this derives from the hypothesis that all human languages share fundamental characteristics of linguistic form, and thus our understanding of linguistic form can only be achieved fully by understanding as much as possible about as many other languages as possible. Similarly, literary linguists might look at literatures other than their own, in order to better understand the general ways in which linguistic form can be exploited in literary form. A comparison of different literatures, to see ways in which they are similar, can be very revealing. This is the general strategy of the present book, which touches on the literatures of around a hundred different languages.

One of the descriptive issues which arises when working on the verbal arts of a culture is whether to take an etic or an emic approach. These terms refer primarily to the ways of classifying the verbal behaviour of the culture. An etic approach is an approach which applies a generalized terminology, suitable for any culture, to this particular culture – thus it is the application of an outsider's understanding to the culture's practices. In contrast, an emic approach attempts to formulate an account of the culture from within, trying to understand the culture as an insider, a member of that culture, understands it.

If we wish to take a comparative approach to verbal art, we must be dominated by an etic perspective; the notion of 'verbal art' itself (as a kind of verbal behaviour which can be looked for in any culture) is an etic notion – though arguably the notion of 'literature' is an emic one, specific to a particular set of related cultures. However, we would be unwise to ignore the advantages of an emic approach, and the insights which can be brought to an analysis by an insider, whether a native speaker of a language, a composer of verbal art, or a member of its audience.

Linguists are used to being asked how many languages they speak. Many linguists know just one or two: but they work on many more. This is possible because a language can be investigated in parts: it is possible for example just to work on the syllable structure of the words of the language, and for this it may not be necessary to understand what any of those words mean. For a full understanding of the verbal art of a culture, it is of course necessary to know the language and also to have other kinds of knowledge shared by people in that culture. But it is possible to work on verbal art without fully understanding the texts, and it is possible to illustrate some basic issues with texts without fully explaining those texts. This is the strategy of this book. Always, something will be lost by this partial approach; but the gains come with the variety of material which we can thereby examine.

Another reason for the diversity of materials in this book is curiosity about other people's verbal art. Here, the book is ambitious in its geographical and historical reach, but must be modest in the extent to which it can really reveal anything about another literature. The texts discussed are all very short, the longest texts being some very short stories, and in all cases are discussed from just one or two angles. The danger faced by this approach is that other people's literatures can seem to present simple, and perhaps easily solved, problems. It is always the case that more detailed study of any verbal practice always reveals complexities at first unsuspected: the better we become at reading something, the harder it is for us to read. That's how aesthetics works, or at least one of the ways in which it works – the creation of difficulty is one of the functions of verbal art.

1.4.3 Ethical problems

The study of what other people do always introduces ethical problems. This is true for the study of other people's languages, but is particularly acute in the study of other people's literatures. Here, for example, are three kinds of ethical problem which arise.

The first problem relates to ownership of texts and rights of reproduction of those texts. Determining ownership is not always straightforward: consider for example a text which incorporates formulaic material from another text, is structured according to generic conventions, is interpreted by appealing to general cultural knowledge, and yet as a whole is unique to a particular performance by a particular person. The most obvious owner of that text is the performer – but there are other contributors, from both within and outside the culture, and in some sense these might also be argued to have some share in ownership. Of course, while the determination of ownership is not unproblematic, it is clear that a composer or performer has rights with regard to a text and its performance, and thus that these rights must be respected by anyone else who would like to make use of that text. At a minimum, the author or performer should have his or her name recorded and reproduced with the text. One of the persistent and damaging problems with the reproduction of art from many cultures is that the authors of texts are forgotten, their names lost, as though they came from the distant unknowable past, their individual skill lost in some general notion of tradition. More complexly, when an author or performer grants rights of reproduction, they risk losing any control over the texts involved, how they are reproduced in subsequent texts (such as this one), and how they are talked about. In the case of the present book, most of the materials were gathered by a third party from the original performer, and where possible I have attempted to gain the permission of that third party for further reproduction. It is unlikely that the original performers or authors will ever see how their texts are used in this book, which demands a particular attention to making sure that the texts are used with respect.

This leads to the second major ethical problem, which is how to talk about someone else's verbal art from a generalizing, universalizing, etic perspective. While it is possible to partially address this problem by looking at a verbal art from within, with an emic perspective, the fact nevertheless remains that we are outsiders with outsiders' agendas. In this book, extracts from texts are used to illustrate generalities; the specific serves the general. This is as true of Alexander Pope's texts as it is of K— W—'s text (both in chapter 6), and I have tried not to distinguish unnecessarily between highly valued canonical 'English literature' texts and unknown, previously unpublished texts from cultures which most readers will not previously have encountered (like the Buru culture to which K— W— belongs). As far as this book is concerned, there is in principle no difference between them: all kinds of text are equally suitable for the exploration of the linguistic bases of verbal art. However, while this approach tries not to skew the discussion of texts in terms of assumptions of cultural value, those assumptions nevertheless inform everyone's perspective on the cultures to which they belong. Thus it can in principle be quite annoying to have someone take a highly valued cultural artefact with its very specific significance and meaning within a culture, and discuss that artefact from an alien perspective which takes away its specialness. One of the complaints about both linguistics and the literary practices, such as structuralism, which emerged from linguistics is that the persistently etic perspective of linguistics fails to recognize the cultural specialness of great works of literature; when Roland Barthes undertook a structuralist analysis of the classic French dramatist Racine in the early 1960s, he did so precisely as a way of defying cultural conservatives and their protective attitudes towards the classics of French literature (Barthes 1964). In this book I avoid questions of cultural value; texts are chosen because of what they can tell us about the language of literature, and particularly given the fragmentary manner in which they are presented, the best assumption to make is that what we see is not what someone from within the culture sees: thus, we should assume that from the fragments presented here we can know very little about any of the literatures illustrated here.

There is another side to the question of etic analysis and cultural value. Among their goals, linguists have sometimes included goals relating to value. Some have used linguistic analysis as a way of reinforcing the special status of already canonized texts. Others have attempted to argue to outsiders that the textual products of a particular culture are of demonstrable value. Thus both Labov's work on oral storytellers in New York and Hymes's work on Native American literatures from the North West Coast were both intended to demonstrate the presence of previously unsuspected complex aesthetics, and hence the value of the resulting texts. This latter approach involves risks of its own, partly arising from the fact that it is often addressed to outsiders by outsiders, and may not feed back into the original culture. Consider for example the fact that there are texts in the present book, used as material for exercises; some of these texts have spectacularly complex structures which can be discovered by an etic analysis (by doing the exercise), but those discoveries may circulate entirely between outsiders and will not return to the authors of those texts.

The third major ethical problem relates to the first two. The first problem was who owned the rights of reproduction of the text; the second was that the text might be discussed in a manner which failed to address its meaning from within the culture. The third problem relates to restrictions on the use of texts. Some varieties of verbal art are restricted in who can have access to them, or to how they can be performed. For example, some genres of stories in some Native American cultures are restricted to being told in the winter. In general, it can be assumed that if an author or performer gave permission to an outsider to publish a text, then that text is not restricted in access; it is not uncommon, in fact, for there to be deliberate gaps in representing the texts of a culture, in order to respect these issues of access. Thus for example Wassmann (1991) published a reproduction and analysis of texts from the Pulau clan of the Iatmul (New Guinea: Middle Sepik); his book begins with a photographed document, hand-written and signed by the councillor of Kandingei village, which explicitly gives permission for texts to be reproduced in Wassman's book, but forbids the repro-duction of hidden or secret names and stories (knowledge of which can be used within the village in claiming land rights, or to do harm by magical means).

1.5   Description and explanation in literary linguistics

Linguistics describes language, both at the level of being able to describe the formal structure of any piece of language, and at the level of characterizing a language as a whole, possibly in terms of its exploitation of the universal possi-bilities of language. These descriptive goals are shared by literary linguistics, which should be able to provide an analysis of the use of linguistic form in literature, and to characterize any particular tradition (or genre within a tradition) in terms of the forms which it chooses to exploit. Large parts of literary linguistics are primarily descriptive at least at the level of form, and are devoted to a charac-terization of exactly how linguistic form is exploited in literary form. Much of this book is also taken up with describing these things.

However, linguistics also attempts to explain why language has the forms that it does, and for many linguists this is its primary aim. Furthermore, many linguists seek a single explanatory model for the formal aspects of all the dif-ferent languages spoken by humans. This raises the question of the explanatory goals for a literary linguistics. What exactly might we try to explain? And can we formulate universals-oriented explanations along lines similar to the universalist explanations found in linguistics? We can distinguish two general explanatory goals.

The first is to discover rule systems which involve language and which are specific to the language of literature, and hence which cannot be discovered simply by looking at language in general. This is analogous to the discovery of phonological rules as an explanation for the regularity of phonological form. The clearest case of this in literature is metrical form and some of the para-metrical phenomena associated with it: it is likely that metrical regularities can best be explained by formulating a metrical rule system. For a particular met-rical practice, the rule system would be explanatory in predicting exactly which varieties of metrical text can arise. More ambitiously, a rule system might be formulated more abstractly as a set of universal possibilities which are then subject to parametric variation such that all the variant kinds of metrical poetry would be characterized by this more abstract understanding of what metrical form is. An example of work along these lines is Hanson and Kiparsky's (1996) attempt to formulate a general parametrizable account of metrical systems. This rule system – whether specific or generalized and universal – would have psychological reality (which gives it its causal force in determining the regularities in behaviour), in just the same way as phonological rules have psychological reality. Thus we would explain metricality as a characteristic of texts by reference to a psychological metrical rule system, a sub-component of human cognition.

The second explanatory goal is less ambitious, in that it does not necessarily formulate a new rule system to characterize literary regularities. Instead, it would look at which aspects of linguistic form are exploited in literary form. In this case linguistics gives us an explanatory account of the rule systems which characterize linguistic form. What we might investigate is which aspects of the linguistic rule systems are accessible for use in the construction of literary form. We might also ask to what extent the rules of the linguistic systems can be 'bent' to create the marked language characteristic of literature, and attempt to explain how such 'bending' is possible. (This is exemplified for example by Austin's (1984) exploration of systematic rule-bending in Romantic poetry.) In this mode we explore the use of language in literary texts as part of the broader goal of linguistics itself, to understand the nature of linguistic form, what it is, how it can be used, and how components of linguistic form relate to one another.

1.6 Further reading

Crystal (1987) is a one-volume reference work on all aspects of linguistics. On formalist linguistics see Newmeyer (1983). *The New Princeton Encyclopaedia of Poetry and Poetics* (Preminger and Brogan 1993) is an invaluable source of definitions, information about literatures, and further reading. Finnegan (1970, 1992a) comments on the oral–written difference and the fact that some general notion of literature cross-cuts it. Other general surveys include Finnegan and Orbell (1995), Okpewho (1992) and Edmonson (1971). The collections of essays by Freeman (1970, 1981) include many classic articles on literary linguistics; see also Sebeok (1960), Fabb et al. (1987) and Lodge (1988). Jakobson is one of the most influential authors in literary linguistics, and Pomorska and Rudy (1987) collects together some of the major articles. Pilkington (1992) and chapter 4 of Sperber and Wilson (1995) are specifically devoted to literary meaning and style. Stylistics as a linguistic approach to literature is exemplified by Leech (1969) and Widdowson (1975). Its suitability to the teaching of literature has made it the basis for a number of textbooks, including two co-written by the present author: Durant and Fabb (1990) and Montgomery et al. (1992). Wales (1989) gives an encyclopaedic overview of stylistics and various related fields, and representative anthologies include Carter (1982), Toolan (1992) and Weber (1996). See also Traugott and Pratt (1980). Fabb (1988) and Macmahon (1995) comment on the misuse of linguistics in literary studies. Osmond-Smith (1985) discusses an explicit adaptation of linguistics (and structuralism) in aesthetic practice, by the composer Luciano Berio in his *Sinfonia*. On the use of materials from another culture, see Marcus and Myers (1995), Price (1989), Said (1978), Hymes (1987a). On relevant ethical problems see Finnegan (1992b), Woodbury (1993) and Myers (1992).

1.7 Exercises

1.7.1 *Linguistic form and literary form*

(a) Suggest three examples of linguistic form in the following text. These must be aspects of the language of the text which are not specific to literature.

(b) Suggest three examples of literary form in the following text. These must be aspects of the text which are characteristically (though perhaps not solely) found in literary texts.

(c) For each of the three kinds of literary form which you chose in (b), discuss whether they are an adaptation of linguistic form.

Text: Shakespeare, sonnet 40

Take all my loves, my love, yea, take them all,
What hast thou then more than thou hadst before?
No love, my love, that thou mayst true love call,
All mine was thine before thou hadst this more:
Then if for my love, thou my love receivest,
I cannot blame thee, for my love thou usest,
But yet be blamed, if thou this self deceivest
By wilful taste of what thy self refusest.
I do forgive thy robbery gentle thief,
Although thou steal thee all my poverty:
And yet love knows it is a greater grief
To bear love's wrong, than hate's known injury.

Lascivious grace, in whom all ill well shows,
Kill me with spites; yet we must not be foes.

1.7.2 *What kinds of verbal behaviour can be considered verbal art?*

(a) Telling a joke.

Instruction

Consider a specific example of telling a joke, and decide whether it can be characterized as verbal art.

(b) Crying out the name of the newspaper.
People whose profession is to sell newspapers or magazines in the street usually cry out the name of the newspaper (and may add other words or phrases).

Instruction

Choose a specific example of this which you are familiar with and decide whether it can be characterized as verbal art.

(c) Naming a Hopi individual.
According to Whiteley (1992), a Hopi individual may be ritually named many times in his or her life. Specific people are permitted to name as part of specific rituals; naming takes place while the subject's hair is washed in yucca suds. The name is always meaningful and its meaning relates to the clan associations of the person who assigns the name – thus it will often imply a particular animal. A name is always considered to have a determinate meaning, though the meaning may not necessarily be known, and hence someone might interpret and speculate over the meaning of a difficult or obscure name. The name *Sikyakwaptiwa* (spelled Sekaquaptewa) is structured from the following morphemes:

sikyangpu	*kwapta*	*-tiwa*
yellow, yellowness	he/she put some things(pl.) above on high	a male name suffix

The name-giver in this case was a member of the Coyote clan. The implied animal is the yellow fox *sikyaatayo* which is conventionally associated by the

Hopi with the stage of dawn at which there is yellow light *sikyangnuptu*. This association is found both in myths and in rituals where an actual yellow fox or fox-skin is produced at the moment of yellow dawn.

Instruction

Whiteley, on the basis of a large number of examples, argues that Hopi names are 'literature' (verbal art). Does the cited example provide justification for this claim?

2 Meter and Linguistic Theory

Chapters 2–5 are concerned with 'metrical form', a kind of literary form which is an adaptation of the type of linguistic form called prosodic phonological form. Texts have metrical form when they can be divided into lines which are governed by a rule system called a meter ('meter' is the American spelling for this term; the British spelling is 'metre'). The account of meter in these chapters draws primarily on the approach called generative metrics, which is a sub-part of generative linguistics; however, the aim is also to give a reasonably comprehensive overview of kinds of metrical practices, not all of which have been discussed in a generative framework.

2.1 The metrical text

2.1.1 Identifying a text as metrical

A text has a prosodic phonological structure, which consists of its sounds, organized into syllables, organized into words, organized into phonological phrases, and so on. Some texts are organized into sections (which we'll call lines) where some part of the prosodic phonological structure conforms to a pre-existing pattern. Texts of this kind are called metrical texts. Consider for example the ending of Milton's *Paradise Lost*, viewed as a continuous text:

Some natural tears they dropped, but wiped them soon; the world was all before them, where to choose their place of rest, and Providence their guide: They hand in hand with wandering steps and slow, through Eden took their solitary way.

This text can be divided into five sections – five lines:

Some natural tears they dropped, but wiped them soon;
the world was all before them, where to choose

> *their place of rest, and Providence their guide:*
> *They hand in hand with wandering steps and slow,*
> *through Eden took their solitary way.*

The prosodic phonological structure of each line conforms to a pre-existing pattern (called 'iambic pentameter'), and it is this which identifies it as metrical. We'll return to a more detailed analysis of this pre-existing pattern later in this chapter, but it can for the moment be stated as: stressed syllables in polysyllabic words tend to be even-numbered syllables in the line.

POLYSYLLABIC WORDS	STRESSED SYLLABLES IN THE WORD	POSITION IN THE LINE
natural	na	second syllable
before	fore	sixth syllable
Providence	pro + dence	sixth and eighth syllables
wandering	wan	sixth syllable
Eden	e	second syllable
solitary	so + ta	sixth and eighth syllables

In this case the pattern refers to some of the even positions within the line (here stated in terms of which number syllable is involved, but this will be restated later), and to a specific aspect of the prosodic phonological structure of the line: the stressed syllables which are in some of the words. The important point is that the meter's control over the text is only partial: *some* but not all of the positions relate to *some* but not all of the components of phonological structure. Thus it is possible for iambic pentameter lines to vary considerably from one another in their prosodic phonological structure, while nevertheless all sharing the same basic pattern. This is typical of all meters: a meter controls some aspect of the prosodic phonological structure of a text while not completely controlling it, and thus allows for prosodic phonological variation between lines.

2.1.2 Para-metrical phenomena

A meter is a set of rules which constrain some aspect of the prosodic phonological structure of the line of text. However, many genres of metrical text are also characterized by additional kinds of regularity which are not themselves metrical but which relate to the meter and to the meter's division of a text into lines. These are para-metrical phenomena. In chapter 5 we look in detail at the two most common kinds of para-metrical phenomena, which are sound-patterning

rules and word-boundary rules. Sound-patterning rules (mostly kinds of alliteration and rhyme) are sensitive to the division of a text into lines and may con-
nect lines together. Word-boundary rules are rules which stipulate that a word
boundary must or must not fall between two metrical positions in the template.
A caesura rule is the most common kind of word-boundary rule, which requires
a word boundary between two constituents; this means that a polysyllabic word
cannot be spread across these two positions in the line. A bridge rule has the
opposite effect – forbidding a word boundary between two positions, which means
that a polysyllabic word must be spread across these two positions. Sound-
patterning rules and word-boundary rules are rules which supplement the metrical
rules, and at the same time are sensitive to them (or – putting it another way
– parasitic on them). These para-metrical rules can be illustrated from the following metrical text:

Dob líonmhur ar leirg an   locha
were numerous on plain of the loch

laoch láidir is   óigfhear   oll
hero strong and young man great/tall

iomdha um   thriath Tatha   taoiseach
many a about the Lord   (of-) Tay leader

sgiath flatha   agus craoiseach corr.
shield of prince and spear   pointed

'Numerous on the lakeside were the stalwart heroes and tall young men; around
the lord of Tay was many a leader, many a shield of prince and taper spear'
(from the elegy on Sir Duncan Campbell of Glenorchy, who died in 1603; cited
by Watson 1959: xxxvii)

This text is governed by *séadna*, a medieval Irish/Gaelic metrical system (see Knott
1957: 16), which includes a meter, a word-boundary rule, and sound-patterning
rules. The meter counts syllables into lines: it requires the first and third lines
to have eight syllables and the second and fourth lines to have seven syllables.
There is a bridge rule operating in the first and third lines, which requires the
seventh and eighth syllables to belong to the same word (i.e. a word boundary
is forbidden between seventh and eighth positions). And there are several sound-
patterning rules, including the requirement that the second and fourth lines must
rhyme. In this text, *oll* rhymes with *corr*: notice that even though the sounds are
different they are counted as equivalent in this tradition for the purposes of
rhyme. This phenomenon of equivalence of different sounds is one of the more
interesting problems in the linguistics of sound-patterning, and we discuss it

in 5.5. Another sound-patterning requirement in *séadna* is that there must be alliteration within each line – for example in the repetition of [l] in *leirg* and *locha*
– and across lines in specified cases such as between the first and second lines,
where *locha* alliterates with *laoch*. In addition to sound-patterning rules which
relate individual sounds with other individual sounds, there is a patterning between
the sequence of sounds in line 3 and the sequence of sounds in line 4: this might
be thought of as a kind of sound-pattern parallelism (and we discuss it in 6.3).
Both word-boundary rules and sound-patterning rules have some effect in shaping the prosodic phonology of the texts which they apply to, and thus have an
effect which is similar to meter: however, we will treat them as distinct from the
meter and explain why in chapter 5.

A metrical text is divided into lines, but in some texts different lines conform
to different meters. Where all lines conform to the same meter (as in *Paradise
Lost*) the text is called isometric; where different lines conform to different
meters the text is called heterometric. The Greek genre of ode is typically characterized by heterometric structure, and more recent imitations often have a
similarly heterometric structure as in these lines from Coleridge's 'Dejection.
An Ode':

> *Those sounds which oft have raised me, whilst they awed,*
> *And sent my soul abroad,*
> *Might now perhaps their wonted impulse give,*
> *Might startle this dull pain, and make it move and live!*

The first of these four lines has ten syllables, the second has six, the third has
ten and the fourth has twelve; the basic 'iambic' rhythm is the same in each line,
but the lines are of different lengths, thus making this heterometric. One of the
questions which arises for heterometric texts is whether the rules which regulate
the sequence of meters are themselves sensitive to linguistic structure (and thus
might be thought of as extensions of the meter in some way).

A meter involves the division of a text into metrical lines, but metrical texts
can also have a structure larger than the metrical line. Thus metrical lines can
often be paired or grouped into larger units which we can call stanzas or
strophes (and texts organized in this way can be called strophic texts, as distinct
from stichic texts where the line is the largest unit of structure). This grouping
into larger units is dependent on metrical structure in several ways. First, the
possibility of grouping lines depends on the division into lines, which is an effect
of the meter. Second, the grouping of lines into stanzas may relate to sound-
patterning rules such as rhyme, which are themselves dependent on metrical
structure. Third, lines may be grouped into stanzas according to a particular
heterometric pattern. Thus the organization of lines into larger constituents can
be thought of as another para-metrical phenomenon.

2.2 Prosodic phonological structure

The prosodic phonology of a language gives an utterance its rhythm: its pattern of more and less prominent parts. The prosodic phonology of an utterance also gives the utterance its constituency, its shape as a sequence of units interrupted by pauses. Prosodic phonology is a characteristic of all spoken utterances, and is not itself a part of verbal art – but metrical texts are a case where verbal art exploits the pre-existing prosodic patterns of the language to develop specifically literary ways of organizing utterances into literary texts. This section is a brief overview of some issues in prosodic phonology which will have particular relevance for the study of meter, word-boundary rules and sound-patterning rules.

Utterances have both prosodic phonological structure and syntactic structure. At the level of syntactic structure, an utterance consists of words which in turn are grouped into syntactic phrases and into sentences. The prosodic phonological structure is a parallel but distinct organization of the utterance as a sequence of sounds which are grouped into other kinds of constituent structure, parallel to the organization into words and sentences, but distinct from it. The relevant levels of prosodic phonological structure for our purposes are: (i) the segment: the smallest prosodic unit corresponding roughly to the individual sound; (ii) the syllable and its component parts – onset, nucleus and coda, and morae; (iii) the word and its permeable or flexible boundaries; (iv) the organization of words into phonological phrases; (v) the organization of syllables into strong and weak members of a hierarchical structure which expresses rhythmic patterns such as stress.

2.2.1 *The phonological segment*

The basic building-block of prosodic phonological structure is the phonological segment. A segment can be thought of as a sound-carrying unit. Which sound the segment carries is determined by the articulatory instructions attached to the segment. For example we can think of the word *fortification* as a sequence of segments:

The first segment is defined by articulatory instructions which make the sound consonantal, labial, voiceless and continuant (i.e. the sound [f], as indicated here). The second and third segments are co-defined by the articulatory instructions which make the sound a vowel which is back and mid-height (i.e. the sound [ɔ]). The fact that the same vowel is spread over two segments means that the vowel is 'long' here. In comparison the vowel [ɪ] seen later in the word is attached to single segments and so is always short. The difference between long vowels (taking up two segments) and short vowels (taking up one) is important for syllable weight, as we see below.

2.2.2 *The syllable and its component parts*

Segments are grouped into syllables. At the centre of each syllable is a segment with a high degree of sonorance: in English, high sonorance usually means a segment which is a vowel but can also mean a semivowel, a liquid (like [l] or [r]) or a nasal (like [n] in *fortification*). The segment or segments (where two segments in a row are matched with a long vowel or diphthong) which are at the centre of the syllable are called its nucleus. If we take a word like *gentlemen* we can identify three highly sonorant segments, and hence three syllable nuclei (and hence three syllables):

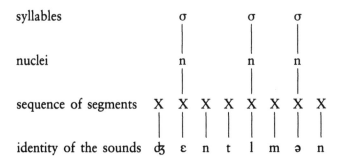

The less sonorant segments which come between nuclei are contained within the syllable, either grouped with the following nucleus as the onset of the syllable, or grouped with the preceding nucleus as the coda of the syllable:

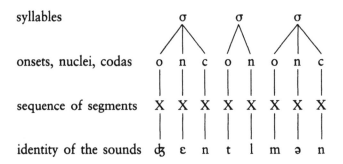

As a general rule (which holds across languages), a non-nuclear segment is put into an onset by preference – that is, it is grouped with the following nucleus rather than the preceding one. However, there are two kinds of situation in which a non-nuclear segment must be put into a coda. The first is when this is the final segment of a word: in *gentlemen* the final [n] must be the coda of the syllable because there is no later syllable for it to attach to. The other situation arises when a sequence of segments is forbidden in an onset. In English, an onset cannot begin with [nt . . .]; thus the [n] which is the third segment of this word cannot be put into an onset and must be part of a coda with the preceding nucleus.

There is a further aspect of structure, which is that the nucleus and coda together constitute a sub-constituent of the syllable, called the syllable rime. Grouping these two elements together is one way of explaining the fact that these two elements contribute to the weight of a syllable while the onset does not.

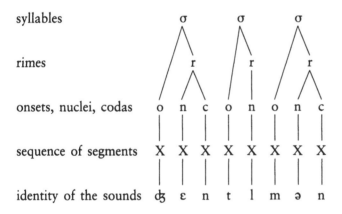

The organization of the syllable into onset–nucleus–coda is relevant for sound-patterning because systematic kinds of sound-patterning are usually defined in terms of the sections of the syllable which they involve: alliteration in a particular tradition can be defined as involving just the onset, for example, and rhyme can be defined as involving both the nucleus and the coda. (There are, however, some kinds of sound-patterning which pick out other components of the syllable, thus suggesting perhaps that the onset–nucleus–coda structure is less central than might at first seem: see 5.3.4.) The organization of the syllable into constituents such as onset, nucleus and coda is also relevant because it is the basis of the definition of the weight of the syllable.

In many languages, syllables can be differentiated by weight into heavy and light syllables. This weight difference is the basis of other aspects of the phonology of the utterance: for example, the patterns of heavy and light syllables in English words partly determines their patterns of stress. The weight of a syllable is based on the number of segments in the nucleus and coda combined (i.e. in the rime), and is measured in morae. A mora is a prosodic unit, made from segments in the nucleus and coda of the syllable, and itself forming part of the syllable: morae can be argued to be part of the prosodic phonological structure because they directly contribute to the rhythmic structure of an utterance. In English, morae are calculated from a syllable as follows: (i) count the first segment in the nucleus as one mora; (ii) if there are any further segments in the syllable (in either the nucleus or the coda) count these as totalling one further mora. Thus a syllable can have one or two morae. The moraic structure of *gentlemen* can be represented as follows:

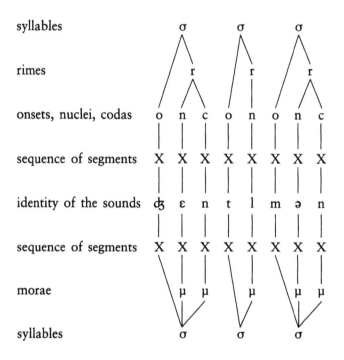

In this diagram, the organization into morae has been distinguished from the organization into onset, nucleus and coda. This is because these appear to be related but distinct dimensions of organization of the syllable, which can therefore be understood as simultaneously organized in the two different dimensions. In most theoretical accounts, the syllable is formulated either as fundamentally organized into onset, nucleus and coda (the top part) or as fundamentally organized into morae (the bottom part): for discussion see Hayes (1995). In this word, the first syllable has two morae and is thus heavy, the second has one and is thus light, while the third has two and is thus heavy.

    Languages vary in how they calculate morae from segments. Each segment in a nucleus counts as a mora, with the consequence that a long vowel always counts as two morae. However, segments in the coda are sometimes counted differently. For example, in Somali a syllable with a CVC structure would contribute one mora (i.e. the single consonant in the coda counts for nothing), while in Arabic the same syllable structure CVC would contribute two morae, with the consonant contributing to the weight. The calculation of morae is very important in some kinds of verse – particularly mora-counting and quantitative verse. Here, the exact number of morae in a line is what makes the line metrical. In practice, each language must be approached on its own terms to decide how the sequence of segments are organized into morae.

(Note: in some descriptions heavy and light syllables are referred to instead as long and short syllables respectively, with syllable weight referred to instead as syllable length. In this book, the terminology of weight is used to differentiate syllables, with the terminology of length used to differentiate vowels.)

2.2.3 *The word and its boundaries*

Central to the notion of a word is that it is a linguistic unit which can exist in isolation and which has some independent meaning: this characterizes what are called lexical words, such as nouns, verbs, adjectives and adverbs. We also use the term 'word' to describe various grammatical units whose function is to enable lexical words to be put together into meaningful sentences: this characterizes what are called grammatical words, such as articles, quantifiers, pronouns, auxiliaries, modals, negators, and prepositions. The notions of lexical word and grammatical word are dependent on domains of linguistic structure such as the lexicon and syntax; when we look at phonological structure, we can formulate a notion of phonological word. Prototypically, a phonological word is coextensive with a lexical word, but understood in terms of the word's phonological structure: it is another side of the same object. However, there is a complication when it comes to grammatical words; sometimes a grammatical word can be understood as a phonological word on its own, but at other times a grammatical word attaches to a lexical word and together they constitute a larger kind of phonological word sometimes called a clitic group.

There is another problem with the notion of word, which relates to the syllable structure of a word (and for that matter also the identity of the segments in a word). When words follow one another in an utterance, they can affect each other's phonological shape. In particular, a syllable in one word can lose one of its component segments to a syllable in a neighbouring word, thus potentially changing the pattern of morae and thus syllable weights. This is best illustrated by a Greek example (which is discussed again in 5.2.1). The Greek word *eridi* has the following syllable structure in isolation:

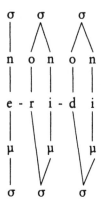

And the Greek word *ksuneeeke* has the following structure in isolation:

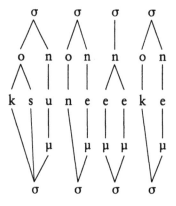

However, when the two words are put together, the initial [k] of *ksuneeeke* re-attaches to become the final segment in the preceding word: and thus adds a mora to that syllable, making it heavy. Thus the overall number of morae in the sequence increases because the segment has moved from an onset where it had no weight to a coda where it does have weight.

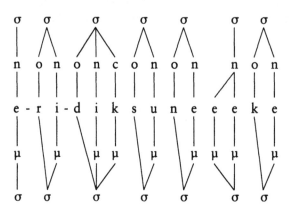

2.2.4 *Phonological phrases*

The word is a lexical and syntactic notion and also a phonological notion –
and the two coincide for the most part, though not always. The same is true
of the phrase. When words are organized into syntactic structures, they are first
organized into phrases – so that a sentence is a structure made from phrases
which ultimately contain words. The same appears to be true of utterances,
where phonological words are organized into phonological phrases. The phonological phrases are sometimes coextensive with syntactic phrases and sometimes not.

   One of the most important characteristics of a phonological phrase from
the perspective of verbal art is that it can typically be followed in performance
by a pause. Thus Dresher (1994) discusses a transcription system used by tenth-
century editors of the Hebrew Bible; this involves a complex system of diacritic
symbols which were intended to preserve the ancient pronunciation and performance of the Biblical text. Some diacritics appear to be used as an indication
that two or more words belong together in the same phonological phrase.
Dresher suggests that other diacritics are intended to indicate the length of
pauses between phonological phrases. He suggests that phonological phrases
are hierarchically grouped, with shorter pauses between phrases lower down
on the hierarchy and longer pauses between phrases higher up in the hierarchy.
The hierarchical complexity of a particular text is its 'grain'. Drawing on this
hypothesis, he suggests that the edited text of the Bible indicates when the performer should speak deliberately (with a greater quantity of pauses) and when
less deliberately.

2.2.5 *Rhythm and stress*

In most languages there is a fairly salient rhythmic pattern to an utterance,
which is composed partly of the inherent rhythmic patterns of words, and partly
of the rhythmic decisions made by the speaker in putting the utterance together.
In English, the rhythmic pattern is realized as relative stress on syllables.
Stress is a rhythm within the word, which is realized by a combination of
several features: stressed syllables are typically louder, longer and higher in
pitch. (See Hayes 1995, chapter 2 for a very detailed discussion of what
stress is.)

   In thinking about English stress, it is necessary to distinguish between stress
within a lexical word and stress within the utterance as a whole. The latter is
constrained primarily by performance considerations, and can be very variable:

the same sequence of words can be given very different patterns of stress within the utterance as a whole. This is called the postlexical stress pattern of the utterance.

Stress within a lexical word, on the other hand, is rigidly constrained by phonological rules of the language, and is part of the basic identity of the word. Thus the words *differ* and *defer* are differentiated in their sound-patterns primarily by the different patterns of stress (*differ* has a stressed–unstressed pattern, while *defer* has an unstressed–stressed pattern). Lexical stress of this kind is not variable at the whim of the speaker (unlike postlexical stress). The various lexical stress patterns of English words are regular, but are also subject to complex rules: a considerable amount of work has been put into trying to understand these in a generative framework since the 1960s, and the matter is still not fully settled. Thus I will present a very simplified account of how stress works within a lexical word.

The basis of stress within a word is that the syllables of the word are organized into constituents (called phonological feet). Consider for example the word *fortification*. The syllables are organized into phonological feet as follows:

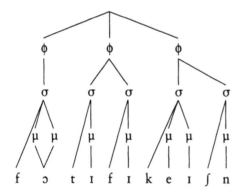

The phonological foot typically contains two morae – either a two-mora (heavy) syllable as in the first and third feet, or two one-morae syllables as in the second foot. The final syllable is 'extrametrical', and appended to the preceding foot. Where there is more than one syllable in a word, some syllables are stronger than others: in a two-syllable word like *differ* the first syllable is said to be a strong constituent relative to the second syllable which is a weak constituent. Where there is more than one phonological foot within the word, the feet also differ from one another in strength. Stress is attracted to strong constituents. Where there are three or more syllables in a word, there will often be more than one strong constituent, and here the strong constituents are strong or weak relative to one another. The patterns of strength in this word are as follows:

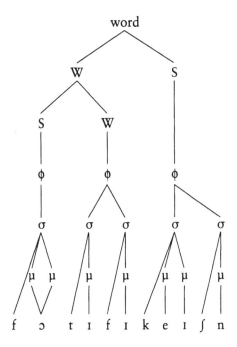

The first syllable containing [ɔ] has stress because it is in a strong foot relative to the neighbouring weak foot containing [tɪfɪ]. This pair of feet are then weak relative to the foot containing [eɪ], which therefore has the strongest stress. Stress within a polysyllabic lexical word is thus dependent on the relations of strength between the syllables.

However, stress can also be assigned where there is no relation of strength: this happens in lexical monosyllables such as *see*. This word has stress on its single syllable, but not because this syllable is relatively strong – there is no other syllable in the word for it to be strong in comparison with. The distinction between stress which is assigned to a monosyllable directly, and stress which is assigned on the basis of strength within a polysyllable, is very important for understanding stress-based meters in English verse, as we now see.

2.3   Shakespeare's iambic pentameter: the problem of rhythmic variation

Iambic pentameter is a meter which is found throughout English poetry, and characterizes some of the major works of the tradition: for example, much of

Chaucer's, Shakespeare's, Milton's and Wordsworth's verse is in this meter. However, despite its familiarity, the meter remains difficult to characterize, and there are disagreements between analysts about the best way to understand its structure. To illustrate the issues which arise, this is a text by Shakespeare in iambic pentameter:

> *Let me not to the marriage of true mindes*
> *Admit impediments, love is not love*
> *Which alters when it alteration findes,*
> *Or bends with the remover to remove.*
> *O no, it is an ever fixed marke*
> *That lookes on tempests and is never shaken;*
> *It is the star to ev(e)ry wand(e)ring barke,*
> *Whose worths unknowne, although his highth be taken.*
> *Lov's not Times foole, though rosie lips and cheeks*
> *Within his bending sickles compasse come,*
> *Love alters not with his breefe hours and weekes,*
> *But beares it out even to the edge of doome:*
> *If this be error and upon me proved,*
> *I never writ, nor no man ever loved.*

The rhythm of this text is manifested as a pattern of stressed and unstressed syllables. However, this text can be quite adequately performed with almost every line having a different pattern of stressed and unstressed syllables. Thus the text can be performed with stresses on the underlined syllables below:

Let	me	not	to	the	ma	rriage	of	true	mindes	
Ad	mit	im	pe	di	ments,	love	is	not	love	
Which	al	ters	when	it	al	te	ra	tion	findes,	
Or	bends	with	the	re	mo	ver	to	re	move.	
O	no,	it	is	an	e	ver	fi	xed	marke	
That	lookes	on	tem	pests	and	is	ne	ver	sha	ken;
It	is	the	star	to	ev	(e)ry	wan	d(e)ring	barke,	
Whose	worths	un	knowne,	al	though	his	highth	be	ta	ken.
Lov's	not	Times	foole,	though	ros	ie	lips	and	cheeks	
Wi	thin	his	ben	ding	si	ckles	com	passe	come,	
Love	al	ters	not	with	his	breefe	hours	and	weekes,	
But	beares	it	out	even	to	the	edge	of	doome:	
If	this	be	e	rror	and	u	pon	me	proved,	
I	ne	ver	writ,	nor	no	man	e	ver	loved.	

This rhythmic variation from line to line in performance is entirely typical of iambic pentameter, and of many other meters as well. There are basically two ways of understanding it.

One approach, which is more or less the traditional one, is to formulate iambic pentameter as a pattern of stressed and unstressed syllables which is approximated to by actual lines of text, with a certain degree of allowed variability. Thus iambic pentameter might be formulated as a pattern of ten syllables with every even syllable stressed.

σ σ́ σ σ́ σ σ́ σ σ́ σ σ́

Actual lines would then correspond approximately to this pattern.

The alternative approach is associated with a theoretical approach called generative metrics, presented in detail by Halle and Keyser (1971), and subsequently developed by other phonologists working in the generative linguistics tradition (which includes generative grammar and generative phonology). The notion of a generative grammar was formulated by Noam Chomsky, with the parallel notion of a generative phonology formulated by Chomsky with Morris Halle. The generative grammar of a language is a set of rules which can characterize any sentence as grammatical or ungrammatical: the grammar generates all and only the grammatical sentences in the sense of being able to create just these sentences. The generative phonology of a language is a set of rules which can characterize a word as having a phonological structure which is acceptable in the language. Similarly, a generative metrics for a meter is a set of rules which can characterize any line's rhythmic pattern as metrical or unmetrical: it should be able to specify that a particular line is metrical or unmetrical – and hence the vast majority of actual iambic pentameter lines should be specified as metrical by the rules.

Whereas the traditional approach to metrics is based on a notion of 'approximation', the generative approach is based on the notion of 'abstraction'. The generative approach formulates iambic pentameter at a sufficiently abstract level such that all the rhythmic variations in actual performance in fact have an identical rhythmic pattern if examined at that level. Generative metrics exploits the linguistic structure of the utterance, to show that once we have a better understanding of the linguistic structure we can also see the underlying regularities which are hidden beneath the apparently random variations of rhythmic patterns. In the case of iambic pentameter, the fundamental insight (as formulated for example by Kiparsky 1977) is that while the meter involves stress, it involves some kinds of stress and not others. We saw that it is possible to distinguish three kinds of stress in an English utterance: (1) the stress within a polysyllable which depends on strength relations between the syllables in the word, (2) the stress on a monosyllable which is assigned directly (and not on the basis of strength), and (3) postlexical stress, the stress pattern of the utterance above the level of the word, which is dependent on the communicative aims of the speaker and is not fixed for a particular sequence of words. Of these three kinds of stress, it is primarily (1) which is relevant to iambic pentameter.

Consider for example postlexical stress. The same sequence of words can be given different patterns of postlexical stress when uttered, sometimes with clear communicative consequences, and sometimes without. Thus if we take the sonnet cited above, the postlexical stress patterns assigned to it could have been different in a different performance. Take for example the first line. Perfectly acceptable alternative realizations of the postlexical stress patterns of this line include:

Let me <u>not</u> to the <u>ma</u> rriage of <u>true</u> <u>mindes</u>
<u>Let</u> me <u>not</u> to the <u>ma</u> rriage of <u>true</u> <u>mindes</u>
Let <u>me</u> not to the <u>ma</u> rriage of <u>true</u> <u>mindes</u>
Let <u>me</u> not <u>to</u> the <u>ma</u> rriage <u>of</u> true <u>mindes</u>

And so on. This variability in possible postlexical stress patterns means that the meter must be formulated to ignore postlexical stress: it is simply irrelevant to the meter. This is because the meter controls the composition of the text rather than its performance, and thus is able to control only those aspects of the prosodic phonology of the text which are invariable (i.e. lexical stress but not postlexical stress).

Thus we are left with lexical stress – on polysyllables and on monosyllables. These kinds of stress are invariant: the stress pattern on *marriage* for example does not vary at the whim of the performer. This means that iambic pentameter must be understood at a more abstract level: as a meter which controls the placement in the line of lexical stress patterns. The basic intuition about iambic pentameter is that there is a difference between odd and even positions: even positions in the line are somehow related to stressed syllables. We now see that this must specifically be the stressed syllables in lexical words. If we look at the sonnet, however, we find that lexical monosyllables are not obviously constrained to appear in either odd or even syllables. In this first line, *true* appears in an odd position (the ninth), for example. But the lexical polysyllables are constrained in their location: it turns out that all the polysyllables *are* placed in lines so that their stressed syllables are in even positions. In the diagram below, polysyllables are boxed:

	even		even		even		even		even	
Let	me	not	to	the	ma	rriage	of	true	mindes	
Ad	mit	im	pe	di	ments,	love	is	not	love	
Which	al	ters	when	it	al	te	ra	tion	findes,	
Or	bends	with	the	re	mo	ver	to	re	move.	
O	no,	it	is	an	e	ver	fi	xed	marke	
That	lookes	on	tem	pests	and	is	ne	ver	sha	ken;
It	is	the	star	to	ev	(e)ry	wan	d(e)ring	barke,	
Whose	worths	un	knowne,	al	though	his	highth	be	ta	ken.
Lov's	not	Times	foole,	though	ros	ie	lips	and	cheeks	
Wi	thin	his	ben	ding	si	ckles	com	passe	come,	
Love	al	ters	not	with	his	breefe	hours	and	weekes,	
But	beares	it	out	even	to	the	edge	of	doome:	
If	this	be	e	rror	and	u	pon	me	proved,	
I	ne	ver	writ,	nor	no	man	e	ver	loved.	

Thus we see the fundamental organizing principle of the iambic pentameter:

> Stress in lexical polysyllables must be in even positions in the line.

That's basically it, though there are plenty of supplementary comments to make. In effect, iambic pentameter controls the rhythmic structure of a line by controlling only those words which have their own internal rhythm. Now we need to formulate this basic principle as a set of metrical rules.

2.4 A generative meter for iambic pentameter

Most theories of meter begin with a metrical template, a sequence of metrical positions which are matched with phonological constituents in the line of poetry. A traditional meter typically stops with the template, and requires the lines of poetry to approximate to the metrical template without necessarily exactly fitting it. A generative meter attempts to formalize exactly which patterns in the line fit the meter and which do not, and this is achieved by formulating sometimes quite abstract rules for matching the metrical template with the line of poetry. Thus a generative meter has two parts: the metrical template and the rules which match the template to the lines.

2.4.1   A metrical template

A metrical template is fundamentally a series of positions. For iambic pentameter there are ten positions. In rhythmic meters like iambic pentameter, the positions are differentiated as strong and weak positions. The series of positions in iambic pentameter is a sequence of weak–strong–weak–strong . . . etc. The template can thus be formulated initially as:

W   S   W   S   W   S   W   S   W   S

There are at least two reasons for thinking that the template might also have a hierarchical constituent structure. The first is that the pattern of positions is periodic, repeating a weak–strong sequence. Thus we could formulate the template as five weak–strong constituents. The second reason for positing a hierarchy is that notions such as strength and weakness are relative notions: the first position is weak relative to the second which is strong. This can be formalized by organizing the line into five binary constituents characterized by the second part of each constituent being stronger than the first. For these two reasons, the template can more fully be represented as organized in constituents: the pairs of metrical positions are called metrical feet, symbolized with F:

For the moment, we will have relatively little to say about the internal constituency of the metrical template, and we will think of iambic pentameter more simply as a sequence of weak and strong positions.

2.4.2   Matching the template to syllables: a first formulation and extrametricality

The template must correspond to all lines which instantiate the meter. In the case of iambic pentameter, the majority of lines have ten syllables and so as a preliminary attempt we could formulate a matching rule: each syllable in the line must fit into a metrical position in the metrical template. This means that all ten-syllable lines are, at least in this sense, metrical.

However, just as there is variability in the stress pattern of lines, so there is also variability in the number of syllables in a line, and so if these variable-length lines are to be considered metrical, our matching rule must be reformulated to accommodate these lines. One kind of variation is where there is an eleven-syllable line ending on an unstressed syllable: this can be interpreted as resembling a typical ten-syllable line but with an extra syllable at the end. There are two such lines in the sonnet, of which this is one:

That <u>lookes</u> on <u>tem</u> pests and is <u>ne</u> ver <u>sha</u> ken;

Lines where there is an extra syllable after the final stressed syllable can be interpreted as involving 'extrametricality' (a possibility discussed in detail by Kiparsky 1977). The final syllable is extrametrical which means that it is permitted not to match a position in the metrical template. This possibility of extrametricality must be incorporated as part of the matching rules.

If extrametricality was allowed freely, there would in effect be no meter. In fact, there are two characteristics shared by extrametrical syllables which limit their occurrence: they are always unstressed, and they are always found in certain kinds of position. The most common position is at the end of a line, as here. In Shakespeare's iambic pentameter, extrametrical syllables can also appear in the middle of a line, but preceding a pause. These two positions turn out to have something in common: they are both at the end of the large prosodic phonological constituent called the phonological phrase. Thus the rule permitting extrametrical syllables is sensitive to phonological constituent structure at this level.

The following line (cited by Kiparsky 1977: 231) illustrates two extrametrical syllables, one at the end of the line and one in the middle. Both are at the end of a phonological phrase (indicated by square brackets):

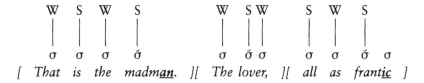

Kiparsky suggests that in iambic pentameter the extrametrical syllable must come after a syllable which corresponds to a metrical strong position, as it does in the line quoted above. A line-final extrametrical syllable in iambic pentameter will of course always be in this position (because the final metrical position is strong); the generalization is more interesting when it comes to line-internal extrametrical syllables. Notice that this generalization means that in iambic pentameter there will not be two extrametrical syllables one after another, though as the above example shows there might be two in the same line after different metrical positions. Finally, Kiparsky points out that English poets differ in what kinds of syllable they will allow to be extrametrical. For example Shakespeare, as here with *madman*, permits the second half of a compound word to be extrametrical, while Milton does not.

2.4.3 *The metrical template and stress*

There are three kinds of stress in the line of poetry: stress within a lexical polysyllable, stress on a lexical monosyllable, and postlexical stress (including stress on grammatical words). It is basically the first kind of stress which is controlled by iambic pentameter. If for the moment we just think of this as 'polysyllabic stress', we might consider how exactly it is matched with the metrical template. The template has S and W positions, and where there is polysyllabic stress it is found only in S positions. But S positions are not devoted entirely to polysyllabic stress – other kinds of stress are found here, and there may also be an unstressed syllable in an S position. For example, the following line has *the* and *to* matching strong positions, but neither word carries polysyllabic stress, and in fact on most performances of the line neither word carries any (postlexical) stress at all.

```
W    S    W    S   W   S   W   S   W    S
|    |    |    |   |   |   |   |   |    |
Or  bends with the re  mo  ver to  re  move.
```

This suggests that the matching constraint is not a constraint on S positions but should be seen from a different angle as a constraint on W positions: specifically, that a W position within the metrical template must not match a 'polysyllabic stress'.

How does the meter differentiate between polysyllabic and monosyllabic stress? The difference is that a polysyllabic stress pattern is derived from the relative strengths of syllables within a lexical word: there is no relative strength pattern within a monosyllable because there is nothing for the single syllable to be strong relative to. Hanson and Kiparsky (1996) suggest that this therefore means that the matching constraint should be reformulated so that it does not directly refer to stress at all, but instead refers to strength. A stressed syllable in a polysyllabic word is also a strong syllable, and is the only example of a syllable which is strong within a word. Thus the matching constraint can be reformulated like this: a weak position in the metrical template must not match a strong syllable within the word. This is a radical suggestion about iambic pentameter because it means that the meter does not in fact directly control stress: it has an effect on stress patterns only indirectly through syllables via their strength and only thereby controlling stress.

2.4.4 The metrical template and the phonological foot

One of the variations in the iambic pentameter line involves extra syllables within the line, which cannot be considered extrametrical because they are in the middle of phonological phrases. It is common to find two light syllables between two strong syllables: this situation must be accounted for by the meter, but cannot be accounted for by the matching rules which exist so far. Consider for example this line from *Othello* (cited by Hanson and Kiparsky 1996):

```
 W   S   W   S   W    S   W       S   W   S
 |   |  /\  |   |   |   |      |   |   |
 σ   ŏ  σ σ  ŏ  σ    ŏ   σ   σ    ŏ   σ   ŏ   σ
This for ti fi ca tion  gent le men,  shall we see it?
```

This line has an extrametrical syllable at the end, *it*. The syllable *men* could also be accounted for by saying that it is extrametrical. But this is not the case for the extra syllable in the word *fortification*. Here there are two syllables between the two strong syllables, but only one weak position for these two syllables *ti* and *fi* to fit into. Hanson and Kiparsky suggest that this problem is resolved by looking at the prosodic phonological structure of the word (as shown in 2.2.5), where *ti-fi* constitutes a single phonological foot (comprising two light syllables). They suggest that it is the phonological foot rather than the syllable which is matched to the metrical position.

The problem with *fortification* arose not from Shakespeare's compositional decision but from the structure of the word: this word always has two light syllables between two strong syllables. However, extra syllables can also arise from the composition of the line, where for example two grammatical words come between two strong syllables, as in the following line:

```
 W  S  W  S  W    S       W    S   WS
 |  |  |  |  |    |       /\   |   ||
 σ  ŏ  σ  σ  σ   ŏ  σ    σ σ  ŏ   σ ŏ
A sample to the youngest; to the more mature
```

This line has two extra syllables in it (it has twelve syllables). One extra syllable, the *-est* of *youngest*, is extrametrical: it is at the end of a phonological phrase. However, *to* and *the* must be considered as two light syllables belonging to a phonological foot, and are permitted to combine to fill a single metrical position because of this.

These are examples where the two-syllable phonological foot is matched to a weak metrical position. However, it is also possible for a two-syllable phonological foot to match a strong metrical position. In the following line from *Henry V*, the two syllables in *many* fill a single strong position: they are both light syllables, even though one is stressed. Note that in this line the pair of light monosyllables *in one*, which constitute a single phonological foot, also fill a single metrical position:

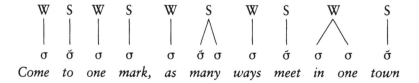

Thus the structure of English words and the compositional practice of Shakespeare both suggest that in his iambic pentameter, the metrical position, while it will normally match a syllable, may also match a phonological foot (i.e. a prosodic phonological constituent containing two light syllables).

2.4.5 Initial freedoms

We have seen that strong syllables may not match weak positions. However, there is a position in the line where this requirement appears to be relaxed: the first position of the line. Here it is not uncommon to find a polysyllabic word with initial stress, even though the first metrical position is weak. Thus a strong syllable matches a weak position. We might expect this phenomenon to be incorporated into the matching rules for the meter. However, there are some reasons for thinking that it manifests a general principle for metrical texts and thus that it should not be incorporated into specific rules. In most meters, and most strikingly in meters in the Indo-European tradition, the metrical matching rules appear to be relaxed at the beginning of a line – but adhered to firmly in the later part of the line. This phenomenon in iambic pentameter might be a reflex of this general phenomenon.

Hayes (1983: 382) suggests that in fact in iambic pentameter the principle of relaxation of matching rules at the beginning relates not to the line but to the phonological phrase: thus 'inversion' of the foot occurs at the beginning of the line and after a pause in the line – both are the beginnings of phonological phrases.

W	S	W	S		W	S	W	S	W		S
|	|	|	|		|	|	|	|	|		|
σ̆	σ	σ	σ̆		σ̆	σ	σ	σ̆	σ		σ̆

[**Ri** cher than wealth][**Prou** der than gar ments cost]

Thus again it seems that certain kinds of variation which are permitted in the matching rules are sensitive to the boundary of a phonological phrase (this was the case also for extrametricality): phonological phrase boundaries appear to allow certain kinds of metrical looseness.

2.4.6 In summary: the metrical rules for Shakespeare's iambic pentameter

In summary, we can formulate Shakespeare's version of iambic pentameter as follows:

1 There is a metrical template:

   W S W S W S W S W S

2 There is a set of matching rules:

   Each metrical position must be matched with a phonological constituent no larger than a phonological foot (and normally with a syllable);

   A weak position in the metrical template must not be matched with a strong syllable within a word.

3 There are stipulated exceptions to the matching rules, which apply at the edges of phonological phrases:

   A syllable at the end of a phonological phrase may be ignored by the matching rules (= extrametricality);

   A weak position in the metrical template may match a strong syllable within a word when that syllable is at the beginning of a phonological phrase.

This is a simplified account of the meter, which nevertheless expresses the basic ideas (for example it does not indicate the foot structure within the metrical template). Other poets modify the meter in various ways, as Hanson and Kiparsky (1996), Hanson (1996) and others have argued.

What, finally, is the relation between this formulation of iambic pentameter and any line of iambic pentameter poetry? The meter fully constrains certain aspects of the prosodic phonological structure of the line: specifically, it constrains the number of syllables, and the placement of strong syllables. Other aspects of the phonological structure of the line are not constrained by the meter: these include the postlexical stress patterns. Thus the meter partially determines the prosodic phonological structure of the line. This will be true of all meters: the problem for analysis is to decide which aspects of prosodic phonological structure are determined, and how they are determined.

2.5 Generative metrics and the formulation of a meter

Thus a meter is a template and a set of matching rules and other rules: the meter is a description of the regularities in a certain kind of linguistic behaviour (the composition of a metrical text). This formulation of a meter is associated with generative linguistics, and generative linguistics takes a specific view of the reason for regularities in linguistic behaviour: regularities in linguistic behaviour arise because linguistic behaviour is generated on the basis of linguistic knowledge. Linguistic knowledge in turn can be formulated in part as a set of rules for building linguistic structures. Thus linguists look at regularities in linguistic behaviour in order to discover the nature of the knowledge which underlies linguistic behaviour, a knowledge which is understood in terms of rules. The same principle carries over to metrics: the regularities in a metrical text are understood as arising from the 'metrical knowledge' of the composer of the text. This metrical knowledge is the meter, consisting of the template and the set of rules.

It is worth noting that the knowledge which underlies the regularities in our behaviour, and from which our behaviour is generated, is not necessarily explicit knowledge. This is clearly the case for language: most people can produce utterances which are fully regular, without having any ability to make explicit the rules which characterize those utterances. Furthermore, even where there is explicit description of the rules which characterize the regularities in linguistic behaviour, that explicit description may be incorrect: people have demonstrably false beliefs about their own linguistic behaviour. The work of linguistics is to discover what the actual rules are which determine the regularities in our linguistic behaviour. These comments can be carried over from linguistics to metrics. Thus an author may compose fully regular texts without being able to describe what he or she is doing, and on the other hand there are often detailed theories of metrical composition contemporary with practice (and sometimes formulated by practitioners) which are not fully accurate in their characterization of actual practice. The bottom line for generative metrics is that there can only be one correct characterization of a metrical practice – only one way of formulating a particular meter; the task of metrics is to work out what that formulation is, by

identifying exactly what the regularities are in the prosodic phonological structure of metrical texts.

2.5.1 *Some terminological issues*

One of the minor metatheoretical problems of doing metrics is that technical
terms are used in different ways. In part this is a reflex of the fact that many
traditions of metrical practice are accompanied by their own theoretical traditions,
with their own terminologies – and as terminologies are adapted to new purposes,
possibilities of confusion arise. The aim of this section is thus to clarify how some
of the more complex terms are used in the present book.

We use the term 'meter' to describe the set of rules which consists of metrical
template, matching rules and any related adjustment rules or permitted variations. 'Meter' is sometimes used to describe these rules plus rules of sound-
patterning and other genre conventions, but the term is not used with this
meaning here. For example, for us 'iambic pentameter' is a meter because it
constrains just the prosodic phonological structure, but 'blank verse' is not a
meter because it adds a constraint relating to sound-patterning (i.e. that there
is no rhyme). Where we need to refer to meters plus other related rules, particularly rules of sound-patterning, we'll use the term 'metrical system'. Thus blank
verse is a metrical system, as is *séadna*; the latter is a metrical system which
includes a meter (which counts syllables) plus other rules of sound-patterning,
etc. Word-boundary rules have a somewhat ambiguous status here – it is not
clear whether they should be thought of as part of the meter or as part of the
broader metrical system (we return to this in chapter 5). 'Prosody' is also sometimes used to describe metrical structure; we restrict the term here to an aspect
of linguistic structure, and generally combine it with 'phonological' to make this
clear. Thus we speak of the 'prosodic phonological structure' of an utterance,
which in itself has nothing to do with literary structure (though it is exploited
by a meter). The term 'meter', which we are restricting to literary texts, is itself
sometimes used for purely linguistic structure (hence there is a theory of 'metrical phonology', which in itself has nothing to do with literary texts).

The terms 'meter' and 'prosody' are one terminological source of complications. The other relates to the names for metrical constituents, and here there
is a clash between emic and etic approaches. The largest metrical constituent is
called a 'line' here; a single metrical line can sometimes be thought of or written
down as a long-line (German *Langzeile*) or a couplet. We define a line as the
stretch of text which is matched with the metrical template, however it is con-
ceived or written down. Within a line, the smallest metrical constituent above
the metrical position is normally called a 'foot'. If there is another intermediate level of constituency between the foot and the line, we'll generally call it a

'half-line' or 'metron' (borrowing the term from Greek metrics); the two terms really mean the same and we could perhaps have a single term for both. However, we'll distinguish them for convenience by using 'half-line' when the line falls into two such constituents, and 'metron' in other cases.

There are some other terminological pitfalls. 'Caesura', for example, is sometimes used to mean a pause in performance, and sometimes just a rule which requires that a word end at a particular place in the line: we will use the term in this second sense. Finally, there are complications involving classificatory terms such as 'verse', 'poem' and 'song'. To some extent these terms are used interchangeably in this book; if a distinction can be made, we might perhaps use 'verse' to describe any text organized into lines (whether metrical or not), 'poem' to describe any text which is metrical, and 'song' to describe any text which is set to music (which may not be metrical or divided into lines).

2.6 Summary: linguistic form (prosodic phonology) and literary form (meter)

In this chapter we have seen one of the most extensively discussed examples of the adaptation of linguistic form to literary form. Metrical structure is a kind of literary form, involving the division of a text into constituents each of which has its prosodic phonological structure adapted to a certain pattern. The possibility of metrical structure, as a kind of literary form, is entirely dependent on prosodic phonological structure which is a kind of linguistic form that is found in all spoken language (whether literary or not). Thus the meter is sensitive to certain kinds of prosodic phonological constituency, both as the units which are matched (syllables, strong positions, etc.), and as constituents which have boundaries which are places of metrical variation (phonological phrases). Metrical structure is one of the few areas of literary linguistics where there may be some involvement of specialized cognitive mechanisms: thus the possibility of metrical verse may be based on aspects of human cognitive structure, just as the possibility of language is based on aspects of human cognitive structure.

2.7 Further reading

Prosodic phonology and its application to metrical theory is discussed by Nespor and Vogel (1986) and Hayes (1989). Kenstowicz (1994) is a comprehensive introduction to phonological structure; see also Hogg and McCully (1987).

Ladefoged and Maddieson (1996) and Pullum and Ladusaw (1986) are useful reference works for phonetics. Generative metrics has consistently returned to the problems presented by iambic pentameter; key discussions which illustrate the development of ideas about the meter can be found in Halle and Keyser (1971), Kiparsky (1977), Hayes (1983, 1988, 1989), Youmans (1986) and Hanson and Kiparsky (1996). Hanson (1996) explores the history of iambic pentameter, both in its origins and in its development. Attridge (1982, 1995) and Tarlinskaja (1989) present influential alternative approaches to iambic pentameter; a traditional approach can be found in Fussell (1979); see also Cureton (1994). Kiparsky and Youmans (1989) is a useful anthology on metrics.

2.8   Exercises

2.8.1   *Holinshed and Shakespeare*

This exercise is intended to give you some practice in matching a metrical template to lines of poetry; it also offers an opportunity to look at the working methods of one of the major practitioners of the iambic pentameter meter, Shakespeare.

Instructions

Work on the text line by line (i.e. do all questions for the first line, then the second line). Lines particularly worth paying attention to are 12 and 13.

(a) Identify all the syllables in each line, and write σ above each one.
(b) Identify polysyllabic words and work out which syllables have stress in each word.
(c) Match the iambic pentameter template to the sequence of syllables. There are some extrametrical syllables and some cases where two light syllables fit into one metrical position.
(d) Is each line metrical, according to the rule for Shakespeare's iambic pentameter formulated in this chapter?
(e) Discuss any changes which Shakespeare made to identifiable pieces of text in the source version (by Raphael Holinshed); can these changes be explained in terms of his need to reshape the lines into iambic pentameter? You might explore this by trying to rewrite parts of Holinshed's text in iambic pentameter and comparing your efforts with Shakespeare's.

Sample answer

As an illustration of what you should do, here is the analysis of the third line.

(a)   Syllables are indicated:

    σ   σ   σ   σ σ σ   σ   σ   σ   σ
    Joined with an enemy proclaimed and fixed

Note that the spelling of the words does not necessarily tell you how many syllables are in them: *joined* is a monosyllable (the written vowel *e* is not pronounced).

(b)   Lexical stressed syllables are marked with an accent:

    ő   σ   σ   ő σ ő   σ   ő   σ   ő
    Joined with an enemy proclaimed and fixed

(c)   There are no extra or missing syllables in this line. This is the matching of syllables to template:

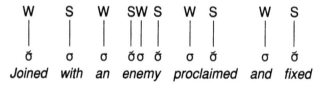

    W   S   W   SW S   W   S   W   S
    │   │   │   │││   │   │   │   │
    ő   σ   σ   ő σ ő   σ   ő   σ   ő
    Joined with an enemy proclaimed and fixed

(d)   This line is metrical: all syllables fit into the template, and there are no cases where stressed syllables in the polysyllables *enemy* and *proclaimed* (i.e. strong syllables) match weak positions.

(e)   There is very little of this line in the Holinshed text with the exception of the word *enemy*, which is placed here in a metrically acceptable position.

Texts

> KING HENRY:
> *God 'quit you in his mercy. Hear your sentence.*
> *You have conspired against our royal person,*
> *Joined with an enemy proclaimed and fixed,*
> *And from his coffers*
> 5   *Received the golden earnest of our death,*
> *Wherein you would have sold your king to slaughter,*

> *His princes and his peers to servitude,*
> *His subjects to oppression and contempt,*
> *And his whole kingdom into desolation.*
> 10   *Touching our person seek we no revenge,*
> *But we our kingdom's safety must so tender,*
> *Whose ruin you sought, that to her laws*
> *We do deliver you. Get ye therefore hence,*
> *Poor miserable wretches, to your death;*
> 15   *The taste whereof, God of his mercy give*
> *You patience to endure, and true repentance*
> *Of all your dear offences. – Bear them hence.*

This iambic pentameter text by Shakespeare (from *Henry V*, 1623 edition) is a development of a prose text from Raphael Holinshed's *Histories* (1587):

Having thus conspired the death and destruction of me, which am the head of the realm and governor of the people, it may be (no doubt) but that you likewise have sworn the confusion of all that are here with me, and also the desolation of your own country. To what horror (O lord) for any true English heart to consider, that such an execrable iniquity should ever so bewrap you, as for pleasing of a foreign enemy to imbrue your hands in your blood, and to ruin your own native soil. Revenge herein touching my person, though I seek not; yet for the safeguard of you my dear friends, and for due preservation of all sorts, I am by office to cause example to be showed. Get ye hence, therefore, ye poor miserable wretches, to the receiving of your just reward; wherein God's majesty give you grace of his mercy and repentance of your heinous offences.

2.8.2 *Monosyllabic adjective + noun sequences in Shakespeare and Milton*

This exercise (based on a comment by Kiparsky 1976: 89) begins with a selection of unconnected lines taken from the first 500 of Book V of Milton's *Paradise Lost*, in each of which there is a sequence of monosyllabic adjective plus monosyllabic noun. In ordinary speech, the postlexical stressing of such a sequence would tend to give both parts fairly similar stress, with a slight tendency towards stronger stress on the second member.

(a)   Are the monosyllabic adjective–noun sequences (such as *best gift*, *fresh field* etc.) consistently placed with regard to strong and weak metrical positions in the line? (Note: where there is a sequence of adjective–adjective–noun as in *last best gift*, focus on the final adjective–noun sequence. Treat 'heaven' as a monosyllable.)

> *Heaven's last best gift, my ever new delight*
> *Awake, the morning shines, and the fresh field*
> *At such bold words vouched with a deed so bold*
> *Wild work produces oft, and most in dreams*
> *So cheered he his fair spouse, and she was cheered*
> *Their maker, in fit strains pronounced or sung*
> *And when high noon hast gained, and when thou fall'st*
> *With the fixed stars, fixed in their orb that flies*
> *Vary to our great maker still new praise*
> *To hill, or valley, fountain, or fresh shade*
> *Among sweet dews and flowers; where any row*
> *With pity heaven's high king, and to him called*
> *Left to his own free will, his will though free*
> *A phoenix, gazed by all, as that sole bird*
> *Of his cool bower, while now the mounted sun*
> *Of God inspired, small store will serve, where store*
> *Rough, or smooth rind, or bearded husk, or shell*
> *Mean while our primitive great sire, to meet*
> *At heaven's high feasts to have fed: yet what compare?*
> *Springs lighter the green stalk, from thence the leaves*
> *No inconvenient diet, nor too light fare*

(b) The following lines have a monosyllabic quantifier + monosyllabic noun sequence: *all things* and *each hand*. How do these compare with the adjective + noun sequences in terms of their placement with regard to metrical constituent structure?

> *And nourish all things, let your ceaseless change*
> *On each hand parting, to his speech gave way*

(c) Based on your findings in (a) and (b), how does Milton's iambic pentameter differ from Shakespeare's iambic pentameter (as described in 2.4.6)? Rewrite one of the matching rules to capture this difference.

(d) Now we look at some adjective + noun sequences taken from the first 500 lines of Shakespeare's *The Rape of Lucrece*. Kiparsky comments that Shakespeare allows greater variety in the placement of monosyllabic adjective + noun sequences. Based on this example, is Kiparsky right?

Of Collatine's fair love, Lucrece the chaste
O rash false heat, wrapp'd in repentant cold
Which Tarquin view'd in her fair face's field
In their pure ranks his traitor eye encloses
In that high task hath done her beauty wrong
And decks with praises Collatine's high name
The silly lambs: pure thoughts are dead and still
That from the cold stone sparks of fire do fly
As from this cold flint I enforced this fire
Fair torch, burn out thy light, and lend it not
O impious act, including all foul harms!
Who fears a sentence or an old man's saw
And with good thoughts make dispensation
Fearing some hard news from the warlike band
Sad pause and deep regard beseem the sage
Full of foul hope and full of fond mistrust
But his hot heart, which fond desire doth scorch
He in the worst sense construes their denial
Huge rocks, high winds, strong pirates, shelves and sands
That his foul thoughts might compass his fair fair
In his clear bed might have reposed still
Without the bed her other fair hand was
From this fair throne to heave the owner out
As the grim lion fawneth o'er his prey

3   Kinds of Meter

Chapter 2 introduced a way of understanding what a meter is: a combination of metrical template and matching rules. In this chapter, we describe the different kinds of metrical verse in terms of this approach to meter. Metrical texts come in basically two varieties. In one variety, the metricality of the text relates to the number of prosodic phonological units in each line – these units normally being either morae or syllables. Texts of this kind are governed by what we can call 'counting meters'. In the other variety, the metricality of the text relates to the pattern of prosodic phonological units in each line (which incorporates a counting of the number of units as part of the pattern); the units in this case are differentiated into some kind of rhythm based on stressed and unstressed syllables or heavy and light syllables. Texts of this kind are governed by what we can call 'patterning meters'. Iambic pentameter is a patterning meter. In this chapter, we see a variety of different kinds of counting meter and patterning meter: the aim here is partly descriptive, to give a sense of the variety of metrical traditions and to suggest some of the issues which might arise in a further study of a wide range of meters.

3.1   'Counting' meters

We begin with counting meters. In principle, a counting meter involves a template in which the metrical positions are not differentiated into strong and weak; the matching rules relate simply to how the positions match with phonological units in the line, and do not differentiate between kinds of phonological unit. It is necessary to add 'in principle' because meters can have indirect effects on the prosodic phonology of a line. Just as the iambic pentameter appears to control stress while actually controlling strength, so in principle we might find that a meter which appears to control simply number of syllables in fact does so indirectly through a covert patterning of types of syllable.

3.1.1   *Syllable-counting meters*

Syllable-counting meters are characteristic of Celtic poetry, and our example comes from the Celtic language Welsh. The following is a stanza in a meter called *englyn penfyr* (from *The Red Book of Hergest*, cited in Williams 1953: 233). The meter determines that the stanza should have three lines, of 10 + 7 + 7 syllables. In addition there are para-metrical constraints requiring a caesura towards the end of the first line (i.e. forcing a word boundary), and a complex pattern of sound-patterning.

Sta-vell   Gyn-dy-lan   am er-wan – pob   awr
(the) hall (of) Cynddylan pains-me   – every hour

gwe-dy mawr ym-gy-vyr-dan
after   great   conversing

a   we-lais ar dy   ben-tan.
which I-saw   on your hearthside

We might deal with the variability in line length by having two metrical templates, or by having a single long metrical template for the whole stanza. On the assumption that we have two templates, this is what the template would look like for the seven-syllable lines:

X X X X X X X

The realization rules would then specify that each metrical position should match a syllable in the line of text. The second line would scan as follows (the letter *y* represents a vowel in Welsh orthography):

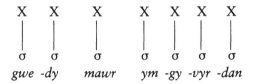

This is a simple account of the meter which assumes that the basic realization rule matches syllables to metrical positions. However, many Celtic syllable-counting meters allow certain kinds of variation and it is possible in principle that a deeper analysis of the meter could show that it is not syllables but some other unit of structure which is matched with the metrical template.

3.1.2 Mora-counting meters

We saw that for iambic pentameter there was a question about whether the
metrical positions matched syllables or phonological feet. The possibility of
varying the size of prosodic phonological constituent which is matched to the
metrical position is the basis of the difference between syllable-counting and
mora-counting meters. In a mora-counting meter, each metrical position matches
a mora.

The Japanese *haiku* genre is governed by a mora-counting meter. The requirement is that the first line has five morae, the second seven, and the third five.
A short vowel constitutes one mora, a long vowel is two morae (e.g. *doo*) and
a syllable-final [n] constitutes a mora. In the transcript below, moraic divisions
within words are indicated with a dash.

na-ra na-na-e
Nara seven

shi-chi do-o   ga-ra-n
seven   temples big temples

ya-e   za-ku-ra
eight-fold petalled cherry blossoms

'Nara (town) is sevenfold, a complete seven-part temple complex, a double-
flowered cherry tree' (cited by Poser 1990)

The operation of the meter can be illustrated for the second line:

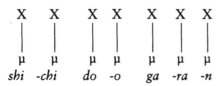

Notice that this line has five syllables, but seven morae: hence it fits the seven-
position requirement by virtue of counting morae rather than syllables.

The use of the numbers five and seven as the typical numbers of morae in the
line in Japanese meters may reflect the seventh-century influence of Chinese
poetry which was already using meters based on five and seven (Brower 1972:
42). In Chinese prosodic phonology the syllable is a more significant unit of
prosodic phonological structure, for the purposes of phonological rules, than the
mora; in Japanese, the mora has greater significance (for example in the assignment of pitch-accent within a word). These differences between the languages

are mirrored in the differences between the meters: a seven/five-syllable counting meter in Chinese becomes a seven/five-mora counting meter in Japanese. When the *haiku* is borrowed into other languages where syllables are more important, such as English, it becomes a syllable-counting meter again: English *haiku* have five + seven + five syllables (not morae). As is generally the case, the linguistic form of the language shapes the possibilities available to the literary form.

3.2 Patterning meters: basic issues

A counting meter has a metrical template consisting of undifferentiated metrical positions. Each metrical position is matched to a prosodic phonological constituent, typically either a syllable or a mora. In contrast, a patterning meter has a metrical template consisting of two kinds of metrical position, with the matching rules being sensitive to differences between the two kinds. Iambic pentameter is a patterning meter, where there are two kinds of metrical position, labelled S and W, and the matching rule is sensitive to the difference: it specifies that a strong syllable in a lexical word must not match a W position in the metrical template. Because the differentiated positions are typically matched to differentiated prosodic constituents (e.g. heavy and light syllables, or stressed and unstressed constituents), a patterning meter determines a rhythmic pattern in the prosodic phonology of the line, and can thus also be called a rhythmic meter. Where the matching rules differentiate syllables on the basis of weight, the patterning meter is more precisely called a quantitative meter. Where the matching rules differentiate syllables on the basis of stress, the patterning meter is more precisely called an accentual meter.

One of the fundamental characteristics of a patterning meter is that the metrical template has differentiated metrical positions. If we consider iambic pentameter, we can see that the differentiation is required for the matching rule, but also appears to arise from the constituent structure of the metrical template. Thus we need to differentiate W from S positions so that we can specify that a strong syllable in the word must not match a W position. But the W position is also 'weak' within the metrical template relative to the 'strong' S position which is its partner within the foot; thus the weak (W)–strong (S) distinction arises purely within the meter independently of the prosodic phonological structure to which it is matched. This is why the W and S positions are so labelled, rather than just being called, for example, x and y or + and –: they arise from relative strength within a metrical constituent. This notion of relative strength is straightforward for iambic pentameter, where the two kinds of metrical position are grouped into binary constituents: each foot has an S member and a W member.

Wherever we can understand a patterning meter as a binary meter, we can think in terms of relative strength. However, if we look at other patterning meters we find two kinds of problem. First, some feet seem to be ternary (or larger). Consider for example the following line from Key's *The Star-Spangled Banner*, which is sung with the indicated syllables most strongly stressed:

σ σ ő   σ   σ   ő σ σ ő   σ σ ő
O-oh say does that star-span-gled ba-nner yet wave

The line would appear to be organized according to a metrical template whereby feet are organized into W W S metrical positions (i.e. a ternary structure):

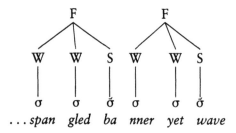

The strongest syllable in polysyllabic words is matched only with S positions. However, there is another constraint involving other stressed syllables in poly-syllabic words – such as *span* in *spangled*. Kiparsky (1977: 227) proposes that in this text (and in this meter generally), stressed syllables in polysyllabic words are matched to metrical positions in a way which differentiates between the two W positions: the stressed syllable may match only the first W position and not the second. This suggests that the foot is not in fact flat in its structure: the first two positions are weaker than the third, but the first position is stronger than the second, a structure which could be realized as follows:

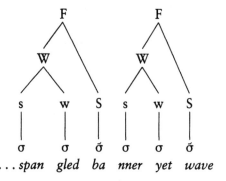

We will see another argument that an apparently ternary foot can be reanalysed as a complex binary foot in 5.2.1.

There is, however, another problem in quantitative meters which cannot be resolved in this manner. Thus for example in the classical Sanskrit meters, heavy and light syllables are controlled by the meter but in runs of heavy and light syllables. An example is illustrated in the next section, from the *mandākrāntā* meter. Here we must differentiate metrical positions in the meter, but the meter will then have for example four of one kind of position (matching heavy syllables) followed by five of the other kind of position (matching light syllables). Here we can use the symbols S and W to differentiate the metrical positions in the template, but these cannot be interpreted as relative strength within the template. Thus the symbols have a somewhat different interpretation from the same symbols used in iambic pentameter. Chen's (1979) account of Chinese regulated verse (3.5) uses the S and W symbols in yet another way, which also does not respect notions of relative strength. This is a theoretical problem which might in principle be solved by a more advanced metrical theory.

It is not always simple to decide whether a particular meter is a counting meter, a quantitative meter or an accentual meter, and conventional classifications may prove to be incorrect. This is partly because stress patterns within a word are sometimes difficult to determine (typically because the languages are no longer spoken), and may have a close relation with syllable weight patterns within a word. Thus meters which appear to be counting meters or quantitative meters might in some cases be reinterpretable as accentual meters. We see an example of this in 3.4.3.

3.3 Quantitative meters

In a quantitative meter, the metrical line has a pattern of heavy and light syllables. This can in principle be formalized by differentiating two kinds of metrical position: S and W. As explained in the previous section, the symbols 'S' and 'W' sometimes imply a relation of strength within the metrical template and sometimes do not. If we assume a metrical template with positions labelled S and W, the traditional approach to quantitative meters then progresses as follows: a W position matches a single light syllable; an S position matches a single heavy syllable. Some metrical positions are designated as anceps positions, which means that they are symbolized as X rather than as S or W and may match either a heavy or a light syllable. Some designated S positions may alternatively match two light syllables: this is called resolution (and has the effect of increasing the number of syllables in the line though not its overall length in morae). Some designated pairs of W positions may alternatively match a single heavy syllable: this is called contraction (and has the effect of reducing the number of syllables in the line though not its overall length in morae). These two alternatives both exploit the equivalence of one heavy syllable (two morae) to two light syllables (one mora plus one mora). The metrical positions are organized into feet and feet may then be organized into larger metrical constituents within the line. As with all traditional notions of metrical structure, the actual workings of a meter may be quite different from its apparent workings as described by a traditional approach.

3.3.1 Greek iambic trimeter

Iambic trimeter is the meter most commonly used in dramatic dialogue in Classical Greek plays (see West 1987). It can be illustrated with the first three lines of Sophocles' *Oedipus Tyrannus*; patterns of heavy and light syllables are indicated above the lines, with a macron (¯) indicating a heavy syllable, and a breve (˘) indicating a light syllable.

˘ – ˘   –   –   – ˘ – ˘ –   ˘ –

o tek-na   kad-mou   tou pa-lai ne-aa   tro-phee
O children of Kadmos   of   old   new   infants

˘ –   ˘   –   –   – ˘   –   ˘ – ˘ ˘

ti-nas po-th hed-raas   taas-de moi tho-ad-ze-te
why   to   the throne   to   me   do you hurry

–   – ˘ – ˘   – ˘   – ˘   –   ˘ –

hik-tee-ri-ois kla-doi-si-n   ek-se-stem-me-noi
suppliant   (olive) branches   stretching out

(Note that the calculation of syllable weights takes resyllabification into account, whereby a consonant at the end of a word can re-attach to the following word.) Each of these three lines has a different pattern of heavy and light syllables. In tragic drama – as here – variation is typically in the first, fifth, ninth and final positions. These positions can be designated anceps positions (i.e. matching heavy or light syllables). Thus the metrical template can be laid out as:

X S W S   X S W S   X S W X

An S position matches a heavy syllable, and a W position matches a light syllable; an X position matches a syllable of any quantity – it is an anceps position. Imitating the traditional approach we might organize pairs of positions into feet and pairs of feet into constituents called metra (singular = metron). Because the feet have a W–S pattern (iambic) and because there are three metra in the line the meter is called iambic trimeter.

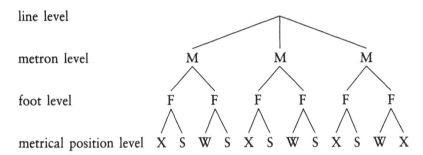

Prince (1989) suggests that the traditional approach is correct and in fact enables us to dispense with explicit anceps positions. Instead we can formulate the template like this:

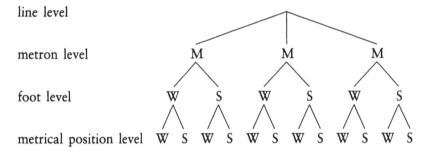

In this approach, where not only metrical positions but also feet exist in relations of strength and weakness, we can see that the first position in each metrical constituent is super-weak, being the weak metrical position within a weak foot. This super-weakness might be sufficient without extra stipulation to result in its being an anceps position, where the quantity of the syllable it matches is irrelevant. There is another way of understanding why the first metrical position in a metron might be an anceps, which is that it might be a general manifestation of the general principle that initial metrical positions are positions of variation: here the variation arises because the position is first in the metron. This is a different approach because it does not refer to the super-weakness of the position as derived from the hierarchical constituent structure. (See Hayes 1989 for discussion of the weakness of initial positions.) Either of these approaches suggests that the initial anceps positions in 1, 5 and 9 are different in kind from the final anceps position in 12. What may be happening in this position is that a final light syllable can fit into an S metrical position because the pause which follows the line-ending can supply a one-mora 'rest' which fills out the light syllable as though it were a heavy syllable: this phenonemon is called 'brevis in longo' (short in long), and is found in many metrical traditions.

Another characteristic kind of variation in a quantitative meter is resolution, where two light syllables are found in a position where we might normally expect one heavy syllable. Here it seems that the two morae of the two light syllables count as equivalent to the two morae of one heavy syllable, thus allowing the two light syllables to match an S position. This suggests that the matching of metrical positions to linguistic material is based on morae rather than syllables, with an S position matching two morae and a W position matching one. The following line (cited by West 1987: 26; from Euripides' *Orestes* 643) shows resolution in the first three S positions:

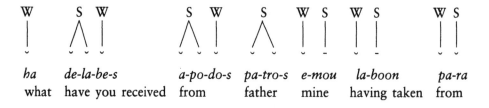

ha	de-la-be-s	a-po-do-s	pa-tro-s	e-mou	la-boon	pa-ra
what	have you received	from	father	mine	having taken	from

Note that, in each case, the resolved syllables are all within the same word; in this tradition, it is common for them to be part of a three-syllable word, and where the resolved syllables are in different words they are 'closely linked . . . by phrasing' (as West 1987: 26 puts it), at least in tragedy. This suggests that resolution occurs within a phonological word and thus that the meter may be sensitive to aspects of prosodic phonological structure above the mora and syllable.

There is another aspect to this meter which has so far not been discussed, which is that there is also a caesura rule. A caesura rule stipulates that a word boundary must fall in a particular place in the line, with 'place' defined in terms of the metrical template. In this meter, there must be a word boundary either after fifth position (as in lines 1 and 2 of the *Oedipus Tyrannus* text, and the line from *Orestes*) or after the seventh position (as in line 3). Note that the caesura does not coincide with a metrical constituent boundary, but always falls inside a foot – and always falls one position away from the middle of the line. This mismatch between caesura and metrical boundary is found in many traditions (see 5.2.1).

3.3.2 Sanskrit

The basis for metrical organization in Sanskrit is syllable weight, measured in morae (or *mātrā*, as morae are called in Sanskrit poetic theory). The overall length of the metrical line (called a *pāda*) involves either a specific number of morae (e.g. thirty morae in the first *āryā* line), or a specific number of syllables (e.g. seventeen syllables in the *mandākrāntā* line). Many Sanskrit meters involve a mixture of counting and quantitative patterning, and can broadly be divided into three kinds (see Preminger and Brogan (1993: 600) for an overview):

1 The line involves a fixed number of syllables with a fixed pattern of heavy and light syllables.
2 The line involves a fixed number of syllables, but only part of the line has a fixed pattern of heavy and light syllables (the latter part of the line is more fixed than the initial part).
3 The line involves a fixed number of morae with some restrictions on patterns of heavy and light syllables.

Each of these metrical kinds will be illustrated in turn. We begin with the *mandākrāntā* meter. There are seventeen syllables in the line in a fixed pattern of heavy and light syllables, with caesurae (requiring word boundaries). A heavy syllable is indicated here with ¯, a light syllable with ˘, and a caesura with a colon symbol.

```
 ¯   ¯   ¯   ¯ :  ˘  ˘  ˘  ˘  ˘  ¯ :  ¯    ˘    ¯   ¯  ˘   ¯  ¯
```
ut-sañ-ge vā ma-li-na-va-sa-ne saum-ya nik-ṣip-ya vī-ṇām

```
 ¯    ¯    ¯   ¯ :  ˘  ˘  ˘  ˘  ¯ :  ¯  ˘    ¯    ¯  ˘  ¯  ¯
```
mad-got-rāñ-kaṁ vi-ra-ci-ta-pa-dam ge-yam ud-gāt-u-kā-mā

'Or perhaps placing her lute on her lap, whose dark garment proclaims her grief, she will seek to sing a song wherein she has worked my name ...' (from the *Meghadūta* by Kālidāsa; in Keith 1920: 101)

(A note on the calculation of heavy and light syllables in Sanskrit. A heavy syllable annotated with a macron (¯) can be identified in the sequence of segments as containing (a) a long vowel, i.e. [ā], [ī] and [ū] whose length is indicated with a macron, and [e] and [o] which are always long; (b) a diphthong such as [au]; (c) a vowel followed by two consonants (which can be in the following word) – the vowel and first following consonant together constitute a heavy coda.)

How would we formalize this meter? In the metrical template, we would have seventeen metrical positions, which match syllables. We would need to differentiate: the two kinds of metrical position would match either a heavy or a light syllable. For convenience we might use S and W to differentiate the two kinds of metrical position:

S S S S W W W W W S S W S S W S S

It is worth noting that S and W would then not be defined relationally with regard to one another: in periodic meters, a strong S position is strong relative to an adjacent W position, but this is not the case in the kind of meter illustrated above, where there are long runs of heavy or light syllables.

Now we consider the rather different kinds of meter which are found in the earliest Sanskrit texts, the *Vedas*. Consider for example the following sequence of lines, annotated with their patterns of heavy and light syllables:

˘ ˘   –   –   ˘   –   ˘ ˘

sva-yú-r   ind-ra   s-va-rā́-ḷ   a-si

–   –   –   ˘   ˘   ˘   –

smád-diṣ-ṭiḥ   svá-ya-śas-ta-raḥ

˘   –   –   ˘   –   –   –   ˘ ˘

sá   vā-vṛ-dhā-ná   ó-ja-sā   pu-ruṣ-ṭu-ta

˘   –   –   –   ˘   –   ˘   –

bhá-vā   naḥ   suś-rá-vas-ta-maḥ

'Indra, you are lord, ruling at will
just and most glorious.
So, having grown in might, much-praised one,
be most gracious toward us'

(From the *Rigveda* (before 1000 BC), 3.45.5; cited by Watkins 1963:198. Note on the calculation of syllable weights: (a) there is resyllabification across words in calculating syllable weight here; (b) the final syllable may be counted as heavy or light.)

The lines of this text fit into two distinct meters: the first, second and fourth lines are eight syllables long, and the third line is twelve syllables long. While there may appear at first to be a random pattern of heavy and light syllables, the two types of line can in fact be partly formalized as a pattern. Thus the eight-syllable lines scan according to the following metrical template, with X matching a syllable of any weight, W matching a light syllable, and S matching a heavy syllable:

X   X   X   X   W   S   W   X

The meter for the twelve-syllable line (called *jagatī*) can be formalized as having anceps positions towards the beginning of the line, and a fixed pattern towards the end, such as the following (which is one of several possible versions):

X   X   X   X   X   X   W   S   W   S   W   X

(Note, incidentally, that as Watkins (1963: 198) points out, the actual *jagatī* line in this text has a regular iambic rhythm, and closely resembles its metrical cousin, the Greek iambic trimeter; not all lines in this meter are so regular, however.)

The general pattern in both the eight-syllable and twelve-syllable meters is (a) metrical positions match syllables, and (b) metrical positions in the latter part of the line are differentiated and match heavy or light syllables. The freer first half of the line is called the 'free initial'; the rigid second half of the line is called the 'fixed cadence'. Note that the final metrical position in the line is anceps, matching a syllable without specifying weight: this is true in all Sanskrit meters (and in many other metrical traditions as well: it is related to the 'brevis in longo' phenomenon mentioned earlier, where a light syllable at the end of the line can fill a strong position). The vedic Sanskrit meters discussed here may be quite close to the meters used in the composition of verse by the Indo-Europeans, the ancient people whose language became the basis of many European and Asian languages, including for example Hindi, Greek, Latin, Welsh and English. One area of research in metrics is to look for traces of the hypothesized Indo-European meters (hypothesized partly on the basis of vedic Sanskrit) in later metrical traditions. Thus, for example, the division of the line into a free initial and a fixed cadence can be found to some extent in many different metrical traditions. For discussion of these issues see for example Watkins (1963) and Sweetser (1988).

The third kind of Sanskrit meter we consider is one in which the overall length of the line is calculated not in syllables but in morae. An example of such a meter is *āryā*. The verse (= line) is divided into two half-verses (= half-lines). One of the half-verses has 30 morae overall, while the other may be shorter, having 27 morae overall. This is a verse/line in *āryā*, split into the two half-verses/half-lines:

μμ μ μ   μ μμ μ μμ μμ   μμ μ μ   μμ μμ   μ μμ μ μμ   μμ μμ
gac-cha-ti   pu-raḥ   śa-rī-raṃ,   dhā-va-ti   paś-cād   a-saṃ-sthi-taṃ   ce-taḥ

μμ μμ μ μ   μ μ   μμ μμ   μ μ μμ μμ   μμ μ μμ μμ μμ
cī-nāṃ-śu-ka-m   i-va   ke-toḥ   pra-ti-vā-taṃ   nī-ya-mā-nas-ya

'(as I think of the girl I have just parted from) my body moves forward, but my unsteady mind runs back, like the silk of a banner being carried into the wind' (from Coulson 1992: 255)

While a half-verse may have an overall count of 30 morae, the pattern of light and heavy syllables within this is not completely free. Thus while we might at first model the metrical template as a sequence of thirty metrical positions, we need to organize these into constituents (called *gaṇa* and equivalent to feet) of four morae each, with syllable boundaries coinciding with *gaṇa* boundaries. There are eight feet in each half-verse, but the eighth foot is always short (it has two morae) and in the second half-verse the sixth foot is short (it has one mora):

1	2	3	4	5	6	7	8

μμ μ μ | μ μμ   μ|μμ μμ | μμ μ μ| μμ μμ |μ μμ   μ | μμ μμ|μμ

gac-cha-ti   pu-raḥ   śa-rī-raṃ,   dhā-va-ti   paś-cād   a-saṃ-sthi-taṃ   ce-taḥ

1	2	3	4	5	6 7	8

μμ μμ |μ μ   μμ |μμ μμ | μ μμμ|μμ μμ|μ|μμ μμ|μμ

cī-nāṃ-śu-ka-m   i-va   ke-toḥ   pra-ti-vā-taṃ   nī-ya-mā-nas-ya

Thus the line is organized into a sequence of four-mora constituents each of which contains between two and four complete syllables: (a) light–light–light– light; (b) heavy–heavy, (c) heavy–light–light, (d) light–light–heavy; and (e) in the second and fourth and sixth *gaṇa* the pattern light–heavy–light may (but need not) also be found:

1	2	3	4	5	6	7	8

H LL | LH   L|H H |H L L |H H |LH   L |H   H|H

μμ   μ μ | μ μμ   μ| μμ μμ | μμ μ μ| μμ μμ |μ μμ   μ |μμ| μμ

gac-cha-ti   pu-raḥ   śa-rī-raṃ,   dhā-va-ti   paś-cād   a-saṃ-sthi-taṃ   ce-taḥ

1	2	3	4	5	6 7	8

H H| L L   L L|H H |L L LH| H H |L | H H|H

μμ   μμ| μ μ   μ μ| μμ μμ | μ μμμ|μμ μμ|μ |μμ μμ|μμ

cī-nāṃ-śu-ka-m   i-va   ke-toḥ   pra-ti-vā-taṃ   nī-ya-mā-nas-ya

An example of what this meter rules out would be a line which begins [light– heavy–heavy . . .] because the third syllable would be split between the first and second *gaṇa* of the line. This meter is an example of a mora-counting meter which has constituent structure in its metrical template. It is possible that the constituent structure relates to an implicit accentual meter underlying the mora- counting meter, as in the Hindi meter discussed later in this chapter.

3.3.3 *Somali*

Somali poetry (often sung: see 4.4.1) is characterized by a unique set of quantit- ative meters, some based on mora-counting and some based on syllable-counting.

While it has long been recognized that Somali poetry was metrical, the meters were not understood and described until the mid-1970s, by Maxamed Xaashi Dhamac 'Gaarriye' and Cabdullaahi Diiriye Guuleed. The discussion in this section is based on Banti and Giannattasio (1996) for the *masafo* and *geeraar*, and Johnson (1984) for the *gabay*; these accounts have been restated in the terms of this chapter (and various complications have been ignored for the purposes of the exposition); see also Johnson (1996) and Orwin (1996) on the prosodic phonology of Somali and its implications for meter.

The *masafo* meter is a quantitative meter which is sensitive to morae. Metrical positions are differentiated (labelled with S and W) depending on whether they match two morae or one mora respectively. Where a metrical position matches two morae it may match either a heavy syllable or two light syllables.

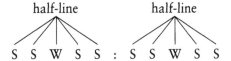

The line is divided into two metrical constituents (half-lines), with a caesura between them. The first position in each half-line is subject to considerable variation in matching, and can match up to four morae instead of the expected two. The first half-line can also end with a heavy–light sequence. There is a caesura between the two half-lines (i.e. requiring there to be a word boundary here), and there is alliteration in each half-line (see 5.4.1). This is an example of *masafo* by the Sayid (Maxamed Cabdille Xasan):

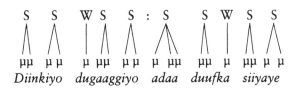

'It is you who reduced them to eating tortoises, beasts of prey, and filth' (cited in Banti and Giannattasio 1996: 90)

Note that S positions match heavy syllables and pairs of light syllables, and that the first S position in the second half-line matches three morae rather than two. Each half-line has at least one word alliterating in [d], which will be true throughout the poem.

In contrast, the *geeraar* is a quantitative meter which is sensitive to syllables. Metrical positions are either S (matching a heavy syllable), W (matching a light syllable) or X (matching any syllable). There are three basic patterns identified by Banti and Giannattasio:

(X) X X S W W S   pattern A
(X) X X S W W S X   pattern B
(X) X X S W W S W X   pattern C

The first position is optional (i.e. it may remain unmatched, indicated here by putting it in brackets). Note again the common phenomenon in quantitative meters of having anceps positions towards the beginning of the line and differentiated positions towards the end (except in the last position which is also anceps). Here is an example of three lines from a text in *geeraar*:

(X) X X S WW S   X   pattern B (with first position unmatched)

    Sidii aarkiyo goosha
'Like the lion and lioness'

(X) X X S WW   S X   pattern B (with first position unmatched)

Oo gabnihii laga   laayay
'Whose young have been slain'

(X) X X   S W WS   pattern A (with first position unmatched)

    Gurxan maygu batay?
'I would make much clamour!'

(From Banti and Giannattasio 1996: 85; singer's name not given)

The *masafo* is a quantitative meter which is basically sensitive to morae, and the *geeraar* is a quantitative meter which is basically sensitive to syllables. The *gabay* is a quantitative meter which is sensitive both to morae and to syllables. The basic template is – like the *masafo* – made of positions which match one- or two-morae units.

(W) S S W S S W S : S W S S W

A W position matches a light syllable (one mora), and an S position matches either a heavy syllable or two light syllables (two morae). Note that this is one of the few Somali meters where metrical positions can be grouped into feet (with the pattern S S W). In addition, there is also a syllable-counting constraint, which is that there must be exactly six syllables after the caesura (with the consequence that one and only one of the two-mora positions must match a pair of light syllables). Here is a line by the Sayid in *gabay*:

'O Hussein, do not speak obstinately: you are my friend' (cited by Johnson 1996: 79)

The mixed nature of this meter – counting both morae and syllables – makes it somewhat unusual, and difficult to describe in our system.

3.4 Accentual meters

A counting meter controls the number of units in the line. A patterning meter controls the pattern of different types of unit in a line. Where the units involve differences in stress (or 'accent' as it is sometimes called), the meter is called an accentual meter. Where the units involve differences in syllable weight, the meter is called a quantitative meter. This is a traditional division which may not divide up meters fully accurately. Thus while an accentual meter has the end result that the lines have a rhythmic pattern based on stress, this may be achieved only indirectly: the meter itself might or might not directly refer to stress. Thus for example iambic pentameter is an accentual meter which does not refer to stress: stress is controlled indirectly through syllable strength. In this section we consider an Italian accentual meter which is related historically to iambic pentameter, and an Old English/Germanic accentual meter. Each meter controls a different aspect of the prosodic phonological structure of the line.

3.4.1 *Italian* endecasillabo

The Italian *endecasillabo* (eleven-syllable) meter is analogous in many ways to English iambic pentameter, both structurally and in its importance – it is the basic meter used by poets from Petrarch and Dante to Foscolo and Leopardi. Different poets used different versions of *endecasillabo*, and here we describe primarily the practice of Petrarch, based on the account of Nespor and Vogel (1986) and Hanson (1996). *Endecasillabo* lines typically have eleven syllables, but there are several kinds of variation. The strongest stresses in the line are found in the tenth position and either the fourth or sixth position. In terms of the prosodic phonological structure within each line, these strongest stresses are the strongest stresses within a phonological phrase: thus each line typically has two phonological phrases, with the main stress within each phonological phrase falling in position 4 or 6 and position 10. Thus the meter involves syllable-counting and constrains the rhythm of the line in terms of stress: where it differs from iambic pentameter is basically that *endecasillabo* relates to stress within the phonological phrase while iambic pentameter relates to stress within the polysyllabic lexical word.

In formulating a meter, we must first decide how to account for the variability in line length. Here, the basic kind of variation in length involves extra syllables. In Italian metrics there are rules of elision and synaloepha which fit two syllables into one metrical position: elision is a process whereby two adjacent vowels are pronounced as a single syllabic peak, and synaloepha is a process whereby the two adjacent vowels are more distinct but are also fitted into a single metrical position. The other kind of extra syllables come at the end of a line. The tenth metrical position always matches a stressed syllable; since many Italian words have penultimate stress this means that there is usually an unstressed syllable after the tenth syllable (i.e. the line has eleven syllables, which is the typical situation). Where the final word has final stress there are ten syllables in the line; where the final word has antepenultimate stress, there are two syllables after the tenth (stressed) syllable and hence there are twelve syllables in the line. Nespor and Vogel suggest that syllables following the final stress are extrametrical – that is, they do not fit into the metrical template. (Note the similarity with iambic pentameter.)

Thus we formulate a metrical template which has ten positions, each of which is matched with a syllable, with line-internal means of adding syllables, and extra syllables possible at the end. This takes care of the syllable-counting aspect of the meter; the rhythm is dealt with by working out the hierarchical structure of the template as follows – with binary feet, and feet grouped into half-lines along one of two patterns, (a) or (b). Each template is shown matched to one of the lines from Petrarch's *Rime cxl* (from Hanson 1996).

(a)

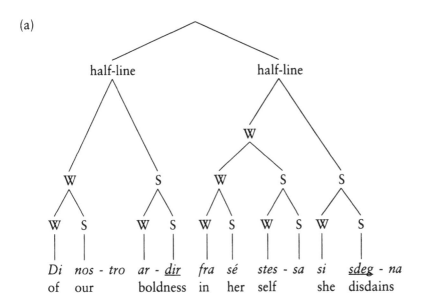

(b)

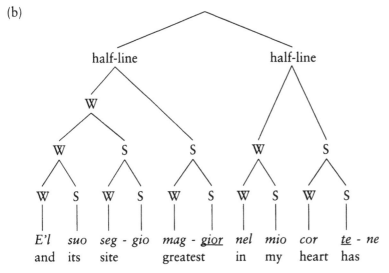

These hierarchical metrical templates permit us to formulate the matching rule. The strongest metrical constituents in the line are the fourth and tenth (a) or the sixth and tenth (b). We match meter to prosodic phonology by requiring the strongest metrical constituent in each half-line to match the strongest stress in each phonological phrase. Thus in the line matched with template (a), the strongest stresses in the phonological phrases are on -*dir* and *sdeg*-; note incidentally that there is also elision in the third metrical position and an extrametrical syllable -*na*. In the line matched with template (b), the strongest stresses in the phonological phrases are on -*gior* and *te*-.

These hierarchical metrical templates have more structure in them than is strictly needed for determining the rhythm of the line: in each case, it is only the final metrical position in each half-line which matters for the matching rule. In principle only the final foot in each half-line need be marked as having a W S pattern of metrical positions, and other positions in the half-line could be left undifferentiated and not even organized into feet: this is a very typical pattern in a meter, where the metrical template becomes increasingly structured towards the ends of metrical constituents.

3.4.2 *The Old English 'strong stress' (alliterative) meter*

We now turn to the Old English meter which holds of *Beowulf* and which is sometimes called the 'strong stress' meter. In addition to the meter there is systematic alliteration (which we return to in 5.4.2, and 9.3.2). Our account of the meter follows Russom (1987), who argues that though the meter does control the patterns of stress in the line, the control of stress is mediated through the control of words. As in most accounts of this meter, Russom proposes that the metrical line (or 'long-line') consists of two half-lines (or 'verses'), and each half-line consists of two feet. The prototypical foot matches a lexical word, and contains one syllable with primary stress; thus a prototypical line would have four lexical words and four primary stresses. Many lines do not fit this simple pattern: there may be more than four words, and there may be fewer than four primary stresses, for example. These variants arise partly from the ways in which grammatical words are handled, and from the ways in which compound words are handled.

Russom's approach to the meter begins with the foot, which is subject to a matching rule (note that in other meters it is normally metrical positions rather than feet which are subject to matching rules). The foot matches a word – with some flexibility in what counts as a word. In addition to the single lexical word, a compound of two lexical words may count as a word (it is structurally ambiguous in that it may also count as two words), as may certain other combinations. Grammatical words (and some morphemes such as prefixes) can be extrametrical – that is, not matched to the foot constituent. This matching of feet to words is what gives the line its prototypical composition of four lexical words, with variations relating to compounding and the presence of grammatical words.

The foot and the word are units which are also involved in determining those aspects of the line which are more normally controlled by an accentual meter: the number of syllables and the pattern of stress. There is an inventory of possible foot patterns, interpreted in terms of three metrical positions: S, s and x. These metrical positions are matched with syllables. The S metrical position corresponds to a stressed syllable (by preference, primary stress). The s metrical position corresponds to a stressed syllable (by preference, secondary stress). The x metrical position corresponds to an unstressed syllable. As is common, while it is typical for one metrical position to correspond to one syllable, there are also ways of fitting two syllables into single metrical positions in some cases. There are nine possible feet, which are parallel to the various patterns of stress which are found in words of the language (i.e. another link between feet and words):

feet of one metrical position: x   S
feet of two metrical positions: xx   Sx   Ss
feet of three metrical positions: Sxx   Ssx   Sxs
feet of four metrical positions: Sxxs

A half-line consists of two feet, and there are constraints on the possible pairings of feet so that a verse will not contain two very short feet or two very long feet; thus some principle operates to control the overall number of syllables.

Here are examples of two half-lines, matched to the metrical template (cited from Russom 1987: 35):

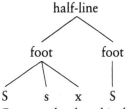

Bīo - *wul* - *fes   biorh*
'Beowulf's barrow' (half-line 501b)

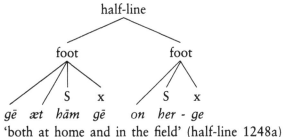

gē *æt hām gē   on her* - ge
'both at home and in the field' (half-line 1248a)

These half-lines illustrate three of the possible foot types, as well as showing the way in which the sizes of feet balance out (to some extent) across the half-line, and the possibility of extrametrical words – the grammatical words in the second example.

3.4.3 Prosodic phonological organization and counting meters

One of the fundamental problems for linguistic research on meters is to decide what aspects of prosodic phonological organization are actually relevant to a meter. For any particular meter, the explicit conventions or traditional approach may need to be revised, as was the case for iambic pentameter. One area for research has been into syllable-counting and mora-counting meters, to discover whether there is any implicit presence of a rhythmic, periodic meter such as an accentual meter: Klar et al. (1984) argues this for Welsh, and Poser (1990) for Japanese. Bryant (1992) offers another example of research in this area, which re-examines medieval Hindi meters, focusing on the texts of the medieval poet Sūrdās. The traditional approach to these meters sees them as involving the overall number of morae in the line; thus they are considered to be mora-counting meters. A common pattern for the line would be for the first half to have sixteen morae and the second twelve morae. We could in principle formalize this as a counting meter by having a 28-position metrical template:

XXX	XXX	XX	XXX	XXX	X	X	X	XX	XXX	XX	XXXX
μμμ	μ μμ	μμ	μμμ	μμμ	μ	μ	μ	μμ	μ μμ	μ μ	μμ μμ
$kūp^a$	$ṣ^an^an^a$	jal^a	$ās^a$	$sūr^a$	pr^abhu	$bh^aw^an^a$		$m^ad^an^a$	$d^ahı$	$jaihai$	

(Retransliterated version of text cited by Bryant 1992: 212)

However, Bryant argues that there are further restrictions on the composition of the line which are revealed by considering how words of different lengths are placed within the line. This would seem at first to suggest that the meter is sensitive to the placement of initial word boundaries; thus a common pattern is for words to begin on the first, fifth, ninth, and thirteenth metrical positions (i.e. a half-line of four 4-morae words). However, Bryant shows that it is not word boundaries but stress which the meter is sensitive to, and that this in turn controls the placement of word boundaries because most words begin with a stressed mora. Thus the 16-position half-line template can be reanalysed as being organized into foot-like constituents, with stress on the first mora of each constituent. Thus we can rewrite the template to differentiate metrical positions into S and W, with an S metrical position matching the strongest mora in the word (which carries stress); usually the first mora in the word. This appears to give us three basic metrical templates for the 16-position half-line, as follows:

```
A:  S W W W    S W W W      S W W W      S W W W
B:  S W W W    S W W    S W W    S W      S W W W
C:  S W W    S W W    S W    S W W    S W W    S W
```

Thus the line cited above can be put to the following metrical template which combines C as its first half-line with B (minus the first foot) as its second half-line:

SWW SWW SW SWW SWW S   W | S WW   S WW S W SWWW
μμμ   μ μμ   μμ   μμμ   μμμ   μ   μ   μ   μμ   μ μμ   μ μ   μμ μμ
kūpᵃ *ṣᵃnᵃnᵃ* *jalᵃ* *āsᵃ*   *sūrᵃ* *prᵃbhu* *bhᵃwᵃnᵃ* *mᵃdᵃnᵃ* *dᵃhɪ* *jaihai*

Bryant suggests that these three metrical templates are related to each other by a relation similar to that of 'transformation' in transformational grammar. Thus the basic pattern is the first, and any sequence of SWWW + SWWW can be replaced by a sequence of SWW + SWW + SW. Bryant's article is a reanalysis of what appeared to be a mora-counting meter, to show that it is in fact an accentual meter: this involved looking for generalizations about what kinds of lines appear in the poems and what kinds of lines do not, and recognizing that the generalization is based on the presence of lexical stress.

3.5 A tone-based patterning meter: Chinese regulated verse

While most patterning meters result in a rhythm based on syllable weight or on stress, there are some examples of meters which result in a rhythm based on lexical tone; in this section we discuss the classical Chinese Tang dynasty genre of regulated verse (*lü shih*) in a discussion based on Chen (1979) and particularly Yip (1984); see also Xue (1989).

Poems are made from eight five-syllable lines or eight seven-syllable lines. Chinese syllables have lexical tone, and the syllables must be arranged to give certain permitted patterns of tone (with some variability, i.e. anceps positions). The patterns – in the pronunciation of the time – differentiate level tones on the one hand from the various kinds of oblique (rising or falling) tones on the other. While the differentiation is seen as one of tone, it is possible that it is also or instead based on syllable weight; there is some reason to think that in the stage of the language at the time of composition, level-toned syllables were heavier than oblique-tone syllables. Thus this tonal meter bears some relation to a quantitative meter.

The following text is the first half of a regulated verse poem by Wang Wei; syllables which would have had level tone at the time of writing are underlined.

kong *shan* *xin* yu hou
tian qi wan *lai* qiu
ming yue *song* *jian* *zhao*
qing *quan* *shi* shang liu

'A deserted mountain after new rain / air like an autumn evening / clear moon shining through the pines / pure spring flowing over the stones' (the first four lines of 'Autumn Evening in the Mountains' by Wang Wei (AD 701–61); from Yip 1984: 355)

Each of these lines must match one of the possible sequences of tones permitted by the meter. The first and fourth lines both have a sequence of level–level–level–oblique–oblique, which is exactly one of the permitted sequences. The second and third lines show certain permitted deviations from possible sequences, as we discuss shortly.

   Chen suggests that we should understand the various permitted sequences of tones in regulated verse as expressing a hierarchically structured metrical pattern in the line. Thus, the first and fourth lines have the following structure:

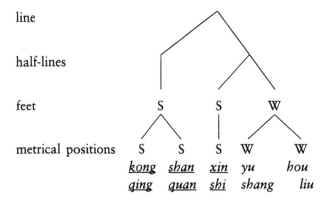

line

half-lines

feet

metrical positions

Chen's proposal has several interesting consequences, which provide support for it. Thus it is possible to formulate rules which predict which possible hierarchical structures may be constructed, and hence predict which tonal sequences are possible. For example, one principle is that within a foot the two metrical positions are identical, either both S or both W (note that this is very different from the kinds of feet we saw in iambic pentameter). A second principle is that within a half-line the two feet must be of different tonal types. Chen suggests various other principles which we will not go into here; he also suggests ways in which we can predict the sequence in which different types of tonal sequence will be found in a poem (Wang Wei's poem does not in fact conform to these rules of sequence, but much regulated verse does).

The second interesting consequence of Chen's proposal relates to the possibility of variation, where matching is less constrained (i.e. anceps positions). The anceps positions are always the first positions in a foot, and are usually the first position in the half-line. This can be seen in lines 2 and 3 of the poem. In the second line, the first syllable is level tone but in a W position, and the third tone is oblique but in an S position; in both cases, the mismatched syllable is first in its foot and also first in its half-line:

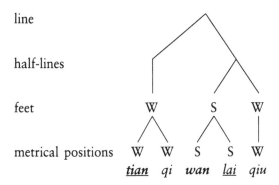

In line 3 we have the same pattern of mismatches:

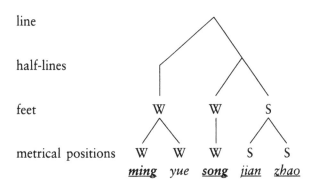

Note that the patterning of anceps relative to the hierarchical structure is similar to that found in Greek iambic trimeter: the anceps position comes at the beginning of a metrical constituent.

3.6 Extra syllables and missing syllables

While we might expect lines of verse in iambic pentameter to have ten syllables, they may also have extra syllables and missing syllables, as we saw in chapter 2.

For example, in iambic pentameter, an extra syllable may appear at the end of a phonological phrase (most commonly at the end of a line), where it is extrametrical and thus need not be matched to the template. And extra syllables can also arise because the metrical position in iambic pentameter can match a phonological foot (which can contain two syllables). In this section we look at two meters in which there are more or fewer syllables than might be expected, and consider how the meter can cope with these variations.

3.6.1 Rules for syllables: the French alexandrine

We begin with the French *alexandrine* meter. This is a syllable-counting meter: each line must have twelve syllables. Consider, however, the following lines from a poem by Charles Baudelaire:

J'ai longtemps habité sous de vastes portiques
que les soleils marins teignaient de mille feux

'I lived for a long time beneath vast doors which the seas' suns tinted with a thousand fires' (Baudelaire, from 'La vie antérieure', 1855)

The complication presented by these lines relates to the status of the final vowel in words such as *vastes*, *portiques* and *mille*. In everyday speech, these words do not have a final pronounced vowel. However, the final vowel of *vastes* and *mille* is pronounced here (as schwa, [ə]), while the final vowel of *portiques* is not. The pronunciation of these vowels means that the lines do in fact add up to twelve syllables each. Whether the final vowel is pronounced or not depends on the following word. If the final -*e* vowel is followed in the same line by a word which begins with a consonant, then this vowel is pronounced; otherwise it is suppressed and hence not pronounced. This kind of phenomenon, where the existence or nature of a sound depends on neighbouring sounds, is called a phonological rule. In this case we might propose that all words with 'final -*e*' start out with this vowel, but that when the words are combined into a line, the phonological rule applies: the vowel is deleted if it is not followed by a consonant. (Phonological rules are discussed again, in more detail, in 5.5.)

3.6.2 Glides, vowels, and syllable counting in the Rigveda

We now explore a complex and widely discussed problem involving syllable counting in the *Rigveda*, and focus particularly on the phonological rule-based solution to this problem proposed by Kiparsky (1972). The problem relates to whether a glide (semivowel) counts as a syllable nucleus, or not. We can illustrate the problem by citing the following line:

ā ṣaṣṭyā́ saptatyā́ somapéyan
'(come) here with sixty, seventy to drink Soma' (cited by Kiparsky 1972: 177)

This line is written according to the *triṣṭubh* meter which requires eleven syllables in the line and a caesura after the fourth or fifth syllable (as in other vedic Sanskrit meters, as discussed in 3.3.2, the pattern of syllable weights is fixed in the latter part of the line, but this is not relevant here). The problem in this line is to decide whether the palatal 'y' glide (= [j]) in the second and third words should be counted as the nucleus of a syllable. This question often arises with glides in many languages, because glides are highly sonorant sounds and hence are often capable of being syllable nuclei. There are three possibilities: (a) neither glide is counted as the nucleus of a syllable; (b) both glides are counted as the nucleus of a syllable; or (c) one glide – e.g. the first one – is counted as the nucleus of a syllable, but not the other. As the following counts illustrate, only the third possibility has the right syllable count and caesura placement (the caesura is indicated by a colon):

(a)

1	2	3	4	:	5	6	7	8	9	10
ā	ṣaṣṭ	- yā́	sap	- tat	- yā́	so	- ma	- pé	- yan

(b)

1	2	3	4	:	5	6	7	8	9	10	11	12
ā	ṣaṣṭ	- y	- ā́	sap	- tat	- y	- ā́	so	- ma	- pé	- yan

(c)

1	2	3	4	:	5	6	7	8	9	10	11
ā	ṣaṣṭ	- y	- ā́	sap	- tat	- yā́	so	- ma	- pé	- yan

While (c) appears to be correct as far as the poetic rules are concerned, it is odd linguistically, because the word *saptatyā́* ('seventy') ends in the same suffix as *ṣaṣṭyā́* ('sixty'), and on the surface one would expect a similar syllable structure within that suffix. The solution to this problem was suggested by the philologist Sievers. Sievers' Law is a phonological rule which states that the glide is a syllable nucleus when it is preceded by a heavy syllable – and is not a syllable nucleus when it is preceded by a light syllable. In Sanskrit a heavy syllable (i.e. a two-mora syllable) consists of a long vowel or a vowel followed by at least two consonants:

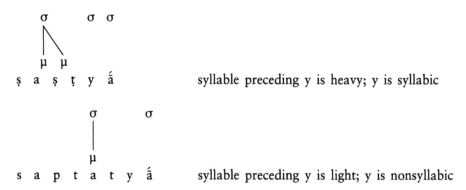

ṣ a ṣ ṭ y å   syllable preceding y is heavy; y is syllabic

s a p t a t y å   syllable preceding y is light; y is nonsyllabic

(Sievers' Law also applies to the labiovelar glide v (= [w]), which syllabifies as
the vowel u.)

Sievers' Law predicts that the same suffix (as here) will sometimes have a glide
as syllable nucleus and sometimes not, depending on the word stem to which
it is attached. But the following lines show that the situation is more complex.
These lines come from a hymn in which the meter shifts from the twelve-syllable
jagatī meter (described in 3.3.2) to the eleven-syllable *triṣṭubh* meter. This is
achieved in these lines only by having the glide [v] in *áyugdhvam* be a syllable
head in (i) and not a syllable head in (ii):

(i)
1   2   3   4   5   6   7   8   9   10   11   12
vṛ́ - ṣa - vrā - tā - saḥ   pṛ́ - ṣa - tīr   á - yug - dhv - am
'(when) you have harnessed the dappled mares with your strong hosts' (last line
of stanza 4 of *Rigveda* hymn 1.85, in 12-syllable metre)

(ii)
1   2   3   4   5   6   7   8   9   10   11
prá - yád   ra - thé - ṣu   pṛ́ - ṣa - tīr   á - yug - dhvam
'when you have harnessed the dappled mares to your chariots' (first line of
stanza 5, in 11-syllable metre)

Since the word is the same in both lines, it is impossible to predict on linguistic
grounds whether the glide will be a syllable head or not. Hence Sievers' Law
does not work in this case.

We now consider three ways of explaining this apparent irregularity. The first
and earliest explanation comes from Edgerton (1934, 1943), who argued that
the exceptions to Sievers' Law (e.g. the above optionality) reflected a situation in
which the poets had 'imperfect linguistic control'. In other words, the exceptions
to Sievers' Law arise because the poets are using a language in their poetry of

which they are 'non-native speakers' – perhaps because it was an archaic language for them – and hence in which they make unpredictable errors. However, linguists in the generative tradition which is fundamental to this book are sceptical (at least at first) of appeals to imperfect control of a system or blind adherence to tradition. Following this principle, Kiparsky (1972) argues that while there is optionality in whether or not a glide can be a syllable nucleus, this optionality is not random – as Edgerton suggests – but is in fact part of the language of the *Rigveda*. His argument centres on the claim that the optionality is found in some suffixes but not others. The conclusion of Kiparsky's argument is that in *áyugdhvam* the [v] is not a syllable nucleus in its underlying representation but is a syllable nucleus in its surface representation (after the application of a phonological rule which is in effect Sievers' Law). Hence the poet has the option of choosing either the underlying syllabification (as in line (ii)) or the surface syllabification (as in line (i)). Kiparsky's analysis has been challenged by Hock (1980), who presents a third possible analysis. Hock argues that there is greater optionality than Kiparsky allows – and that this optionality cannot in the end be analysed as a choice between underlying or surface forms. Hock agrees with Kiparsky, however, that the poetry reflects the actual language of the poets, and not an archaic language which they 'imperfectly control'. Following the theory of the sociolinguist William Labov, he proposes to treat the variation by allowing for variable application of phonological rules (i.e. the coexistence of different phonological systems for the same user, with choice between them).

3.7 Summary: kinds of meter and metrical theory

This chapter has briefly introduced examples of meters from some of the world's major metrical traditions, and has attempted to formulate those meters in terms of the template and matching rules model described in chapter 2. Work on these meters in the generative tradition tends to be somewhat preliminary, with relatively less work having been published on them than on English. Thus for example various problems are presented by these meters (such as the status of differentiated positions in patterned meters) for which a universal solution is not at present obvious. And the issue of variation within the meter has only barely been touched on in this discussion; for iambic pentameter, variation is the key to the meter, and a similar finding is likely to arise from more detailed work on some of these other meters. Generative metrics has universal ambitions: the aim is to formulate the general principles of metricality with an eye to implications for cognitive structure and its realization in metrical form. Given these ambitions, there are a large number of metrical traditions which need to be re-examined or examined in greater depth using the generative framework.

3.8   Further reading

Wimsatt (1972) is a useful overview of different metrical traditions. McCully and Anderson (1996) is an anthology of recent work on English meters, including Old English. Welsh meters are outlined in Williams (1953); see also Klar et al. (1984), Sweetser (1988) and Griffen (1981). Irish meters are outlined in Murphy (1961). Linguistic approaches to Greek meters can be found in Allen (1973), Prince (1989), Devine and Stephens (1984); West (1982, 1987) are standard textbooks on Greek meters. Arnold (1905) is a standard description of vedic Sanskrit meters: see chapter V on syllable structure; Keith (1920) lists the classical Sanskrit meters; see also Coulson (1992). On *endecasillabo* see Nespor and Vogel (1986), Abondolo (1996). An anthology which is primarily devoted to Somali poetry is Hayward and Lewis (1996); see also Johnson (1984) and Andrzejewski (1972) and Andrzejewski and Andrzejewski (1993), the latter an anthology of translations. Zeps (1963) was an early proponent of a generative approach to missing syllables, focusing on Latvian songs; see also Zeps (1973, 1989). Attridge (1974) discusses the attempt to develop quantitative verse in English.

3.9   Exercises

3.9.1   *Gerard Manley Hopkins: sprung rhythm*

Gerard Manley Hopkins developed his own unique meter which he called 'sprung rhythm'. This is a difficult-to-understand meter which has recently been described in a generative framework by Kiparsky (1989), Hanson (1991) and Hanson and Kiparsky (1996).

Instructions

(a) The following text is in the 'sprung rhythm' meter. Formulate the meter as specifically as you can. This will involve specifying (i) a metrical template, which may have differentiated positions and hierarchical structure; (ii) matching rules between metrical positions and phonological constituents, which enable you to state any restrictions on the number of syllables in the line; (iii) matching rules which enable you to state any restrictions on the stress-based rhythm of the line.

> *Hint: work out a meter for the first line first, and then develop and modify your account of the meter on the basis of the rest of the poem.*

(b)   This poem is a sonnet; English sonnets are normally in iambic pentameter. Describe the differences between the 'sprung rhythm' meter and iambic pentameter.

> *Hint: one difference is that in this text, each line must have five stresses, while an iambic pentameter line will tolerate fewer than five stresses. Your description of the difference should take account of this.*

(c)   Why did Hopkins decide that some metrical stresses had to be explicitly marked (in lines 2, 3 and 12)? Try to explain each case.

(d)   Why did Hopkins need to mark some syllables or pairs of syllables as 'outrides'? Try to answer this question in as general terms as possible.

(e)   There is much alliteration in this poem. What is its relation to the meter?

Text

In his manuscript of this poem, Hopkins used an acute accent for 'the metrical stress, marked in doubtful cases only' and an arc which 'under one or more syllables makes them extrametrical: a slight pause follows as if the voice were silently making its way back to the highroad of the verse'. (These are Hopkins's own explanations.) Hopkins called the arc an 'outride'.

The Windhover
To Christ our Lord

I caught this morning morning's minion, king-
   dom of daylight's dauphin, dapple-dáwn-drawn Falcon, in his riding
   Of the rólling level úndernéath him steady aír, and stríding
High there, how he rung upon the rein of a wimpling wing
In his ecstacy! then off, off forth on swing,
   As a skate's heel sweeps smooth on a bow-bend: the hurl and gliding
   Rebuffed the big wind. My heart in hiding
Stirred for a bird, – the achieve of, the mastery of the thing!

Brute beauty and valour and act, oh, air, pride, plume, here
   Buckle! AND the fire that breaks from thee then, a billion
Times told lovelier, more dangerous, O my chevalier!

No wónder o͟f i͟t: shéer plód makes plough down sillion
Shine, and blue-bleak embers, ah my dear,
  Fall, gall themselves, and gash-gold vermillion.

3.9.2 *The Serbo-Croatian epic decasyllable*

The text for this exercise is cited by Jakobson (1966: 418) as part of a very detailed analysis of the Serbo-Croatian epic decasyllable meter (*êpskī desetérac*); the questions incorporate parts of his analysis.

Some information about the language: syllables, length and stress

Syllable nuclei can be any of the five vowels [a e i o u], or in some cases [r]. Each of these can be either long or short, and accented or unaccented. Length and accent are indicated by diacritics above the nuclei, as follows:

	long	short
accented	ˆ or ´	˵ or ˋ
unaccented	‐	no diacritic

Text

pâ jȍš da ti vȉšē jȁde kâžēm

štȍ se âjka hási učìnila

proz ájtara m̀ŕka kàurina

pâ na svéca psȕjē muàmeda

svȅ no štȍ je káza i kȁko je

e kad mújo sȁlušā alíla

pâ ovàkō bèsjediti zádje

'"And to tell you something sadder / It's that Ajka has become an infidel! / for the sake of the damned giaour! / and she blasphemes the Holy Mohammed." / He told everything as it was. / And after Mujo had heard Alil out, / he began to speak in this way' (composed/performed by T. Vučič; reproduced by permission of Mouton de Gruyter)

Instructions

(a) Jakobson says that each line has ten syllables. Do adjacent vowels belong to the same syllable or to different syllables?

(b) Jakobson says that there is a caesura after the fourth syllable (i.e. a word must end here). Is this true of the above text?

(c) Jakobson says that there is a bridge between the third and fourth syllables and between the ninth and tenth syllables. This means that the third and fourth syllables must belong to the same word, as must the ninth and tenth syllables. What notion of 'word' is involved here? (Recall the discussion of 'word' in prosodic phonological structure, 2.2.3, and assume that short words are potentially part of larger phonological words along with adjacent longer words.)

(d) Jakobson says that even syllables tend to be unaccented. Are there any examples of accented syllables in even positions in this text, and can you generalize about where these are found? Can you explain why accented even syllables might be found in these positions?

(e) Now attempt to formulate the epic decasyllable meter as a metrical template and matching rules.

(f) Jakobson says the first syllable of a word is usually an odd syllable. Where a word begins with an even syllable, its final syllable must also be even. How does this fit with other aspects of the meter, and what is meant by 'word' here?

(g) The weight of syllables is relevant towards the end of the line. Syllables 7 and 8 tend not to be accented heavy syllables, and syllable 9 is never an accented light syllable and is usually a heavy syllable. Check whether these generalizations hold for the quoted text, and suggest an explanation for them. Why would you expect specifically these syllables to be associated with constraints relating to weight (and not earlier syllables, or syllable 10)?

(h) Jakobson says that there is a preference for open syllables (syllables which end in a vowel), particularly in the final syllable of the line. Suggest a possible reason for this (bear in mind that these texts are sung, with a pause between lines).

(i) On the basis of your answers to f–h, make any adjustments which might be needed to your meter. (You may find that no changes are necessary.)

4 Issues in Metrical Theory: Metrical Constituents, and Music and Meter

This chapter addresses two directions for metrical research. We begin by exploring in more detail some of the issues which arise in the study of metrical constituent structure. We then discuss the relation between the meters of some sung texts and their musical structures.

4.1 The metrical line

A meter has two essential components: metrical positions (the smallest metrical constituent) and the metrical template (the largest metrical constituent). Metrical positions must be matched systematically with constituents at some level of the prosodic phonological structure. In addition there is a second level of matching: it seems that in all meters there is a match between the metrical template as a whole and some definable constituent of textual structure; this definable constituent of textual structure is the line, and cross-linguistically lines have certain characteristics in common. In this section we look at some of the characteristics of lines in metrical texts.

The line, as a textual constituent, typically corresponds to linguistic constituents – both prosodic phonological constituents and syntactic constituents. In the prosodic phonological structure, the line ending typically coincides with a major constituent boundary such that a pause is possible; this may be responsible for some of the line-ending effects which we mention in the next section. In the syntactic structure, the end of the line will often coincide with a major phrase boundary, and often with the end of a clause. At a minimum, a line boundary will usually coincide with a word boundary, which in some traditions sharply distinguishes the line from metrical constituents such as the half-line/metron or the foot, which in some cases are required to cross-cut word boundaries. Allen (1973: 113) points out that in vedic Sanskrit verse the line (*pāda*) resembles a sentence in various linguistic features, such as that the finite verb is normally accented only if it begins a sentence – or if it begins a line.

An odd but cross-linguistically attested characteristic of lines in some traditions is that their beginnings can be 'read vertically' down the lines rather than in the sequence of words. Thus the initial letters in each line of a written text may be added together to form a word or phrase (i.e. an acrostic pattern). Or we may find the situation described by Watkins (1995: 39) for some vedic Sanskrit and Greek texts, where we can add together the first words of three successive lines and derive a coherent phrase from it which is a crucial contribution to the meaning of the lines. Another characteristic of lines in some traditions is that the line of text is transportable: it can easily be picked up and moved to another place, or copied, to create a new text. Thus Dixon (1980: 57) describes a Girramay song, sung by Paddy Biran and recorded in 1963. The song consists of six six-syllable lines, most of which independently have a coherent meaning. The six lines were put together into a song of twenty-three lines by repetition and re-arrangement; the same lines were also recorded by Dixon as sung by another singer, Jack Murray, in a different order. Thus the line is in some traditions a recombinable unit of structure.

The line is the largest metrically governed unit of text. However, there is also some (basically para-metrical rather than metrical) regulation above the line. Thus for example sound-patterning rules typically refer to units of textual structure larger than the line. And in heterometric texts where different lines match different templates the placement of a line within the text may determine which metrical template it is matched with (e.g. in Japanese *haiku* 3.1.2, or Welsh *englyn penfyr* 3.1.1).

4.1.1 The end of the metrical line

Ends of lines show various distinctive kinds of irregularity, across metrical traditions. Cross-linguistically, extrametrical syllables are most likely to be found here (though these can also be found at the ends of other large constituents within the line). In Serbo-Croatian poetry, there is an avoidance of consonant-final syllables at the end of a line (i.e. syllables end with a vowel here). And the final position in the line is in many traditions an anceps position: in particular, a light syllable may often fill a metrical position which we might expect to require a heavy syllable ('brevis in longo', 3.3.1). Some of these general characteristics might relate to the fact that in many traditions there may be a pause at the end of the line, which coincides with the end of a major prosodic phonological constituent. We might perhaps suggest that extrametrical syllables fall into this pause, and are thus able to escape the meter; and on the other hand, the pause might itself be counted as standing for textual material and allowed to fill out a one-mora syllable into a two-mora position.

Hale (1984) discusses another distinctive line-final phenomenon in two Australian traditions: Aranda and Warlpiri. Hale cites an Aranda song:

m-arnkentyele rreytenge
l-arnkentyele rreytenge
l-erwamperrkele nepene
m-erwamperrkele nepene

'Where far-flung their hollows stretch with firelight aglow they will ever dwell' (text from Hale 1984: 260; poetic translation from Strehlow 1971: 689)

A common practice in Australian aboriginal poetry is the repetition of lines; a poem/song may consist of just two lines which are repeated many times in a particular performance (sometimes changing the order). The second process, specific to Aranda poetry, involves the transfer of the consonant of a line-final suffix to the beginning of the following line: *rreytenge* would in ordinary language be *rreytengel*, *marnkentyele* would in ordinary language be *arnkentyele*, *nepene* would in ordinary language be *nepenem*, and so on. Hence we could see the above version of the poem as based on a more abstract version of the poem, which acts as a kind of template or script for the full text:

arnkentyele rreytengel   Line X
erwamperrkele nepenem   Line Y

The performed poem is now built by two processes. First, lines are repeated (line X is repeated once, and line Y is repeated once); then consonants are carried over. Note that the very first word of the performance acquires its consonant *m-* from the very last word of the performance, *nepene(-m)*.

This poem is sung by men belonging to the Honey Ant (*yurrampi*) ancestral group, to which men from other Australian cultures, and speaking other languages, also belong. When Warlpiri-speaking men sing this poem, they sing it slightly differently. Their version can be represented as:

l-uraimpaiyerrkeila nooupaayanoou
l-uraimpaiyerrkeila nooupaayanoou
m-arnkiintyala rreeitengeei
m-arnkiintyala rreeitengeei

(from Hale 1984: 258: translation as above)

(We ignore the differences in word phonology, and line order, which are irrelevant to our purposes.) We can see an interesting difference from the Aranda version, suggesting that for the Warlpiri men, the performed version is based on essentially the same abstract version but realized by a different order of processes; first the consonant is transferred, and then the lines are repeated.

4.1.2 *Free initial and fixed cadence in the metrical line*

One of the most striking cross-tradition characteristics of metrical lines is that the earlier part of a line tends to be metrically freer than the later part of a line. This is seen, for example, in the vedic Sanskrit meters. Thus the *gāyatrī* metrical template has four anceps positions followed by three quantitatively fixed positions (and a final free position). The line is said to have a free initial and a fixed cadence.

initial (anceps positions)				cadence (fixed quantities)			final anceps
X	X	X	X	W	S	W	X

An interesting problem for metrical theory relates to the fact that many traditions have metrical tendencies of this kind – with a free initial and a fixed cadence within the line. Hayes (1989) remarks that the 'free initial' characteristic of lines is also found in smaller metrical constituents, such as metra and half-lines, and we saw examples of this in Greek and Chinese.

This is an example of a generalization which holds across traditions, and in principle might be explained in various ways. We might try to explain it historically by suggesting that as a pattern it originates with Proto-Indo-European verse, and has been inherited by other metrical traditions. This assumes that all the relevant metrical traditions (including some non-Indo-European ones) are the inheritors of the Indo-European tradition. While this is not impossible (e.g. Chinese could have been influenced by the Indian meters via Buddhist texts), it nevertheless places great faith in historical explanations. An alternative approach would be to see the organization of the line as reflecting some universal aspect of metricality, perhaps relating to the ways in which all humans process metrical verse.

4.1.3 *The line in non-metrical texts*

A text which is not governed by a metrical template is not divided into metrical lines. However, texts can also be divided into various kinds of non-metrical constituent, and among these are consituents which resemble metrical lines – and which are often referred to as (non-metrical) lines. In some cases, non-metrical lines and metrical lines share characteristics, a fact of particular interest for an understanding of literary form. Thus there might be a version of the free-initial fixed-cadence structure, and the ends of non-metrical lines might show special characteristics. (It is, however, also the case that what appear to be non-metrical lines may turn out on closer examination to be metrical: the key is the discovery of constraints on prosodic phonological structure, which suggests the presence of a meter.)

Here we consider five justifications for segmenting non-metrical texts into lines. The first relates to syntactic structure, and basically assumes that a line is syntactically coherent and bounded (often a clause); in some accounts of narrative constituency, it is argued that each line contains a verb. The second relates to performance and involves pausing – or the possibility of pausing (e.g. the possibility of phonological phrase endings) – at the end of a line. Both of these arguments for division of a text into lines are strengthened if there is some consistency, such that the syntactically bounded 'line'-type units are relatively equal in length throughout, or if the performance units are relatively equal in length throughout. The third argument looks for consistent components, usually at line boundaries: for example each line in a narrative might end in a particular way (with a hearsay particle, for example) or might begin in a particular way (with a connective like 'then', for example). The fourth and fifth arguments bring non-metrical lines closer to metrical lines. The fourth argument for lineation looks for regular numbers of words in the line. Some genres of ancient Hebrew poetry organize their texts into lines by counting not syllables but words; thus some of the Hekhalot hymns and Talmudic epigrams and poetic passages have a consistent four words to the line, and Carmi quotes a poem on the binding of Isaac which has consistently three words to the line (Carmi 1981: 60). The fifth argument, which we explore in greater detail in chapter 6, looks for parallelism between adjacent stretches of material, and divides the text into lines such that adjacent lines are parallel. Foster (1975, 1980) uses this as a diagnostic for whether Ancient Egyptian texts are prose or verse.

We can summarize this discussion by reference to (Southern African) Tswana praise poems as discussed by Schapera (1965). On the basis of Schapera's presentation, there is no reason to think that these texts are metrical: they cannot be organized into lines on the basis of counting syllables or features of syllables. Nevertheless, there are a number of other reasons to think that they are organized into lines. Thus the 'line' as proposed by Schapera has four out of the five diagnostic characteristics drawn from our above list: (i) it is syntactically coherent; (ii) in performance the final stressed syllable may receive extra emphasis and be followed by a brief pause; (iv) in most lines (84 per cent in his sample) there are three or four words in the line; (v) many adjacent lines are parallel. In addition there are other kinds of evidence for lines. First, as the texts were transmitted historically they tended to lose component parts which tend to be whole lines or groups of lines, suggesting that lines are stored as separate units which can be lost as wholes. Second, literate Tswana have intuitions about the division of texts into lines (thus providing a literary-linguistic version of Sapir's discovery that people could have intuitions about underlying sound structure). We should conclude by noting that the question of constituency in much African poetry continues to be a matter of discussion; a complicating factor is that some traditions might be metrical but have not been recognized as such – as we argue for Luganda below. Thus for example Rycroft and Ngcobo (1988) look at Zulu praise poetry but suggest that there is no clear sense in which this poetry is organized into lines. This may, of course, reflect a difference between the Tswana and Zulu literatures, or it may reflect a difference in analytical approach.

4.2   Metrical constituent structure and other kinds of constituent structure

4.2.1   *Portable metrical components*

The kinds of metrical constituent which we have seen so far are periodic. Thus the iambic pentameter line is divided into a repeating sequence of five identical feet; and the Greek iambic trimeter has a repeating sequence of identical feet and of identical metra. Where a metrical template lacks periodic structure, we have not in general claimed that it has constituent structure. However, there is reason to think that there is another kind of metrical constituent which is not periodic, but which is identifiable because it is shared between different meters within a tradition. This can be illustrated from Sanskrit. While the classical Sanskrit meters are quantitative, they are not periodic: many of them control the line by requiring non-periodic runs of heavy or light syllables. However, some of the sequences of positions are apparently shared between different meters (this was pointed out to me by John Smith, and the following discussion is indebted to his comments). For example, here are the sequences of heavy and light positions used in four meters. All four meters end in the same pattern of seven positions, which can thus be thought of as a 'portable metrical constituent':

mandākrāntā	− − − − : ˘ ˘ ˘ ˘ ˘ −	: − ˘ ˘ − ˘ − −
mālinī	˘ ˘ ˘ ˘ ˘ ˘ − −	: − ˘ ˘ − ˘ − −
śālinī	− − − −	: − ˘ ˘ − ˘ − −
sragdharā	− − − ˘ − − : ˘ ˘ ˘ ˘ ˘ ˘ −	: − ˘ ˘ − ˘ − −

Similarly, internal runs are also shared between meters. Thus compare these three meters:

mandākrāntā	‐ ‐ ‐ ‐	: ˘ ˘ ˘ ˘ ˘ ‐	: ‐ ‐ ‐ ‐ ˘ ‐ ‐
hariṇī	˘ ˘ ˘ ˘ ˘ ‐	: ‐ ‐ ‐ ‐	: ‐ ‐ ˘ ˘ ˘ ‐
śikhariṇī	˘ ‐ ‐ ‐ ‐ ‐	: ˘ ˘ ˘ ˘ ˘ ‐	: ‐ ˘ ˘ ˘ ‐

Here the first and second runs in *mandākrāntā* and *hariṇī* are the same but in a different order, and one of the runs is also found in *śikhariṇī*. The implication for the meter is that the metrical template is divided into constituents whose boundaries match word boundaries (i.e. there is a caesura or line-edge at the edge of each of these portable constituents), which can be borrowed from one meter to another. This is a different sense of what a metrical constituent is from the notion of metrical constituent discussed so far.

4.2.2 *The structure added in performance*

Jakobson (1987a: 79) uses the term 'verse design' to describe the meter of a text, and 'verse instance' to describe the lines of text which are permitted by the verse design. Thus a Shakespeare sonnet may have one verse design underlying all fourteen lines and fourteen different verse instances (one for each line). The meter governs both the verse design and the verse instance. But there is a third manifestation of the text which is not directly governed by the meter at all, which is what Jakobson calls the 'delivery instance', the structure of a line as performed. The meter does not directly govern how that text is performed, and this can be illustrated with iambic pentameter. It is perfectly possible in most cases to perform an iambic pentameter text in a very regular rhythm, stressing every even syllable and de-stressing every odd syllable. But this is not relevant to the metrical structure of the text: the meter governs how the words can be combined based on invariants of their stress patterns (i.e. the stresses within polysyllabic words), not on variable aspects of how they are pronounced. In principle, we might propose that the performance of an iambic pentameter text in a very regular rhythm is governed by what we could call a 'performance template', which would either relate to the meter of the text or would directly relate to the text itself. Thus the delivery instance might be regulated in a manner analogous to the way a meter regulates the verse instances by specifying the verse design.

There are some traditions where texts appear to be governed by distinctive performance templates of this kind; in some cases these performance templates are very different from the meters which govern the text. Poser (1990: 80) offers an example of a tradition of recitation of Japanese *haiku* poetry. The meter determines that each line of poetry must have five or seven morae (as described in 3.1.2). But one style of performing this poetry involves the insertion of mora-length pauses or the lengthening of morae such that each line (whether it abstractly has five or seven) is roughly equivalent in performance to eight morae. The line thus ends up with an even number of morae, and Poser argues that this derives from a phonological fact about Japanese – that morae are grouped into two-mora feet. This would be an example of a performance template which, though it is not metrical, nevertheless is sensitive to the phonological structure of the language.

4.2.3 *Metrical constituent structure and other constituent-based systems*

Metrical texts are often performed in combination with other structured systems, such as music. This is considered in detail in the next section. The basic question is whether, when a metrical text is set to music, the meter mediates the matching of text to music or whether the music is set directly to the prosodic phonological structure of the text. In addition to considering the relation between the constituent structure of music and the constituent structure of a meter, we might in principle also consider the relation between the constituent structure of bodily movement (e.g. in dance) and the constituent structure of a meter. While we might find that dance is always mediated through music before it matches with meter, it is also possible in principle that meter might have a direct relation with dance structure in some traditions (e.g. traditions where dance or other gestures accompany a text without a musical accompaniment).

4.2.4 *The distinctive characteristics of metrical constituent structure*

A meter is a template plus matching rules, and miscellaneous other rules. The template can have its own internal constituent structure. One of the striking characteristics of this constituent structure is that it involves counting beyond two. In this, metrical constituent structure is probably unlike prosodic phonological constituent structure – where it is unlikely that counting beyond two is permitted as part of the rules of structure. Generalizations in prosodic phonological constituent structure can generally be captured by building binary structures and having rules which refer to these binary structures. Thus there is no equivalent, for example, of the possibility of counting nineteen positions into a metrical line, or five feet into a line, or three metra into a line. In this sense, the processing of metrical structure apparently draws on cognitive abilities other than linguistic abilities – perhaps the cognitive abilities which are associated with music (where complex counting is also found).

Finally, we might ask whether metrical constituent structure is subject to any limits on its size. There appear to be no significant limits on the number of constituents within a metrical unit, as the Sanskrit meters for example show. However, there may be limits on the number of constituent levels within the line. Some meters have just the minimum two kinds of metrical constituent which are required to build a template – the metrical position and the metrical line (e.g. most counting meters probably have this structure). Others have three levels of metrical constituent: the metrical position, the foot and the line (iambic pentameter might be an example of this, though there is some weak evidence for a half-line constituent as well). A further possibility is four levels of metrical constituent: the metrical position, the foot, the half-line or metron, and the line (most periodic meters have such a structure). However, there may be no meters with five levels of metrical constituent, and it is worth asking why.

4.3   Songs: basic issues

Many texts are sung, which means that the text is set to a musical structure. For our purposes, we'll distinguish three aspects of musical structure (in a very oversimplified and generalized manner). These are temporal structure, rhythmic structure and melodic structure. A piece of music need not have all of these elements of structure. We can illustrate them by quoting a short section of song: the text is a sonnet by Petrarch, set to music by the early sixteenth-century Italian composer Bartolomeo Tromboncino. This is the beginning of the vocal line of the song (there are also several accompanying instrumental lines).

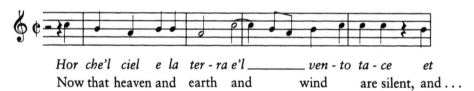

Hor che'l ciel   e la   ter - ra e'l _____ ven - to ta - ce   et
Now that heaven and   earth   and   wind   are silent, and . . .

(from Rooley 1980: 56; performed on the Decca LP set *Musicke of Sundrie Kindes*)

The musical structure can be thought of as a sequence of notes and rests. The notes in the above piece are notated as ♩♩♪; the rests are notated as ♪. A note has a pitch value and a duration; a rest is a silence which has a duration. The changing sequence of pitches is the melodic structure, and is something which we will not discuss here. Instead our main interest is in the duration of notes. Duration can in principle be measured by fixing a basic unit of duration and measuring notes in multiples and fractions of that unit; we'll use the term 'pulse' to describe the basic unit of duration in a piece (sometimes the term 'beat' is used also for this basic unit of duration). Thus in the above musical extract, we can fix on the length of a pulse as equivalent to a crotchet (= quarter-note in American terminology). Thus the above piece is twenty pulses long. We can thus restate its structure focusing just on the pulses as follows:

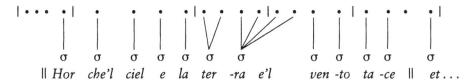

This clarifies the matching of pulses to prosodic phonological units in the song (here syllables – taking contraction into account), which will be our main focus in our discussion of music and meter. Some pulses remain unmatched (these are the rests), while in other cases a syllable is held over several pulses (long notes). The lines of text are bracketed by ‖ – thus this is the first line and the first syllable of the second line of the sonnet.

The vertical lines (bar lines) divide the sequence of pulses into four-pulse constituents; the theory of musical constituency is complex (and shares some characteristics with metrical constituency). We will not discuss it in detail here except to say that in this musical setting, the first pulse in each constituent is the strongest (i.e. accented), partly as a result of the accompanying instrumentation, which also picks out this constituent-initial pulse; the third pulse in each constituent is also fairly strong but is less strong than the first. This gives the music its rhythmic structure. The rhythmic structure of the music matches the rhythm specified by the meter of the text. This text is in the *endecasillabo* meter; in this meter the two strongest positions are fourth or sixth and tenth positions. In this line, the sixth position (filled with *ter-* of *terra*) and the tenth position (filled with *ta-* of *tace*) are matched with pulses at the beginning of musical constituents, which in this musical structure are accented pulses. In other lines of the song, the sixth and tenth positions are sometimes matched with accented pulses, as here, and at other times are matched with constituent-internal sequences of two or more pulses (long notes), another manifestation of musical prominence. Note, incidentally, that the constituent structure of the music does not coincide with the metrical constituent structure of the text: line divisions indicated by ‖ fall inside musical constituents. This does not mean that the musical setting is insensitive to metrical constituency, however: thus there are rests in between metrical lines.

The question we must now ask about the setting of this text to the music is whether it is the prosodic phonological structure of the text which is directly matched to the musical structures (temporal and rhythmic) or whether these are mediated by the metrical structure of the text. In fact, there is reason to think that the meter has some role since it is precisely the two aspects of prosodic phonological structure which the meter governs (syllables as the matched units, and the sixth and tenth syllables as the rhythmically dominant units) which are also most specifically matched to the musical structure. Note for example that the fourth bar begins with a rhythmic pulse which does not match any single syllable – thus the text is not accented here, and at the same time this is a section of text whose rhythm is not governed by the *endecasillabo* meter. Furthermore, given the high incidence of elision and synaloepha (squashing two syllables into one position) in the song, we might argue that the pulses are in fact matched to metrical positions rather than to syllables. Thus we might argue that the meter mediates the matching of text to music in this case. In general, where a metrical text is set to a musical structure, we would always want to ask whether the matching of text to music matches prosodic phonological structure, or matches the metrical template. The issue is partly one of how much prosodic phonological variation the musical matching rules are sensitive to: if they are sensitive to considerable variation in the text then they are likely to be matching prosodic phonological structure directly. If they are insensitive to variation in exactly the way that the meter is, then they reach the text by matching first with the metrical template.

4.4   Metrical texts and musical structure: some examples

This section explores some of the issues relating to metricality which arise when we consider texts which are set to music.

4.4.1   *The Somali* masafo, *set to music*

Work on the meters of Somali poetry began by looking at the texts alone, but more recent work has integrated an account of the meters of the text with an account of the music to which the text is sung (e.g. Johnson 1996, Banti and Giannattasio 1996). In this section we return to Banti and Giannattasio's account of the *masafo*, to discuss briefly how the meter of the line relates to the musical structure to which it is set. They analyse performances by contemporary singers, and suggest that the rhythmic structure of the music is as follows. There are nine pulses in each half-line, with a rest between half-lines (the half-lines are also differentiated by melody). Each pulse matches a mora; thus the (typical) nine morae of each half-line match the nine pulses of each half-line. The third, sixth and ninth pulses are accented in singing. To illustrate, here is a line (from 3.3.3) as sung by Sheekh Jaamac. In the transcription, • is a pulse, : is an accented pulse, and a vertical line marks a constituent boundary in the music.

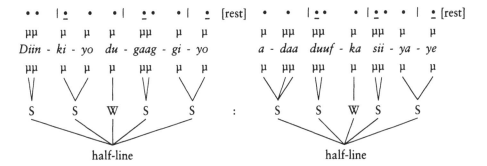

The timing structure of the music corresponds to the metrical structure of the text: both are sensitive to the mora as a basic unit of prosodic phonological structure. However, the rhythmic structure of the music does not correspond to the meter: the musical rhythm is ternary and the text is organized by a basically binary rhythm (but there is a relation between musical rhythm and meter, as we see shortly). Nevertheless, the melodic structure (not shown here) of the music does correspond to the metrical structure, in that the melody differentiates the two halves of the line.

While the musical rhythm and the meter do not correspond, there is an interesting relation between them at the beginning of the half-line. Here, in the musical rhythm, there is a constituent consisting of just two pulses (instead of the expected three). This musical constituent corresponds exactly to the first constituent of the meter (the first S position), which is subject to considerable variation in matching. There may be up to four morae in this first constituent, and fundamentally two ways of fitting these extra morae into the musical structure. One possibility is to contract a long vowel down to one mora in performance; thus for example the long vowel in *adaa* is fitted into two pulses in this position by pronouncing the word as *ada*, shortening the second vowel. A second possibility is to add a pulse, so that three syllables can be fitted into this constituent: this is possible because the rhythmical constituent of the music generally has three pulses, and a third pulse can in principle be added to this otherwise anomalous two-pulse initial constituent. Thus the organization of the musical rhythm, with a 'short' initial rhythmic constituent which can be expanded, conspires with the organization of the meter where the first position can be expanded in the number of morae it can contain.

4.4.2 Are Luganda court songs metrical?

It is sometimes said (e.g. by Greenberg 1960) that outside the reach of Arabic
meters (via Islam), African verse tends not to be metrical. The usual assumption
is that canonic parallelism (see chapter 6) governs African verse structures. However, work on African literatures is now revealing otherwise unsuspected metrical
systems; this section briefly outlines an account of the structure of Luganda songs
based on Katamba and Cooke (1987), and proposes that the texts of these songs
might be thought of as metrical.

The songs in question are part of the court music of the Buganda kings of
Uganda (the language is called Luganda). The musical structure of some of the
songs involves a basic line-sized constituent of thirty-six pulses corresponding
to a line of text; the line is divided into two half-lines, and the soloist may sing
the first half-line (the call) and the chorus the second half-line (the response);
in some performances, the soloist sings both parts. Accompanying handclaps
divide the line into six 6-pulse constituents. There are two reasons for thinking that the text might be matched to the music in a manner which is basically
metrical. First, there is a matching of positions to units of prosodic phonological
structure: pulses in the music are matched with morae in the line, with a mora
matching a pulse and very few unmatched pulses (rests) internal to the half-line.
Second, the music is divided into constituents (36-pulse units) which match
textual constituents (a complete call and response sequence in the text of the
song). This suggests that the text might be controlled by a meter, which is either
parallel to the musical structure or somehow incorporated into it.

Morae are calculated from a text as follows. A long vowel counts for two morae,
as does a vowel preceded by a glide (hence *kwa* counts for two morae); where
a vowel is followed by two consonants – even if they are in the next syllable, or
the next word – the vowel also counts for two morae. (Perhaps one of the two
consonants resyllabifies from being part of the onset to being part of the preceding
coda.) The following is a line from the song of Ssematimba and Kikwabanga
as performed by Blasio Busuulwa. Pulses are indicated by •, and a pulse which
can be accompanied by a handclap (i.e. implicitly accented) is indicated by •.

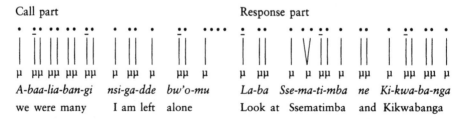

(Note: the letter 'k' in *kikwabanga* is pronounced as [tʃ] and hence makes the
preceding syllable count for two morae) (cited by Katamba and Cooke 1987: 52)

Several points need comment. First, there are some pulses which are not matched with syllables. In general, unmatched pulses never appear within a half-line; but either they may appear (in small numbers) at the end of either half-line, as here, or if the half-line is very short the first part of the half-line may be empty. There is also a section in this text where three pulses are matched to two morae, in the first two syllables of *Ssematimba*; here, the vowels appear to be lengthened slightly in performance.

If we were to hypothesize a meter for this text it might be as follows:

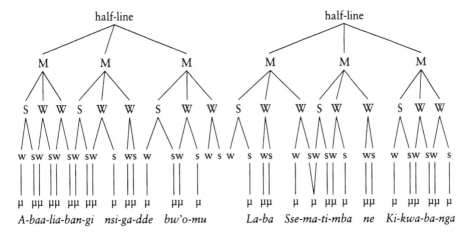

In this meter, the line is divided into two half-lines, each of which contains three metra, each of which contains three iambic feet. In matching music and meter, the handclap falls on the strongest metrical position within each metron.

Various justifications can be proposed for this meter. First, there are some unmatched positions (i.e. the lines are shorter than the metrical template), but these positions tend to be at the ends of half-lines. The end of a major constituent is a typical place for there to be some metrical variation, and this recalls the 'brevis in longo' phenomenon seen in 3.3.1. Any other unmatched metrical positions within the line would have to be examined in detail, to see if there are constraints on their position: finding constraints would further justify this hypothetical meter. The grouping of metrical positions into strong and weak is justified primarily by the special status of the first strong position in each metron, which in the musical rhythm matches the handclap. We differentiate this metrical position not for musical reasons (which are in themselves irrelevant to a meter's structure) but for linguistic reasons: there appear to be constraints on how this position is matched to the prosodic structure of the text. The first constraint is that the syllable it is matched with is 'prominent' (i.e. carrying perceived stress): thus for example the word *Ssematimba* must be aligned so that the most prominent syllable *ti* matches the position. (This is why the preceding syllables must be lengthened slightly, as mentioned earlier.) Exactly what 'prominence' means remains to be determined (e.g. whether it is lexical stress, postlexical stress, etc.), as must the nature of the matching rule. The second constraint, probably related to the first, is that if this position matches a two-mora syllable, the position will match with the first of the two morae: another phonological constraint which suggests that this is a meter which has differentiated metrical positions. Note finally that while the organization into half-lines in the above line involves an empty position at the beginning of the second half-line, in many other lines this position (the first w position in the half-line) is filled with the first syllable in the second half-line; for example in a performance of this line by Albert Ssempeke, he replaces *laba* (= 'look at') with *mulabe* (= 'you look at'), thus filling the first weak position. We return to this song tradition in 9.3.3.

Thus there is some reason to think that the matching of music to text in this song tradition implies the presence of a metrical template. The metrical template constrains the textual structure of the song, and the musical template is then matched to the metrical template (and hence indirectly to the text).

4.4.3 The discovery of a metrical text inside a non-metrical sung text: the Rajasthani Epic of Pābūjī

Smith (1979) proposes that the Rajasthani *Epic of Pābūjī* can be thought of as existing in three versions: (a) the underlying text, (b) the sung text (technically referred to as the *gāv*), and (c) the declaimed spoken text (technically referred to as the *arthāv*). The underlying text is fixed and is metrical. The sung text is adapted to the musical meter by adding words and vocables to the underlying text. The declaimed text has some added material which appears to survive from the performer's experience of singing the text but is close to the underlying text. (This discussion is extended, with musical examples, in Smith 1991.)

For example, this is the underlying text for the first line of a couplet:

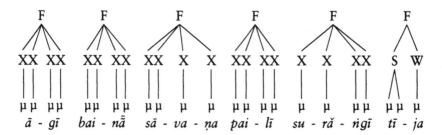

'Sisters, the lovely festival of *Sāvaṇ rī Tīj* has arrived'

The meter consists of five constituents of four morae followed by a fixed cadence of a heavy + light syllable in the first line and a fixed cadence of a heavy + light

+ heavy syllable in the second line. This mixture of mora-counting and a quantitative cadence can be achieved, as a first try, by stipulating a matching rule which states that a metrical position may match a mora or a syllable but matches a mora by default, and that an S position matches a heavy syllable and a W position matches a light syllable. The text of the epic follows this meter; however, this is never the text as performed. When it is performed – either sung or declaimed – the text is not metrical.

When sung (the *gāv* version), the text will have various words and vocables (see below) added which add morae. These extra morae are required to match the units of the musical meter (in at least some musical settings, each mora matches a musical unit): the text has 48 morae per couplet, but the musical meters for this text typically have many more than 48 musical units, and so extra morae are added to fill the gaps. Thus in one sung performance of the above line, it is added to as follows:

e jī āya-gī sayelyā̃ hamẽ bainā̃ jī
sāmaṇa to jī e pailairī jī suraṅgī o tīja o

Added to the underlying text are (a) the vocables *e, jī, to* and *o*; (b) the word *hamẽ* which means 'now' and adds no significant meaning; (c) the word *sayelyā̃* which means 'girlfriends' and is a redundant vocative term of address which again adds no significant meaning. There are other alterations of the underlying text which also change its overall mora count. The total number of morae in the underlying text line was 23; the total number of morae in this sung version of the text is about twice as many.

An alternative mode of performing the text is when it is declaimed (i.e. spoken rather than sung). This is the same line again, in one declaimed version:

āy-gī saiyā̃ jo sāvaṇa pailī surăṅgī tīja

This is quite close to the underlying text, and is almost metrical with the exception of the added vocable *jo*. Declaimed versions are typically closer to the underlying text but may not exactly correspond to it. Smith suggests: 'there is a strong tendency for some or all of this verbiage [added in singing] to "stick" – to become so integrally associated with the [underlying] text in the performer's own mind that he cannot fully distinguish one from the other' (Smith 1979: 353, my additions in square brackets).

This example illustrates the complementary situation to that for Luganda. In Luganda songs, the metricality of the text is revealed in the singing of the text, and can be seen in an examination of the musical structure and its matching with prosodic phonological structure. In the Rajasthani songs, the metricality of the text is concealed in the singing of the text, because the musical structure requires the text to be altered in ways which make it unmetrical.

4.5 Vocables

A vocable is made from speech sounds organized into syllables, but is not a word of the language. Vocables are found in many literatures; examples of lines made from vocables in English songs and poems might be 'eeny meeny miney mo' or 'hey nonny nonny no'. Vocables are interesting in the context of this book for a number of reasons. First, since their meaning is obscure, their use is a good example of the exploitation of linguistic form for literary functions other than straightforward communication. Second, since they are not words in the language, they present a case of literary-linguistic innovation from a base of linguistic form, and we might consider to what extent their innovatory use remains constrained by linguistic principles.

Vocables have been extensively cited as components of Native American songs, and we choose Navajo for our discussion of them, based on Frisbie (1980). Navajo vocables have a CV or VCV structure, and may be strung together tightly (into 'words') or loosely (giving the effect of a string of words). Their phonetic structure is mainly dependent on the phonetic possibilities of the language, but involves a restricted range of sounds: thus the consonants [n], [y] and [h] are very common in vocables, while glottalized (ejective) consonants are not found. In some cases, the vocables might have originated as now archaic words in the language, or might be foreign words which have been imported. In other cases the vocables appear to have been invented. Navajo vocables may be improvised for the song, or may be fixed and re-usable – in effect a kind of poetic diction. Fixed vocables may symbolize the speaking or calling of specific deities and specific animals and birds; thus *haʔaʔaʔá* is a transcription (by Washington Matthews) of the call of the deity 'Monster Slayer', while *háaaá* is his transcription of the call of the deity 'Born for Water'. The improvisation of vocables, which remains within the general phonetic constraints on vocables, is undertaken for various reasons. Thus a singer may forget the words of the song and use the vocables to cover the lapse: Frisbie cites one singer's line *heye neye ya ŋa ŋa naŋa na*, which the singer later acknowledged to be an error replacing the line which begins with two non-vocable Navajo words *nitliz iłtas aŋ a ŋa naŋa yei*. A contextually defined function for improvised vocables is the replacement of obscene words with vocables in a song performed for recording and reproduction outside the culture.

Frisbie speculates on various functions for vocables. One function is to mark the constituent structure of the (non-metrical) songs. Thus vocables introduce a song, with specific vocables being associated with particular songs, and may also indicate the arrival of the song's ending; this is clearly analogous to the use of fixed and sometimes meaningless words to begin and end narratives in many traditions, such as English '*snip snap snover, the story's over*' (see also 8.3.1).

Vocables are also used to mark the transition between verse and chorus; again, Frisbie suggests that a chorus–verse linking vocable such as *holaghei* is analogous to the use of a connective like *áádóó* ('then') in narrative. Just as for narratives, particular singers may have their own preferences for particular vocables as constituent markers; thus while the singer Frank Mitchell prefers *holaghei* as a verse–chorus marker, the singer Tłaah used *xa ŋayeye xa ŋeyeye* in the same structural position. A second function for vocables appears to be the expression of emotion and mood; thus one song (cited by Leland Wyman) begins *ʔe-ye ʔe-ye ʔe-ni* and describes this as 'an expression of affection'. This is an interesting area since it involves the problem of sound symbolism. Sounds appear to be capable of symbolizing in three ways: (i) by conventional association between sound and meaning, (ii) by resemblance between sound and some other sound, (iii) by the inherent meaning of sounds. The first two possibilities are reasonably convincing as explanations, but in many cases (iii) represents an emic view which can be reduced to (i) in an etic perspective: that is, an outside observer will usually suggest that while speakers may think that a sound has inherent meaning, this must be understood as a conventional association within the culture. We might speculate on a third set of functions for vocables, along lines which we discussed in 1.2.1; vocables, because they are not words of the language, may make songs difficult in various ways – they are difficult to understand (if they even have a meaning), they may be difficult to remember, or even to discern while listening to or learning a song. Thus the correct reproduction of vocables is an act which emphasizes meanings of faith, the esoteric, and the culturally conventional, and thus fits with deliberate kinds of obscurity found in other literatures and cultures.

4.6   Summary: the characteristics of a meter and its relation with other systems

Metrical texts appear to be governed by structures (metrical templates, and the matching rules) which have some psychological reality, suggesting that the composition (and perhaps reception) of metrical verse is mediated by some kind of metrical processing system. The metrical templates are possibly governed by universal principles which control their overall complexity, permit various options such as counting, and allow for phenomena such as free initial and fixed cadence. One of the more intriguing aspects of metrical structures is their relation to musical structures. Metrical texts may be set to music, but it is an empirical question in any particular case whether the matching of text to music is a matching of prosodic phonological structure directly to musical structure, or whether it is mediated through the metrical structure of the text. The relation between metrical processing and musical processing is an area which has remained more or less untouched by any generative approaches: it offers rich possibilities for future work.

4.7 Further reading

Prince (1989: 49) offers two subtle arguments for the foot as a metrical constituent, comparing iambic and trochaic meters. Poser (1989) discusses the relation between phonological and metrical feet in Diyari. Halle (1987) illustrates one way of discovering a meter in a Biblical text thought not to be metrical.

Myers (1992) is an exhaustive introduction to ethnomusicology; the accompanying volume Myers (1993) discusses research in different traditions. Brăiloiu (1984a) discusses a song tradition where syllable structure determines musical structure. Wade (1993) is a useful collection on music and meter with an emphasis on Indian traditions. On songs in Luganda see Katamba and Cooke (1987), de Vale (1984), Gray (1992), Kiguli (1996). Schuh (1989) discusses the relation between music and meter in Hausa songs. On some Polynesian song traditions see Moyle (1987), Love (1991). A very detailed account of Dyirbal songs (Australia) is given in Dixon and Koch (1996). On linguistic aspects of the connection between meter and music see Jackendoff (1989); on linguistics and music more generally see Monelle (1992), and on music and cognition see Sloboda (1985). The two exercises for this chapter focus on children's songs. Two classic discussions of the metrical and rhythmic structures of children's songs and the cross-linguistic similarities between them are Brăiloiu (1984b) and Burling (1966). Frisbie (1980) is a good starting point for reading about vocables; see also Powers (1992) on vocables in Lakota.

4.8 Exercises

4.8.1 *Alphabet songs*

The texts for this exercise are five songs which teach the alphabet. Each song represents a solution to the problem of how to fit the 27- or 28-syllable English alphabet into a song for children. (Of the 26 letters, all are monosyllables except W which is either two or three syllables long.)

Instructions

Answer the questions below for all of the texts.

(a) Is the text metrical?
(b) Divide the text into metrical lines, and explain how the division into lines is reinforced by the text (e.g. when things happen at line-ends).
(c) Are metrical positions organized into feet? Justify your answer.
(d) Text B1 differs from the A texts in that there is a length difference between syllables, with stressed syllables being performed to be approximately twice as long as unstressed. Does this difference correlate with any other differences between B1 and the A texts?
(e) In the first half of each of the A texts, the sequence L M N O is sung rapidly, with two syllables to a pulse. (i) Is there a reason for these syllables in particular being chosen for being sung rapidly? (ii) In A3 it is this sequence which is repeated: can you explain why?
(f) If you know how to sing any of these versions, or any other version of this song – and can do some basic musical transcription – speculate on the relation between the melody of the song and its metrical structure.

Texts

Texts are given as the sequence of letters, and their phonetic transcriptions (ignoring variations in vowel qualities between dialects). A pulse is indicated by • and a stressed pulse by ⁞. Where a pulse matches two syllables they can be taken as each lasting half a pulse; where the pulse is accented it is the first of the two syllables which carries the accent.

   Texts A1–4: all of these have the same first half (A–P), and vary in the second half. This is the first half:

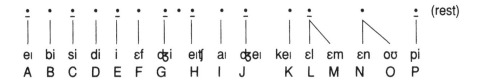

These are the second halves:

(A1) Learned in England (Midlands and London), 1930s. Note that Z is pronounced as zɛd.

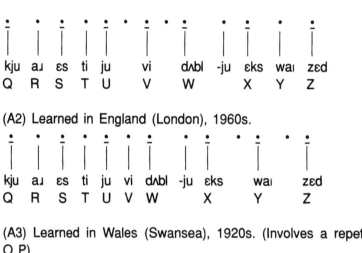

kju	aɹ	ɛs	ti	ju		vi		dʌbl	-ju	ɛks	waɪ	zɛd
Q	R	S	T	U		V		W		X	Y	Z

(A2) Learned in England (London), 1960s.

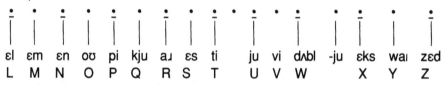

kju	aɹ	ɛs	ti	ju	vi	dʌbl	-ju	ɛks		waɪ		zɛd
Q	R	S	T	U	V	W		X		Y		Z

(A3) Learned in Wales (Swansea), 1920s. (Involves a repetition of L M N O P)

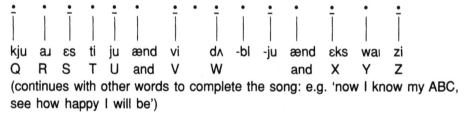

ɛl	ɛm	ɛn	oʊ	pi	kju	aɹ	ɛs	ti		ju	vi	dʌbl	-ju	ɛks	waɪ	zɛd
L	M	N	O	P	Q	R	S	T		U	V	W		X	Y	Z

(A4) Learned in USA (New York), 1950s. Note that Z is pronounced as zi.

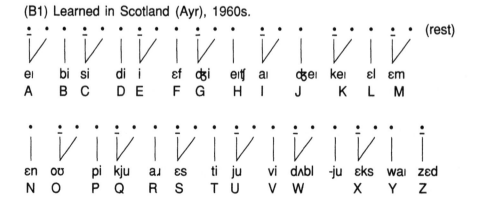

kju	aɹ	ɛs	ti	ju	ænd	vi		dʌ	-bl	-ju	ænd	ɛks	waɪ	zi
Q	R	S	T	U	and	V		W			and	X	Y	Z

(continues with other words to complete the song: e.g. 'now I know my ABC, see how happy I will be')

Text B1: the division into two halves is different.

(B1) Learned in Scotland (Ayr), 1960s.

eɪ		bi	si		di	i		ɛf	dʒi		eɪtʃ	aɪ		dʒeɪ	keɪ		ɛl	ɛm	(rest)
A		B	C		D	E		F	G		H	I		J	K		L	M	

ɛn	oʊ		pi	kju	aɹ	ɛs		ti	ju		vi	dʌbl	-ju	ɛks		waɪ	zɛd
N	O		P	Q	R	S		T	U		V	W		X		Y	Z

4.8.2 *Are Tongan children's songs metrical?*

This exercise addresses another children's verbal art tradition, this time from Tonga. The texts and explanation of their contexts are from Moyle (1987), where discussion of the structure of the texts and music can be found (see especially p. 235). Versions of these songs can be heard on *Traditional Music of Tonga*, notes by Richard Moyle, Hibiscus LP record HLS–65. The musical transcription from Moyle (1987) has been rewritten in terms of pulses.

Instructions

Two songs are provided; do the exercise for both of them (you may find that there are different answers for each text).

(a) Are there any rules for the matching of pulses with syllables (or any other constituent of prosodic phonological structure)?
(b) Are syllables with short vowels dealt with differently from syllables with long vowels (a long vowel is written with a macron above it)?
(c) How are sequences of vowels dealt with (whether in the same word or in adjacent words)?
(d) Is there any basis for saying that the text itself is metrical? [*Hint: In my view both texts can be argued to have a metrical structure, though the structure is different in each text.*] If you think there is evidence for a meter, formulate the meter. If you think there is no evidence for a meter, explain why.

Text A: Motuku

'One of the more widespread children's songs in Tonga relates to the heron (*motuku*). This bird is often seen on the reef, at low tide, poking about in the shallow water searching for food. When children spy a heron, they break into song' (from Moyle 1987: 225).

motuku talitali	the heron waits expectantly
si 'ono heke mai	it glides in our direction
ke fai 'etau kai	to make our meal
te u heke au ki tahi	I will glide to the sea
'o pūlou mei ai	and cover myself from it

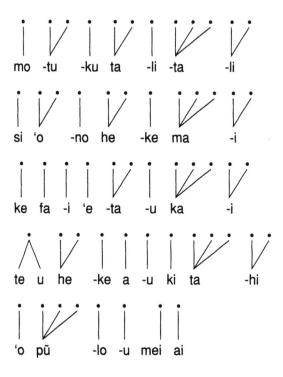

mo -tu -ku ta -li -ta -li

si 'o -no he -ke ma -i

ke fa -i 'e -ta -u ka -i

te u he -ke a -u ki ta -hi

'o pū -lo -u mei ai

Text B: Mahina

'Moonlit nights are a favourite time for children's play. . . . they often walk about, striking postures which will produce the most unusual or grotesque shadows. They sing the following song as they do so' (from Moyle 1987: 223).

māhina mo e kalipa   The moon with its cusps
mou punou ki he la'ā   all of you bow down to the sun
taha ua tolu fā   one two three four

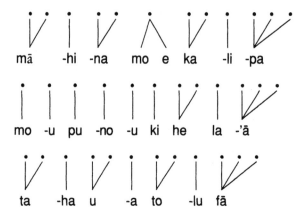

mā -hi -na mo e ka -li -pa

mo -u pu -no -u ki he la -'ā

ta -ha u -a to -lu fā

5 Para-metrical Rules: Word-boundary Rules and Sound-patterning Rules

In this chapter we look at two very different kinds of para-metrical rule. We begin with rules which control the placement of prosodic phonological constituent boundaries, typically word boundaries. Word-boundary rules are para-metrical rules which are very closely tied to the meter, and specifically to the metrical template. In contrast, sound-patterning rules, which we discuss in the remainder of the chapter, are less closely tied to the meter though they are sensitive to metrical structure.

5.1 The control of phonological constituent boundaries

A metrical template is matched to a metrical line by controlling certain aspects of the prosodic phonological structure of that line. To some extent, this control involves a control of prosodic constituents. Consider for example a metrical template where a metrical position matches a pair of morae. In some traditions, it is not possible for two distinct adjacent heavy syllables to supply those morae, such that the second mora of one syllable and the first mora of the next together fill the metrical position. In this case, the placement of syllable boundaries is being controlled by the meter. Similarly, many meters require the line ending to correspond to a large phonological constituent boundary (such as the ending of a phonological phrase).

In this and the next section we focus on one particular kind of phonological constituent, the word, and how the placement of words is related to the metrical template by word-boundary rules. Word-boundary rules are rules which refer to a metrical template and stipulate whether word boundaries must or must not fall between the syllables matching two metrical positions. There are two types of word-boundary rule: a caesura rule requires a word-boundary while a bridge rule forbids one. Thus a caesura marks a point in the line where a word must begin or end, while a bridge must always fall within a word. Both kinds of rule can be illustrated by reference to the Serbo-Croatian meter *êpskī desetérac* (epic decasyllable). The meter can be characterized (loosely) by a metrical template with ten positions, with each position matched to a syllable; you may have worked out a more precise version when you did exercise 3.9.2. A caesura rule stipulates that between the fourth and fifth positions there must be a word boundary (this is annotated with a colon : in the metrical template), and two bridge rules forbid word boundaries between the third and fourth and ninth and tenth metrical positions (annotated with an equals sign = in the metrical template). The effects of these rules can be seen in actual composition, where the third and fourth syllables always belong to the same word, and the fourth syllable is always at the end of a word, while the ninth and tenth syllables also always belong to the same word:

X	X	X = X	:	X	X		X	X = X

kad   se-je-ny   serb-sky   tsar Stje-pa-ne
na   da-le-ko   za-pro-sy   dje-voy-ku
u   Le-ja-no   gra-du   la-tin-sko-me

'When the Serbian tsar Stepan gets married, he proposes to a girl from far away, from Lejano an Italian city' (the first three lines of *The Marriage of Dushan*, anonymous, 12th or 13th century)

Sometimes caesura and bridge rules relate to performance, for example with pauses at caesura positions, and can be understood as arising from performance requirements. This is not the case for Serbo-Croatian epics, however, where the line is sung rapidly without a pause, and where the composers themselves are usually unaware of any rule controlling word boundaries; thus Jakobson says that when a line is composed which has the word boundary in the wrong place, the poet may say that it is 'out of tune' but is unable to explain why.

   Relatively little linguistic work has been done on word-boundary rules, and it is not clear how they should best be formulated. They are not really part of the meter (they may act as a separate, counterpointing system, as we see below), but are parasitic on the meter. The best approach might be to see them as annotations of the metrical template, as here. Notice, however, that it might be possible in some cases to achieve word-boundary effects indirectly (just as stress patterns can be controlled indirectly in iambic pentameter). Thus for example if words have particular prosodic characteristics, we might be able to control the placement of word boundaries by controlling those prosodic characteristics: if the strongest stress is always on the first syllable of a word then we might be able to force or forbid a word to begin at a particular syllable by controlling the stress on that syllable.

5.1.1   What counts as a word?

One of the interesting characteristics of word-boundary rules is that they are complicated in some cases by the issue of which prosodic phonological constituent counts as a word. There are two levels of phonological constituent which might be thought of as a word. One is the lexical word. The other is the lexical word plus preceding or following grammatical words such as conjunctions, or articles, or prepositions: these can cluster together to form a 'clitic group', a kind of phonological word which is larger than the lexical word. Devine and Stephens (1984) show that in classical Greek poetry the 'word' to whose boundary the bridge rule is sensitive can be interpreted sometimes as the lexical word and sometimes as the clitic group. In looser genres (e.g. in comedies), the clitic group can count as a word – hence a clitic-group internal boundary between a grammatical word and a lexical word may be allowed in a bridge position. In stricter genres (e.g. in tragedies), the lexical word is the relevant unit – hence a boundary between a grammatical word and a lexical word is ruled out in a bridge position. This may correlate with deliberateness of speech style. A more deliberate speaking style, as in tragedy, involves a more finely grained hierarchical structuring of the phonological string, and hence boundaries within clitic groups will be more prominent and hence forbidden in bridge position.

This variability between different sizes of phonological constituent in what counts as a 'word' for caesura and bridge rules is seen also in other literatures. Thus Keith (1920: 417) discusses caesura rules in Classical Sanskrit poetry and says that while the caesura normally coincides with the end of the inflected word, in some cases it coincides with an internal morpheme boundary (after a prefix) or the internal boundary between the two parts of a compound. Keith does not comment on whether these variations are correlated with any other aspect of the text in question, as Devine and Stephens show for Greek.

5.2   The relation between metrical template and word-boundary rules

5.2.1   Counterpoints

Word-boundary rules relate primarily to the bottom level of a metrical template, the sequence of metrical positions. However, there are reasons to think that in some cases word-boundary rules are sensitive to higher levels of metrical structure. In particular, one of the peculiarities of caesura and bridge rules is that they sometimes operate to prevent word boundaries coinciding with higher-level constituent boundaries.

This is the case, for example, in the Greek dactylic hexameter, the meter used in Homer's *Iliad* and *Odyssey*. Prince (1989) argues that the metrical template for this line has the following structure (slightly adapted here):

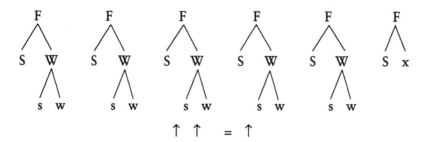

A major metrical position – an S or W metrical position – matches a two-mora syllable (i.e. a heavy syllable), while a minor metrical position – an s or w metrical position – matches a one-mora syllable (i.e. a light syllable). (There are further restrictions.) This gives sub-sequences of heavy–light–light and heavy–heavy syllables. There must be a caesura in the line, and it must appear in one of the three positions marked with an arrow. Note that the caesura falls within a foot, and does not fall at the middle of the line (where there is a bridge position). In other words, there must not be a word boundary at the middle of the line and there must be a word boundary just next to the middle of the line. Thus the caesura and bridge rules counterpoint the metrical structure rather than fitting directly into it. West (1987: 19) points out that the hexameter line, when divided in the third foot, falls into two parts which are independently found in other meters: they are the portable non-periodic metrical constituents (cola) discussed in 4.2.1.

Prince argues further that the three positions where the caesura can fall are statable very simply: the caesura must be at most one major metrical position from the centre of the line. The meter can be illustrated with the following line. The word *eridi* crosses the middle of the line (where the bridge is), and the caesura requirement is met by either the beginning or the ending of this word.

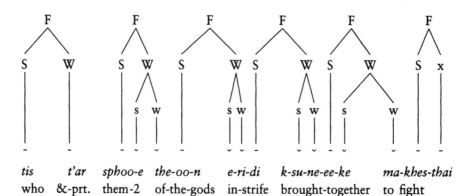

tis	t'ar	sphoo-e	the-oo-n	e-ri-di	k-su-ne-ee-ke	ma-khes-thai
who	&-prt.	them-2	of-the-gods	in-strife	brought-together	to fight

'Which of the gods brought these two together to fight in strife?' (*Iliad* I.8, cited in Prince 1989: 61; ¯ indicates a heavy syllable, ˘ indicates a light syllable. Word-internal syllable divisions are indicated in the text with a dash. See 2.2.3 for a discussion of the resyllabification)

Prince suggests that this approach provides evidence that the apparently ternary foot is organized into a complex binary structure as shown here.

5.2.2 Complete control of the placement of word boundaries

Complete control of the placement of words within the line is rarer, and is not obviously the same kind of thing as a caesura or bridge rule; in the 'complete control' case, control of word placement is the basic principle governing the text. An example is furnished by the literature of the Dyirbal-speaking peoples (Northeastern Australia), who have a song-type called Gama (Dixon 1984; Dixon and Koch 1996). As is the case in many Australian aboriginal songs, the song consists of a few lines which are repeated many times. Here are the two lines making up one such song, whose content is a single image. The metrical template for the line has eleven positions, matched with syllables; there are two obligatory caesuras after the fifth and seventh positions, and one optional one after the second position. Bridges come between all other positions.

X = X (:)		X = X = X :	X = X :	X = X = X = X
mimimimi-gu			*galu*	*gagara-gu*
new moon			out there	moon
waga		*bulma-gu*	*galu*	*wanda-ŋu-gu*
calf		new moon	out there	hang up

'[Look at] the new moon, hanging out there like the calf (on a leg)' (sung by Jimmy Murray, 1963; in Dixon 1984: 225 and Dixon and Koch 1996: 94. Four performances of this song can be heard on the Larrikin Records CD *Dyirbal Song Poetry* (LRF 378).)

Thus the placement of words is constrained with unusual rigidity; these are the only two possible sequences of word-lengths in the genre. As is often the case, however, a particular literary-linguistic requirement often fits the formal possibilities of the language. In this case, the formal possibilities include the possibility of having very free order of words in a sentence in ordinary speech (which carries over to songs). There are also two possibilities allowed the song-composer: he or she may clip suffixes off words to bring them down to length, and may also invent words of the right number of syllables. In this song, *mimimimi* and *bulma* are invented words given the meaning 'new moon' by the composer.

In some languages, such as Chinese, the word is typically monosyllabic: here metrical positions match with words at the same time as matching with syllables and so words are controlled as a side-effect of syllable control. Sustained rigid control of words can be found also in some non-metrical poetry. For example, in some Hebrew post-Biblical poetry the number of words in a line was fixed at three or at four, with this being one of the basic organizing principles (Carmi 1981: 60).

5.2.3 Can word-boundary rules be stated independently of the metrical template?

Texts can be divided into non-metrical lines, and in some traditions (e.g. Mongolian), sound-patterning rules can refer to these non-metrical lines. Can word-boundary rules similarly apply within non-metrical lines? In principle this should be possible – for example, each non-metrical line, no matter how long it is, might be required to end on a disyllabic word. However, I am not aware of any traditions where word-boundary rules operate over non-metrical texts. This might be taken as evidence that word-boundary rules are specified on the positions in a metrical template, and can thus only be specified for a metrical text.

5.3 Sound-patterning rules

5.3.1 Systematic and unsystematic sound-patterning

The rest of this chapter is devoted to systematic sound-patterning, primarily alliteration and rhyme. There is an important distinction to be made between systematic and unsystematic sound-patterning. Systematic sound-patterning is the result of a rule which stipulates that sounds must be repeated in a regular and predictable pattern. Thus for example if a text is organized into stanzas where every second and fourth line rhyme, this is systematic sound-patterning.

Unsystematic sound-patterning is not the result of a rule; for example, in texts with unsystematic sound-patterning one line might have a lot of alliteration while the next has none. It is perhaps worth distinguishing two kinds of unsystematic sound-patterning. One kind exists as a marked effect within an otherwise un-patterned text, and thus might have some special communicative effect (as in sound symbolism) or might function to draw the hearer's attention. Thus, for example, the alliteration which emerges at the end of this Lakota story is marked and perhaps functions to indicate the ending of the story:

ecel śina oowa-śa nais to nais gi, sapa koko kaḣpapi na hankeya mazawakan na woyuha koko kaḣpapi śkeʔ. hetan nakeś oyate kin woyuha waśteśte yuhapi śkeʔ.

'even blankets . . . guns and fine possessions, came down. And that was the beginning of such things in the tribe, they say' (from the story of White-Plume Boy, cited in Rice 1992: 284)

The other kind of unsystematic sound-patterning is where a particular kind of text is characteristically highly patterned, but not systematically. Thus for example we might find a tradition where lines typically have much internal repetition of sounds – but this is unsystematic because there are no fixed numbers of repetitions, some lines may lack repetitions completely, and the repeated sounds may not come from the same parts of the syllable (a restriction found in systematic sound-patterning). The general tendency across traditions is for alliteration to be unsystematic and for rhyme to be systematic, though there are exceptions to these general tendencies. This chapter will have nothing further to say about unsystematic sound-patterning.

5.3.2 The relation between sound-patterning rules and prosodic phonological structure

The syllable is the level of prosodic phonological structure which is of most relevance to sound-patterning rules. Sound-patterning rules are sensitive to the internal division of the syllable into onset, nucleus and coda. This can be seen in two ways. First, systematic sound-patterning always involves a repetition of the same parts of the syllable: thus we find onsets repeating onsets, but we never find systematic cases where codas repeat onsets. Second, systematic sound-patterning never involves the repetition of just a whole syllable: there is always some difference within the syllable. Thus rhyme involves identical nuclei and codas but different onsets.

Other aspects of prosodic phonological structure can also be relevant. In some traditions, syllables involved in sound-patterning must be prosodically prominent; thus in Old Icelandic *dróttkvaett* alliteration the alliterating syllables must carry stress. In other traditions, syllables involved in sound-patterning must fall at a word boundary; thus in Somali alliteration, the alliterating syllable must be at the beginning of the word (and need not be stressed).

5.3.3 The relation between sound-patterning rules and the metrical template

Sound-patterning rules are typically sensitive to the metrical template in the sense that they are sensitive to metrical constituent structure. Thus rhyme will often be defined as holding at metrical constituent ends (often lines). As we will see shortly, alliteration may be subject to a constraint that it must hold between adjacent constituents. On the other hand, sound-patterning rules are also found in non-metrical texts, as we now see. This makes sound-patterning very different from word-boundary rules, since the latter require the metrical template for their specification.

5.3.4 Systematic sound-patterning in non-metrical texts

Sound-patterning rules can operate in non-metrical texts, if those texts have some other way of being organized into constituents such as lines. An example of this is Mongolian epic and lyric poetry. Here, lines are defined by parallelism (and perhaps also by any musical setting of the texts). In some genres, adjacent lines alliterate at the beginning of the line. Here is one example (another, from epic poetry, can be seen in exercise 6.7.1), two stanzas from a lyric about the seasons. The beginnings of lines alliterate (and there is rhyme in the first three lines of each stanza, with the fourth lines rhyming with each other between stanzas).

xaŋ   gadzar gesedž
khan earth   thawing

xaluuŋ salxi salxildž
warm wind blowing

xarisaŋ šuwuu iredž
returned birds   coming

xawar tsagiiŋ dox^jool ene   wää džaa.
spring time's sign(s) this (these) indeed

'The King's earth is thawing, warm wind blowing, birds are returning; these are indeed the signs of spring time'

dzüseŋ   xur   orodž
gentle, steady rain precipitation falling

dzüitee   nar gartš
proper/fitting sun rising

dzülgiiŋ   nogoo sergedž
meadow's green   refreshing

dzuŋ   tsagiiŋ dox[i]ool ene   wää džaa.
summer time's sign(s) this (these) indeed

'Gentle rain is falling, the proper sun is rising, the meadow's green is refreshing; these are indeed the signs of summer time'

(from Poppe 1958: 196)

Note, incidentally, that this alliteration appears to involve both the onset and the nucleus of the syllable, a pattern found also in Finnish (and which involves a sequence of segments which together do not form a sub-constituent of the syllable).

5.3.5 Sound-pattern parallelism

In this book, I distinguish between sound-patterning and sound-pattern parallelism: the latter involves parallelism between two discontinuous sequences of sounds. We saw in 2.1.2 a possible example of this in the Gaelic poem; to illustrate this again, consider the following lines of Welsh poetry:

Doe'r   oeddwn dan   oreuddail
yesterday I was   beneath leaves

Yn aros gwen,   Elen ail,
awaiting a maiden, Elen's peer

A   gochel   glaw dan   gochl   glas
And sheltering (from) rain beneath (the) mantle green

Y   fedwen, fal ynfydwas.
(of) the birch,   like (a) madman

(Dafydd ap Gwilym, 14th century: the first four lines of 'Ei Gysgod')

In this poem, pairs of lines rhyme: here, in *-ail* and in *-as*. This is systematic sound-patterning. In addition, within some of the lines there is a parallelism between two identical sequences of consonants within the line (a practice called

cynghanedd by Welsh poets and discussed more fully in 6.3.1). Thus in the first
line the sequence *r–dd* is repeated, in the second line there is no repetition, in
the third line the sequence *g–ch–l–gl* is repeated, and in the fourth line the
sequence *f–d–w*. This is (unsystematic) sound-pattern parallelism. Sound-pattern
parallelism clearly resembles sound-patterning, and perhaps we should see a
continuum between them, rather than sharply distinguishing them. However, in
general, sound-pattern parallelism is best discussed in the context of parallelism
between sections of text (chapter 6).

Sound-pattern parallelism as represented by *cynghanedd* is less tightly
constrained than sound-patterning in several ways. First, it is generally not as
sensitive to metrical constituent structure. Second, it can involve sounds which
emerge at a postlexical level (see 6.3.1). Third, there are cases where the repeated
sounds are in different parts of the syllable (i.e. a mixing of syllable-final 'rhyme'
and syllable-initial 'alliteration' which is not found in systematic sound-patterning);
this is illustrated by the following line cited by Morris-Jones (1980: 144):

rhoi angen un rhwng y naw

Here the repeated sequence is *rh-ng-n*. The 'n' of *angen* is syllable-final in the
first case (there is no resyllabification with the following word *un*), and is
repeated by a syllable-initial 'n' in *naw*. (I am grateful to Alan Thomas for
suggesting this example.)

5.4   Distinctions between alliteration and rhyme

Sound-patterning can be classified into kinds depending on which components of
the syllable are involved. Alliteration is a kind of sound-patterning which includes
the onset (it may also include the nucleus as well as the onset, as in the Finnish
Kalevala). 'Rhyme' is a general cover term for kinds of sound-patterning which
include the rime. More specifically, rhyme proper includes both nucleus and coda,
while assonance includes just the nucleus and consonance includes just the coda.

Rhyme is much more common as a kind of systematic sound-patterning than
alliteration is. Alliteration most commonly appears unsystematically. We might
expect this distinction because rhyme involves those parts of the syllable which
are also controlled by a meter: the nucleus and coda. Alliteration, on the other
hand, involves a part of the syllable – the onset – which has very little significance for a meter. (Possible exceptions to this generalization about onsets and
meters are Luganda song, where complex onsets may contribute morae, and
Chleuh (Berber) songs, where Jouad (1993) argues that every segment in the line
is counted by the meter.)

5.4.1 The adjacency of alliteration

Where we do find systematic alliteration, it appears to be subject to a distance constraint of a kind not found with systematic rhyme. This is that the items which are linked by alliteration must be within the same metrical constituent or within adjacent constituents. In the case of non-metrical texts, systematic alliteration holds within the line or between adjacent lines as we saw in Mongolian. Thus we find sequences of alliterating words within adjacent constituents, but we do not appear to find any of the patterns commonly found with rhyme where a constituent can be hopped (AAzA) or the pattern intersects (ABAB). We might formulate a generalization:

> Systematic sound-patterning which involves the onset (i.e. alliteration) must hold between items within the same constituent or within adjacent constituents, where a constituent is a metrical constituent or a non-metrical line.

Consider for example Somali, one of the few reported traditions which has systematic alliteration. In Somali (Banti and Giannattasio 1996), alliteration (*qaafiyad*) plays the role – elsewhere played by rhyme – of linking large metrical constituents. The large metrical constituents in question are lines, or – in genres which have them (*masafo*, *gabay*, etc.) – half-lines. In most cases, the same alliteration is sustained throughout the text, so that for example a *gabay* might be 'in d' – with every half-line having at least one word which begins with [d]. The alliterating segment is always at the beginning of a word: this means that it is not necessarily on the most strongly accented syllable. Any vowel alliterates with any other (Somali poetic theorists consider vowel-initial words to begin with an initial glottal stop – hence vowel alliteration can be interpreted as alliteration of a glottal), but there are no other equivalence sets (*contra* Greenberg 1960). Systematic alliteration holds between adjacent metrical units (and there are no genres where, for example, every second line alliterates, or the first halves of lines alliterate, or where there are intersecting patterns of alliteration).

However, in the light of a possible constraint on alliteration whereby it must hold between adjacent constituents, a genre of particular interest is the *buraambur*, the meter of a text typically sung by women during a special women's dance of the same name. The meter can be described as follows:

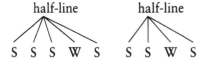

This has some similarities to the *masafo* meter discussed in 3.3.3; in particular, the first position in each half-line may match three morae (instead of just two).

This is one of the reasons for thinking of the meter as having two half-lines; another is that there must be two alliterating words within the line (as is typically found in lines divided into two half-lines). However, there is a complication: there is no caesura, and the second alliterating word can actually begin in the first half-line and continue into the second half-line. The following line is an example of this:

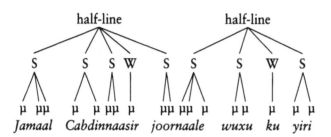

'Gamal Abdel Nasser said in a journal' (from Banti and Giannattasio 1996: 107)

This meter requires alliteration in each half-line, but here the two instance of the alliterating [j] are both in the first half-line. This would seem to leave the second half-line without an alliterating word, which would therefore be a gap which we would not normally expect in systematic alliteration. Perhaps the way to analyse the constraint regarding alliteration is to recall that alliteration is sensitive to word structure (it is the first segment of the word which alliterates), and that the constraint may simply require each half-line to contain (or partly contain, as here) a word which alliterates; it need not contain the actual alliterating segment. It is also worth noting that in texts of the *buraambur* meter, alliteration may also change between lines: that is, the text might begin with alliteration in [d] every half-line, and then shift to having alliteration in [b]. Whether these two kinds of relaxation of the requirement on alliteration are connected is a subject for further study.

If it is true that alliteration is subject to some kind of closeness requirement, while rhyme is not, we could try to find a reason for this. We might pursue two alternative lines of enquiry. The first would be to look at the relative differences in salience between alliteration and rhyme and derive the difference from this. Thus rhyme typically involves the syllable nucleus while alliteration typically does not: this might give rhyme a greater acoustic prominence and hence enable it to stay in memory for longer. However, there are traditions (such as Finnish and possibly Mongolian) where the nucleus is involved in alliteration, but where alliteration conforms to the adjacency constraint. It would be interesting to find out whether cases of true consonance (i.e. not involving the nucleus) are also subject to an adjacency constraint of the kind found with alliteration. An alternative way of looking at the difference relates to the positions of rhyme and alliteration within a constituent. Rhyme (because it comes at the end of a syllable) is able to come at the end of a constituent, which is impossible for alliteration. This may be the key difference: perhaps the end of a constituent is a position whose contents can be retained in memory longer than material elsewhere in the constituent. To test this, we might look at rhymes which are not constituent-final, to see whether these can hold over long distances. The explanation for this difference between alliteration and rhyme at present remains undecided.

5.4.2 *Alliteration in* Beowulf

Systematic sound-patterning has two components. First, the scope of the repeated material must be specified (which parts of the syllable, how many syllables, what sounds count as equivalent, etc.). Second, the position of the repeated sound must be specified (e.g. a rhyme may be required to fall at the end of a line). 'Position' in a text is a notion which makes sense only if the text has an internal constituent structure, and so systematic sound-patterning requires a text to have internal constituent structure, whether metrical or arising via parallelism. The sound-patterning must be specified as holding either between two named constituents or within a named constituent. This is normally the line: it is common for rhyme to hold between lines and alliteration to hold within lines, for example. The line is the most commonly invoked constituent in sound-patterning rules, though there are some cases where other metrical constituents are invoked, and we now discuss an example of this: a Germanic meter where alliteration holds between distinct feet.

We begin with the alliteration patterns found in *Beowulf*. The line is divided into two half-lines (usually called verses), the a-half-line and the b-half-line, each of which contains two feet; see 3.4.2. There are three typical patterns of alliteration across the four feet as indicated here (A means that there is an alliterating strongly stressed syllable):

a-half-line + b-half-line				example from *Beowulf*
A	A	A	z	*modgan maegnes, Metodes hyldo*
A	y	A	z	*wine Scildinga, worold of-laetest*
y	A	A	z	*tha waes on salum, sinces brytta*

We now attempt to answer three related questions about the b-half-line: (i) why does it always have the same pattern while the a-half-line may vary, (ii) why if there is one alliterating part must it be the first part, i.e. A z rather than z A, and (iii) why can both parts not alliterate, i.e. A A? We consider three different (but possibly complementary) approaches to these problems.

We begin by suggesting that this pattern can be accounted for by referring to the adjacency of alliteration. Following Russom (1987), the line can be organized into metrical constituents as follows:

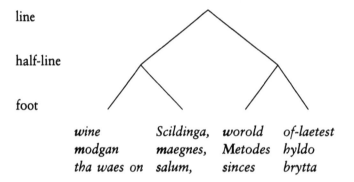

line

half-line

foot

wine	*Scildinga,*	*worold*	*of-laetest*
modgan	*maegnes,*	*Metodes*	*hyldo*
tha waes on	*salum,*	*sinces*	*brytta*

We make an initial assumption, that alliteration is on the first main stressed syllable in a constituent. Now we see that all three kinds of alliteration are adjacent but are found at different levels of metrical structure in different kinds of half-line. In the AyAz case, alliteration is initial in each half-line. In the AAAz and yAAz cases, alliteration falls in adjacent feet. We can now see why zA is not a possible pattern for the b-half-line; since its placement at the beginning of a foot but not the beginning of a half-line means that it is a foot-level alliteration, it must therefore have jumped a foot – which would make it non-adjacent. Why can alliteration not fall in every foot, to give AAAA? We cannot explain this by adjacency, and in fact we have seen other alliterative patterns where this is the pattern; thus our account must be supplemented by some other explanation here.

We now consider another account of the pattern, which interprets it in terms of a strong–weak alternation at the metrical level. Russom proposes labelling the feet and half-lines in an S W pattern:

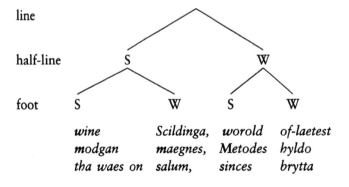

line

half-line   S   W

foot   S   W   S   W

wine	*Scildinga,*	*worold*	*of-laetest*
modgan	*maegnes,*	*Metodes*	*hyldo*
tha waes on	*salum,*	*sinces*	*brytta*

This labelling means that the final foot is super-weak since it is the weak member of a weak constituent. Since alliteration appears to be tied to strong stress, the lack of alliteration in the final foot could derive from its super-weakness. This answers all three questions (and also correctly predicts that AAAy and AyAz should be more common than yAAz, since the latter pattern fails to have alliteration on the super-strong first foot). It is worth noting, however, that it does not by itself explain why AAAA is impossible; furthermore it might be interpreted as implying that the attested yAAz should be impossible exactly because it does fail to have alliteration on the super-strong first foot.

Our third account of the pattern comes from Suzuki (1988). Suzuki places Germanic alliterative verse in its diachronic (historical) context, suggesting that it can best be understood as a development of certain possibilities in the ancestral Indo-European poetry. Suzuki first suggests that the rigidity of the b-half-line is an example of a fixed cadence, while the freedom of the a-half-line is an example of a free initial; both are possible inheritances from Indo-European. Next he suggests that the b-half-line pattern of Az rather than zA is an inheritance from Indo-European, where the caesura (here, the break between a-half-line and b-half-line) is followed by a strong position. This can be seen both in the quantitative meters of Sanskrit, where a heavy syllable follows the caesura, and the stress-based meters of Irish where a stressed syllable follows the caesura. Suzuki presents other arguments relating to the pattern of alliteration which we do not discuss further here. In principle, we might suggest that all three approaches presented here might combine to overdetermine a particular pattern of alliteration in the line.

5.5   Sound-patterning rules and phonological structure

5.5.1   *Syllable-internal prosodic structure and sound-patterning rules*

We can see that sound-patterning rules are sensitive to the internal structure of the syllable because a particular rule always designates which parts of the syllable are involved in a pattern (thus differentiating alliteration from rhyme). In this section, we look at ways in which more subtle aspects of the structure of the syllable are referred to by two conventions of alliteration in Germanic alliterative verse (and some other traditions).

In Germanic poetry (as in fact in many alliteration-based systems, including Irish and Somali) vowel-initial words alliterate with one another, irrespective of the vowels involved. We would not want to analyse this as involving an equivalence set of all vowels, partly because this would be a far too loosely defined set, and also because there are no cases of equivalence sets of all consonants. Furthermore, alliteration in Germanic involves only the onset. In vowel-initial words there appears to be no onset – but this is perhaps the key to the analysis. We could hypothesize that there is a structural position for the onset which as a position is still present at the beginning of the syllable, but unfilled with any sound. All syllables beginning with a vowel thus begin with an identical onset, identical because empty. Thus vowel-initial syllables are actually empty-onset-initial syllables and thus may alliterate with one another (this argument is outlined by Kiparsky 1970: 170). Thus again a sound-patterning rule is sensitive to syllable structure even in the absence of actual sound.

A second characteristic of alliteration in Germanic poetry involves some onsets which do not alliterate though we might expect them to. Normally any two words will alliterate if they begin with the same sound. This is not a matter of repetition of the whole onset but just of the first sound in the onset: thus *sunu* (son) alliterates with *sweord* (sword). But a word beginning in [s] will not alliterate with a word beginning in [sp], [st] or [sk], and similarly a word beginning in [sp] will not alliterate with a word beginning in [st], [sk] etc. It is as though [s], [sp], [st] and [sk] count as different 'initial sounds'. The explanation for this can perhaps be found by looking at the structure of a syllable beginning with [sp], [st] or [sk]. Such syllables are unusual in Germanic because they are the only syllables which can have *three* consonants in the onset (e.g. [spl . . .], [skr . . .] etc.). Kenstowicz (1994: 258) suggests that the initial [s] in [sp], [st] and [sk] clusters is appended to the onset by a special rule. We might hypothesize that the syllable onset then has a distinctive shape such that the appended [s] cannot on its own alliterate, but can only alliterate in combination with the following consonant. This would suggest that the rules for identity are sensitive to underlying aspects of the syllable structure of the words. Further suggestive evidence comes from the ancient Germanic language Gothic. Kurylowicz (1970: 13–16; cited by Russom 1987: 64) points to the fact that the Gothic language has a morphological rule which reduplicates the first consonant and adds a vowel spelled [aí] – so that *slēpan* becomes *saí-slēp*. But [sp], [st] and [sk] are picked up as though they are a single consonant – to give for example *skaidan* → *skaí-skaith*. Here too [sk] etc. are treated by the phonological rules as though the [s] is attached in some special way to the following consonant such that the pair counts as a single segment.

One of the interesting issues which arises in the study of sound-patterning is cases where the convention for which segments are involved appears to override the constituent structure of the syllable. Thus in some traditions (e.g. the Finnish *Kalevala*) the alliteration involves the onset and nucleus, which together is not a well-formed constituent of the syllable; similarly Greenberg (1960) suggests that rhyme in Tuareg involves the nucleus and the final consonant of the onset (ignoring intervening consonants) – again, not a well-formed constituent part of the syllable. A better understanding of these traditions would help us understand the relation between sound-patterning rules and prosodic constituent structure within the syllable.

5.5.2 *Sound-patterning rules which refer to phonological features*

It is common to find that where a tradition has systematic sound-patterning rules, it also has conventions about which different sounds can be counted as the same for the purpose of the rules. These conventions are sometimes explicit, as for example in medieval Celtic poetries, and sometimes implicit – poets may compose with them without being aware that they are doing so. The linguistically interesting point about these conventions is that the sounds which are considered equivalent are often also phonologically related. Linguists have argued for two kinds of phonological relationships which may hold between such equivalent sounds: based on phonological feature-sharing, and based on underlying representations. In this section we look at equivalence based on phonological feature-sharing.

Sounds which are counted as equivalent for the purposes of sound-patterning rules constitute a literary-linguistically defined group of sounds. Sounds can also be organized into groups on a purely linguistic basis. One reason for organizing sounds into groups is when they are articulated in a similar manner. For example, the sounds [b], [d] and [g] are members of a set of sounds all of which are articulated by keeping the vocal cords relatively tight: they are called voiced sounds. In contrast, the sounds [p], [t] and [k] are members of a set of sounds which are articulated similarly to one another, by keeping the vocal cords relatively slack: they are called voiceless sounds. Another reason for organizing sounds into groups is that they 'behave' in a similar manner in a particular language. The 'behaviour' of sounds includes the ways in which sounds affect other sounds which are next to them, as formalized by phonological rules. Typically, the behavioural groupings of sounds are related to the articulatory groupings of sounds. Thus for example [b], [d] and [g] – which are articulatorily a single group – also form a unified behavioural group in English because a noun which ends in one of these sounds will have [z] as the plural affix (e.g. 'dogs' *dɔgz*). And [p], [t] and [k] form a unified behavioural group because a noun which ends in one of these sounds will have [s] as its plural affix (e.g. 'docks' *dɔks*). Note, incidentally, that we just saw another reason for grouping [p], [t] and [k] in English: these are the only three consonants which can come in the middle of a three-consonant onset in an English syllable.

In linguistic theory, the grouping of sounds is understood by the hypothesis that a linguistic sound is made from phonological features, and sounds group together articulatorily or under phonological rules because they share phonological features. Thus we can say that [b], [d] and [g] have the phonological feature [+voiced] while [p], [t] and [k] have the phonological feature [−voiced]. Many features are defined in this way, as a feature for which a sound can be specified as having a positive value or as having a negative value. Phonological features must be discovered by phonological theory, and the same features exist in all languages (though they will combine differently to create the different sounds of different languages): thus for example in all languages which have the sound [b], that sound has the feature [+voiced].

[b], [d] and [g] group together by virtue of sharing the feature [+voiced], but they are also distinct sounds. This distinctness comes from the fact that each sound also has features not shared by the other sounds. There are various ways of understanding how these sounds differ: each sound involves the mouth being closed off, but in each case a different part of the mouth is closed off and is closed off by a different articulating part of the mouth. Thus for example [b] involves the closing off of the mouth by the lips (the labial articulator), while [d] involves the closing off of the mouth by the blade of the tongue (the coronal articulator), and [g] involves the closing off of the mouth by the back of the tongue (the dorsal articulator). These differences can be expressed by differences in the features which comprise the sounds. Thus for example (in one system for understanding phonological features: see Kenstowicz 1994: 146), [b] alone of the three has the feature [labial], [d] alone of the three has the feature [coronal], and [g] alone of the three has the feature [dorsal]. Thus each linguistic sound is defined by a unique set of features: the whole set of features expresses its identity and uniqueness, while each component feature expresses the fact that it can be grouped with other sounds with the same feature.

The interest of this for sound-patterning is that the groups of sounds which count as equivalent for sound-patterning often form a group on phonological grounds: that is, they share some phonological features (while differing in others). Where this is the case, the sound-patterning rule can be expressed not in terms of whole sounds but in terms of phonological features. For example, it is very common to find that labial sounds such as [l] and rhotic sounds such as [r] are counted as equivalent in sound-patterning rules (this is for example the case in the Scottish Gaelic example cited in 2.1.2). These sounds are also phonologically alike by virtue of sharing many phonological features: both are sonorant consonants (having the features [+consonantal] and [+sonorant]) and both are anterior coronal oral sounds (having the features [oral], [coronal] and [+anterior]). They differ basically in that [l] has the feature [+lateral]. Thus the sound-patterning rule can refer to the rhyme as involving the cluster of features shared by these two sounds: this is the identity which is required for the rhyme, and the presence or absence of the feature [+lateral] is ignored.

As an example of a fully worked-out system of equivalences, Greenberg (1960: 946) cites the equivalences found in Tuareg texts (North African Berber). These texts require lines to rhyme. The rule for rhyme is complex in its reference to syllable structure: the syllable nucleus must be identical and the final consonant in the coda must be equivalent. (Other consonants are apparently ignored: thus in one poem *-at* rhymes with *-art*, and also with *-ayt* and *-ant*, and *-alt*.) There are various equivalence sets. Thus [t], [k] and the uvular consonant [q] are equivalent: these are all plosive sounds [−continuant] which are also voiceless [−voiced]. The voiced plosives also group together as an equivalence set. The sounds [f] and [s] group together: these are fricative sounds [+continuant] which are also voiceless [−voiced]. The sounds [l] and [r] are grouped together: these are the oral sonorant consonants as described above. And the sounds [m] and [n] are grouped together: these are the nasal consonants [nasal]. Thus in Tuareg we can (as a preliminary attempt) say that segments with the following features are equivalent: (i) [−continuant, −voiced], (ii) [−continuant, +voiced], (iii) [+continuant, −voiced], (iv) [+consonantal, +sonorant, oral, coronal], (v) [nasal]. To complete our account we would need to look at what other sounds exist in Tuareg, and whether this description of features makes inaccurate predictions. (Greenberg describes this system only briefly.)

Zwicky (1976) presents an account of a rather different way in which an equivalence set might function. This relates to the rhymes found in English-language rock songs. Zwicky points out that in these songs, while vowels tend to be identical, consonants in codas may be different. One approach to this would be to say that these songs have assonance (i.e. involving just the nucleus) rather than full rhyme (i.e. involving both nucleus and coda). But Zwicky argues that the coda is involved, because while different consonants in the coda may be counted as equivalent, not every consonant can rhyme with every other. Specifically, he argues that a consonant in a coda may rhyme with a consonant in another coda if they differ in just one phonological feature. Thus *heart* may rhyme with *dark*: the consonants [t] and [k] differ in that the former has the feature [coronal] while the latter has the feature [dorsal]. And *light* and *died* can rhyme because the consonants [t] and [d] differ in that the former has the feature [−voiced] and the latter has the feature [+voiced]. But *died* and *bike* do not rhyme because [d] differs in two features from [k]: they differ in voicing and position of articulator.

Relatively little work has been done on equivalence sets, and what work has been done now needs to be reanalysed in the light of new developments on phonological feature theory (as described by Kenstowicz 1994). In terms of research that might be undertaken, it is worth looking again at traditions where a sound-patterning has been described as assonance (or consonance). These might be reanalysed as rhyme, involving equivalence sets. Assonance and consonance are like rhyme except that either the coda or the nucleus differs between the paired syllables. In these cases we should ask whether the differences conceal underlying similarities: thus for example the Berber example described above might at first appear to be an example of assonance and only on further examination be shown to be an example of rhyme which incorporates equivalence sets.

5.5.3   *Sound-patterning rules which refer to underlying representations*

One of the fundamental claims of (most kinds of) phonological theory is that the sequence of segments which constitutes the uttered form of a word may be a transformed version of a sequence of segments which constitutes the underlying or stored (in memory) form of a word. Thus for example the English words *critic* and *criticism* appear to contain the same component word *critic*, but as a sequence of segments this word ends with [k] in the first case [krɪtɪk] and [s] in the second [krɪtɪsɪzəm]. It seems that the pronounced word [krɪtɪsɪzəm] is best understood as comprising [krɪtɪk] plus [ɪzəm], with the [k] changed to [s] by a phonological rule because the [k] is followed by the sound [ɪ]. Thus the features of the segment are altered under the influence of the segment which follows it. The word 'criticism' thus has two levels of representation: its underlying representation is [krɪtɪkɪzəm] and its surface representation is [krɪtɪsɪzəm], with the surface form derived from the underlying form by a phonological rule. In this section we see several cases of sound-patterning where it seems that it is the underlying representation of a word which is involved in the sound-patterning rather than its surface representation.

One argument to this effect is proposed by Kiparsky (1970). The Finnish *Kalevala* has (semi-systematic) alliteration within the line, with alliteration involving the onset and the nucleus. Hence *luvan* alliterates with *luoja*. However, there are some oddities. For example, *hiekka* does not alliterate with a word beginning in *hi-* as we might expect it to, but does alliterate with a word beginning in *he-* such as *helkki*. There are other similar patterns, which cannot be explained on the basis of equivalence sets (partly because *hiekka* does not alliterate with apparently identical onset–nuclei sequences). Kiparsky argues that the alliteration refers to an underlying version of the words, before the operation of a certain phonological rule which alters the vowels. In particular, the word which has *hiekka* as its surface form has *heeka* as its underlying form: this is why it alliterates with a word beginning in *he-* and not with a word beginning in *hi-*, on the assumption that alliteration refers to the underlying form of the word and not the surface form of the word.

A similar argument is presented by Malone (1988a) with regard to alliteration in Irish poetry. There are complex equivalence sets in Irish poetry which can be adequately explained on the basis of feature-sharing (see exercise 5.8.1). However, not all equivalences can be explained along these lines. In particular, feature-sharing cannot explain why in one text which he cites, a word pronounced *mán* (mbán = white) alliterates with a word pronounced *ßó* (bho = cow) but does not alliterate with a word pronounced *mór* (mór = great). Here, he argues that the alliteration refers not to these surface forms of the words – and the consonants which begin them on the surface – but to the underlying forms of the words. The initial sounds [m] and [ß] in the first two words are both derived from [b] by separate phonological rules, the former by a rule of eclipsis which nasalizes the sound, and the latter by a rule of lenition which turns it into a continuant. In their underlying forms, the first two words begin with the same consonant [b], and are *bán* and *bó*, and it is at this level that they alliterate with each other and not with the word whose surface and underlying form is *mór*. Thus again the sound-patterning rule refers to the underlying rather than the surface forms of the sounds.

This was an example of a phonological process which changed a feature. However, phonological processes can also add a feature to a segment which is not fully specified for features. Some segments are incomplete in their underlying representations, and receive their full complement of features, thus fully defining a sound, only once those segments are put together into full words. This is commonly the case for affixes. Consider for example the prefix which expresses negation in the words *impossible* (= not possible) and *indecent* (= not decent). The prefix is the same in both cases but is realized as *im* in the first word and *in* in the second word. The phonological rule in this case takes a feature from the segment at the beginning of the word and copies it onto the prefix: thus the [labial] feature of [p] means that the prefix has a [labial] sound [m], while the [coronal] feature of [d] means that the prefix has a [coronal] sound [n]. Thus it seems that the prefix consists underlyingly of the vowel [ɪ] followed by a segment which is specified only as [nasal]. Exactly which of the nasal sounds is realized by this segment depends on whether the segment receives a [labial] or [coronal] feature from the sound next to it when the prefix is attached to a word. We say that the segment of the prefix is underspecified, and that the feature spreads from the following sound onto this prefix in order to specify it fully.

The fact that many affixes exist in underlying forms with underspecified segments appears to be relevant to sound-patterning in Turkish. Malone (1982) cites the following stanza:

dört kitaptan bize haber verildi	But to us four scrolls of knowledge are given
kâmal olan akıl başa derildi	And into our minds full wisdom from Heaven;
iblis lâin merdud olup sürüldü	While accursèd Satan from hence is driven
hakkın buyruğuundan döneldenberi	Being bereft by himself of God's guidance.

(the second stanza of an anonymous poem, 'Ahi Ali Baba', translated by Malone; translation of the whole poem by Malone in the literary magazine *Paintbrush* XI and XII, 1984–5)

The first three lines rhyme, with rhyme involving the nucleus and coda of the final syllable in each line. This means that the [i] of lines 1 and 2 is equivalent to the [ü] of line 3. Malone shows that this equivalence – and other equivalences between vowels in other rhymes – cannot be explained by referring to the features of the vowels. However, as it happens these final syllables are all manifestations of the same suffix. This suffix consists of the consonant [d] followed by an underspecified vowel which just has the feature [+high]. A Turkish vowel requires two more features to be fully specified – these being the features [back] and [round], and these features are spread in these words from the preceding segment. So in one case the suffix surfaces with a front and unrounded vowel in -*di* because the preceding vowels are non-back and unrounded (e, i), and in the other case the underlyingly identical suffix surfaces with a front and round vowel in -*dü* because the preceding vowels are non-back and round (ü). The point is that the rhyme involves identical segments at an underlying level (when the vowel is underspecified) but not on the surface. In a later article, Malone (1988b) points out that *yürür* can rhyme with *hür*; underlyingly the final vowel in *yür-ür* is underspecified as just [+high], while underlyingly the final vowel in *hür* – where there is no suffix – is fully specified as [+high, –back, +round]. Hence if we say that the equivalence set is defined in terms of underlying representations, the crucial factor is not identity (these are not identical vowels underlyingly) but nondistinctness (there is no clash between the vowels under-lyingly – one is just incomplete).

Phonological processes sometimes change or add features to already existing segments. However, phonological processes can also add segments to or remove them from a word. We saw examples of this in 3.6, where phonological rules changed the number of syllables in a word with consequences for the metrical rules. Here we briefly consider an example where such a process relates to a sound-patterning rule. In modern Chinese there is a rule which deletes a segment which is the vowel [ə] (called 'schwa') when it follows another vowel, in certain cases. Thus a word has the underlying sequence of segments *nuəŋ* which becomes the surface sequence of segments *nuŋ*, from which the schwa vowel has been removed by the phonological rule. Chen (1984) shows that it is the under-lying form of the word which is involved in rhyme in poetry, because the schwa is involved in the rhyme (even though it has been lost from the actually pro-nounced version of the word). Thus the words *fəŋ*, *t'iŋ* and *nuŋ* rhyme with one another not because of their surface vowels (which are different) but because underlyingly they are represented as *fəŋ*, *t'iəŋ* and *nuəŋ* and thus underlyingly all end in -*əŋ*.

5.6 Summary: word-boundary rules and sound-patterning rules

In this chapter we looked at two kinds of regularity which are often also found in metrical verse, in addition to the meter itself. Word-boundary rules are best understood as rules which depend on the meter, because they are defined in terms of the metrical template: these rules may be found only in metrical texts. Some explanation must be found for the fact that in some traditions (e.g. Greek iambic hexameter) the word-boundary rules place word boundaries so that they do not coincide with metrical boundaries. Word-boundary phenomena might need to be redefined in some cases as side-effects of metrical rules – and thus there might not need to be any specific statement of the placement of word boundaries. In contrast, sound-patterning rules appear to be much more independent of the meter, and can be found as systematic structural devices in non-metrical texts. Nevertheless, there is some reason to think that sound-patterning rules are sensitive to constituency (whether metrical or not) and that rhyme and alliteration are distinguished in whether they are able to jump over constituents. Finally, we have seen that apparent irregularities in sound-patterning turn out to be regularities at a more abstract underlying level of linguistic structure. Relatively little work has been done on the phonological identities which underlie various kinds of sound-patterning, and much of the work which has been done was carried out in older frameworks of phonological theory, and in many cases would benefit from a rethinking in current frameworks. Thus this is a fruitful area for future research.

5.7 Further reading

Joseph Malone has published linguistic accounts of equivalence in various languages and literatures: Irish (1987, 1988a), Turkish (1982, 1988b), Sephardic Hebrew (1983), Chaha (1991). Kiparsky's (1970) article has been very influential. Jakobson's work on equivalence sets in Czech and Russian rhyme is summarized by Worth (1977). Árnason (1991) is a generally sceptical account of equivalence sets (and other issues in metrical theory). A recent overview of generative work on rhyme (and a new approach based on optimality theory) is Holtman (1996). On Tuareg poetry in its social context see Chadwick and Chadwick (1940). On Germanic, see Suzuki (1988) for further aspects of its complex argument which relates both to sound-repetition and to meter in general; see also Suzuki (1985). On Welsh meters see Williams (1953), Rowlands (1976) and Morris-Jones (1980);

on Irish meters and equivalence sets see Knott (1957) and Grijzenhout and Holtman (1995).

5.8 Exercises

5.8.1 *Equivalence sets in Irish rhyme*

Equivalence sets are used in medieval Irish poetry. The sound-pattern called *comhardadh slán*, meaning 'perfect rhyme', holds between two words when (i) they have identical stressed vowels, and (ii) the consonants which follow the stressed vowels belong to equivalence sets.

Question

Work out a characterization of the various different equivalence sets based on the phonological features of the sounds involved. *Hint: you should end up with four equivalence sets.*

Data

These are some pairs of words which are found in perfect rhyme in actual texts (drawn from Knott 1957). The first vowel in each word is stressed. These are the ways in which the words are spelled; for the sounds which the spellings represent, see below.

eibhe	meile	
eich	beith	
foda	coda	
gad	lag	
géag	séad	
ionadh	iodhan	
leanab	sealad	
life	ithe	
lot	cnoc	sop
maca	slata	
neamh	feadh	
sgeach	cleath	
taraidh	adhaigh	
teagh	treabh	

These are the phonetic values of the consonant letters:

letter	sound	some of the defining features of the sounds		
		voiced	continuant	sonorant
b	b	+	−	−
p	p	−	−	−
bh, mh	v	+	+	−
f	f	−	+	−
d	d	+	−	−
t	t	−	−	−
dh, gh	y	+	+	−
l	l	+		+
r	r	+	+	+
n	n	+	−	+
g	g	+	−	−
c	k	−	−	−
ch	x	−	+	−
th	h	−	+	−

5.8.2   *Toda phonological rules and song-specific vowel-insertion rules*

Toda is a Dravidian language spoken in South India. Toda songs (as outlined by Emeneau 1966) are governed by a meter which counts three syllables into each line. Where the line would otherwise be short a syllable can be added to the line by inserting the vowel [e] or the vowel [i] into one of the words in the line. This exercise looks at the relation between this process, which is found only in songs, and phonological rules which are found in all forms of the language.

One of the characteristics of phonological processes is that they can apply in a particular order, with one process being required to take place before another. This is the problem addressed in this exercise (based on Emeneau 1966: 326).

The insertion of the vowel [i]

This vowel is added before a suffix which expresses location ('in' or 'on'). Here are some examples of lines of song in which the vowel has been added to bring the syllable count up to three:

m o r j i ʃ m o x   'on-the-lap child'
n i t j i ʃ   x oˑ s   'on-the-forehead coin'
m a ɖ i ʂ   ŋ iˑ r   'on-the head water'
n oˑ t i ʂ   θ oˑ r   'in-the-places important-men'

The phonologically interesting thing about this locative suffix is that it is under-specified, taking some of its features from the preceding consonant. Thus if the preceding consonant is the palatal glide [j] the suffix is the palatal consonant [ʃ], while if the preceding consonant is an alveolar consonant such as [t] or [d], the suffix is the alveolar consonant [ʂ]. In the normal language, if the preceding sound is a (voiced) vowel such as [i], the suffix is the voiced consonant [ẓ].

Question

(a) Does the specifically literary-linguistic rule which adds the vowel [i] add the vowel before or after the general phonological rule which specifies the features of the suffix?

The insertion of the vowel [e]

This vowel can be inserted at the end of any word, to bring the length of the line up to three syllables. The sequence of words *pin* (= golden) and *poˑθ* (= ridge-pole) is found in songs in two alternative forms, both of which incorporate the added vowel [e]:

p i n e b oˑ θ   golden ridge-pole
p i n e f oˑ θ   golden ridge-pole

Note that the initial consonant of *poˑθ* is [b] in the first example and [f] in the second. These changes are the result of phonological processes, which are found in the language more generally. In the language in general, *poˑθ* becomes *foˑθ* if the preceding sound is a vowel, and becomes *boˑθ* if the preceding sound is a nasal consonant.

Questions

(b) Does the specifically literary-linguistic rule which adds the vowel [e] add the vowel before or after the general phonological rule which alters the first sound in the word *poˑθ*?

(c) How do the processes of the insertion of [i] and the insertion of [e] differ? Speculate on possible reasons for these differences.

6 Parallelism

6.1 Parallelism

Parallelism is a 'sameness' between two sections of a text, and can be structural or semantic. Structural parallelism holds between two sections of text when they are the same at some level of structure (for example, when they have the same phrase structure). Semantic parallelism holds between two sections of text when they can be interpreted to be the same in some component of their meanings.

6.1.1 Structural parallelism

Structural parallelism involves similarity of structure. The structure involved may be syntactic, morphological or phonological. As an example of syntactic parallelism, consider the last two lines of Andrew Marvell's poem 'To his Coy Mistress':

> *Thus, though we cannot make our Sun*
> *Stand still, yet we will make him run.*

The parallel parts are the two sentences *though we cannot make our sun stand still* and *yet we will make him run*. These sentences are parallel in that (with minor exceptions) they have the same phrase and word classes in the same orders, and these phrase and word classes have the same functions in the clause in both parts. Thus both sentences have a basic sequence of:

coordinating conjunction + subject noun phrase + modal + verb + subordinate clause
though   *we*   *cannot* *make* *our sun stand still,*
yet   *we*   *will*   *make* *him run.*

They differ in that the first sentence also has negation (attached to the modal, in *cannot*). The subordinate clauses in each part are also parallel, consisting of a subject noun phrase *our sun* or *him* followed by an intransitive verb *stand still* or *run*. Again there are some minor syntactic differences: the subject noun phrase is a full noun phrase in the first sentence and a pronoun in the second, and there is an adverb *still* in the first sentence which completes the meaning of the intransitive verb. Overall, however, we can say that the two parts of this text are syntactically parallel to one another. Note that they are also semantically parallel; semantic parallelism often accompanies syntactic parallelism.

Consider now an example of morphological parallelism, a parallelism which involves sub-parts of words (morphemes). This is typically very similar to syntactic parallelism, in that the morphemes involved may carry syntactic information (i.e. they are often inflectional morphemes), as in the following case cited by V. Hymes (1987: 74) from a narrative by Hazel Suppah in the Sahaptin language (USA: Oregon):

*Naxš áyat **iwínana** míi ꞏ ꞏ ꞏ mi.*	A certain woman **went** lo-o-ong ago.
Ixásunaitima nišákni íčn	**She rode** (horseback) from her house **to**
waníči tiičám Šítaikt.	**here** The place called Shitike.
*Kwníin áuku **ixásutuxa** anáštk'a.*	From there then **she rode home**, towards evening.

The parallelism in this text is morphological, and holds between the three verbs in boldface. Each Sahaptin verb is complex (as can be seen by the fact that a Sahaptin verb can require several English words to translate it). This is the division of the verbs into their component morphemes:

i			*wína*		*na*
i		*xásu*	*naiti*	*m*	*a*
i		*xásu*	*tux*		*a*
third person singular		'on horseback'	'go'	'towards here'	past

Notice that the elements which are parallel are elements which in another language (such as English) might have been expressed as independent words in the syntax: thus a morphological parallelism in Sahaptin might be equivalent to a syntactic parallelism in English.

As an example of phonological parallelism, consider the following example from an eighteenth-century Scottish Gaelic song:

Mo *chreach,* ***Teàrlach*** *ruadh* **bòidheach** *bhith fo*	**bhinn**	*aig Rìgh*
My ruin! Charles red handsome to be under	sentence of	King

Deòrsa nam **biasd!**
George of the beasts!

B'e **dìteach** *na còrach, an* **Fhirinn** *'s a* **beòil** *foipe* **sios;**
T'was denial of justice, the Truth with its lips under it down

Ach a **Rìgh,** *ma's e's* **deòin** *leat, cuir an* **rìoghachd** *air* **seòl** *a*
But oh King, if it's will Thy, put the kingdom on a course that
  chaidh **dhinn,**
  went from us

Cuir rìgh **dlìgheach** *na* *còrach ri* **linn** *na* *tha* *beò os ar* **cinn.**
Put king rightful of the justice to generation that's alive over our heads

'Alas that the bonnie, red-headed Charles should be at the mercy of George of the beasts! That would be a denial of justice, a stifling of the lips of truth. But, O Lord, if it be your will, restore the kingdom to the course we have lost; restore the rightful king over us in the generation of the living' (from John Roy Stewart, 'Culloden Day', cited by Dunn 1972: 140)

Each line has five stressed words (a pattern determined by a meter), indicated in boldface in the text above: stress is on the first syllable of each word. With the exception of the first stressed word *Teàrlach* the stressed vowels in all four lines are:

. . . ì . . . ò . . . i . . . ò . . . i . . .

Thus the lines are phonologically parallel in that each of them realizes this same sequence of sounds: it is what we called a sound-pattern parallelism in chapter 5. Phonological parallelism resembles both meter and (para-metrical) sound-patterning, an issue we return to below.

6.1.2 *Semantic parallelism*

Semantic parallelism holds where two sections of text can be interpreted to have parallel meanings, where 'parallel meanings' covers a range of possibilities, with the two most common kinds being similarity of meaning and opposition of meaning. Often, semantic parallelism arises as a result of lexical parallelism, where two words are interpretable as being parallel to one another; the relation of meaning between the two words determines the relation of meaning between the two larger sections of text which include those words.

One way in which this might arise is where the two words are the only points of difference between two otherwise identical sections of text (i.e. the texts which surround the words are structurally parallel in all ways). A first example comes from a prayer in Zinancatecan (a dialect of the Mayan language Tzotzil, spoken in Mexico: Chiapas):

1 *ʔana yaya tot,*	Well grandfather,
ʔahvetik:	Lord:

2 *kʼu yepal mi liʔ čamala hlumale?*	How long have you been waiting here for my earth?
mi liʔ čamala kačʼelale?	How long have you been waiting here for my mud?

3 *¢obolon tal;*	I am gathering together here;
lotolon tal.	I am meeting here.

This extract is analysed by Bricker (1989: 369). The layout of lines on the page here makes clear the parallelism between the two halves of each verse. In verses 2 and 3, the parallel sections are identical in all ways (fully structurally parallel, and with identical words) except for one word which differs. In verse 2 the words which differ are *-lumal* 'earth' and *-ačʼelal* 'mud': thus the text puts them into comparison. In verse 3 the words are *¢ob-* 'gather together' and *lot-* 'meet'. In both cases, the words have similar meanings which means that the parallel texts which contain them therefore also have similar meanings.

In our second example (from an eighteenth-century English poem by Cowper, 'The Task'), the words are likewise put into comparison by being embedded into parallel structures. Here, however, the semantic parallelism is that the two sections of text can be interpreted as implying an opposition:

God made the country, and man made the town.

We can lay out the text to bring out the structural parallelism, which encourages us to look for the lexical parallelism.

	noun phrase (subject)	verb	noun phrase (object)
	God	*made*	*the country,*
and	*man*	*made*	*the town.*

God and *man* are made lexically parallel by the text, as are *country* and *town*. Furthermore, the two sets of lexical parallel words align so that the pair *God/country* is parallel to the pair *man/town*.

Lexical parallelism typically involves a pairing of two words. The examples we have seen so far (including the examples of structural parallelism) all involve expected lexical parallels. In contrast, an example of an unexpected lexical parallel is the following, from Alexander Pope's 'Essay on Man':

> *Who sees with equal eye, as God of all*
> *A hero perish, or a sparrow fall,*
> *Atoms or systems into ruin hurl'd,*
> *And now a bubble burst, and now a world.*

Here, structural parallelism presents us with word-pairs which are antonyms (the words have opposed meanings or associations): *hero* and *sparrow*, *atoms* and *systems*, *bubble* and *world*. These are not conventional pairs. Unexpected lexical parallels of this kind require very salient surrounding structural parallelism to draw attention to the comparison between the two words; otherwise the two words will not be recognizable as parallel. Whether a text has expected or unexpected lexical parallels is likely to be tied to the tradition and genre to which the text belongs. Pope's poetry has unexpected lexical parallels because he is writing satire, for example. Most examples of lexical parallelism, however, involve expected parallels, and we now examine expected parallels in greater detail.

Expected lexical parallels will often involve two words which have the same reference or which refer to similar things. Thus for example in the Zinancatecan text discussed above, -*lumal* 'earth' and -*ač'elal* 'mud' is a pair of words which are synonyms or near synonyms, as is the pair *¢ob-* 'gather together' and *lot-* 'meet'. The pair in the first verse, *yaya tot* 'grandfather' and *ʔahvetik* 'Lord', both refer to 'elders' and thus are similar in meaning. In the Sahaptin text, there are three different verb roots for 'go', the first two of which mean 'go' and the third, *tux*, means more specifically 'go homeward': again, a similarity in meaning (though not identity in meaning). Sometimes a pair might be fully synonymous as a result of the borrowing of one member from a different language. Thus Bricker cites a prayer in which a saint is named in the two parts of a lexical parallelism, the first using the Zinancatecan noun *ʔan¢* and the second using the Spanish noun *sinyora*: both have the same meaning of 'woman' (Bricker 1989: 381):

čiʔuk li č'ul mariya rosaryo,   With holy Mary of the Rosary,
  vinahelal ʔan¢,   Heavenly Woman
  vinahelal sinyora.   Heavenly Lady.

Lexical parallelism can also involve two words which are in opposition (as we saw in the Cowper text above). In this case, the opposition can draw on a pre-existing cultural opposition: in the Cowper text the pre-existing opposition is between the good countryside and the bad town – an opposition pervasive throughout English literature (R. Williams 1973). Thus various kinds of lexical parallelism can draw on expected relations of meaning between words, whether similarity or opposition.

When we find lexical parallelism in a text, it is worth asking whether the parallelism draws upon a pre-existing set of words: that is, whether the words are already organized into an 'equivalence set' and this equivalence set is exploited for lexical parallelism. Thus in the Hebrew scriptures, it can be shown that there are eighteen pairs of lines which contain a lexical parallelism between the words meaning 'hills' (*gᵉbaoth*) and 'mountains' (*harim*). Here is one example:

w^ethishiphuu he-harim   asis
shall drip   the mountains sweet wine

w^ekhal   hag^ebaoth   tithmogg^enah
and all   the hills   shall melt
(Amos ix.13)

The same pair of words is found also in Ugaritic literature, showing that the pair exists independently of any actual text as an equivalence set and can be borrowed across traditions. As we will see, in some literatures, the existence of such equivalence sets is explicitly formulated as part of the poetic practice – analogously to the explicit use of equivalence sets of sounds in Irish or Welsh poetic traditions (5.5). In other cases (e.g. Hebrew) there is no recorded explicit acknowledgement of the presence of equivalence sets, and we must hypothesize their existence on the basis of an analysis of the texts.

6.1.3 Canonical parallelism and meter

Parallelism can hold intermittently or occasionally in a text, or it can be characteristic of a text as a whole. Where it is a basic principle of organization which holds of the text as a whole it is called canonical parallelism. (Fox (1977: 60) uses the phrase 'canonical parallelism', based on Jakobson's (1987b: 146) phrase 'canonic parallelism'.) Canonical parallelism is similar to meter in that both are organizing principles for a complete text. Note, however, that there is a fundamental difference between canonical parallelism as an organizing principle and meter as an organizing principle. Meter involves a division of the text into sections (typically 'lines'): each section is matched to an external template, and thus – in an isometric text at least – a section may resemble other sections because they all resemble the same template. The result is a kind of parallelism, but as a side-effect of meter (notice, however, that not all metrical texts have parallelism: if the text is heterometric, lines will not be parallel with one another though they will all be metrical). Parallelism as an organizing principle, in contrast, divides the text into sections (typically 'line pairs') and then requires the second half of each section to resemble the first half. There is no external template to which they are matched.

Where sections of a text are matched to an external template, it is always the prosodic phonological structure of the text which is matched. In principle, we might expect to find meter-like systems where sections of a text are matched to an external template on the basis of their syntactic structure: thus, for example, every line in a text might have a strict subject–verb–object structure. However, there are no reported kinds of 'syntactic meters' of this kind and it is worth asking why. Note, in comparison, that parallelism generally involves syntactic parallelism (with some lexical parallelism involved as well); while phonological structure can be involved in parallelism, it is relatively rare. Thus the systematic organization of prosodic phonological structure on the whole (though not exclusively) falls to meter, while the systematic organization of syntactic structure apparently exclusively falls to parallelism: the two distinct organizing principles govern different components of linguistic structure.

While meter and parallelism are distinct as organizing principles, they do nevertheless interact with one another. Parallelism requires the division of a section of text into two halves – and a section of text can also fall into two halves in terms of its organization by metrical rules, or by caesura rules or sound-patterning rules. On the other hand, it is also possible for a parallelism to constitute an alternative structuring of a text, distinct from the metrical structuring. Our first example of syntactic parallelism, from Marvell's poem 'To his Coy Mistress', is an example where the metrical divisions do not correspond to the divisions of parallelism. Whether a parallelism coincides with metrical structure or mismatches with it may be explicitly theorized in a poetic tradition: we see an example of this in the Welsh system of *cynghanedd*, discussed shortly.

An interesting example of apparent interaction between meter and parallelism has been claimed for the Welsh early medieval poem *Gododdin* by Sweetser (1988: 151). She argues that the stanzas of the poem are subject to organizatory principles which give them cohesion and regular structure, but that this work of organization is divided between syntactic parallelism as an organizing principle of some of the stanzas and (the para-metrical system of) rhyme as an organizing principle of others.

Where parallelism is the norm, a lack of parallelism is marked. Canonical parallelism involves the organization of a whole text, such that all the parts of the text should be divided into parallel halves. However, it is not uncommon for otherwise fully parallel texts to have isolated non-parallel lines at the beginning and sometimes also at the end of the text; this is found in many different traditions and thus must derive from some basic principle. Jakobson (1987b: 156) cites examples from Chinese texts, Russian folk poetry, Finnish folk poetry and the Biblical Hebrew psalms; we also see an example in a Rindi text discussed below. One way of interpreting this functionally is to suggest that the lack of parallelism is a way of marking the boundaries of the text, the beginning and end, as a bracketing device. Jakobson suggests that there might be another functional reason: that isolated lines at beginnings or ends can be used to emphasize a key idea at the beginning or end. Again emphasizing the marked use of non-parallelism for particular effects, Hanson and Kiparsky (forthcoming) point to a use of non-parallel lines (which they call 'orphans') within a generally canonically parallel text (part of the Finnish *Kalevala*): these lines typically mark moments of transition in the narrative.

6.1.4   *Functions for parallelism*

Parallelism has perhaps three basic functions in verbal art, though not all functions may be realized by any particular example of parallelism. The first function is to be an organizing principle, a means by which the text takes form. In this, canonical parallelism is like meter.

The second major function relates to the first. The effects of parallelism and meter are salient – very noticeable to the hearer – with the result that the text itself is ostentatiously put forward as something which has been put together as a formal object, revealing the structural principles of the language itself. This drawing attention to the text itself is what Jakobson called 'the poetic function' – thus implying that 'poetic' is a characteristic tied to overt formal structure. He said: '. . . on every level of language the essence of poetic artifice consists of recurrent returns' (Jakobson 1987b: 145). Thus both parallelism and meter, because they involve 'recurrent returns' (though for different reasons), are basic means of carrying out the poetic function, the drawing of attention to the form of the text.

Given the role of parallelism as a way of indicating that a text is verbal art, it is interesting to note that in some cultures, ordinary conversation may be structured by parallelism: here parallelism may have some function other than drawing attention to the 'message'. Thus Brody (1986: 260) illustrates with a typical kind of conversational pattern in Tojolabal (Mexico: Chiapas):

A: *b'a aya mi=ša Ø-h-lah-aw-Ø ha aktobus=i.* Then I didn't meet the bus
B: *mi=ša Ø-a-lah-aw-Ø ha aktobus=i.* You didn't meet the bus
A: *mi=ša Ø-h-lah-aw-Ø.   aktobus=i.* I didn't meet it. Bus.

Parallelism is found also in the verbal art of this culture (like Zinancatecan, which we saw earlier, and other Mayan languages/cultures). Thus cultures may differ in the extent to which parallelism by itself indicates verbal art; we see another example of this in Nage in 6.4.1. The above example involves parallelism within a dialogue, with one speaker producing a text which is parallel to that of another speaker; this is found not only in conversation but also in verbal art in some cultures.

The third major function of parallelism is to express parallelisms in cultural thinking. This might be the expression of cultural oppositions, as we saw in the Cowper text above. But it has also been argued that in some cases the pervasive use of parallelism in verbal behaviour, and particularly in verbal art, reflects a pervasive dualism underlying the principles of conceptual organization of a society. Bricker argues this for Tojolabal, suggesting that the use of parallelism (in couplets) 'is the verbal expression of a dualistic principle that is pervasive in

Zinancateco culture' (Bricker 1989: 378). Thus Zinancatecos classify certain aspects of the physical, spiritual and social worlds into contrasting and parallel pairs. This principle of pairing extends both to the form of (some) texts and in some cases also to their performance: thus for example rituals are performed by a pair of religious practitioners. This function of parallelism might be reflected in the duality of conversation in the related Tojolabal culture (as illustrated above). Along similar lines, Foster (1975, 1980) has argued that the two-part parallelism which he finds in various Ancient Egyptian texts reflects the particular centrality of dualistic thinking in Ancient Egyptian culture with its geographical distinctions between the two lands of Upper and Lower Egypt, the two sides of the Nile east and west, the two horizons where the sun sets and where it rises: 'Twoness – the fusion or pairing of dualities – lies deep in ancient Egyptian consciousness; it would be natural for it to occur also in the ancient poet's style of expression' (Foster 1975: 14).

Parallelism clearly functions in other ways as well. In texts which are not organized systematically by parallelism, a parallelism can have a stylistic effect, drawing the hearer's attention to a particularly important part of a text, for example, or communicating a particular meaning.

6.2 Syntactic parallelism

Syntactic parallelism is the commonest kind of structural parallelism. At its simplest, syntactic parallelism involves structural identity between two sections of text in three simultaneous senses. First, each section of text contains the same classes of phrase and word. Second, corresponding phrases bear similar grammatical and thematic relations to the predicator. Third, the corresponding phrases and words are in the same order in both sections of text.

In principle, each of these basic possibilities can be varied. We now consider an example of each of these types, beginning with an extract from Alexander Pope's poem 'Epistle to Dr. Arbuthnot' which has multiple syntactic parallelism:

> *What walls can guard me, or what shades can hide?*
> *They pierce my thickets, thro' my Grot they glide,*
> *By land, by water, they renew the charge,*
> *They stop the chariot, and they board the barge.*

The most complete syntactic parallelism here is in the fourth line. Here the same constituent types are in the same order. Note that there is also some identity of words (particularly grammatical words: *they, the*):

	noun phrase (subject)	verb	noun phrase (object)
	They	*stop*	*the chariot*
and	*they*	*board*	*the barge*

The first line has a syntactic parallelism whereby each half can be seen as having the same structure, but in the second half there is a gap – an implied object rather than a repeated one. This is common in syntactic parallelism where a constituent in one part is identical with a constituent in another.

	noun phrase (subject)	auxiliary	verb	noun phrase (object)
	What walls	*can*	*guard*	*me*
or	*what shades*	*can*	*hide*	**GAP**

We consider gapping further below.

We can also interpret the second line of the extract as having an internal parallelism in that the two halves have a subject–verb–complement structure, but the structural similarity between the parts is weak for several reasons. First, the complement of the verb is displaced in the second part, disrupting the parallelism of sequence. Second, the complement of the verb is a noun phrase in the first part and a preposition phrase in the second. Third, the complement of the verb has a somewhat different thematic relation to the verb in each case, being the object acted upon (*my thickets*) in the first part and the place of action (*thro' my Grot*) in the second.

preposition phrase	noun phrase (subject)	verb	noun phrase (object)
	They	*pierce*	*my thickets,*
thro' my Grot	*they*	*glide,*	

While there is some aspect of syntactic parallelism between these two parts, the parallelism arises primarily at a semantic level: the two halves mean more or less the same thing. Thus syntactic parallelism can exist in a text to variable degrees, and has a relation with semantic parallelism.

The reordering seen in this line is not uncommon in structural parallelism. There are various kinds of reordering. One of the most common is chiasmus, where the components are the same in both parts of the line but in mirror-image order. Syntactic chiasmus requires a freedom of phrase order which is not easy to achieve in English; the following is an example from Robert Browning's 'Parting at Morning':

Round the cape of a sudden came the sea,
And the sun looked over the mountain's rim.

preposition phrase (location)	verb	noun phrase (subject)
Round the cape [of a sudden]	*came*	*the sea,*

	noun phrase (subject)	verb	preposition phrase (location)
And	*the sun*	*looked*	*over the mountain's rim.*

Here each clause contains the same type of phrase in the same relation to the verb, but the order is reversed in the second half. (The phrase *of a sudden* is an extra preposition phrase in the first half which has no parallel in the second.)

6.2.1 *Gapping*

One of the variant types of syntactic parallelism involves a gap in one of the sections of text, which corresponds to a phrase or more in the other section of text. Austin (1984) discusses Alexander Pope's and John Dryden's uses of gapping in some detail, and we draw on his findings here.

Gapping is found in ordinary spoken English; it typically involves a missing phrase in the second of two similar constituents. This typical pattern is violated in poetry, for example in the poetry of Alexander Pope, where the first of two elements may be gapped:

*Now leaves _ the trees, and flowers **adorn** the ground*

Or there might be a gap in the first and third parts of the text:

> *While Fish _ in Streams, or Birds **delight** in Air,*
> *Or in a Coach and Six _ the British Fair.*

Here the two halves of the first line involve similar order of constituents, but the first half has a gap which 'looks forward' to the second half for its completion (it is called a forward-looking gap). The second line has a backward-looking gap and at the same time reverses the linear order of constituents. A second way in which Pope and also John Dryden go against the tendencies of the standard language is that the gapped elements do not necessarily together form a single syntactic constituent. Thus Dryden offers us this example:

*Thy Tragic **Muse gives** smile, thy Comick ____ ____ sleep*

Here, the gapped elements are a noun *muse* followed by a verb *gives*. Together, these do not constitute a single constituent, as we can see by looking at the syntactic constituent structure:

[NP *Thy tragic* [N *muse*]] [VP [V *gives*] *smile*]

If we gap the two elements, we do so by taking one out of the subject noun phrase, and the other out of the verb phrase, in both cases leaving material behind:

[$_{NP}$ *Thy comic* [$_{N}$ ____]] [$_{VP}$ [$_{V}$ ____] *sleep*]

There are some ways in which we can reorient our understanding of double gapping of this kind. We could interpret double gapping as two separate gappings, each of a single constituent. And in some cases, the gap is not filled by a single syntactic constituent but would be filled by a single postlexical phonological constituent:

Happy the man, . . .
Whose herds ____ ____ *with milk, whose fields* ____ ____ *with bread,*
*Whose flocks **supply him** with attire*

Here we could plausibly group the two words *supply him* as a single phonological phrase even though it is not a single syntactic constituent; this returns us to the question we raised earlier, whether we should interpret structural parallelism as involving syntactic or postlexical phonological constituents. (Note, however, that not all double gaps can be handled in this manner: the Dryden example does not involve a complete phonological unit.)

6.3   Phonological parallelism

6.3.1   Cynghanedd: *sound-patterning in Welsh poetry*

Cynghanedd (harmony) is an explicit classification of kinds of line-internal sound-patterning established for Welsh poetry in the fourteenth century (the following discussion is based on Williams 1953). Many of the kinds of *cynghanedd* involve parallelism between sequences of sounds. *Cynghanedd gystain* involves the repetition just of a sequence of consonants, and there are various sub-kinds of this. *Cynghanedd groes* has the parallel sequences adjacent:

troes dilyw tros y dalaith
tr s d l   tr s   d l

'flows a flood across the land'

Cynghanedd draws allows a gap between the two sequences (i.e. with other consonants intervening):

tristach yw Cymry trostyn
tr st   tr st

'sadder are the Welsh over them'

Cynghanedd groes o gysswllt is a variant of *cynghanedd groes*. In *cynghanedd groes* the two sequences fall on either side of the pause which divides the line into two: thus parallelism reinforces an already existing constituent structure (perhaps derived via a para-metrical caesura rule). In *cynghanedd groes o gysswllt*, however, the parallelism does not coincide with this division; in the following example the line is divided metrically into two after *rois*, but the sound-pattern parallelism does not respect this division:

serch a rois ar chwaer Esyllt
s rch   r s r ch   r

'he sent his love to sister Isolde'

    While these kinds of *cynghanedd* involve just consonants, there is another kind which involves both consonants and vowels. This is *cynghanedd sain*:

llygaid a ddywaid i ddoeth
   aid   dd   aid   dd

'eyes speak for the wise'

    Griffen (1981) demonstrates that the sounds which are patterned in *cynghanedd* can be sounds which arise as a result of postlexical phonological rules (this is not strictly his argument, but his argument can be interpreted along these lines). Thus the following line has a *cynghanedd draws* pattern:

onid hen yw cerddi'n tud
 n t   n t

'are-not old the poems of our country'

However, the first [t] is not the lexical sound but arises as a result of a postlexical process devoicing [d] before [h]. Thus sound-pattern parallelism, like other kinds of sound-patterning, can hold of the postlexical phonological structure.

6.3.2 *Parallel patterns of tone in Efik riddles*

Efik tone riddles are an example of sound-pattern parallelism in very short texts. This discussion of Efik (spoken in southern Nigeria and Cameroon) is based on

Simmons (1958). Tone riddles exploit the fact that the language has lexical tone, with words identified not only by their segmental composition but also by the tones on the syllables. The Efik use the term *ŋke* to name a group of genres which include tone riddles, folktales, tongue twisters, puns and proverbs; some Efik distinguish tone riddles as a distinct way of speaking called *ukabádé íkɔ* (= word change), though there is no further theorization within the culture of how the parallelism works. The tone riddle is in two parts, usually two clauses, which are similar or identical in the sequence of tones. The first part of the riddle is said by one person, and a second person says the second part. The meaning of the riddle is typically the explicit meaning of just the second part, whereas the first part may have no meaning on its own. The pairing is often arbitrary in the sense that it is purely the tonal similarity which links the parts, but at the same time it is conventional such that the second person should know the right response to the first part. This can be exploited in various ways. Thus, an innocent first clause can have an erotic clause as the second part, and this first clause alone can be used in private greetings, or to embarrass a member of the opposite sex. Similarly, a person may without penalty curse another person by addressing them with just the first 'innocent' part of a riddle whose conventionally associated but unspoken second part expresses the curse.

In tonal parallelism in Efik tone riddles, the pattern of tones in the second line is based on the pattern of tones in the first line. Thus this is not metrical: there is no external template which consistently governs the tonal patterns in the text. Here are two examples:

ńtēm ntém ḿben úsuŋ ŋ́kpi ébót ɔ́kpɔ́	I cut sticks near road I cut goat's bone
ńdīa udía úfɔk owo ńtre útóm ńdínám	I eat food of house of person I fail work to give

The meaning of this riddle is: 'I eat a person's food and fail to work for him' (Simmons 1958, no. 35).

(An acute accent on a syllable indicates high tone, a macron indicates middle tone and an absence of diacritic indicates low tone; thus *ńtēm* is high + mid, and *úsuŋ* is high + low. Note that nasal consonants can act as syllable nuclei and thus carry tones.)

mbakárá ébuhɔ kɔ́kpɔ́ úsuŋ	Europeans are buried on main road
ikpɔŋ ákpa ntéyén únen	person without family dies like child of fowl

This riddle constructs a comparison between Europeans who die in Africa and a person who dies without a family, neither of whom have anyone to perform proper funeral rites for them (Simmons 1958, no. 28).

The first example illustrates the possibility of altering the ordinary language to make it fit the tonal requirements; instead of the more usual ɔ́kpɔ́ ébót, the word order is reversed to give ébót ɔ́kpɔ́. Here we see a way in which sound-pattern parallelism adapts the ordinary language to fit the formal requirements of parallelism (in a manner similar to meter).

A question not raised by Simmons but which we might raise is whether the parallelism should be interpreted as a parallelism of tonal shifts, or as a parallelism of syllables with specific tones. This makes a difference for the degree of parallelism in the second example, which has an identical parallelism of tonal shifts but where the actual pattern of tones on syllables is not exactly parallel because there are two extra high syllables at the beginning of the first line:

pattern of syllables with tones:
L L H H   H L L   H H   H L
mbakárá   ébuhɔ   kɔ́kpɔ́   úsuŋ
L L   H L   L H H   H L
ikpɔŋ   ákpa   ntéyén   únen

pattern of tonal shifts:
  L H   L   H   L
mbakárá   ébuhɔ   kɔ́kpɔ́   úsuŋ
L   H L   H   L
ikpɔŋ   ákpa   ntéyén   únen

Notice that whichever pattern constitutes the parallelism, word boundaries are clearly irrelevant; it is the sequence of tones or syllables and tones which makes the lines parallel, while word boundaries can only disrupt this. Thus we see that parallelism is able to exploit a particular level of the linguistic structure of the utterance while ignoring other aspects. The question of which pattern constitutes the parallelism is an interesting one; Efik speakers are able to recognize and control the patterns, which thus have psychological reality, but are unable to explicitly describe them. Hence the question of which pattern is used is also a question about psychological representations of tone.

Incidentally, Simmons implies that where parallelisms of tone are not exact (it is likely that he means parallelism of tone and syllable), the ends of the line are more likely to be exactly parallel than the beginnings. We might ask whether this is related to the 'cadence' phenomenon seen in metrical verse, where the second half of the line tends to be more metrically structured and consistent (4.1.2). If it is a manifestation of cadence-based variation, then we appear to have a parallelism practice which comes close to meter in some of its characteristics.

6.3.3 *Tonal dissonance in Yoruba* ijala

Efik tone riddles are an example of parallelism arising from similarity. Sound-pattern parallelism can also arise when two elements are conventionally paired not by similarity but by opposition; thus parallelism can be 'dissonant'. An example of dissonant tonal parallelism comes from another Nigerian literature, the *ijala* chants of the Yoruba. This is a segment of a chant, cited by Bamgboṣe (1970: 110):

èmi ò rójú apérémọpéte   I have no time for arguments
èmi ò rójú apèrèmọpète   I have no time for arguments

The two lines are identical with the exception of the tones on the word *apérémọpéte*; in the second line this word's high tones (acute accent) are all changed to low tones (grave accent). The resulting word *apèrèmọpète* is not a Yoruba word. It is interesting that the mid tone (on the vowels [a] and [o] in this word) in this poetic practice is typically unaffected by these changes, given that the mid tone is linguistically distinct in its behaviour from high and low tones (Pulleyblank 1990: 271). This suggests again that our understanding of tonal parallelism in verbal art must be tied to our linguistic understanding of tone; it also suggests that sound-pattern parallelism is able to access levels of phonological representation other than at the surface.

6.4 Lexical parallelism

Two words may be paired – that is, be lexically parallel – by having various kinds of semantic relation to one another. The words may have the same reference, they may relate as part to whole, they may belong to the same semantic field (e.g. they might both refer to kinds of weather), or they may be interpretable as antonyms (having opposed meanings).

6.4.1 *Lexical equivalence sets in Eastern Indonesia*

Much work has been done on parallelism in the ways of speaking in Indonesian cultures, where it is clear that lexical equivalence sets are an important resource for the construction of parallel texts (see e.g. the collection of articles in Fox

1988). In particular, there is an extensive use of conventional pairings of words, which Fox calls dyadic sets. These dyadic sets may in some cases be shared by different cultures: for example in several of the cultures of Eastern Indonesia the words which mean 'banana' and 'sugar cane' are frequently paired. This section reviews some of the findings of work on lexical parallelism in Indonesia.

The following text, which is the first three lines from a Rindi funeral oration recorded in 1975, illustrates the use of equivalence sets in the context of a structural parallelism (from Forth 1988: 159):

Mu patinginya Hingitana	You listen to it, Hingitana,
Lànga tàka nàhu jàka ta njara mera ndewa	most definitely now, as if we are horses of equal spirit [destiny],
Jàka ta ahu mera ura	as if we are dogs of equal fortune [soul].

Parallelism holds here between the second and third lines. The lines are structurally parallel, and involve an aligned lexical parallelism between two word pairs *njara* and *ahu* (horse and dog) and *ndewa* and *ura* (spirit and fortune). Each pair of words belongs to a conventional lexical equivalence set for use in ritual language. (Note, incidentally, that the first line of the text, seen here, does not participate in parallelism – a common feature in otherwise fully parallel texts, as was mentioned earlier.)

Where a single word can be paired with one of several other words, we might ask whether this is a single multi-word lexical equivalence set or a collection of two-word sets. Forth, discussing East Sumbanese, interprets the multi-word relation as a collection of dyadic sets and suggests that the word's meaning may be inflected differently when paired with different other words. Thus *tana* (earth) can be paired with *rumba* (grass) or *pindu* (gate), and either of these pairings brings out the sense of earth as land or soil. But when *tana* is paired with *wai* (water), the meaning of 'earth' which is brought out is its cosmological significance as 'the earth' as opposed to water. *Tana* can also be paired with itself – a repetition of the word – and here the meaning of the earth as a spiritual sustainer of life is brought out. There are interesting questions here about the classification of the vocabulary, as well as the productive possibilities of words in context and the extent to which their precise meanings are created by their entextualization. Fox (1988: 25) shows that in different languages, a particular word – like the word for earth – may pair off differently, and so bring out different aspects of its meaning. Thus East Sumbanese *tana* may pair with water words, while Rotinese *dae* (also meaning 'earth') may pair with *tua* meaning lontar palm. The association of East Sumbanese *tana* with *pindu* (gate) emerges because *tana* is associated with meanings of 'domain', while the Rotinese equivalent *dae* is associated with directional meanings, and hence can be paired with directional terms such as *dale* (outside) or *dulu* (east).

Forth (1988: 147) argues for Rindi that the larger formal parallelism whereby one line parallels another is a secondary process which is parasitic on the fundamental parallelism based on lexical equivalence sets. Thus in one text which he discusses, most pairs of lines are parallel, but some lines are not. But these single lines typically have an internal pairing of words (without structural parallelism); thus the pairing of words is more consistent in the text than the pairing of lines and can thus be interpreted as prior.

As we saw earlier in this chapter, in cultures where parallelism is pervasive in the verbal art, parallelism may also characterize ways of speaking which are everyday or mundane, and thus not verbal art; in this case, parallelism in everyday speech may differ in kind from the parallelism found in the verbal art. An example of this is provided by Forth (1996) in a discussion of Nage (Indonesia: central Flores). The vocabulary of everyday Nage is characterized by a particular kind of compounding, where lexically parallel words are juxtaposed. An example is *mosa laki* which refers to the 'nobility', political and ritual leaders; this combination is used in everyday speech. *Mosa* means 'adult male' and is used on its own in everyday speech; *laki* is less commonly used on its own and has a range of possible glosses including 'noble', 'male' and 'husband'. Thus the two component words are apparently lexically parallel and are combined into a dyadic set which is used in the everyday language. In ritual speech, the same components can also be combined into parallelism, but here the process is more elaborate. While in everyday speech two words A and B are combined together as AB, in ritual speech two pairs of words A, B and Y, Z are intertwined to become AYBZ: in ritual discourse a wealthy nobleman would be described as *mosa bhada, laki watu*, intertwining *mosa laki* with the expression *bhada wea* which means 'wealth'. Thus while lexical parallelism characterizes both everyday and ritual speech it is different and more complex in the latter, which is verbal art.

6.4.2   Ta-poman: *lexical equivalence sets in Asmat songs*

An interesting use of lexical equivalence sets is found in the composition of Asmat songs, as described by Voorhoeve (1977); Asmat is spoken in Irian Jaya (Indonesia). These are three verses from a song sung by Simni, chief of the Yew Awor in Suru village (Voorhoeve 1977: 30, reproduced by permission of *Pacific Linguistics*):

> verse 1
> *Ay yipio yow: awayisama ayiro::*
> *áya na mewero-awocaia*

as api enama imi apeàyi
nar awar ipi ope yowa fa: foro:tama: paya: ayirá::

verse 2
yici: yipi: yesia: awayisama ayiro
aya na isamaawoca:
pow ipi ename imi apeayi
nara yinim ipiyi upe yesi fa foro:tama: paya: ayio::

verse 3
powkaw ipi: piri awayisama ayiro:
aya na yewerawoca
minuk upi enama imi apeayi
nara: semen ipi: upi pira fa: foro:: tama:: paya ayo::

The three verses are interpreted as each having the same meaning and can thus each be translated as: 'Here he is! at the mouth of the Ay river the sun is rising. Hi! I am the red-parrot woman, I have come to defecate, as I always do. For you, sun, who is shining above, I have opened my dress, here I am!' Thus the words are semantically parallel from verse to verse. This semantic parallelism is based on the syntactic parallelism between the three verses and on the fact that where words differ, the variant words all belong in the same equivalence set. Thus *ay* in the first verse is replaced by *yici* in the second and *powkaw* in the third. These three words are all considered to have the same meaning when used in a song: they all refer to a particular river.

However, the three words in the ordinary language have different meanings (they refer to different rivers), and this is a significant characteristic of lexical equivalence sets in Asmat songs. Asmat poetic theory groups words into lexical equivalence sets for the purpose of their use in songs, and considers them exact synonyms. One word in the set defines the meaning of all of them; the Asmat call it an *arcer* word. The other words in the set are conventionally assigned the same meaning as the *arcer* word; they are called *ta-poman* words. (The terms allude to a river: *arcer* is the mainstream of the river, and *ta-poman* is the other side of the river.) Thus for example the word *yow* is the *arcer* word (it means 'sun' in both the ordinary language and in poetry), with *yesir* (= *yesia*) and *piri* as *ta-poman* words in the same set. *Yesir* means 'morning star' in the ordinary language, but means 'sun' in a poem; *piri* means 'moon' in the ordinary language but again means 'sun' in a poem.

In the poem, the first verse has *arcer* words. In the second verse, each *arcer* word is replaced by a *ta-poman* word from the same set, and the same is done in the third verse. Because the *ta-poman* words are considered by convention to mean the same as the *arcer* words, the meaning of the verses remains stable. These are the substitutions in the poem:

verse 1		verse 2		verse 3	
arcer word	meaning in ordinary language and in the song	*ta-poman* word	meaning in ordinary language	*ta-poman* word	meaning in ordinary language
Ay	river name	*yici*	river name	*powkaw*	river name
yow	sun	*yesir*	morning star	*piri*	moon
mewero	red-parrot	*isama*	? fire	*yewar* (= *yewer*)	kind of parrot
as	faeces	*pow*	soft mud	*minuk*	hard lump of clay
awar	dress	*yinim*	young sago leaves	*semen*	rope made from young sago leaves

The pattern whereby the first word used from the lexical equivalence set is the *arcer* is described by the Asmat in terms analogous to the ranking of people: thus the older brother (the *arcer* word) comes first. Voorhoeve is uncertain whether there is a strict ordering between other terms in the group – whether for example we would expect *yesir* always to precede *piri* as it does in this song. Some *ta-poman* words are used only in literature, and hence constitute a specialized literary vocabulary of a kind found in other literatures. These kinds of *ta-poman* words are sometimes used to the exclusion of the *arcer* words – so for example there is an ordinary (*arcer*) word for 'alas' (*sawnak*), but this word is not used in songs, where only the replacement *ta-poman* word is used (*newàyipi*).

The grouping of words into a lexical equivalence set raises interesting questions: first, what is the basis on which words are grouped together, and second, are there any specialized functions performed by the grouping of words in this way? The grouping of words reflects similarities between the objects – for example the dog (*yuwur*) is the *arcer* for a group of *ta-poman* words which include those naming the wallaby, rat, flying squirrel and so on: all are furry animals. 'Similarity' of course is determined only partly by external considerations, and is also determined by cultural convention, the classifications existing within the society which, for example, might classify pigs with humans. Interestingly, it is generally and perhaps exclusively animate objects which are grouped into these lexical equivalence sets (i.e. 'animate' as defined within the culture; thus the sun, morning star and moon are considered to be living beings). This is reflected in the Asmat term *ofew* (kinship group) to refer to the concept of a similarity set, and in the terminology of 'older and younger brothers' to describe members of the set.

6.4.3 *Parallel names in a Tswana praise poem*

Where a text is consistently about a particular person – for example an epic about a hero, or a text praising a person – that person will need to be repeatedly named. In some cases, the person is assigned a set of different names, which are thus synonymous in that they have the same reference, though in many cases they also characterize the person in different ways, either by attributing characteristics to him or her ('brave', 'noble' etc.) or by metaphorically identifying him or her with other things ('lion' etc.). As we see in 9.3.2, this can become a resource for poetic composition, where the poet has a selection of different names for the same person which can be drawn upon depending on metrical requirements. But the practice can also be exploited in parallel texts, where the structural parallelism co-occurs with the use of the set of names. This is illustrated by the following beginning from a Tswana praise poem (from Southern Africa):

1 *Tsamayang lobolêlêlêng kwagôMorêmi aMathiba,*
   go   tell this   to Moremi   son of Mathiba

2 *lobô lotsênang kagôôMoêpêdi,*
   also call on   the Mopedis

3 *lore   kwaMokube lefatshe leasenyêga,*
   report that at Mokube   the land is being torn apart (troubled)

4 *mapôdisi aalesotlha.*
   the police are causing disorder.

5 *Mme galeise leutlwa   Leisantwa;*
   but   yet   has not heard Leisantwa

   ('But Leisantwa has not heard yet': Leisantwa might refer to the hero's age-set (see below) or might be used just to refer to the hero himself as a great warrior)

6 *motlhang leutlwa   letlatsoga   bosigo,*
   the day   he knows he will rise very early

7 *Rralesêgô otlaphêtha lesôlê   molala,*
   Rralesego will wring the soldier's neck
   (Rralesego = father of Lesego, i.e. a respectful term of address)

8   *aba asôka lepôdisi   phidikwê;*
    and break the policeman's spine;

9   **Segopê**   *abôkôlêlêla   lesôlê,*
    the elephant will trumpet over the soldier

10 *agala   mogatêng   lalepôdisi,*
    while bellowing will trample over the skull of the policeman

11 **lefenya**   *lesôka   mhagô tsêjwana,*
    the conqueror will break off an ear for provision
    (i.e. as a symbol that the warrior has subdued his victim, and as testimony
    that there will be no more war – hence the next line)

12 *phefô   eba   etlhaba,* **Rramoswaana**
    the breeze of calm is felt,   the fair complexioned man
       yôokwagaNgwakêtse.
       of the land of Ngwaketse
    (i.e. the fair complexioned man brings the breeze of calm, meaning that
    there is peace)

(Source: the beginning of *Kgang lebahurutshe* (dispute with the Hurutshe), by
Seokwang Kuana, late nineteenth century. Tswana text in Schapera (1965: 166;
reproduced by permission of Oxford University Press).)

This poem praises Bathoen I, the chief from 1889 to 1910 of the Ngwaketse
section of the Tswana, and is about his role in a boundary dispute. Bathoen is
never named directly but he is indirectly named by five different names (indicated
in boldface in the text). The first name is *Leisantwa*, which is the name of the
age-set to which he (and others of his age) belong. Next he is named *Rralesego*
after his eldest child. Then he is given an animal's name, *elephant* (later in the
poem, Bathoen is also called 'bull of the plateau'), followed by *conquerer*, and
finally *fair complexioned man of Ngwaketseland* (a reference to Bathoen's light
skin colouring). The distribution of names is not random. Based both on the
interpretative parallelism between pairs of lines and on the parallel syntactic
structures between pairs of lines, we can organize the twelve lines into six two-
line constituents. The hero is named in each constituent from the third onwards,
and is named twice in the final constituent (lines 11 and 12) of this unit; after
this beginning to the text he is not named with anything like the same density
again, and this initial density might function to imply that the beginning constitutes
a distinct section of the text. This case of parallelism draws particular attention
to the connection between lexical parallelism and metaphor. In lexical parallelism,
equivalent phrases are put into sequence; in metaphor, one phrase replaces
another. In both cases, words and phrases with meanings which are in principle
distinct are drawn together.

6.5   Summary: parallelism and linguistic form

Parallelism is widespread in the verbal arts of the world; as canonical parallelism it is a basic structuring principle analogous to meter in metrical poetry. Jakobson suggests that parallelism and meter considered together as involving 'recurrence' constitute the fundamental linguistic contribution to literary form, the most basic way in which form can draw attention to itself. Parallelism nevertheless is significantly different in its functioning from meter: it can involve syntactic as well as phonological form, and does not appear to require a separate rule system as meter does. Thus for example there is no equivalence in parallelism of the metrical template. No general account at present exists of the ways in which parallelism can access linguistic form; thus while parallelism often exploits abstract linguistic form, it is not clear how tightly constrained it is by linguistic form, and it is also not clear whether parallelism can exploit underlying form as meter can. Parallelism also offers some interesting insights into the relations between words in the lexicon, though again it is not clear to what extent the operation of parallelism is constrained by the structure of the lexicon. In general, the question for a generative linguistic account of parallelism (an account yet to be attempted) is whether parallelism simply exploits linguistic form or whether it is also constrained by linguistic form.

6.6   Further reading

For Jakobson's views on parallelism see for example Jakobson (1987a, 1987b). Fox (1977) is a discussion and extension of Jakobson's work. Leech (1969) discusses parallelism in the stylistic analysis of English texts. De Moor and Watson (1993) is a collection of essays on Hebrew, Egyptian and other ancient Near Eastern literatures, many of which raise questions relating to parallelism; de Moor (1993) discusses gapping in Ugaritic poetry; see also Foster (1975, 1980) on Ancient Egyptian. Yoder (1972), from Wimsatt's compilation on meter, is a short and clear summary of Hebrew meter. Gillingham (1994) is a recent account of Hebrew poetry, all examples in English. Baker (1973) discusses Lowth's original work on parallelism. Babalola (1966) is a survey of Yoruba *ijala* chants; he concludes with some interesting comments about the constituent structure of the chants which he argues is metrical and based on stress. On parallelism in praise poetry in Africa see Okpewho (1992); literature-specific studies include Schapera (1965), Rycroft and Ngcobo (1988) and Anyidoho (1991). On parallelism in Indonesian cultures see Fox (1988), Phillips (1981) and Forth (1996). Fox (1982, 1991) discusses the mixing of Christianity and traditional religion, and Malay and Rotinese in parallel structures, in Rotinese prayers and sermons. Hale (1971) discusses the use of antonym sets (as opposed to the lexical equivalence sets discussed in this chapter) in the construction of Warlpiri ritual speech. Fox (1989) shows that dualism is a basic principle which is exploited in complex ways by Indonesian societies to construct an understanding of their own social structure.

6.7 Exercises

6.7.1 *Mongolian epic*

The following is an extract from a Mongolian epic. (You might find it helpful to look again at the Mongolian lyric poem discussed in 5.3.4.)

Instructions

(a) Look for and describe (i) parallelisms involving sound (including sound-repetition, remembering also to uncover possible equivalence sets), and (ii) parallelisms involving syntax and meaning.
(b) Comment on the relation between the various kinds of parallelism: do they coincide or intersect?
(c) Speculate on the functions of parallelism in this text.

Text

1 *xöliiŋ   xumas*
   leg/foot-of nail(s)/claw(s)

2 *xödöö   teeši   maadžisaŋ*
   countryside towards grasped/scratched

3 *xöxö tömör degee bolsoŋ*
   blue iron   hook(s) became
   'Whose toenails scratched at the countryside and became blue iron hooks . . .' (Note: the identity of the 'whose' is revealed later in the passage – it is the Mangus, a demon.)

4 *gariiŋ   xumas*
arm/hand-of nail(s)/claw(s)

5 *gadaa teeši   maadžsaŋ*
outward towards grasped/scratched

6 *gaŋ tömör xuurai bolsoŋ*
steel   file(s) became
'. . . whose fingernails grasped outwards and became steel files . . .'

7 *armag tarmag saxal*
here and there beard

8 *ardzaidž negeŋ   xadxasaŋ*
bristling one/once attached
'. . . whose beard was wild and bristling . . .'

9 *arwaŋ tawaŋ tolgoi*
ten   five   head(s)

10 *širwidž   negeŋ   xarsaŋ*
casting unfriendly glance one/once looked around
'. . . his fifteen heads looked around with unfriendly glances . . .'

11 *atagar   xar maŋgas xürtš irdž*
malevolent black Mangas arriving coming
'. . . the malevolent black Mangas (a demon) came.'

12 *xaaŋ   širee bulaanaa*
Khan('s) throne (will) snatch

13 *xatad xüüxed awxa gedž*
ladies children take saying

14 *iredž   jawana gedž*
coming goes   saying

15 *uural ugaa   xataŋ dzüüdelwee*
Uural Ugaa('s) queen dreamed
'Ural Ugaa's queen dreamed and said that he will come to seize the king's throne and seize the women and children.'

(Source: Mongolian text from Poppe 1958: 197; thanks to Alan Sanders for help with this and other Mongolian texts.)

6.7.2   *When Pope imitates Chaucer*

This exercise uses an extract from Geoffrey Chaucer's *The Canterbury Tales* and a rewritten version of the extract by a teenage Alexander Pope.

Instructions

(a)   Do the two texts have parallelism between the same kinds of constituent?
(b)   Do they have the same quantity of parallelism?
(c)   Is there the same kind of relationship between parallelism and metrical structure in each case?
(d)   Adjective–noun pairs are particularly characteristic of eighteenth-century poems; are they used differently with regard to parallelism in the two texts?
(e)   Try to explain any differences you found between the two texts.

Texts

> But in due time, when sixty years were o'er,
> He vow'd to lead this vitious life no more;
> Whether pure holiness inspir'd his mind,
> Or dotage turn'd his brain, is hard to find;
> But his high courage prick'd him forth to wed,
> And try the pleasures of a lawful bed.
> This was his nightly dream, his daily care,
> And to the heav'nly pow'rs his constant pray'r,
> Once, ere he dy'd, to taste the blissful life
> Of a kind husband and a loving wife.
> (Pope, translation/imitation of Chaucer, 'The Merchant's Tale', 1709)

> And whan that he was passed sixty yeer,
> Were it for hoolynesse or for dotage,
> I kan nat seye, but swich a greet corage
> Hadde this knyght to been a wedded man
> That day and nyght he dooth al that he kan
> T'espien where he myghte wedded be,
> Preyinge to oure Lord to graunten him that he
> Mighte ones knowe of thilke blisful lyf
> That is betwixe an housbonde and his wyf,
> And for to lyve under that hooly boond
> With which that first God man and woman bond.
> (Chaucer, from 'The Merchant's Tale', late fourteenth century)

6.7.3 *The Buru* Epic of Latsamane

The text for this exercise is a short extract from the *Epic of Latsamane*, in Buru (a Malayo-Polynesian language spoken on Buru Island, Indonesia). This version was sung by K— W—, about 1972, and recorded by Chaumont Devin, who kindly provided it for this book.

Instructions

(a) List the parallelisms in this text.
(b) How does the performance of this text relate to the parallelisms in the text? Does it, for example, reinforce the parallelism or complicate it? (If you are able to do so, consider both the rhythmic organization of the text and its melody.)
(c) Speculate on the function of the vocables in this text (vocables are meaningless syllables: here, *le, o* and *e*).
(d) Speculate on some functions for the parallelisms in the text, and comment on any formal features which recall the use of parallelism in other Indonesian texts.
(e) (If you have any knowledge of music, try this question.) This epic song is in principle made up of a very large number of verses, each sung to the same melody. What features of this melody might correlate with this basic fact about the text?

Text

Each verse is sung to the same melody with slight variations (illustrated for the first line). The singer stops for several seconds between verses. The verse is sung to a series of pulses (with no rests – so the words are in a continuous stream); in the transcription a monosyllable corresponds to a single pulse, and multi-pulse words are divided with hyphens to indicate the number of pulses: e.g. *bo-ot* is two pulses, *ba-de-fo* is three. Vocables are similarly divided: thus *o-o-o-o-o-o-o* is a continuous 'o' which lasts seven pulses. In this performance, the penultimate syllable in a word is stressed (this does not apply to vocables); thus *fa-fan* has stress on the first syllable, while *ba-de-fo* has stress on the second syllable. The extract from the epic begins with the hero Latsamane getting back under way after destroying a fleet of twelve sailing ships that challenged him on the high seas.

bo-ot fa-fan po-lo o-o-o-o-o-o-o le ge-ran ru-a wa-gar fa-fan po-lo e-e-e-e-e-e· e ge-ran ru-a do-o-o-o

bo-ot fa-fan po-lo o-o-o-o-o-o-o le ge-ran ru-a wa-gar fa-fan po-lo e-e-e-e-e-e-e ge-ran ru-a do-o-o-o
boat deck ten   plus two boat   deck ten   plus two then
'twelve sailing ships, twelve sailing ships' (note: *boot* is a more recent word and *wagar* a more ancient word, both meaning 'boat')

le o-laʔ tu-ren   o-o-o-o-o-o-o le gam-na be-raŋ   o-laʔ tu-ren   o-o-o-o-o-o-o-o-o gam-na be-raŋ   e-e-e
sea piece-of   like   red-cloth   sea piece-of   like   red-cloth
'That stretch of sea was like scarlet cloth, that stretch of sea was like scarlet cloth' (i.e. because of the blood; pieces of red cloth are traditionally worn by warriors in the Moluccas)

le riʔ ba-se-a e-e-e-e-e-e-e-e fen   wa-li si-ra   wa-gar fa-fan po-lo e-e-e-e-e-e-e ge-ran ru-a
he pray   thus: my brothers-in-law boat   deck   ten   plus   two
do-o-o-o
then
'he said to them respectfully my brothers in law (fellow men), twelve ships . . .'

le kim ba-de-fo o-o-o-o-o-o-o-o-o le de-fo na-a tu ya naŋ to-hon o-o-o-o-o ba-re-ma he-de e-e-e-e
you sit/remain   sit   here for I my path   is long   yet
'. . . you remain here (respectfully), remain here, for my path is still long . . .'

kim ba-de-fo e-e-e-e-e-e-e-e-e le de-fo na-a tu ya naŋ to-hon e-e-e-e-e ba-la-wa he-de e-e-e-e
you sit/remain   sit here for I my path   soars   yet
'. . . you remain here (respectfully), remain here, for my path still soars (i.e. remains long)'

7 Narrative: The Storyline

7.1 General characteristics of narratives

Stories can be told in many media, and do not require language; thus narrative form is medium-independent. Like any kind of formal organization, narrative form is able to exploit the particular characteristics of the media which it uses: thus film narrative or television narrative will exploit the characteristics of those media. Similarly, verbal narrative will exploit the characteristics of language, and this is the topic of the next two chapters. We will be looking at ways in which linguistic form is used to communicate narrative form, either by encoding it or (more commonly) by providing less direct and deterministic evidence for it.

7.1.1 The macro-structure of narratives

The macro-structure (large-scale structure) of narratives is one of the aspects of narrative form which exists independently of language; we will focus on ways in which linguistic form may be exploited as a way of drawing attention to it or providing evidence for it. A basic element of macro-structure is the arc of many narratives from an initial and developing complication to a final resolution of that complication. Thus many narratives begin with something going wrong, and the narrative is brought to an end by the righting of that wrong. Or a narrative may describe a developing situation which is disruptive in some way (e.g. the hero gets into danger) and the narrative ends with the smoothing of that disruption by bringing the situation to an end (e.g. the hero escapes). A narrative as a whole can consist of a number of sub-sequences of complication and resolution. The arrival of the resolution is often signalled by a practice which Labov and Waletzky (1967) call 'evaluation'. The complication and resolution are the two basic components of the storyline of the narrative; in addition there are various components which supplement the storyline. Labov and Waletzky propose that narratives can begin with a component called the abstract and very often also at the beginning have a component called the orientation. The abstract is a brief summary of the story to come. The orientation sets the scene for the narrative, saying when it happened, describing the environment and so on. And narratives often end with a coda, the material which follows the resolution and which can perform various functions; one function of the coda is to return from the narrated time to the narrating time, bringing the audience back to the moment of narration. Putting these components of narrative together gives us the following sequence which is the skeletal structure of many narratives:

abstract
orientation
complication
evaluation
resolution
coda

This is the sequence which Labov and Waletzky (1967) find in many of the verbal narratives which they analyse, and which can be found in narratives in other media. Not every narrative will have every component, though at least the complication and resolution are usually present because these make up the basic storyline.

A second fundamental element of macro-structure is the organization of the narrative into a sequence of episodes. Episodes often begin or end with a change in location, or time, or participants. We look at the organization of narratives into episodes in chapter 8.

7.1.2   The use of linguistic form to communicate narrative form

Narrative form is communicated to the audience: they must be able to follow the narrative, and work out where they are in it (including identifying the resolution, without which the narrative is incomplete). One of the roles of linguistic form in a narrative is to provide evidence for the presence of narrative form. In this and the next chapter we will see how linguistic form provides evidence of continuity or discontinuity in the development of the narrative. In chapter 8 we will look at how linguistic form is used to provide evidence for the initiation of new episodes in the narrative. Shortly we will see how formal differences between two kinds of clause correlate with whether those clauses are found in the storyline or elsewhere.

In the communication of narrative form, linguistic form may encode narrative form or may provide partial evidence for it. The clearest cases of encoding of narrative form can perhaps be seen in fixed phrases such as 'once upon a time' or '*and they lived happily ever after*' which encode the orientation and the coda of the story respectively. We will see other examples of the encoding of narrative form, but on the whole, narrative form is implied rather than determined by the linguistic form of a text.

Perhaps the best example of the use of linguistic form in a non-coded way, simply to provide very basic evidence of narrative form, is the use of linguistic form to create the narrative component called the evaluation. Labov and Waletzky (1967) suggest that a narrative justifies itself when it reaches a resolution which brings to an end the sequence of events which makes up the storyline. The significance of the resolution may depend on the genre of narrative involved. In the stories of personal danger elicited by Labov and Waletzky, the resolution functions to emphasize just how great the personal danger was, and perhaps to inflate the narrator's own role and character as revealed by the resolution. In some genres of European fairytale, the resolution functions to restore symbolic order: a story which began with a disrupted family ends with a marriage. In some stories about mischievous and greedy animals, the resolution functions to demonstrate the consequences of a stupid action and thus has a moral force. In all cases, the story has a purpose which relates to the resolution of the complication or lack set up by the story. This makes it particularly important for a narrator to draw attention to the resolution of the story, and Labov and Waletzky (1967) and Labov (1972) discuss various means by which this is done in the English narratives which they analyse. The process of drawing attention to the resolution of the story (and hence to its significance) is called 'evaluation' by Labov and Waletzky, because it arises from the narrator's evaluation of the significance of the story in the context in which it is told. Labov (1972) later expands the notion of evaluation to recognize that throughout the story its significance may be highlighted, and thus that there are evaluations throughout: but the most important evaluation comes at the moment when the complication is resolved.

There are various means by which a narrator can carry out an evaluation, and there is no single coded means of doing so. The desired result is for the audience's attention to be drawn, and for them to recognize that the story is reaching the resolution; any means available may be used to achieve this. First, a person may explicitly utter an evaluation. The simplest case of this is perhaps when the narrator interrupts the narration to speak directly to the audience; for example, saying '*But it was quite an experience*'. There are increasingly embedded versions of this same practice. The utterance can be embedded under a verb of saying, and attributed to the narrator: '*I said to myself, this is it*'. This has the possible advantage over direct address in that it remains within the past tense of the narrative; in fact, it frames the evaluation inside a narrative clause. (It is irrelevant whether the person really did say to himself '*this is it*'; the sentence is there primarily for its function to emphasize the structure of the narrative.)

The utterance of the evaluation can instead be to a third person. Thus the shift from complication to resolution in one narrative gathered by Labov and Waletzky is marked by this evaluation: '*But that night the manager, Lloyd Burrows, said "you better pack up and get out because that son of a bitch never forgives anything once he gets it in his head".*' The narrator could equally well have presented this utterance as his own, or could have directly addressed the hearer with it.

Labov and Waletzky look at narratives of first-person experience, but the same kind of evaluations are found in narratives of third-person experience. Stout and Thomson (1971: 251) describe a (South American Indian) Kayapó narrative in which the culture hero Xakawã Pò gets lost (complication); the resolution is when he finds home, and it is preceded by a clause '*"Could this be home?" he said*' which performs the evaluation, drawing attention to the resolution. This example also shows that the use of attributed utterance as an evaluation is found in literatures other than English-language literatures. In his analysis of a (North American) Chinookan story told by Louis Simpson, Hymes points out that all but one of the instances of quoted speech occur in the resolution section of the story. He comments: 'Since quoted speech appears to have a special saliency in memory for Chinookan narrators, this concentration of quoted speech in the one part of Mr. Simpson's text seems an especially strong indication of the location of the emphasis in his performance, i.e. in the Dénouement' (Hymes 1981: 108). Another way of looking at it is that Simpson uses quoted speech to initiate and then identify the resolution (= dénouement).

Another device which can be used to enact an evaluation is a shift of tense, from past into historical present. The term 'historical present' is used to describe a use of the present tense form of a verb to refer to past events, and is found in various languages including English. Silva-Corvalán (1983) shows that the shift from past to historical present in several Spanish oral narratives functions simply to indicate the evaluation: it has no significance for the temporal reference of the narrative. Past tense is the unmarked morphological form of the verbs in the narrative clauses; the verbs shift to morphological present (historical present) at crucial moments. In some of the cited examples, there are other markers of the evaluation – such as reported speech, or repetition. Here is an extract from a narrative:

Un día estaba sentada – estaba la barra de salto alto aquí, yo estaba mirando pa' otro lado,	One day I was sitting – the high jump bar was here, I was looking in the opposite direction
y dije, 'Me tengo que dar vueltas porque la niña que va a saltar ahora, que tiene buzo rojo, se va a pegar con la varilla ten la espalda'	and I said, 'I have to turn around because the girl who's going to jump now, who's wearing a red warm-up suit, is going to hit her back against the bar'

Y me <u>estory</u> dando vuelta así, pero <u>iba</u> demasiado lenta,	And I'm turning around like this but I was going too slowly
y en esto la niña <u>viene</u> corriendo así, ¡zaz!, se <u>pega</u> en la espalda con la barra.	and just then the girl comes running like this, bang! she hits her back against the bar

Here we see the shift from past tense (single underlining) to present tense (double underlining) leading up to the resolution, accompanied by a quotation also functioning as evaluation. A similar point is made for the use of the historical present as an evaluating device in English oral narratives by Schiffrin (1981).

Some ways of enacting an evaluation involve simply some kind of interruption; the interruption plausibly can be said to draw the hearer's attention. One form of interruption is the insertion of an orienting clause, a statement about the circumstances, forcing the narrative to a halt just as it is about to reach its crucial moment. Another form of interruption is repetition; the final clause in the complication might be repeated, thus drawing the hearer's attention and signalling that the narrator has something special to say (or is about to say it). Finally, while the text itself can 'peak' with formal elements which perform an evaluation, it is also possible to 'peak' in the performance of a text. A particularly prominent gesture, for example, might indicate a narrative peak. Labov cites the use of gesture to accompany a deictic term like *that* which is part of an evaluation. Modifications of the voice can also draw attention to a particular part of the text: a lengthening of vowels, greater loudness, etc. (Labov 1972: 379)

Thus the function of evaluation, which is a way of drawing the audience's attention to the narrative form, can be performed by a wide range of different linguistic forms. None of these encode evaluation: they can be used elsewhere in the story. But they are sufficiently marked, where they are used, to draw the hearer's attention, and thus provide evidence for narrative form.

7.2   Storyline and non-storyline clauses

7.2.1   *The sequence of clauses and the sequence of events*

The storyline expresses the sequence of events which are the core of the story. In a verbal narrative there is a distinction between clauses which carry the storyline and clauses which do something else (such as giving circumstantial information). In linguistic analyses of narratives, this idea of a distinction between storyline and other clauses can be traced back to an article by Labov and Waletzky (1967) on the structure of a certain genre of narratives, where people told stories about things which had happened to them. This account was reshaped somewhat by Labov (1972). Labov and Waletzky suggested that the referential function of narratives is to represent connected events which happen in temporal sequence (i.e. one after another in time). Language is well suited to this, because clauses are also ordered in temporal sequence (one clause spoken after another in time). Hence a verbal narrative can represent the temporal sequence of events simply by the temporal sequence of clauses: by saying one thing after another we imply that in the events described, the first described event took place before the second described event. This is a sense in which a characteristic of linguistic form (sequentiality) is exploited in literary form.

For Labov and Waletzky, a storyline clause (or a 'narrative clause' in their terminology) is a clause whose position relative to other clauses encodes the temporal location of the event which it describes. Thus, when storyline clauses are reordered the consequence is that the text represents the events as taking place in the other order. Consider for example these two clauses:

I hit him. He hit me.

If these are interpreted as storyline clauses, then the meaning of the text is that first I hit him and then he hit me. If we reorder the clauses, treating them still as storyline clauses, then the meaning changes:

He hit me. I hit him.

We could add an explicit marker of sequence, adding *then* to the second clause, but this is not strictly necessary because the sequence of clauses by itself means that the events took place in this sequence. (Note that this means that when *then* is added, it may have some additional function other than just indicating sequence: for example, it may signal the beginning of a new episode.)

The sequence of actions can be expressed in other ways. We can for example have single clauses which contain subordinate clauses which are introduced by explicit markers of sequence such as *because* and *before*:

He hit me because I hit him.
He hit me before I hit him.

Here Labov and Waletzky argue that the relation between the two actions described is not a storyline or narrative relation. In part this is because the position of subordinate clauses within a clause can often vary freely without changing the meaning of the clause.

Not all clauses in a narrative are storyline clauses. The main other kind of clause is an orientation clause, a clause which describes the location, or the participants, for example. Orientation clauses do not refer to actions which are temporally ordered to form part of the storyline sequence, and they can typically be moved around in a narrative without changing the way in which they refer. For example, we might add a clause *I was angry* to our sequence:

I was angry. I hit him. He hit me.
I hit him. I was angry. He hit me.
I hit him. He hit me. I was angry.

In all three cases, the clause *I was angry* might be interpreted as an orientation clause, describing the speaker's state of mind, with the same meaning arising in each case. (The placement of the clause might, of course, have other effects, but the point is that the situation described remains the same.) Storyline and non-storyline clauses can thus be distinguished by a reordering test: non-storyline clauses can be reordered without changing the situation as described. Labov and Waletzky suggest that orientation clauses are of particular significance when found in two places in a narrative. First, there is the orientation section of the narrative, at the beginning: a section which describes the context before the narrative begins. Second, orientation clauses are sometimes placed at a climax point of the narrative, interrupting the flow of the storyline and thus drawing attention to the storyline at that moment functioning as evaluation.

Storyline and non-storyline clauses can also to some extent be distinguished by their linguistic features. These linguistic features generally correlate with the difference between clauses which describe 'what happens' (storyline) and clauses which describe 'what is' (orientation); in other words, the linguistic differences between storyline and non-storyline clauses seem to arise primarily from their different kinds of meaning. The linguistic form of a clause can thus to some extent provide evidence for interpreting the clause as storyline or non-storyline (and thus helps the hearer to follow the story). However, this is only partial evidence and, as with other kinds of linguistic meaning, there may be other sources of evidence for deciding whether a particular clause is storyline or non-storyline – with the consequence that a clause with a particular linguistic form might in principle perform either function. For example, while it may not be the most likely interpretation, it is not impossible to interpret the *I was angry* clause as describing a change of state caused by the hitting, and thus as part of the storyline (for example, if the clause was said with particular vehemence, this might mark it as describing a change of state). Similarly, consider a situation in which a sequence of clauses describes a location; while in most cases these would be interpreted just as orienting clauses, if these are instead interpreted as the sequential perceptions of the hero, then they might also be interpreted as storyline clauses.

7.2.2 *Word order and the storyline/non-storyline distinction*

The distinction between storyline and non-storyline clauses is based on whether the sequential position of a clause is itself meaningful, encoding the sequence of events in time. However, the distinction may also be reflected in the linguistic form of storyline and non-storyline clauses. Here we see how the placement of the verb may correlate with this distinction.

A verb can in principle occupy various positions in a clause, most typically the first position, the second position and the final position. In some languages, the verb is fairly rigidly fixed in one position (e.g. English where it is basically in second position). In others it occurs in two or more distinct positions depending on syntactic rules: thus in German, the verb is final in subordinate clauses and in second position in main clauses. In languages where the verb may occur in several possible positions within the clause, it has sometimes been argued that the position of the verb correlates with the discourse status of the clause – for example, whether it is storyline or non-storyline. In particular, this has been argued for some of the languages where there is a choice between putting the verb at the beginning of the sentence or in some other position; here it seems that verb-initial position is correlated with storyline. Thus Longacre (1995) considers three languages in which there is a choice between verb-initial or non-verb-initial clauses (a study much extended in Longacre 1990). In Chicahuaxtla Trique storyline clauses are verb-initial; non-verb-initial clauses are used for non-storyline purposes, or in some cases for special effects. In Luwo and Biblical Hebrew, narratives are split into primary and secondary narratives; the primary storylines consistently have verb-initial order, though other orders are possible in secondary storylines. Cumming (1995: 60) says that in Malay, non-storyline clauses have fixed verb-medial order, while narrative/foregrounded clause types have relatively free order including the option of verb-initial order. Hopper (1979: 222) suggests that storyline clauses in the Old English story of Cynewulf from the *Parker Chronicle* tend to be either verb-initial or verb-final (i.e. 'OV' structure), while non-storyline clauses have the verb in the middle part of the clause. There is an interesting twist to the placement of the verb in this text; Hopper says that the verb comes at the beginning in about every fourth narrative clause, with the verb being at the end in the others. He comments that 'the break seems to come as a sort of breathpause or, perhaps, an aesthetic effect: possibly it was considered trite to maintain an unbroken series of OV clauses'.

It is possible that there is a functional explanation for this preference for verb-initial in storyline clauses in so many languages, and various proposals have been made (for example by Harold 1995: 151). It may for example be that fronting of the verb draws attention to the verb, and hence to the eventuality described by it (which in storyline clauses is likely to be a highly transitive action). This would be more important in storyline clauses, which trace out the sequence of actions in the narrative, than in non-storyline clauses. This is one of the areas where work on verbal art has consequences for linguistics more generally. Languages where the verb appears in different places in the sentence are a potential site of conflict between syntax-oriented explanations and discourse-oriented explanations. Syntacticians tend to look for clause-internal explanations for the placement of the verb; discourse analysts on the other hand might argue that the placement of the verb might be correlated with clause-internal features but is ultimately tied into the function of the clause in a discourse. The study of verb placement in narrative thus has consequences for an understanding of verb placement in the language more generally.

7.3   Transitivity

7.3.1   *High transitivity as a characteristic of storyline clauses*

We now turn to another typical distinction in the linguistic form of storyline and non-storyline clauses, which relates to transitivity. The traditional notion of transitivity involves the number of arguments taken by a verb (or other predicator). A verb with two arguments, such as *eat*, is transitive, while a verb with one, such as *sleep*, is not transitive (is intransitive). Hopper and Thompson (1980) and Hopper (1979) suggest that this is just one element of a whole cluster of related 'transitivity' properties which a clause may have. This is because they adopt a very general definition of transitivity as the transfer of an activity from an agent to a patient. Hopper and Thompson (1980: 252) list ten variables for a clause which can each be marked for high or low transitivity. A cardinal transitive clause will have all ten variables marked for 'high transitivity'; a cardinal intransitive clause will have all marked for 'low transitivity'. Many clauses will come somewhere in between, though we should be able to say broadly whether a clause is generally high or low in transitivity. Highly transitive clauses are the typical kinds of storyline clause, and within storylines we would expect the more significant clauses to be the more transitive clauses; this is because if the story is about the transfer of action, as many stories are, then transitive clauses are the best suited to carry the storyline.

   These are the ten variables of transitivity (in each case, H is the high transitivity option, and L is the low transitivity option).

1   *Number of participants: two or more (H) or one (L).* High transitivity
    involves two or more participants, allowing the transfer of the action from
    one to the other. In low transitivity there is only one participant, disallowing
    a transfer. This feature alone is what some grammars mean by 'transitivity'.

2   *Kinesis: action (H) or state (L).* An action (involving an event caused by
    an actor) is highly transitive compared to a state of affairs where there is
    no actor involved. For example *to like* is a verb which describes a state of
    affairs, and hence *Sally likes Mary* is low in transitivity for this variable.

3   *Aspect: the action has an endpoint (H) or does not have an endpoint (L).*
    Highly transitive actions have an endpoint, which can for example be
    expressed by perfective aspect and a completion particle as in *I ate it up.*
    The endpoint means that the action is completely transferred. An action
    without an endpoint, as expressed by the imperfective (progressive) *I am
    eating it*, is low transitive.

4   *Punctuality: the action takes place at a moment in time (H) or is ongoing
    (L).* To *kick* is an example of a verb which expresses an action which takes
    place as a punctual, complete and undivided event, and is thus high trans-
    itive. On the other hand, an ongoing action such as *to carry* would be low
    transitive.

5   *Volitionality: the action is done on purpose (H) or is incidental/accidental
    (L).* Actions which are intended (and therefore have a more apparent effect
    on the patient) are higher in transitivity than actions which are not intended.
    I dropped the vase is ambiguous between a volitional high transitive read-
    ing and an accidental low transitive reading.

6   *Affirmation: an action is said to happen (H) or is said not to happen (L).*
    No matter what type of action is involved, it can be said to be presented
    as more transitive when it is said to happen than when it is said not to
    happen: i.e. *I kicked it* is higher transitive than *I didn't kick it.*

7   *Mode: an action actually happens (H) or has the potential to happen or
    happens in a fictional world (L).* Hopper and Thompson say about this
    difference: 'an action which either did not occur, or which is presented as
    occurring in a non-real (contingent) world, is obviously less effective than
    one whose occurrence is actually asserted as corresponding directly with a
    real event'. This is an interesting feature of transitivity as regards literature,
    since many of the happenings described in verbal art are at some level
    fictional.

8   *There is an agent which causes the action (H) or the action is caused other
    than by an agent (L).* The recipient of an event might be receiving it from
    someone (e.g. when someone deliberately shows his face to me) or might

have access to it without any deliberate action on the other's part (e.g. when I just see someone's face).

9 *Affectedness of the object: the object is totally affected by the action (H) or unaffected by it (L).* This is a feature of transitivity which focuses on the recipient of the action. For highest transitivity, the action must be completely carried over to the object. Thus *I drank all the milk* is higher in transitivity than *I drank some of the milk*.

10 *Individuation of the object: the object is highly individuated (H) or generic (L).* Individuation is in turn a collection of features, such that something might be more highly individuated than something else. The most individuated things are referred to by nouns which are proper (names), human or animate, concrete, singular, count (as opposed to mass) and referential or definite. High transitivity correlates with individuation of the object.

We can summarize the features of a cardinal transitive clause, with the highest degree of transitivity, as follows: The clause will have an agent and an object, which are distinct from one another; the agent is fully agentive and acts purposefully, and the object is totally affected by the action. The eventuality is an action (not a state), viewed in terms of its having an endpoint and being punctual. The clause positively affirms the taking place of a really occurring action.

Transitivity is relevant for the structure of narratives, because as Hopper and Thompson show (and has been widely attested by others), the clauses in a narrative which carry the storyline are high in transitivity. They call the storyline clauses foregrounded clauses; the non-storyline clauses are called backgrounded clauses, these being the clauses which are 'extraneous to the narrative's structural coherence'. Foregrounded and backgrounded clauses thus perform different functions in a narrative. (The distinction between foregrounded and backgrounded clauses extends beyond narrative, to include also for example the key points in conversation as foregrounded clauses.) Hopper and Thompson suggest that in some languages, including English, foregrounded/storyline clauses are higher in transitivity than backgrounded clauses. This has a functional explanation: there is an expected correlation between the clauses which express the storyline and clauses which express actions which are highly transitive, with actors transferring actions to patients. Stories are about actions rather than states, and deliberate rather than accidental actions, and the effects of one individual on another: all characteristics of high transitivity. This is a probabilistic correlation, with no guarantee but rather a reasonable chance that the foregrounded clauses will be the high transitivity clauses and the backgrounded clauses will be the low transitivity clauses; in a survey they undertook, they found that 78 per cent of their foregrounded clauses averaged out as having the ten features of high transitivity, while only 39 per cent of backgrounded clauses did.

While the overall collection of transitivity features might be important in some cases, in other cases storyline clauses correlate with specific transitivity features and their occurrence in foregrounded clauses. Thus for example in some languages such as Tagalog and Malay, 'passive' clauses are most typically the foregrounded or storyline clauses. These clauses are called 'passive' (in inverted commas) because of their analogy with the English passive: in Malay for example there is special morphology on the verb, a *di-* prefix, and the subject is in a preposition phrase with the preposition *oleh* (analogous to the English 'by-phrase' in passives). Unlike English passives, however, these clauses appear to be counted as high transitive when it comes to the storyline, as they are the basic type of narrative clause (Hopper 1979: 229):

maka oleh tuan   itu di-suroh aku berdua
and   by   master the were-told we   two

'And we were told by the master'

In contrast, the so-called 'active' verb is unprefixed and can take an agent directly; these two differences make these analogous to the passive and active verbs of English. But this conceals a fundamental difference in function. It is the passive verb which is used to express eventualities which are perfective, active and really took place – all features of high transitivity – and it is this verb which is used in foregrounded clauses. The 'active' verb in contrast is a formal marker of backgrounding, indicating that the event it describes is outside the main storyline.

7.3.2 The prominence of participants

The notion of 'transitivity' is also used in another way in literary linguistics, relating not to the storyline but to the way in which participants are represented as involved in actions. In stylistics, particularly in the tradition initiated by Michael Halliday, the investigation of transitivity has focused primarily on the choices which clauses offer about how to represent the role of an individual in an action or event. Consider for example an action in which Mary breaks a window. This could be represented by different clauses, all of which describe the same event but which make Mary more or less prominent:

(1) *Mary broke the window*
(2) *The window got broken by Mary*
(3) *The window got broken*

(1) represents Mary as the agent who causes the breaking, as does (2), but (2) de-emphasizes her role; while (3) removes any mention of her at all. Options about how to represent agency, in particular, have been investigated particularly from two perspectives. First, it has been argued that in political reporting of events in newspapers, the representation of agency is biased: thus a right-wing newspaper, in narrating an event in which strikers are beaten by police, might de-emphasize the agency of the police in order not to draw attention to their action (see Kress and Hodge 1979). Second, it has been argued that in some kinds of writing there is a tendency to de-emphasize the agency of women, by choosing to represent them in clauses where they are not agents (i.e. as (2) or (3)). Extending this to the notion of transitivity introduced earlier, it would be interesting to know whether there is a general tendency for patriarchal narratives about women to have lower-transitivity clauses describing the eventualities which involve the women characters.

7.4   Other means of controlling the prominence of participants

The transitivity of a clause relates in part to whether the clause is a storyline or a non-storyline clause. The term 'transitivity' has also been used in discussions of how centrally a participant is represented as part of a storyline. We now look at some other ways in which the prominence of participants in the storyline is controlled by linguistic choices.

7.4.1   *Emphasizing participants: word order in Sinhala and Tamil*

We first consider a use of word order to achieve a similar effect of emphasizing or de-emphasizing participants. The material comes from Herring and Paolillo's (1995) discussion of narratives in Sinhala and Tamil (Sri Lanka etc.). In both languages, the verb is typically final in the clause. In Sinhala narratives, newly mentioned concepts tend to appear immediately before the verb; however, particularly important concepts – concepts which will have an important role in the narrative to come – come after the verb, at the end of the clause. Thus for example in one (written) folktale, in the initial orientation when the setting is being described, when a forest (*kælæ̃ewa-k*) is introduced it is placed before the verb (*tibunaa*), the typical place for relatively low-importance new information:

oya gaňg-en   e-goḏa   eka pætta-k-a   loku kælææwa-k tibunaa.
that river-INSTR that-bank one side-INDEF-LOC large forest-INDEF exist-PAST

'On the far bank of the river a large forest was.'

But when a narratively important particular forest is introduced, where the hero jackal lives, the forest (*kælææwa-k*) is put after the verb (*tibunaa*), thus indicating its greater centrality for the narrative:

gaňg-en   me-goḏa-t   tibunaa kælææwa-k. Oya kælææ-we hiṭiyaa
river-INSTR this-bank-also be-PAST forest-INDEF that forest-LOC live-past
  nariy-ek.
  jackal-INDEF

'On this bank of the river also was a forest. In that forest lived a jackal.'

It is possible that the placement of the noun phrase after the verb draws attention to it either because it is at the edge of the clause (analogous perhaps to the verb-placement phenomena seen earlier) or because it is in an unexpected position.

A similar distinction between a preverbal position and a clause-final position can be seen in Tamil narratives. Here, however, the language permits a different strategy for getting an important concept into final position; instead of placing the phrase after the verb, the verb is omitted so that the phrase becomes final by default. Thus in one oral folktale, the hero (rabbit) and villain (lion) are introduced in clause-final position, with the verb of the clause omitted; other animals are introduced in preverbal position.

7.4.2 De-emphasizing participants: incorporation and other processes

In the previous section we saw that important concepts and participants – which the narrative is 'about' – can be highlighted by syntactic means. It is also possible to do the opposite: to obscure concepts and participants which are mentioned in the narrative but which are of very little importance. We now look at an example of this involving noun incorporation in the Paraguayan language Guaraní. Noun incorporation typically involves a noun which is an argument of a verb being morphologically merged with the verb, resulting in a compound verb. Velázquez-Castillo (1995) shows that it is one of three options for the realization of a verb and object pair in Guaraní. The three options are:

- object–verb as a single word
- object is morphologically distinct from the verb and precedes the verb

- verb is morphologically distinct from the object and precedes the object (perhaps the best candidate of the three as an unmarked option)

The choice between these options communicates different degrees of narrative importance for the object, presumably as a consequence of the degree to which each option makes the object manifest. Incorporation makes the object least important and verb–object order makes it most important. (Notice that the difference between the three might also be understood in terms of degrees of transitivity relating to the high-transitivity 'distinctness of the object' feature, with the incorporated object being low transitive.) Velázquez-Castillo illustrates this by comparing an utterance (1) from a story about the monkey and the crocodile with an invented alternative (2):

(1) *ka'i*   *o-ñe-ndy-moko, o-ñe-mbe-su'u, o-jete-poka*
    monkey saliva-swallows, lip-bites,   body-twists

(2) *ka'i*   *o-mokõ h-endy,   oi-su'u h-embe, oi-poka h-ete*
    monkey swallows his saliva, bites   his lip, twists   his body

In (1) the body parts are incorporated into the verbs and hence are not marked as of independent importance, unlike in (2) where they are postverbal objects and hence of independent importance in the narrative; (2) would be used if the body parts themselves were significant in the story.

    Velázquez-Castillo suggests four somewhat distinct functions for noun incorporation, all of which have the same basic function of ensuring that the incorporated noun is not marked as important. In three cases, the incorporated noun names a body part. The result may be to express an emotional state, as in the previous example. Or it may reflect attitude, as when the monkey moves his tail (described in an incorporating verb) expressing his irreverence. Or the incorporation of the body part may reflect its permanent physical qualities as applied to the person. Thus the story ends by the monkey telling the crocodile that the women think the crocodile is ugly; here the noun describing the body part is incorporated into a predicator with an adjectival function:

jakare   *tuja ape-korocho, resa-kua-ku'e, juru-guasu*
crocodile old surface-rough eye-hole-move mouth-big

'That old rough-skinned crocodile, with eyes trembling in their sockets, big mouth.'

The body parts are incorporated into predicators which describe the subject (the crocodile) because they are unimportant in themselves but important specifically in that they characterize the crocodile: it is the saying of these things about the crocodile which brings the story to its resolution. Finally, the fourth case of noun incorporation involves a verb describing routinized activity, as in the following example describing the eating of the pakuri-fruit:

a-ha'aro-a-ina che-irū-me   ro-ho-hagua   pakuri-'u-vo
I'm waiting   for my friend so that we can go pakuri-eating

Velázquez-Castillo comments: 'the fruit is not important in itself; it is important only insofar as it serves the purpose of characterizing the action as an established type of social activity. Thus it doesn't matter which particular fruits are eaten; what matters is the type of activities people are engaged in when eating that kind of fruit.' (There is another example of noun incorporation in a Koryak narrative – also involving body parts – in exercise 8.7.2.)

Schaefer (1995) presents rather similar data from the Nigerian language Emai, involving choices about the syntactic representation of body parts. His focus is somewhat different, but his findings are similar. There are two syntactic options for the expression of possession: (a) the unmarked case is where the possessed noun comes first, followed by the connecting particle *isi* and the possessor, and (b) the possessor ascension case where the possessor precedes (directly) the possessed. Possessor ascension has the pragmatic consequence of marking the possessor as more important than the possessed. It is most commonly found in narrative clauses, which we would expect if particularly in these clauses the actors must generally be highly important and their body parts low in importance.

7.5   Continuity and discontinuity in the storyline

A storyline is a sequence of situations. Each situation has certain components: characters who have specific roles in the situation, objects, a location, a time when it happens, and so on. The narrative will present that situation to us in a particular way, perhaps drawing particular attention to certain aspects of the situation, or presenting it as though seen through the eyes of one of the participants. Situations change in two ways: either the situation remains generally the same but components of it change, or the situation ends and a new situation begins. In both cases, we can think of situations in terms of their having continuous or discontinuous elements. A character might for example be important for the narrative over several clauses (i.e. a continuity in the central character) and then another character might come to the fore (i.e. a discontinuity in the central character). The discontinuity may coincide with a change from one situation to another, or it might be internal to the situation. In some narratives, we can recognize the presence of major simultaneous discontinuities which constitute a boundary between distinct narrative episodes. Distinct episodes may involve a simultaneous change of location and participants and may involve a jump in time; we will return to these in the next chapter.

In order to understand a story, the audience must be able to understand all these aspects of situations: both what they consist of, and when and how they change. The fundamental requirement is to be aware of any changes – any discontinuities. In this section we look at discontinuities and how they are communicated to the audience. In some cases the discontinuity will be in what is described (e.g. the hero travels to a new location) and in other cases in how it is described (e.g. we shift from seeing events through the hero's eyes to seeing them through the villain's eyes).

Linguistic form can provide evidence of discontinuity, but in some cases there is no overt marking of a discontinuity. Where the discontinuity involves a shift to an unexpected situation it is more likely to be explicitly indicated; where it involves a shift back to an expected situation it is less likely to be explicitly indicated. Where linguistic form provides evidence of discontinuity, that evidence can in some cases be coded into the form; in other cases the linguistic form provides potential evidence for discontinuity which must then be further interpreted by the audience.

7.5.1 *Implied discontinuities in Swahili*

Swahili verbs may be modified for tense, aspect and modality by a large number of prefixes and suffixes and by combination with grammatical verbs. Contini-Morava has argued that the verbal system can only fully be understood once we look at its use in narratives. In particular, certain options within the verbal system seem to function in part to signal narrative discontinuities.

We begin with Contini-Morava's (1987) analysis of the verbal prefixes *li* and *ka* in Swahili written narratives. *li* and *ka* are two among several possible prefixes on verbs; Contini-Morava explores the possibility that *li* communicates discontinuity (while *ka* does not) by looking at two-verb sequences with either of the prefixes attached to the second verb. She suggests that the prefixes differ in how they alert the audience to possible discontinuities. For example, *li* is more likely than *ka* to be found on the second verb when that verb has a different subject from the preceding verb, a kind of discontinuity involving which participants are in primary focus. This is not the only kind of discontinuity which is accompanied by a *li* verb, however. Where there is some lack of continuity in time between the events described by the two verbs, *li* is also found; this might involve a flashback (breaking the temporal sequence) or a longer than expected gap in time between the two events; in the latter case, the *li*-prefixed verb is frequently accompanied by an explicit temporal connective meaning 'then'. *li* is even found with greater than chance frequency on a second verb where there is some unexpected sequence of events, as in '*Wote wa-li-furahi na wa li-lia...*' (= both rejoiced and they cried...). This correlates with the fact that the disjunctive connective *lakini* (= but) is also commonly accompanied by a *li* verb. Thus *li* is found as a prefix on verbs in various cases of discontinuity. Contini-Morava's conclusion is that *li* offers evidence to the audience that there may be a discontinuity (without guaranteeing this) but does not provide any evidence as to the kind of discontinuity. Thus an element of narrative form (continuity) is communicated somewhat indirectly, rather than being coded, by linguistic form.

Our second example, from Contini-Morava (1991a), involves the grammatical verb *kuwa*. This verb, which can be glossed as 'be', adds no lexical information to the clause, and in some analyses is treated as an auxiliary, though Contini-Morava argues that syntactically it is an independent verb. One function of *kuwa* is to code a discontinuity in the reference point by which the reference of a tense form is calculated. For example, there might be a past tense verb with its time reference calculated with reference to the moment of speaking, followed by *kuwa* and a past tense verb, and the presence of *kuwa* indicates that the time reference for the second verb is now calculated with reference to a different moment in time, perhaps the moment in time defined by the preceding verb. This is how *kuwa* works in the following text:

Baadaye maiti alifutwa na kufunikwa	'Then the corpse was cleaned and
guo moja kubwa tangu kwenye dole	covered with a big cloth from head
gumba mpaka utosini. Palitiwa	to toe. There were placed
ubani na uvumba chumbani.	frankincense and perfume in the room.
Wakati huo nyumba ilikuwa	By that time the house had filled/was
imeshajaa wanawake na inahanikiza	full with women and it resounded
kwa vilio na maombolezo.	with laments and dirges.'

(from M. S. Farsy, *Kurwa na Doto* (1960), Nairobi: East African Literature Bureau; p. 42. Cited in Contini-Morava 1991a: 299)

The verbs in the first two sentences are past tense, and are past relative to the moment of narrating. *ilikuwa* (a form of *kuwa*) then comes before the next verb *imeshajaa* to indicate that the past tense is now calculated from a different reference point, defined by the previous verbs: the filling of the room is past relative to the placing of frankincense and perfume. Contini-Morava suggests that, in addition, *kuwa* provides evidence for other kinds of discontinuities, but the exact nature of these must be inferred and is not coded by the word: thus there is a discontinuity in kinds of event, and a discontinuity in subjects.

7.5.2 *Indicating the central participant in Fox: obviative and proximate*

Some of the Algonquian languages of North America, which include Fox, have a formal feature by which one participant referred to in a clause can be marked as proximate and another as obviative (Goddard 1990). The notions of 'obviative' and 'proximate' are particularly associated with these languages, though the terms are sometimes used to describe possibly related characteristics of other languages. The participant marked as proximate is the participant which the narrative is 'about' during this clause; the participant marked as obviative is a participant which the narrative is less about during this clause. Which participants are proximate and which are obviative may shift during the narrative, though the most important character (the hero) will be the unmarked carrier of proximate morphology. Proximate and obviative morphology are applied irrespective of grammatical role (e.g. subjects and objects can be marked either way) and to some extent irrespective of thematic role, though there are some constraints. Proximate and obviative might be coded as part of the verbal morphology, with a pronoun attached to the verb being marked as proximate or obviative, or as part of the noun's morphology where a full noun is used. To illustrate: 'girl' is *iškwe·se·ha*, the proximate form of 'that girl' is *i·na iškwe·se·ha*, while the obviative form of 'that girl' is *i·nini iškwe·se·hani*.

There seem to be several senses in which a narrative can be 'about' the participant who is proximate at any given time, and the audience must infer which sense is implied. First, proximate is associated with general narrative importance, as can be seen by its unmarked association with the hero. This is revealed by the fact that when the narrative alternates from one participant being proximate to another participant being proximate, the shift from non hero to the hero requires less overt indication (it is in a sense a return from a marked state) than the shift from hero to non-hero. The fact that a shift back to the hero need not be indicated (because the hero is expected to be the central character) is rather typical of the indicating of discontinuity shifting: as a general principle in all narrative traditions, discontinuities are less likely to be explicitly indicated when they involve a return to an expected situation and more likely to be explicitly indicated when they involve a shift to an unexpected situation.

In its second sense, proximate appears to relate to local importance: Goddard refers to a character as being 'in narrative focus' or 'at the centre of the narrative', a general notion of focus which can be put to various uses depending on the narrator's requirements (and hence where the audience must decide for themselves what 'in focus' means). To illustrate these first two senses in which proximate morphology relates to 'aboutness', here are two sequential paragraphs from a written narrative (the paragraphs are 1, 2 followed by 3, 4). [P] indicates proximate morphology and [O] indicates obviative morphology.

(In the first paragraph the narrative has the chief in narrative focus: it is the chief who stops and the chief's son who gets worse; the chief is the 'he' who is marked with proximate morphology.)

(1) *o·ni='pi   e·h=naki·či.*
     Then=QUOTATIVE he[P] stopped
(2) *e·h=e·škamesiniči=meko   okwisani.*
     he[O] got worse=EMPHATIC his[P] son[O]
     'And then, it is said, he stopped. And his son got worse and worse.'

(Now in the next paragraph the narrative shifts to having the hero – not the chief or the chief's son – in narrative focus; it is the hero who stops and the hero's mother who speaks. The hero is the 'he' who is marked with proximate morphology.)

(3) *o·ni='pi   e·h=naki·či.*
     Then=QUOTATIVE he[P] stopped
(4) *na·hka=meko=wi·na   okye·ni,*
     again-EMPHATIC-him[P] his[P] mother
     'ayo·hi='škwe   owihowi·kita·we'   e·h=ikoči.
     'here gosh!   let's live'   she[O] said to him[P]
     'And then, it is said, he stopped. And his mother said "Gosh, let's live here."'

(from a narrative written by Alfred Kiyana between 1910 and 1920; in Goddard 1990: 321, emended)

Thus the narrative shifts from having the chief in focus to having the hero in focus. There is no overt indication of this shift, with the possible exception of the connective *na·hka* which sometimes accompanies a shift of reference and hence might be taken as implying a shift without coding it; for the most part, the reader must infer the shift from various kinds of indirect evidence, including the parallelism between sentences 1 and 3, and the development of the narrative. The fact that there is no overt indication of the shift back to the hero fits with the fact that it is the hero (the unmarked bearer of proximate morphology) who is being shifted back to.

A third way in which proximate and obviative are used to express 'aboutness' relates to point of view. In one narrative by Alfred Kiyana, the hero is taken by a Buffalo spirit to see a ceremonial dance held by other spirits. Throughout the description of the dance, the proximate form is used almost uniquely to refer to the hero, though in fact the hero is not mentioned in many of the clauses. Since the narrative at this point is about the dance, it is mainly the dancers who are explicitly referred to rather than the hero, but the dancers are referred to almost entirely by the obviative. Goddard suggests that what the narrative communicates here is that the dance is from the point of view of the hero; the narrative is about the hero (and hence his perspective on the dance) rather than about the dance which is described. Thus the same form can be used to express narrative importance – both generally and locally – and point of view; three kinds of 'aboutness' which are in principle distinct. Thus while the fact of the shift can be coded by use of proximate or obviative morphology, the interpretation of the shift is left to the audience.

7.5.3 Word order as an indication of discontinuity in Malay

We now consider an example where a discontinuity is apparently coded by a syntactic choice, involving word (or phrase) order. This involves a narrative technique in Classical Malay whereby the narrative shifts from a section which is basically about the actions of one character to a section where it is basically about the actions of another character. This is demonstrated by Cumming for a type of narrative called a *hikayat* (written down, but intended to be read aloud to an audience). The text in question is drawn from a royal history, the *Sejarah Melayu* (Cumming 1995: 73; see also Cumming 1991).

> *Maka Sang Nila Utama, anak Sang Sapurba, diabmil baginda akan menantu, didudukkan baginda dengan anaknya baginda yang bernama Wan Seri Beni itu; maka dinobatkan sekali akan gantinya.*
>
> *Maka oleh Sang Sapurba akan ananda baginda Sang Nila Utama itu dianugerahinya baginda suatu makota kerajaan, tiada bahana kelihatan masnya daripada kebanyakan permata dan ratna mutu maknikam yang terkena pada makota itu; dan dianugerahi cap kempa kerajaan, seperti cap baginda juga rupanya.*

'Then she took Sang Nila Utama, Sang Sapurba's son, as her son-in-law, settling him with her daughter Wan Seri Beni; then she crowned him king in her place.

Then Sang Sapurba gave his son Sang Nila Utama a royal crown whose gold couldn't be seen clearly from the quantity of jewels of various sorts which were inlaid in it; and he gave him a royal seal, just like his own seal.'

The first of these two sections has an unmarked word order with just one argument, the recipient *Sang Nila Utama, anak Sang Sapurba* ('Sang Nila Utama, Sang

Sapurba's son') before the verb *diabmil* ('took'). The second section, however, has a marked word order, with two arguments before the verb *dianugerahinya*, both the agent *oleh Sang Sapurba* ('Sang Sapurba') and the recipient *akan ananda baginda Sang Nila Utama itu* ('his son Sang Nila Utama'). The fact that the second segment begins with the marked placement of two arguments before the verb can be interpreted as an indicator of a continuity shift such that the narrative shifts from being about the actions of the queen to the actions of king Sang Sapurba. Cumming implies that the shift in 'aboutness' is communicated partly in a coded manner, with this being a standard method of marking continuity shifts in Classical Malay narrative, and is partly communicated inferentially by its being a marked word order.

7.5.4 *Switch reference and the continuity or otherwise of participants*

Switch reference is a continuity and discontinuity phenomenon found in some languages; this account of it is based on Stirling (1993). Prototypically, switch reference works as follows. One (or more) clauses is subordinated to a main clause, and the subordinate clause may carry one of two kinds of morpheme which we'll refer to as DS and SS morphemes. If the subordinate clause contains a DS morpheme, that clause has a Different Subject (hence DS) from the main clause. If the subordinate clause contains an SS morpheme it has the Same Subject (hence SS) as the main clause.

subordinate clause (contains DS morpheme) + main clause
    Interpretation: the subordinate verb has a different subject from that of the main verb.

subordinate clause (contains SS morpheme) + main clause
    Interpretation: both clauses have the same subject for their verbs.

Stirling shows that the prototypical switch reference system has many variations, and proposes a new way of thinking about switch reference which focuses not specifically on the subjects of the two clauses but on the relationships between the two clauses as wholes. Hence, DS marking can signal not just (or only) that the subjects of the two clauses are different, but, depending on the language, can also signal kinds of temporal relation between the clauses, and so on. Thus switch reference can more generally be seen as a marker of discontinuity or continuity between main and subordinate clauses.

    An example of switch reference marking between different clauses in narratives is provided by Scollon (1985) for Chipewyan (Canada: Alberta). Independent narrative clauses are systematically connected by certain clause-initial elements.

If the two narrative clauses have the same participants, the second clause begins with the connective *huldu* (= 'then'). If the narrative clauses have different participants (usually the object will be different, but the subject will stay the same) the second clause begins with a third person pronoun *ʔɛyi* or *bɛ*. These connectives are used to introduce independent narrative clauses. (Notice that this is not a prototypical kind of switch reference, and is not called switch reference by Scollon; it does, however, fall within the more general characterization provided by Stirling.)

Kayapó (Brazil: Mato Grosso) has a switch reference system whereby a connective at or towards the beginning of the clause codes the subject as the same as the previous subject (SS) or as different from the previous subject (DS). Stout and Thomson (1971) say that these connectives are used also to join compound verbs that have the same or different relations to the subject and object of the clauses in which they occur. The connective *nẽ* is used to mark continuity (same subject):

ba kubī nẽ kukrẽ
'I kill it and (I) eat it'

While the connective *nhüm* is used to mark discontinuity (different subject):

kũm kabẽ nhüm kuʔê
'he spoke to him and he (the other) just stood there'

The particular interest of these connectives is that they appear to be used in an extended sense, at the beginning of larger narrative units which Stout and Thompson call 'paragraphs'. Even if two narrative sections have different subjects, the 'continuity' connective *nẽ* can be used if there is some thematic similarity between the subjects given the meaning of the narrative as a whole. Thus in the story of the culture hero Xakawã Pò which they discuss, there is a section describing the hero's encounter with the alligator; the next section introduces another animal, the coati mundi – and begins with *nẽ*; and the next section is about the hero's encounter with the monkey and begins with *nhüm*. It seems that the paragraph about the coati mundi is represented by the narrative as continuous with the previous paragraph because both are about animals; the next paragraph, however, is about the hero and less about the animal he encounters. Thus we see an adaptation of switch reference marking to indicate an implied continuity at the level of what the story is about as it develops.

One of the interesting characteristics of switch reference markers is that they can be used to differentiate storyline from non-storyline clauses. Stirling (1993: 148) considers the relation between these and suggests that SS marking may sometimes characterize storyline ('foregrounded') clauses. This is partly because

SS marking can function as a signal of narrative continuity, and also because there is a correlation between SS marking and temporal sequentiality between clauses (while DS marking correlates with simultaneity between clauses). Stirling also shows that DS morphology in particular is sometimes used in a language to mark the shifting between storyline and non-storyline material.

It seems that switch reference markers are also used to mark the major discontinuities which hold between distinct narrative episodes (Stirling 1993: 114, citing Roberts, Payne and Woodbury). Thus for example in the Papuan language Amele, a DS morpheme may be found on the first verb of a new episode even if there is continuity of subjects of verbs across the episode boundary. And in the North American language Chickasaw, switch reference is marked on initial connectives; thus *haatakot* is the SS and *haatakō* is the DS version of a 'then'-type connective which is used at the beginning of groups of sentences – the DS version is used if there is a major change of location or time between groups, in other words at an episode boundary.

Thus one formal device, switch reference, achieves a range of functional effects within a narrative – establishing 'aboutness', differentiating the storyline from the non-storyline, and indicating episode boundaries. This multiple functionality of formal devices is characteristic of the exploitation of linguistic form for literary functions.

7.6   Summary: the storyline

The storyline of a narrative is a sequence of clauses which represents a sequence of events. In addition to the storyline, the narrative also contains other material, most obviously information about circumstances, which is most commonly found at the beginning of the narrative but may also be interspersed throughout the story more generally. Clauses which express the storyline are often distinguishable from clauses which express non-storyline material: the former are typically higher in transitivity and may have distinctive word orders; in both cases there may be functional reasons for these correlations. Within the storyline, the narrator may make some characters more prominent than others, and various structural possibilities including transitivity choices, incorporation and word order placement can be used as ways of controlling participant prominence. A characteristic of the storyline is that it changes, and various kinds of change can be communicated by various linguistic means, some highly coded and others less so. In the next chapter we will look at major changes in the storyline, involving the division into episodes, and at ways in which the boundaries of episodes are indicated.

7.7   Further reading

On kinds of clauses see the chapter by Longacre in Shopen (1985). On Labov's approach see Labov and Waletzky (1967) and the final chapter of Labov (1972). On Hopper and Thompson's notion of transitivity see Hopper (1979) and Hopper and Thompson (1980); see also Kalmár (1982). On transitivity and gender see Mills (1995). On word order and a complex theory of storyline structure see Longacre (1990). On continuity in a narrative or other discourse see Halliday and Hasan (1976), Chafe (1980), Givón (1983), Hobbs (1990) and Contini-Morava (1987, 1989, 1991a, 1991b). On the function of word order alternations in narrative see the chapters in Downing and Noonan (1995), several of which are cited in this chapter. On speech in a narrative see Basso (1986). On point of view (one kind of continuity) see Simpson (1993). For textbook surveys of areas of narrative analysis not covered in this book see for example Fowler (1977), Leech and Short (1981), Toolan (1988) and Montgomery et al. (1992).

7.8   Exercises

(Exercises based on longer narratives in other languages can be found in chapters 8 and 9.)

7.8.1   *The Cuckoo-Penners: an English story from Somerset*

Instructions

(a)   For each of the 21 sections, characterize it as high or low transitive (if possible).

(b)   Is there a correlation between a section being high transitive and its being part of the storyline (i.e. a narrative clause)?

(c)   Indicate where the tenses shift in this story (e.g. involving the historical present tense), and where the aspects shift (specifically, where progressive *-ing* forms are used). Try to explain these shifts (and are they related to one another?).

(d)   Comment on the use of parallelism in this story: what functions does it play?

Text

Divided into 21 sections, with one or two verbs/clauses to a section:

 1 *Round April 15th they hold Cuckoo Fair Day down to Crewkerne,*
 2 *'cause when cuckoo do come, they begins to think about putting in the
    'arvest.*
 3 *If 'e come early, they get a good 'arvest,*
 4 *but if 'e come late, well, then they don't 'ave much chance.*
 5 *Well, the Crewkerne wiseacres, they put their 'eads together,*
 6 *and they say,*
 7 *'Well if us kept cuckoo, us 'ud get more 'n one 'arvest in one year.'*
 8 *So they outs,*
 9 *and they vinds a young cuckoo in a dunnock's nest.*
10 *Well, they veeds 'en*
11 *and while they keeps 'en ved and 'appy,*
12 *the rest of the Crewkerne men, they builds a 'edge right round 'en.*
13 *'Now',*
14 *say they,*
15 *'Us'll 'ave three 'arvests this year.*
16 *Look 'ow the 'edge be a-growing!'*
17 *Cuckoo were growing too.*
18 *Well, the 'edge grew nice and 'igh,*
19 *and the cuckoo grew 'is wings,*
20 *and 'e flied nice and 'igh.*
21 *And 'e went!*

(Note: *'en* = him, *vinds* = finds, *ved* = fed. Told by L. Wyatt to Ruth L. Tongue in 1913 in Somerset, England; anthologized in Briggs (1970: A2:51 and 1977: 55), with the title 'The Cuckoo-Penners')

7.8.2 *Three anecdotes from an American autobiography*

The texts for this exercise are three extracts taken from a written unpublished autobiography dealing with the narrator's family (her mother came from Russia) and her own childhood in America.

Instructions

(a) For each story, distinguish storyline clauses from orientation clauses, commenting on any clauses where this distinction is difficult to make.

(b) Comment on the placement of orientation clauses relative to the storyline clauses. How do the orientation clauses contribute to the effect of the storyline clauses?

(c) Comment on the internal order of orientation clauses: what effects arise, for example, when you reorder them?

(d) The first two narratives both comment on the fact that they are stories. What is the purpose of this, and why are these comments placed where they are in the texts?

Texts

(a)

There was one story about family life in Russia. The kitchen was big, lots of time was spent there. There was a big stove for cooking and for warmth. There was a large shelf above the stove, a person could rest there or sleep there, especially when not feeling well, and keep warm and cosy. The story goes that the girls would climb up and down and play there, and one day Mother's twin Sylvia fell off the shelf and hurt herself very badly. She was sick a long time and as a result, it was thought that because of this, Sylvia was different from her twin, and from my recollection, they were different. Mother was taller, quicker, more accomplished. Both of them are no longer living. My Mother Eva died January 20, 1980, and my Aunt Sylvia quite a few years later.

(b)

About a year later, my Mother, Eva, her twin sister Sylvia and sister Vera, after long preparation were ready to join Louis. The girls were about 16 to 18 years old, were outfitted with handmade shoes and wool suits. Sylvia was the most careful, so she carried the small amount of money they had with them. They were young and pretty and ready for this adventure, though fearful. Their father Simcha took them by train to the point of embarkation, and saw them onto the ship. My Mother Eva told stories of the journey – it was long, about 30 days, crowded, most everyone got seasick but some sailors took pity on the three pretty sisters and got them special food and fruit. Sometimes they permitted the girls to go on deck, where there was more space and fresh air. Sylvia had the money in her high shoes, and would dole it out very frugally. Mother told me that to get a nickel for oranges you had to stand Sylvia on her head and shake her. The girls stuck together and eventually the arduous trip was over. They were met by Louie who had made all the arrangements and went to New Haven by train immediately.

(c)

The garden was special, all of it Mother's doing. She had a green thumb and loved her vegetable patch. She spent a great deal of time with tomatoes, cabbages, beans, lettuce and cucumbers. There were canning times, and jelly and jam making and lots of pickling. Mother's sauerkraut, which was kept in a large crock smelling of spices, and her pickles were legendary. I remember one incident when Clare and I decided that Mother had made a mistake in putting all those cucumbers in glass jars and we corrected this when she was out. We took all the jars out of the cellar, opened them and replanted cucumbers, worked hard and were pleased with ourselves. When Mother came home, we proudly showed her how we had saved the cucumbers. There was plenty of screaming, we couldn't understand why we were punished.

8 Narrative Episodes

8.1 The marking of episode boundaries

Episodes are narrative constituents which are characterized by their internal continuity in participants, time and location, and distinguished from one another by discontinuities in these components. There are two kinds of implication for the linguistic structure of narratives across episode boundaries. The first implication is that linguistic form might be used to signal a break between episodes, not just by marking a boundary but more specifically by marking a discontinuity of a specific kind. Thus the discontinuities discussed in the previous chapter might be interpreted not simply as discontinuities in some aspect of the narrative (such as main participant) but more specifically as a break between distinct episodes of the narrative. The second implication is that the break between episodes might have consequential effects upon linguistic forms, such that these must accommodate to the discontinuity and hence special things must be done at episode divisions.

It can be difficult to distinguish these two implications; in many cases, a particular linguistic form can be interpreted both as the consequence of an episode division and also as a marker of the episode division. An example of such a paired explanation in the North American language Chipewyan comes from Scollon (1985). Episodes begin with a connective, either *ʔɛkúʼ* or *kúʼ* (both meaning 'so, then'). *ʔɛkúʼ* is found at the beginning of major constituent boundaries, such as the beginning of the core narrative; *kúʼ* is found at the beginning of smaller constituents such as minor episodes. Scollon comments that the latter is a clipped version of the former; they may underlyingly be the same, but performance patterns may clip the marker in subordinate episodes. Thus the difference between the two connectives is partly a consequence of discontinuities of different sizes, as reflected in performance and possibly then reflected in the phonological form of the words; but it is also possibly a conventionalized pattern of use such that one connective conventionally signals a more major constituent boundary than the other.

The discontinuity arising at major episode breaks (indicated with *ʔɛkúʼ*) in Chipewyan narrative has other consequences relating to pronominals. A subject pronoun is normally optional because the subject can instead be identified by verbal agreement. However, subject pronouns (specifically first and second person) are found most commonly after major episode breaks. Since they are not strictly necessary for the meaning of the clause, we can interpret this use of pronouns as an overt re-establishing of participants at the beginning of a new major episode, and thus as a reflection of the discontinuity between episodes. Scollon suggests that other sequences of pronouns (specifically possessive pronominalizations) which have the same reference are broken at major episode boundaries, as though pronominal reference must be re-established as a consequence of the episodic discontinuity.

In the rest of this section we look at various different kinds of linguistic form which appear to function to indicate the division of the narrative into episodes; most of these are forms which appear at the beginning of episodes.

8.1.1 Connectives as episode-initiators

A 'connective' is a linguistic element which connects one sentence with another (usually with a preceding one). It is often possible to identify a connective in narratives which means something like 'and then'. Connectives may have a second purpose – in addition to connecting sentences to one another, they may also be concentrated at episode beginnings. One such practice is discussed by Ghezzi (1993) for Ojibwe narratives. The connective in question is *ninguting* which Ghezzi translates as 'now presently'. In a narrative she analyses, this is the distribution of this connective relative to the segmental structure; the story can be analysed in terms of its content as consisting of four major episodes (I–IV), each of which contains smaller episodes. N indicates that an episode begins with *ninguting*:

    I
N introduction [begins with *ninguting*; there are three examples of *ninguting* in the first sixteen lines]
    man discovers wife is a manito [an evil spirit]
    man sends the two children away
    man burns manito/wife

    II
N boy receives awl and comb from his grandmother
N   the children hear their manito/mother in pursuit (he throws the awl to stop her)
    the children hear their mother (boy throws comb)

III
N boy receives flint and punk from grandmother
N   hears mother (and throws flint)
N   hears mother (and throws punk)

IV
   the children meet their grandfather Horned Grebe who helps them across
      the river
N mother meets Horned Grebe (and falls into the river).

(Mrs Marie Syrette's narration of 'The Orphans and Mashos', told in 1903–5
to William Jones)

Ninguting is used differently at different parts of the story. At the beginning, it
is used three times within the same basic episode; this initial density is typical
of Ojibwe stories. It is then not used again within that part of the story which
deals with the man and his wife. In the part of the story (II–IV) which deals with
the children, *ninguting* is used at the beginning of most of the episodes; it is not
clear at this level of analysis whether the absence of *ninguting* in two of the
episodes is significant. This analysis suggests two things. First, specific linguistic
forms – here a specific connective – can be used to indicate the beginning of episodes. Second, this use need not be completely consistent. Clues to narrative form
are often used inconsistently; this is what we would expect, if we see narrative
form as something which is communicated. Communication typically involves
the presentation of partial evidence for something and need not be fully explicit.

8.1.2 Hearsay particles as markers of episode boundaries

A hearsay particle is a word which indicates that the eventuality represented by
the sentence is 'hearsay', its truth guaranteed by someone other than the narrator.
Hearsay particles are often translated as 'it is said'. They are discussed in chapter
10; here we see one illustration of the use of hearsay particles to mark episode
boundaries in Lakota stories, based on Rice (1992: 285). Sentences in a narrative
end with a hearsay particle, usually *keʔ* but sometimes *śkeʔ*. Rice suggests that
the phonological shape of the particle, ending as it does in a glottal stop which
causes a momentary cessation of sound, makes it particularly suited to indicating
the end of the sentence, and thus contributes to a strong sense of constituent
structure in the narrative as part of its aesthetic form. The less common particle
śkeʔ begins with an ejective fricative which Rice suggests makes the particle
particularly salient in its sound, and hence makes it suitable as a constituent
boundary marker. The hearsay particle *śkeʔ* is used in three positions in the
narrative instead of *keʔ*: (i) in the first few sentences of the narration and the

last few sentences of the narration, (ii) at the end of major episodes, and (iii) to intensify dramatic events. Here we seem to have a combination of highlighting, exploiting both the phonological possibilities of *ške?* and its choice as the marked form replacing *ke?*, and a conventionalized use of *ške?* at certain structural points in the narrative.

8.1.3   Tense and the marking of episode boundaries

This section presents a use of tense to mark episode boundaries in the South American language Apalaí. Koehn (1976) discusses two Apalaí narratives, the *Frog Legend* and the *Bead Legend*, in the different versions of two narrators. Koehn argues that an episode is defined by having the same setting and participant inventory at beginning and end. Note that this includes but also extends the notion of episode, because it allows the setting and participants to change in the middle of the episode so long as they are restored at the end. This is a conception of episode which fits well with a narrative technique according to which episodes are embedded inside other episodes, as Koehn shows is the case for Apalaí.

Apalaí verbs have a number of different tense suffixes, including *-no* (immediate past), *-ase* (recent past), *-ne* (distant past), and *-ko* (historic past). The historic past suffix *-ko* is found only in narratives which are outside the narrator's experience – for example, in myths in which animals and natural objects have semi-human characteristics – suggesting perhaps that this is thought of as a different kind of time, distinct from the other kinds of past time as marked by the other suffixes. In such narratives, this suffix is found with particular density at the beginning and ending of the core narrative. Here is an example from the ending of a narrative:

xinkutu okohmã-ko	black it-got-dark
okohmã-ko	it-got-dark
oxioxiroh-ko	he-became-feverish
sã xinukutu	next-day black
akuruhtatoh ipunaka	sick very
beH orih-ko	die [ID] he-died

'It became black. It was dark. It was night. He got feverish. Next day by dusk he was really sick. He died.'

(from the *Frog Legend*, told by Coboclo Velho, cited in Koehn 1976: 244)

This tense suffix is also found with particular density at the beginning and ending of episodes in the story, as in the following case, where the sequence of *-ko*-marked verbs both ends one episode (the man's night in the jungle, ending with his returning home) and begins another (the man makes pets of the baby birds):

mame   *apoi-ko* then   grab-them
      kyry apoi-ko   grab [ID] grab
mame   *yto-ko* then   go

'Then he catches them (the birds) and takes them. Then he goes home.'

(from the *Bead Legend*, told by Azuma, cited in Koehn 1976: 245)

Thus *-ko* functions primarily as a tense suffix and secondarily – when used with particular density – as a means of marking episode boundaries.

Koehn notes that there is a correlation between verbs with the *-ko* suffix and ideophones. Ideophones are words which are considered to describe actions by mimicking the action (i.e. similar to onomatopoeia): they are indicated with ID in the translations of the above examples. The ideophone *beH* (= die) is accompanied by *orih-ko*, the verb meaning 'die' with a *-ko* suffix; and the ideophone *kyry* (= grab) is accompanied by *apoi-ko*, the verb meaning 'grab' with a *-ko* suffix. One of the two narrators he studies (Coboclo Velho) uses this correlation between ideophone and *-ko* verb much more extensively than the other narrator (Azuma); Coboclo Velho is in effect using ideophones in combination with *-ko* as a way of strengthening boundary marking.

Koehn notes two further aspects of the use of *-ko*. The suffix is used to mark the first and second part of what he calls a behavioural dyad. The behavioural dyad consists of two statements, A and B; given A, there is a reasonable cultural expectation of B, as in the following example:

pina oema-ko arrow throw-down
kyry kaxi-ko grab [ID] do

'He threw down the arrows and grabbed (the frog)'

(from the *Frog Legend* as narrated by Coboclo Velho, cited in Koehn 1976: 247)

It is of course possible for the two parts of the behavioural dyad to bracket an episode (or the whole narrative), in which case the two functions of *-ko* are combined. Koehn also notes that *-ko* tends to be used with verbs which describe the actions of the main character rather than those of subordinate or background characters; thus it is the main character's narrative which is bracketed as a whole, and episodes which describe the displacement and return of the main character which are particularly likely to be bracketed with *-ko*.

The two narrators differ greatly in their use of *-ko*, even though they tell more or less the same stories. Thus for example in the *Bead Legend*, both narrators present the episodes of the hero getting lost in the forest, but Azuma indicates the getting lost as the beginning of the core narrative (by use of *-ko*) while Coboclo Velho includes it as part of the orientation, before the core narrative begins (by not using *-ko*). And Azuma makes much more use of *-ko* overall in this narrative. A question which we might ask (but cannot answer here) is whether this means that the episodic structure of the two narratives is significantly different, or whether the episodic structure is similar and it is just the marking of the episodes which is different. This question might be answered by further study of this narrative tradition.

8.1.4 *Repetition and parallelism at episode boundaries*

We now see how parallelism (and repetition) can be used as ways of marking an episode boundary. One example of this is provided by the South American language Tojolabal. Brody (1986: 267) says that in addition to fixed phrases which can act as coded markers of episode boundaries, there is also a practice of repetition of a clause at the episode boundary. To illustrate this, Brody cites a section from a narrative; first there is a discussion of what is done with the newborn's umbilica, ending in '*Then it dries*'. Then '*Then it dries*' is repeated exactly, followed by a new narrative episode; the repeated clause codes the boundary between episodes.

In Saramaccan travel narratives from Surinam, each episode (or 'narrative paragraph' as Grimes and Glock 1970 describe it) occurs in a particular place; the episode begins with the hero's arrival there and ends with his or her departure. The beginning of the episode is typically marked by a parallel structure, whereby the first part of the episode is recapitulated or repeated by a clause (which may be the second or a later clause in the episode) which is marked by beginning with the connective *dí* (translated as 'with reference to'). The following is one of the more complex examples cited by Grimes and Glock (1970: 410):

(1) hén-de gó-dóu a-dí-kɔ́ndɛ de-tá-kái kámpu.

(1) Then they went and arrived at the village they call Kampu.

(2) a-dé-áa té-i pasá-a godo hái dí-dán fu-godo gó-n[a]-ɛ́n líba, nóo-yu-dóu a-wan-kɔ́ndɛ de-tá-kái kámpu.

(2) It is not there till you pass by Godo, haul [your boat up through] the falls of Godo, [and] go from it upstream, now you arrive at a village they call Kampu.

(3) naandɛ́ dí-ómi tá-líbi.

(3) Thereabouts the man lived.

(4) dí-dí-wómi gó n[a]-ɛ́n kɔ́ndɛ, a-gó-mbɛ́i wósu d[a]-ɛ́n mamá.

(4) **With reference to the man going to his village**, he went and made a house for his mother.

Here, the recapitulating clause (4) which begins with *dí* (in boldface) picks up material from (1), the first clause in the episode. Note, however, that intervening material such as the identification of 'the man' is also taken into account in the recapitulating clause. Note that the two intervening sentences (2) and (3) are not storyline clauses, but give orienting information; thus (4) is the first narrative clause after (1). The way parallelism works here is for the recapitulating clause to be the first clause in a longer sentence; thus it functions both to mark the beginning of a new episode, and as a transition from the initial description of the travel into the description of actions.

The South American language Kayapó uses repetition as a way of marking transitions between narrative sections. The practice is referred to by Stout and Thomson as sentence-chaining; they give this as an example (Stout and Thomson 1971: 254):

(1) mĩ krã yajà nẽ amũm tẽ nẽ arĩ. (1) He pushed the alligator's head in the water and fled and jumped.

(2) pĩ ʔä mò. (2) Grabbed the tree.

(3) nẽ pĩ o abêr tẽm puro ʔo abi. (3) The recently fallen tree he climbed.

(4) ʔo abi nẽ prõt - nẽ. (4) He climbed and ran.

The chaining here is accomplished by the repetition of the verb *abi* ('climb') in the third and fourth sentences. The function of chaining, according to Stout and Thomson, is primarily to provide a point of departure for the next action; hence it links clusters of actions together. Thus, here there is an unchained sequence of actions, *pushed–fled–jumped–grabbed*, followed by a chained sequence, *climbed–climbed*, which provides a point of departure for the next action, the unchained *ran*. Stout and Thomson suggest that there is also some slight emphasis added to the repeated action; thus again an exploitation of linguistic form is multi-functional in its role in the narrative.

8.1.5 Ring-composition

Finally we consider a practice of marking episode boundaries which is very common in ancient Indo-European (e.g. Greek) metrical poetry. Watkins (1995: 34) calls this ring-composition: it involves a parallelism between a phrase, word or sound-sequence at the beginning of the episode with one at the end. There may in fact be episodes embedded within other episodes in this way; the practice is perhaps reminiscent of that seen in Apalaí. Thus in the Greek text of the

Odyssey, the episode which consists of the recognition between Odysseus and his dog Argos begins with:

an de kuoon kephaleen te ouata kai	The dog lying there raised up his head
keimenos eskhen,	and ears,
Argos	Argos

And the episode ends with:

| *entha kuoon keit Argos* ... | There lay the dog Argos ... |

The repeated part involves *kuoon* ('there'), *kei-* (the verb 'lie' with different inflections) and *Argos* (the dog's name). Watkins comments that this practice of ring-composition, a parallelism between the beginning and the ending of the episode, may be the source of the practice found in Irish poetry (of Indo-European origin) of beginning and ending the whole poem with the same word, phrase or syllable.

8.1.6 Speech and the constituent structure of narratives

We have seen that the constituent structure of narratives can be formally marked by the use of specific kinds of word (such as connectives), or by practices such as parallelism. Where narratives are spoken (as is the case for most of the narratives discussed here), the possibilities of speech can also be exploited to mark narrative constituency. This is the realm of prosodic phonology and includes various kinds of marked intonation and the length of intonation contours, the use of pauses and the length of pauses, the accelerating or decelerating of speech, the use of special speech qualities, etc. One of the interesting questions which arises in regard to the use of speech in narratives is whether the organization of the narrative by syntactic means (e.g. particles, parallelism, etc.) is the same as the organization of the narrative by prosodic phonological means. Thus one of the issues in narrative constituent structure which has engaged analysts of North American Indian narratives is the question of the performer's pauses and whether they are sensitive to constituent structure. Dennis Tedlock's approach to transcription and translation (e.g. Tedlock 1978, 1983) is particularly associated with the idea that the placement and length of pauses is a significant aspect of an oral narrative. In many cases, pauses coincide with constituent structure as indicated by other means; however, where the structure of a narrative as indicated by pauses conflicts with the structure of that narrative as indicated by other constituent markers, we must decide either that one is prior or that there is some kind of counterpoint between the two kinds of structure.

I consider this issue by outlining a discussion by Woodbury (1987) of a Central Alaskan Yupik Eskimo narrative by Evon Mezak, told in about 1972 (USA: Alaska, Nunapitchuk). The genre is *quliraq* (= traditional tale); Woodbury gives the tale the title 'Grandchild and Grandmother'. Woodbury's main concern in his article is to argue for an all-inclusive kind of constituent structure for a narrative which he calls rhetorical structure. Within this he distinguishes five kinds of constituency. In a later article, Woodbury (1992) argues against the hierarchical conception of prosodic phonological structure proposed by Hayes, Nespor and Vogel, and others; however, for convenience, I propose some rough equivalences below. These are Woodbury's kinds of constituency:

- Prosodic phrasing: a constituent defined by an intonation contour. Analogous to the prosodic phonological constituent of 'intonation phrase'.
- Pause phrasing: a constituent preceded and followed by a pause. Analogous to the prosodic phonological constituent 'phonological phrase'.
- Syntactic constituency: i.e. the syntactic constituent structure of the sentence.
- Adverbial particle phrasing: constituents as marked by initial connectives or interjections (as discussed above). This does not clearly correspond to an already existing linguistic constituent and can be seen as unique to the constituent structure of literary texts.
- Numerically constrained form–content parallelism: the hierarchy of constituents counted out into equivalence groups of five and three. This is clearly specific to literary form and not really an adaptation of linguistic form; it is discussed further in the next section.

He then shows that the different kinds of constituency sometimes line up but also sometimes overlap. Larger constituents ('parts' and 'episodes') line up fairly consistently, but smaller constituents may not.

The larger constituents are best defined in terms of the counted hierarchy. The core narrative is in three large groups: the grandson goes upriver, he goes home, and he goes to the *qasgiq* (a ritual building). The first and the third of these groups are each divided into five episodes, each dealing with a different animal. Woodbury argues that in this story episodes tend to correlate exactly with a kind of intonational constituent called an intonational section. An intonational section may begin with a low lead contour or a sudden slowing of tempo; or it may end with an emphatic core contour. Thus intonation helps identify the beginning or end of an episode in the narrative. However, intonational contours function rather differently when it comes to the smaller 'division' constituent of counted structure. The smallest level of counted constituent is the division, typically organized in threes: three divisions constitute an episode. The three divisions can be generalized as a challenge, a response and a result of the response. This is an example from Woodbury (1987: 220):

(PART 1, THE BOY'S JOURNEY; EPISODE 2, HE MEETS THE DUNLINS)

semantic divisions	a pause at the end of each line	intonational groups
(1)	*Tuamte=llu,*	lead
	ayagturaqerluni ceremraagnek tekituq.	core
	Ik':ikika amllerrarluteng!	core
(2)	*'Aullu=wa=i! Aullu=wa=i!*	exclamatory lead
	Ciunemni uitanrici!	exclamatory core
	Aa tua=i,	exclamatory lead
	pisqekum –	
	pisqekumci ꞈtaūgaam piniartuci!'	exclamatory core
(3)	*Tua=i tayima.*	emphatic core

'(1)   Then again / going a little ways further he came upon two dunlins (a kind of bird). / Boy there were lots everywhere!

(2)   "Watch out! Watch out! / Don't you be in my way! / Hey, enough now / but when I – / when I tell you you will carry on some more!"

(3)   And so they were gone.'

In the above example, there are three intonational groups. The first consists of a lead contour (with little or no final fall in pitch at the end) followed by a core contour (ending in a steep fall in pitch). The second group consists just of a core contour. The third group is complex, being made of three sub-groups, each with its own core; based on Woodbury's explanation of a complex group, we can assume that this is a group because of two factors – (a) the intonational parallelism which pairs the two exclamatory sub-groups, and (b) the emphatic core which outweighs the two earlier cores to create a single group from the three sub-groups. The intonational groups do not correspond to narrative divisions – though as expected the episode as a whole corresponds to an intonational section (marked by a final emphatic core contour).

Woodbury interprets the relation between divisions and intonational groups as follows. First, he suggests that there are two unmarked (i.e. expected) cases: either one division corresponds to one intonational group, or one division is made of several intonational groups (as is the case for division (1) above which corresponds to two groups). Then he suggests that the third possibility, where several divisions are grouped together into one intonational group – as above, where (2) and (3) are grouped together – is marked and as such carries a special communicative value. It is common in the story for a division 2 (a command) to be grouped together with a division 3 (a result); Woodbury suggests that 'apparently this reinforces the interpretation of the grandson's orders and the animals' obedience as a linked action-and-response pair'. Since this narrative as a whole is about the grandson's ability to control the animals' behaviour by his commands, unlike the weaker shamans of his village with whom he competes at the end, this special cohesion between his action and the animals' response is appropriate to the theme.

8.2 Pattern numbers

One of the characteristics of episodes is that they may fall into sets, with parallelism between the parts, and with a counting out of the parts. This applies also to characters in a story, who may be organized into twos, into threes, etc., as well as to other objects. Dell Hymes (1992: 93) has argued that the counting of episodes is used extensively in North American (Indian) narrative traditions, such that whole narratives are structured according to numbers which reflect culturally significant numbers. Where episodes or other constituents in a narrative are counted, the organizing principle is called (by Hymes) a pattern number.

Where a number is culturally significant, such that the culture counts things or happenings into a typical number, we similarly say that it is a (cultural) pattern number. We saw examples of dualistic thinking – the organization of the world by the pattern number two – in chapter 6, where we also saw that dualistic thinking is reflected in formal parallelism. Many cultures organize themselves by pattern numbers. Thus the North American Lakota classify their universe according to the pattern numbers four and seven. Four is the pattern number according to which nature (including human nature) is divided, and seven the pattern number according to which culture is divided. Taking four as an example, there are four directions, four seasons, four stages of life, four kinds of living thing, four phases of a plant, four cardinal virtues, etc. (Powers 1986: 128). These pattern numbers also pervade Lakota narratives; thus in his discussion of the Lakota story *White-Plume Boy*, Rice (1992) shows that it is organized into four episodes, each composed of four events (of variable length).

Hymes argues that North American narrative traditions (as well as other traditions) tend to make use of pattern numbers in pairs, a phenomenon which he calls a double correlation. Typically, a narrative tradition will use either four and two or five and three as pattern numbers. Thus the Ojibwe story outlined at the beginning of this chapter is built in fours and twos; there are four major episodes, and of these the last three each contain two smaller episodes. Four things are thrown in the way of the mother, to stop her, and this sequence of four is grouped into two parts. Characters are grouped into pairs: man and woman, brother and sister, grandfather and grandmother. The double correlation of three and five can be seen in the Central Alaskan Yupik Eskimo story analysed by Woodbury (1987), as seen in the previous section. After a short and formulaic opening, the storyline as a whole can be organized into three macro-episodes:

Grandson goes upriver
Grandson goes home
Grandson goes to the spirit lodge (the *qasgiq*)

The first and third macro-episodes are considerably longer than the middle episode, and are both organized into five episodes. Each episode is internally consistent in participants, involving the grandson as hero and (usually) a pair of animals; the five episodes differ in which animals are involved, but the sequence of animals is the same in the first and third macro-episodes. Thus in the first macro-episode, the journey upriver, the grandson first meets two ptarmigans, then meets a flock of dunlins, and so on; in the third macro-episode, where the grandson is in the spirit lodge, he first calls on the ptarmigans to appear, then the flock of dunlins, and so on. Within each of the five episodes, there are three eventualities, showing that the three-and-five pattern extends below episode level to control also the pattern of clauses. Thus each episode in the journey consists of (1) the meeting of hero and animals, (2) the hero saying something, (3) the animals leaving. (An episode from this story is quoted in full above, where I consider the performance structure of the story and its relation to the pattern number organization.) Five and three, the pattern numbers by which this Eskimo story is organized, are found elsewhere in the organization of the culture. Three is associated with repetitions in other arts, such as dance and songs, and is reflected in some ceremonies which count days into threes. Perhaps more central to the culture is the pattern number five, which can also be understood as composed of four plus one. In Central Alaskan Yupik Eskimo culture, four is the number of non-completion and five the number of completion, a pattern considered to be represented in the structure of the hand with four fingers but five digits. This is reflected in the narrative, where the fifth encounter – with wolves – is both different from the others (the wolves are significantly more threatening as animals) and also brings the two macro-episodes and eventually the narrative to a close; in a sense the encounter with the wolves is the 'thumb' which brings the counting of the hand's digits to completion.

Where constituents are counted out, there are various sequential possibilities which arise, as Hymes has shown in many of his analyses (e.g. Hymes 1987b: 51). With a pair of units, the first can be complication and the second resolution, or they might be the starting and ending of an action. With three units, we might find a structure of onset, ongoing and outcome; this is clearly true for the three-part structure of the Central Alaskan Yupik Eskimo story discussed above. The double correlation of two and four as pattern numbers enables the two to be combined as a pair into the four. Hymes suggests that in the double correlation of three and five, two threes are combined into a five by sharing one unit:

```
onset  ongoing  outcome
                 onset        ongoing   outcome
                   ↑
                 PIVOT
```

The outcome of the first sequence is the onset of the second, combining together to make five. Hymes calls this shared unit the pivot. It can be seen in a Kalapuya (North-west USA) narrative by John B. Hudson in which the hero Coyote releases water dammed up by the frogs, thus making water available to all of humankind (Hymes 1987b: 54). The third and final episode in the narrative has this structure:

	onset		Coyote puts his hand into the water to drink
	ongoing		While drinking, Coyote puts his hand where the water is dammed
PIVOT	outcome	onset	When he stops drinking he gets up and scoops the dam aside
		ongoing	The water escapes
		outcome	Coyote says 'All the time water will be everywhere'

Here the pivot is an event which combines the ending of the drinking with the beginning of the releasing of the water.

While some literatures use a single system, either five and three or four and two, in other literatures, two systems are in existence and either may be chosen for a narrative. It is also possible in some literatures for the two systems to be systematically combined within a single text. One function of such mixing might be the general function of marked style, that of highlighting; thus Hymes argues that John B. Hudson uses pairs to intensify the action within the basically three-and-five organized story about Coyote and the frogs. Hymes also discusses two literatures in which the two systems are matched to gender. In the North American language Tillamook, narrative sections involving women are counted in four and two, while narrative sections involving men are counted in five and three. In the North American language Tonkawa the match is reversed. It is worth noting that narrators may not be aware that their practice is governed by pattern numbers. In the North American Chinookan languages, the cultural pattern number is five, while the narrative pattern numbers are a pair of five and three; Hymes reports that Chinookan narrators were aware of the presence of fives in the narrative (presumably because of its salience as a cultural pattern number) but not of the threes. Similarly, a storyteller in an English-language narrative tradition, Charlotte Ross, was aware that her narratives were organized in threes (the familiar pattern number of 'Anglo' cultures) but was surprised to be shown that they were also organized in fives.

8.3   The narrative situation

8.3.1 Bracketing the story

The performance of verbal art often constitutes, or is part of, a cognitive displacement of performer and audience away from their immediate reality into some other reality, which might be imaginary, in the past, in some other place, or in a spiritual realm. One of the problems which must be solved by this practice is how to relate the narrated world to the actual world in which the narration takes place. This section considers some strategies by which this can be done.

In many literatures, narratives have conventional beginnings and endings, which constitute what we might call 'brackets' for the narrative. Thus English fairytales may begin with *once upon a time* and end with fixed phrases like *and they lived happily ever after*, which relate the time of the narrated world to the time of narration. In some cases, the convention for beginning a narrative is to indicate that a journey is under way; thus Kayapó narratives may begin with 'We *were going to the other village*' (Stout and Thomson 1971: 251). Yokuts (California) stories often (but not always) begin with '*people were living there*' or '*so-and-so was there*' or '*so-and-so was going along*'; in contrast, in the neighbouring culture of Western Mono, the story starts by reference to time, with '*in olden times*' or '*long ago*' (Gayton 1964: 379). Thus the conventional ways of bracketing a story vary, though the basic practice is widespread. The conventional beginning and ending of a narrative can be very complex in its construction, involving speech and gesture, some parts meaningful and other parts not, and can involve the audience in conventional action as well as the narrator.

This can be illustrated with the performance of the Zuni (South-west USA) genre of *telapnaawe*, narratives set in the past before the period of European contact, and considered to be fictional. They are told only at night and during winter. According to Tedlock (1983: 160), the *telapnaawe* has its own specific formulaic frame. First the narrator loudly says *so'nahchi* and the audience replies *eeso*; then the narrator loudly says *sonti inote* (stretching out the second word) and the audience again replies *eeso*. Of these words, only *inote* is found in the ordinary language, meaning 'long ago'. Then the narrator gives an orientation, listing the major characters and where they live, beginning loudly and then dropping to a normal speaking level to continue into the story. To conclude, the narrator may make an etiological statement (i.e. a statement of how things in the modern world came to be as a result of the past action of magical beings as described in the story). Then he says *Le'n inoote teyatikya*, meaning 'this was lived (or happened) long ago', and then *Lee semkonikya*, stretching out the first word which means 'enough' – the second word is no longer current in the ordinary language, but Tedlock says that it may once have meant 'the word was short'. During these final fixed phrases the audience begins to stir and then rises and stretches: a formulaic gesture on the part of the audience which is their contribution to the formulaic ending.

Brackets need not be constituted only by fixed and conventional material. Labov and Waletzky (1967: 40) show that the ending of the narrative (their 'coda') can return the narration to the context of narration in various ways. One is to distance the speaker from the narration by referring to the narrated world as *that*; some of the final clauses they quote are '*That was one of the most important*' and '*And that was that*'. Another is to introduce some kind of bridging incident; in one narrative a central character is referred to in the final clause – '*And I see him every now and then*'. A third way to return is to refer to the narrator himself, linking his role as a character in the narrative with his present status – '*I quit you know. No more problems.*'

8.3.2 *Engaging the audience*

The previous section outlined some ways in which a storyteller can link the story to the storytelling context at the edges of the story, at the beginning or the end. It is also possible for a storyteller to link the narrated and narrating worlds in the course of the story. Wiget (1987) shows that gesture is one way of achieving this, in a discussion of Helen Sekaquaptewa's telling of a Hopi (South-west

USA) story. Among these are gestures which Wiget calls iconic gestures, meaning gestures which dramatize the action. These gestures are not inevitably links between the narration and the context but the narrator develops them during the performance such that they take on this role. An early stage of gesture in the narration is a winnowing action, within her own body plane, mimicking the action described by a song at that stage. In some sense, the narrator's body is being drawn into the representation of the narrated world. However, the gestures become larger as the narrative progresses, and eventually the narrator reaches out into the audience's space and touches the audience; such an action is one which mimics the plucking and placing of feathers, and by touching the audience members they are implicitly transformed into characters. This can be seen both as a drawing of the audience and the context of narration into the narrated world, and at the same time as an anchor between the narrated world and the distinct world of the narration.

8.4   A narrative analysis of *Ashey Pelt*

To conclude the two narrative chapters I now analyse a short English-language fairytale, referring to issues raised in these chapters. The story is included in Katharine Briggs's collection of British folk narratives (Briggs 1970: A1: 137, and 1977: 20); it was first published in 1895, and is a representation by M. Damant of a story 'told me by a woman now living, a native of Ulster, aged about 60'. It is worth noting that, like much of the vast amount of material gathered in the nineteenth century (in English and other languages), we cannot be sure how precisely this story represents what the original storyteller said, and how much of it was revised by the contributor and other intermediaries. Also typical is the fact that the storyteller's name was not recorded and reproduced, a decision which tends to de-emphasize her individual skill in shaping this story in just this manner, and instead she is seen as typical of her community as though the story came from the community rather than from her as an individual: this misses the point, since skill is not in the typical aspects of the story but in the individual formal structuring of the story. By a detailed formal analysis, we can begin to reconstruct the narrator's skill in organizing the text.

   In laying out the story I have ignored paragraphing in the printed text, and have divided the text into numbered sections mostly corresponding to independent clauses (with clauses coordinated with *and* treated as independent). Letters indicate what I propose to be episodes within the narrative; I justify this division in the analysis (where I suggest that the text is organized to bring out this episodic division).

1	A	*Well, my Grandmother she told me that in them auld days a ewe might be your mother.*
2		*It is a very lucky thing to have a black ewe.*
3	B	*A man married again,*
4		*and his daughter, Ashey Pelt, was unhappy.*
5		*She cried alone,*
6		*and the black ewe came to her from under the grey-stone in the field,*
7		*and said,*
8	C	*'Don't cry,*
9		*go and find a rod behind the stone*
10		*and strike it three times,*
11		*and whatever you want will come.'*
12	D	*So she did as she was bid.*
13		*She wanted to go to a party.*
14		*Dress and horses all came to her,*
15	E	*but she was bound to be back before twelve o'clock*
16		*or all the enchantment would go,*
17		*all she had would vanish.*
18	F	*The sisters, they didna' like her,*
19		*she was so pretty,*
20		*and the stepmother, she kept her in wretchedness just.*
21	G	*She was most lovely.*
22		*At the party the Prince fell in love with her,*
23		*and she forgot to get back in time.*
24		*In her speed a-running she dropped her silk slipper,*
25		*and he sent and he went all over the country, to find the lady it wad fit.*
26		*When he came to Ashey Pelt's door he did not see her.*
27	H	*The sisters was busy a-nipping and a-clipping at their feet to get on the silk slipper,*
28		*for the king's son he had given out*
29		*that he loved that lady sae weel he wad be married on whaever could fit on that slipper.*
30	I	*The sisters they drove Ashey Pelt out bye to be out of the road,*
31		*and they bid her mind the cows.*
32		*They pared down their feet*
33		*till one o'them could just squeeze it on.*
34		*But she was in the quare agony*
35		*I'm telling you.*
36	J	*So off they rode away:*
37		*but when he was passing the field, the voice of the auld ewe cried on him to stop,*
38		*and she says,*

39   *says she –*
40   K   *'Nippet foot and clippet foot   Behind the king's son rides,*
41   *But bonny foot and pretty foot   Is with the cathering hides.'*
42   L   *So he rode back*
43   *and found her among the cows,*
44   *and he married her,*
45   M   *and if they live happy, so may you and me.*

The narrative can be organized into episodes: B is the initial episode in which the girl is visited by the ewe, D is her reception of the clothing, G ranges from the party to the prince's attempt to find her, I describes the sisters' actions, J is the departure of the prince with one of the sisters; together these form the complicating action to which the final episode L is the resolution. Three of the episodes (D, J and L) begin with *so*, which might be taken as a connective marking an episode beginning. There is also a general tendency for subjects to come at episode beginnings (most strikingly, *the sisters* and sometimes *she*). Episodes are divided from one another by stretches of represented speech (C, K) or orienting material (F, H); the only apparent exception is the division between I and J, but here the clause *But she was in the quare agony I'm telling you* functions somewhat as both orienting material and even as the represented speech of the narrator (hence the explicit *I'm telling you*).

The placement of the two internal orientation sections is particularly note-worthy. F could in principle be put anywhere in the story but by its placement here it serves to separate the preparation for the party (D) from the party itself (G) and the crisis which occurs there, and thus draws attention to the structure of the narrative. Notice also that the clause *she was so pretty* is part of the orientation and then *she was most lovely* is part of the storyline (she was perceived to be the most lovely at the ball as a consequence of her preparations). This parallelism might function to alert the reader to the fact that the second description is not to be taken as general background information but is a specific stage in the narrative; it also may be alerting us to a change of point of view, such that it is specifically the prince (the character in main focus in G) who perceives her as lovely. The second internal orientation section is H. It has an elaborate structural function, as follows. Section G is about the prince while section I is about the sisters, and thus the sections are coherent as regards the characters in main focus, but in temporal order there is an overlap with the prince arriving at the cottage after the events described in I. The orientation section H refers to and reproduces this inverted temporal order (the clipping is described before the order which causes it) but in an orientation rather than a storyline section. Note for example that the verbs *a-nipping* and *a-clipping* are relatively low in transitivity (progressive) relative to *pared* (perfective) in the I section. Thus this orientation section operates to clarify the structure of the story at this moment.

The complicating action of B–J is resolved in L, when the prince discovers and marries the girl. Notice that this resolves not only the general development of the story and all parts of the storyline, but also resolves the action which initiates the story – the inappropriate marriage of the father is resolved by the appropriate marriage of the girl. The resolution is drawn attention to by two devices which are used only here. The first is the repetition in J of *she says, says she* and the second is the song in K. Note also that clause 3 *A man married again* is less transitive (no object) than clause 44 *and he married her*, which corresponds to the difference in significance (3 lies somewhere between orientation and storyline and hence is relatively backgrounded, while 44 is the crucial ending to the storyline and is highly foregrounded).

The coda for the story is a conventional ending, perhaps modified by this storyteller or perhaps conventional (we could find out by looking at other stories in the same local tradition); it is worth noting, incidentally, that storytellers are quite capable of modifying conventional beginnings and endings in idiosyncratic ways. The beginning (A) refers to conventional wisdom, which will then be exemplified by the story (the black ewe coming from under the grey-stone is by implication the girl's dead mother); notice that one thing achieved by this is to make the story something other than a decontextualized fairytale of the kind familiar from books of fairy stories. Instead the story is integrated at some level into cultural knowledge (in an uncertain manner, since we cannot be sure whether the appeal to the grandmother is an appeal to reliable tradition or a dissociation of the narrator from that tradition – or perhaps ambiguously both). This raises the question of pattern numbers, and interestingly while there is a fragment of a 'three' number (*strike it three times*) the story can perhaps best be interpreted as organized in pairs (though this is only rather weakly manifest in comparison with some narratives). The characters and objects are organized in pairs, most obviously the ewe as opposed to the cattle (it is worth asking whether there is a conscious reduction from the threes found in other versions of this story: we have *dress and horses* but no carriage, and the number of sisters is never specified). In the language there is overt pairing, most obviously in the song. And the six basic episodes can be interpreted as organized in pairs (B + D as action and result, G + I as action and result, J + L as false departure and true departure). Note, however, that if we treat the complex overlap between G and I as indicating some kind of unifying episode, we can also see this episode as the pivot between two threes (B + D + G/I and G/I + J + L). This example perhaps illustrates one of the problems of identifying pattern numbers in texts, which is that it is sometimes a somewhat blurry inference about the text rather than being coded into it.

There are, of course, many other things which one could do with the story (such as assessing its intertextual relationship with other versions of the story, which might be assumed as shared knowledge by the storyteller). For example,

we could point to the presence of an apparent evaluation at the end of I, which
signals a possible apparent ending to the story in J – but since most hearers will
be sufficiently knowledgeable either about this story, or at least the genre, all
will recognize this as a fake resolution (preceded by a premature evaluation),
and thus as a further element of narrative elaboration to teasingly delay the real
evaluation and resolution.

8.5   Summary

Many narratives are subdivided into episodes, which can be taken as constituents
of narrative form. Episodes arise to some extent from the organization of the
narrated events: thus a shifting of personnel, or place, or time in the narrated
events will coincide with a shift in episodes. But at the same time, episodes have
their own formal presence, as is illustrated for example by the phenomenon
of pattern numbers: this arises as part of the formal structure of the narrative
and is not simply a reflection of what is happening in some fictional world.
A narrator may communicate this organization into episodes as part of the
organization of the story, even when the narrator does not consciously decide
on a particular episodic division. Like all kinds of communication, this communication takes place at a risk, and hence it is possible for interpreters or an
audience to disagree about exactly how the narrative is divided into episodes.
Linguistic form offers evidence of the division into episodes, but rarely encodes
and thereby determines that division. Thus the division into episodes which is
communicated by the narrative must be inferred by the audience.

   In this chapter we also considered some of the situational aspects of narration, including the leading into and out of the narrative, the shaping of the
narrative in speech, and the use of gesture. The next chapter is devoted to a
fuller exploration of the context of verbal art, as something which is performed.

8.6   Further reading

V. Hymes (1987) on constituent structure in Sahaptin narratives provides an
exhaustive overview of means of marking constituent structure, both by linguistic
forms and by modes of speech. On tense shifts as a marker of episode boundaries
in English narratives see Wolfson (1979) and Schiffrin (1981). Woodbury (1992)
discusses further the relation between prosodic structure and narrative structure

(which he calls thematic patterning). Urban (1986) shows that parallelism between narrative constituents is fundamental to an understanding of a Shokleng myth. D. Hymes (1992: 92–9) summarizes the current findings on pattern numbers.

Anthologies which contain articles on North American Indian narratives (which are where much of the most interesting linguistic work on narrative has been done) include Sherzer and Woodbury (1987), Swann (1983, 1992), Krupat (1993) and Swann and Krupat (1987). Sherzer and Urban (1986) is a useful anthology of South American literatures. *Coming to Light* (Swann 1994) is an anthology of North American literature, primarily stories, translated and discussed by linguists. Hymes's (1981) collection '*In vain I tried to tell you*' is indispensable. Tedlock's views on speech and narrative structure are represented by Tedlock (1983). Tedlock (1978) is a collection of translations of Zuni narratives which attempt to reproduce aspects of constituency as indicated by features of speech. A useful and very large collection of British folk stories is Briggs (1970, with a selection as Briggs 1977).

8.7 Exercises

Note: chapter 9 includes an exercise on the performance of a Madi story, which includes questions drawing on material from chapters 7 and 8.

8.7.1 *The Demon of Ganish: a Burushaski story*

Instructions

(a) Divide the story into episodes.
(b) How does the language of the story relate to the division into episodes?
(c) Is there a pattern number, and if so what draws our attention to its presence?
(d) Comment on the use of *séi báan*: what kind of word is it, and how is it used?
(e) Comment on the splitting of the clause between lines 14 and 17, with other material placed in the middle.
(f) Does the story show any signs of a macro-structural organization into abstract, orientation, complication, evaluation, resolution, and coda?
(g) Comment on any other aspects of the linguistic structure of the narrative which seem particularly relevant to a literary-linguistic analysis.

About the language

Burushaski is spoken in Pakistan, and is a language isolate (i.e. it has no known relatives); the cited story was told in the town of Hunza. The people are called Burúsho (pl.), Burúshin (sg.). Lorimer (1935) is a collection of Burushaski texts and translations, and is one of three volumes, the others being a grammar and a vocabulary. The text was revised for this book by Professor Bertil Tikkanen in a new orthography.

Text

0   *Gánishe   Bilás*
    Of-Ganish ogress
    The Demon/Ogress of Ganish
    (told by Jemadaar Imaam Yaar Bèg to D. L. R. Lorimer, 1923–4)

1   *Cshórum zamaanáulo Gánishulo hin bilásan bom,   séi báan.*
    In-early   times   in-Ganish a   demon she-was they say
    'It is said that there was a demon in Ganish in early times.'

2   *Hitháane   nuúruṭ, hin   ními ke iné iṣhúçhu bom.*
    In-a-certain-place living   a-person went and him eating   she-was
    'If a person went to where she lived, she ate him.'

3   *Altán níman   ke hin phat   ne   hin iṣhúçhu bom.*
    Two   they-went and one released made one eating   she-was
    'If two went, she ate one and released the other.'

4   *Iskén níman   ke altán núṣhun hin phat   échu bom.*
    Three they-went and two   eaten one released she-was-making
    'If three went, she ate two and released the third.'

5   *Béeruman dening qháa akhílaṭe   buṭ sis   uṣhúmo.*
    Several   years for   in-this-manner many people she-ate
    'For several years she ate many people in this manner.'

6   *Ité zamaanáulo Shon Gukúr biṭán   bam.*
    At that-time   Blind Gukur the-wizard he-was
    'At that time, Blind Gukur the wizard was living.'

7   *Inéer qhabár   étuman.*
    To-him information they-made
    'The people told him about it.'

8   *Étasar   Gánishar ními,   séi báan.*
    On-making-(information) to-Ganish he-went, they say
    'When they informed him, he went to Ganish, they say.'

9 *Han díshan bilúm; íte iík   Latoó Har   bilúm.*
One a-place it-was; it   name Lato Ravine it-was
'There was a place; its name was "Lato Ravine".'

10 *Téele hin bilásan bom.*
There one demon she-was
'There was a demon there.'

11 *Íne sis   ushúchu bom.*
She people eating   she-was
'She was eating people.'

12 *Shon Gukúre han chhumáre gílian óotimi,   séi báan.*
Shon Gukur   one of-iron   a-peg made-them-make, they say
'Shon Gukur got them to make an iron peg, they say.'

13 *Nóotan   íne bilás   dam ne —*
Having-done-so he demon spell having-made-(on her)
'Having done so, having made a spell on that demon —'

14 *Téele han búnan bim;   íse iík   Guyó Bun   séi bam.*
There one boulder it-was; its name Guyo's Boulder, they were-saying
'There was a boulder there which they used to call Guyo's boulder.'

15 *Guyó sénas híran bam;   íne   basíulo bim.*
Guyo to-say a-man he-was, in-his garden it-was.
'There was a man named Guyo, it was in his garden.'

16 *— Isé   búnulo iné bilás gíli mudélimi.*
    in-that boulder that demon peg he-hit-her
'— he pegged that demon down into that boulder.' (? perhaps to be
interpreted as: he forced her into the boulder through his spell and then
struck the peg into the boulder to lock her up)

17 *Isé bun   darúm qháa bi,   áma íimo díshcsum,   iílate*
that boulder now   up-to it-is, but from its-own-place, on-its-edge
    bim,   yáare qha   wáli bi.
    it-was, below down it-has-fallen
'That boulder still exists, but it has fallen down from its original site which
was on the edge of a cliff.'

18 *Chhumáre gíli darúm qháa bi.*
Of-iron   peg now   up-to it-is.
'The iron peg still exists.'

8.7.2   *How Amamqut became a cannibal: a Koryak story*

Instructions

(a)   Divide this text into episodes, based on content. You might find it useful to organize the story into a few major episodes, each of which is divided into smaller sub-episodes.
(b)   Name any words or other features of the language which typically mark episode boundaries.
(c)   Is there any evidence of pattern numbers in this text? Look both at the patterned organization of characters and events and at the patterned organization of clauses.
(d)   Can the narrative be divided into narrative macro-constituents along the lines suggested by Labov and Waletzky (see 7.1.1)? Does the narrative use the strategy of evaluation?
(e)   Koryak is a language which has noun incorporation (see 7.4.2). In this narrative, words which refer to body parts are sometimes incorporated into verbs and sometimes not; try to explain why a particular option is chosen in each case.

About the language

Koryak is a member of the Chukotkan group of Paleosiberian languages spoken in Kamchatka and north-east Siberia. The chief figure in mythology is Quy'qinnaqu, the Raven, who also figures in many myths of the American North-West. Bogoras (1917) includes a selection of narratives. The transcription is a slight modification of Bogoras's original, provided for this book by Andrew Spencer, and follows IPA except y = j, ñ = ŋ, g = ɣ, č = ʧ, diacritic ʾ after a consonant indicates palatalization.

Text

How Amamqut became a cannibal
(told by Anna to Waldemar Bogoras in the village of Kamenskoyein, December 1900)

1   *quyqınnʾaquwgi vañvolaike.*
    Raven's people were living.

2   *amamqutinak vʔiyai   gamatalen.*
    Amamqut   Grass(-Woman) married her.
    (i.e. Amamqut married Grass-Woman)

3 *amamqutinak ewañ   ñawɪsˑqatıñ, 'mınnutılatısˑqiw'.*
Amamqut   he said to the woman 'Let us go into the open country!'

4 *gewñıvolen 'qayiñun quyaakuyičvanñıñ'.*
She said   'It seems you are going to do wrong'.

5 *ewañ   'tʔayaqak   ačivan   qayem'.*
He said, 'Why should I? This time I shall not.'

6 *notaitıñ   qanñıvoykin yatikın   elvau*
To the open country he is going, he comes, wild reindeer
   ganmılenau.
   he has killed them.

7 *vʔayuk   gatčewñıvolen   ənñʔaan, gek, vʔayuk   ñeetčıñ,*
Afterwards he passed a night thus,   oh   afterwards twice,
   vʔayuk   amñut.
   afterwards all the time.

8 *ñanyen vʔiyai   əlletı   galqallin, tatkagıtñıyıkıñ.*
That   Grass-Woman to her father went,   to Root-Man.

9 *galalin,   gawasˑvılin yınootñenqo,   maleta gawasˑvılin.*
She came,   looked in   into the vent-hole, quietly looked in.

10 *eʔen Enin   tatkagıtñıın gakaggupəlen   akilʔač amamqutinak*
her (father) Root-Man he split him in two just now Amamqut
   ñano   yuykınin   matalʔan   čininkin.
   that one he was eating him father in law his own.
   (i.e. she saw that Amamqut had just split her father Root-Man in two, and
   was now eating him)

11 *ñanyen vʔiyai   nekaitı   notayaitıñ*
That   Grass-Woman somewhere into the open-country house
   gatalqıwlin.
   entered.

12 *yalku   qolla qai-mımič, qolla aiak   opta*
In the inner room one small louse, one in the storehouse also
   qai-mımič gayoolen.
   small louse she put in.
   (i.e. she put one small louse into the inner room, and another into the
   storehouse)

13 *to, Ennu qoyqınnˑaqoyıkaitıñ   gagıntawlin.*
Oh, she   to the Big-Raven's house fled.

14 *qoyqınn·aqoyıkıñ*   *galalin.*
To the Big-Raven's house she came.

15 *ewañ,*   *'yaqikın*   *amu*   *amamqut'.*
she said, 'What happened to I do not know Amamqut'.
(i.e. she said 'I don't know what happened to Amamqut')

16 *gatuiveñlinau.*
They constructed a raised platform.

17 *gek, amamqut nutayak*   *galalin, ewañ*   *'vʔiyoi'.*
Oh, Amamqut to the country house came, he said 'Grass-Woman!'

18 *yayačıkoitıñ*   *ewañ*   *'a'*
From the house someone said 'Ah?'

19 *aiačıku*   *galalin*   *gemlañ ewañ*   *'vʔiyoi'.*
to the storehouse he came, again   he said 'Grass-Woman!'

20 *aiačıkoitıñ*   *ewañ*   *'a'*
From the storehouse someone said 'Ah?'

21 *ñanyaiñanu qai-mımčıt*   *valomeke.*
Those   two small lice he heard them.

22 *ewañ*   *'ñiyuq*   *tayıñtinuñikin'.*
He said '(curse)! She is deceiving.'

23 *ewañ*   *'qayem ñano-van mınutñanawge'.*
He said, 'Not   those   I shall be able to eat them'.
(i.e. 'I shall not be able to eat them')

24 *vʔayuk*   *gininilin.*
Afterwards he appeared.

25 *uivelqak*   *gañalqıwlinau.*
On the platform they were sitting.

26 *ewañ*   *amamqut 'qayem ñanu mınutñanau.*   *čemyaq*
He said Amamqut 'Not   those I shall be able to eat. Really
    gatuiveñlinau'.
    they constructed a platform.'

27 *galalin*   *čılınmılulatikın.*
He came, with-tongue-licked.
(i.e. he began to lick with his tongue the supports of the platform)

28 *quyqɪnnˑaqunak gathata* čɪlɪɪl *čvitčuykɪnin* ɪmɪñ *čimatikɪn*
Big-Raven   with hatchet tongue he cut at it all   he is breaking
  gatte yɪčičatikɪnin   *gaɪnnɪmčačaivɪlin.*
  hatchet he is examining it it is with broken gums.
(i.e. Big Raven cuts at Amamqut's tongue with a hatchet, and breaks the
hatchet; when he examines the hatchet it is jagged like the broken gums
of an old man)

29 *vaʔak*   *aʔal opta ganˑčičalin*   *opta* ɪmɪñ *gaɪnnɪmčačaivɪlin.*
Afterwards axe also he examined also all   it is with broken gums.
(i.e. by implication Raven tries again to cut the tongue with an axe, breaks
it, and finds again that it looks like the broken gums of an old man)

30 *quyqɪnnˑaqu ewañ 'vʔiyoi*   *čininkin ənin yaqu-ənki'.*
Big-Raven   said 'Grass-Woman own   child what of that.'
(i.e. he tells Grass-Woman to feed Amamqut with Amamqut's own child)

31 *ganayalin*   *kmiñɪpil čɪkɪtñɪk.*
She dropped small son into the mouth.

32 *gatamtɪvalen.*
He spat out bones.

33 *quyqɪnnˑaqunak gewñɪvolen*   'yaqu-ənki   qenavalom.*
Big-Raven   he said to him 'what of that, listen to me!

34 *činit ənñaʔan qitɪ*   *qenavalom uwik vetha-qonom qnuñvon'.*
Since like that you are, listen to me, self just now   consume.'
(i.e. Raven tells Amamqut to eat himself)

35 *vʔayuk*   *uwik gañvolenau vagɪtčɪnu*   *yukka.*
Afterwards he he began   toenail-ends to eat.
(i.e. Amamqut begins to eat himself, starting with the toenail-ends)

36 *to,*   *vʔayuk*   ɪmɪñ *gɪtčat uwikinat ganulinat*
There, afterwards all   legs his own he consumed them,

37 *vʔayuk*   *uwik vʔayuk*   *mɪngɪt vʔayuk*   *čenpɪnmɪn.*
afterwards torso, afterwards arms, afterwards shoulders.

38 *vʔayuk*   *am-elʔeineyɪ amqamatčan gatčɪlin.*
Afterwards mere neck,   mere throat became.
(i.e. Amamqut is reduced to being just a neck or throat)

39 *wʔətču*   *gavʔilin.*
Then only he died.

40 *ganqangawlin   tito-on.*
    They burned him after a long time.

41 *v?ayuk   vos·qeti   guyetveiñelenau   v?ayuk*
    Afterwards in the dark they were with the burnt out fire afterwards,
       yiniañawgutinti   gewñıvolenat
       Yinianawgut and her sister they said
       'mıntomñalqiw'.
       'Let's stop up the smoke-hole!'

42 *gatomñalqiwlinat   v?ayuk giwlinat   gewñıvolenat,*
    They stopped the smoke-hole then   they said, they said,

43 *'če   assakinat   yatiki.*
    'Ah, those two of the other day are coming!

44 *qulumtičitalat   tiwgak   ənin kmiñıpil*
    They carry something on shoulders, it seems, his small son
       gaqulumtilin'.
       he carries on shoulders.'

45 *v?ayuk gewñıvolenat, 'milhon qanalagatča'.*
    Then   they said,   'Fire   bring out'

46 *gamilhınalinat   ginalvalinat.*
    They carried out the fire, they fed the fire.

47 *we?tču   galqıwlinat.*
    They only entered.

48 *qonpə   gankawlin iwak   'mınnutılatıs·qiw'.*
    Altogether he ceased to say 'Let us go to the open country!'

49 *qonpə   am-yayak   vañvolaike, qonpə   gankawlinau*
    Altogether, only at home they stay,   altogether they ceased
       galñıl   menkaitı   yas·qanñık.
       in all directions wheresoever to want to walk.

50 *am-yayak   gana?linau   ənnaniku.*
    Only at home they became (staying) in one place.

51 *ačč̌oč̌.*
    That is all.

9 Performance

Many literary works have two modes of existence: as texts and as performances. The text is just the words. The performance is the words, said in particular ways and perhaps accompanied by gestures, in a particular place and time and performed to an audience in a cultural context. This book up to now has concentrated for the most part on the literary work as a text; this is appropriate to the book's project which is to investigate specifically the linguistic form of literary works, which is best revealed by extracting the text from its context of performance. However, in some cases we may fail to understand certain aspects of the linguistic structure of a text precisely because we fail to think of it as something which is performed. This chapter focuses on the performance of texts in their sociocultural context.

9.1 Speech styles and ways of speaking

We begin by considering the classification of linguistic conduct into types, using the terms defined by Dell Hymes in an important essay on 'ways of speaking' (Hymes 1989). The terms 'speaking' and 'speech' are intended here to cover all kinds of linguistic behaviour, whatever its modality – whether oral, written, or secondary oral (broadcast, recorded, etc.).

A person's linguistic behaviour can be classified into speech styles, with each speech style characterized by its own set of formal features: vocabulary, syntactic structures, phonological rules, phrasal phonology, modifications of the voice, etc. The features can be constant throughout the style, in which case they are called a stylistic mode (tone of voice would be an example). Or they can be a linear structuring of the speech, in which case they are called a stylistic structure; thus the organization of a narrative into complication and resolution can be thought of as a stylistic structure. Most of the aspects of literary form which have been presented in this book are stylistic structures: metrical and parametrical rules, parallelism, and narrative structure.

The speech styles of an individual are to a large extent drawn from the community or communities in which she or he lives, and may well be subject to an emic classification: that is, the community will often have its own names for many of the speech styles (though speech styles can also exist without being explicitly recognized and named). This internal recognition of speech styles is important for an understanding of how literature functions, and in particular is important for understanding the notion of performance, as we will shortly see. However, there are likely to be certain features of even a recognized speech style which the speaker will not be aware of. This is not uncommon for complex literary speech styles which are performed very accurately by performers who may have little explicit knowledge of what they are doing.

Speech styles are associated with particular contexts. If a speech style is typical of a type of situation it is called a register; if it is found only in a particular situation (rather than a general type) it is called a situational speech style. A register is associated with some repeatable kind of typical context, while a situational speech style might be called emergent: it appears in a particular situation, and perhaps may appear only once and not be repeated. A context which is of particular interest in the study of literature is the context of genre. Texts (and their performances) can be classified into genres, and a genre may have its own genre speech style. For example, Greek tragedy and Greek comedy are distinct genres which are associated with distinct speech styles: the formal features which differentiate them include for example different rules about what constitutes a 'word boundary' for the purpose of word-boundary rules (see 5.1.1); thus the genres are differentiated by a stylistic mode.

A particular speech style is likely to be associated with a particular context. A speech style considered in terms of its context is called a way of speaking; a way of speaking is both the formal features of the speech style and the meaning which that speech style has for members of the community. An important characteristic of many speech styles, however, is that they can also be used outside their characteristic contexts. Speech styles which can 'travel' or be 'borrowed' in this way are called significant speech styles. For example, parody may work by embedding a tragic speech style into a comic genre. More generally, the possibility of picking up and re-using either whole styles or component features of styles is the basis of the extensive intertextuality which is enabled by performance, and which is discussed below.

9.2   Performance

9.2.1   *Performance as a way of framing a way of speaking*

The term 'performance' is used in two distinct ways in linguistics. Noam Chomsky first used the term to name linguistic behaviour as opposed to the linguistic system (called 'competence') which underlies that behaviour. In its other meaning, deriving from work by Dell Hymes and Richard Bauman, 'performance' refers to one among various possible ways of framing a speech style. Performance in this sense describes a subset of the kinds of linguistic behaviour characterized as performance by Chomsky. It is Hymes's and particularly Bauman's notion of performance which we explore in this chapter.

For Bauman (1984), performance is a 'frame' (a term borrowed from Gregory Bateson and Erving Goffman). A frame is a set of guidelines which contribute to the interpretation of an utterance; the frame is signalled either by certain formal features of the utterance or by the utterance being recognizably of a type which has the frame conventionally associated with it. Performance is a frame whereby a speaker takes responsibility towards an audience for the correct, complete, and skilled realization of a particular way of speaking. The performer enters into a contract with the audience whereby the performer undertakes to speak in a way which realizes the features of the way of speaking. The audience is thus both enabled and permitted to evaluate the performer's speech in terms of how well it realizes the features of the way of speaking; this requires explicit knowledge on the part of both performer and audience of some of these features. The 'contract' may be implicit or (as in some kinds of poetic competition) explicit.

It is typical for the performance frame to be associated with ways of speaking which we might call 'literature', such as the songs, poems, and stories which have the formal features described in the earlier chapters of this book. Bauman's article (and the book derived from it) is called 'Verbal art as performance', and it is an appeal to think of verbal art as being defined not primarily in terms of its formal and functional features (as Jakobson did) but in terms of its interactional or social features, as something which is defined fundamentally by being performed. Bauman cites Jakobson's characterization of the poetic function as involving reflexivity whereby the text draws attention to its own form (for example, by parallelism, meter, salient narrative structure, etc.: see 1.4.1). If performance involves the performer explicitly committing himself or herself to realizing the formal features of a way of speaking, then on the one hand literature offers a plentiful supply of salient formal features, and on the other hand, the process of drawing attention to form both meets the requirements of performance and also carries out the poetic function. It is the drawing of attention to formal features of the text which enables the performance/text to be evaluated – and evaluation, along with notions of cultural value, is a fundamental feature of 'literature'. Bauman suggests that performance not only requires the audience's special and intensely focused attention (because they must evaluate), but at the same time rewards this work put into the performance by the audience by offering them 'the present enjoyment of the intrinsic qualities of the act of expression itself'. Ways of speaking which are not performed, in contrast, are rarely liable to be considered as literature: these might include technical instructions, trial records, letters, lectures, and so on. In these texts, the fact that form is itself not emphasized and the heavy emphasis on content together relegate these texts to being considered non-literary.

We have seen the term 'evaluation' used before (see 7.1.2), by Labov and Waletzky (1967) to describe a narrator's evaluation of his or her own narrative relative to the context in which it is told: what Labov and Waletzky call the evaluation is the drawing of the audience's attention to the point of the narrative, the thing which makes it worth telling. This is an evaluation by the performer of some component of the text, rather than an evaluation of his or her own performance. Thus the term 'evaluation' means something different in narrative theory, where it describes the narrator's own act, from its meaning in performance theory where it describes the role of the audience. However, there is a relationship between the narrator's evaluation of the narrative and the audience's evaluation of his or her performance of the narrative, in two senses. First, the narrator's act of evaluation is itself likely to be a key of performance; the more overt the evaluation, the more the narration is being keyed as a performance (Bauman 1984: 26). Second, the narrator's evaluation is paralleled by the audience's evaluation in the sense that an audience will evaluate a story in part on whether it has a point for them.

A way of speaking can be framed in various ways, of which performance is only one. Thus for example a story can be performed, but it can also be reported or summarized in a way which does not constitute full performance (and in these forms for example may lack a narrator's evaluation). Performance has a special status as a frame, since it is evaluated by an audience, and so it is important to cue evaluation by identifying the performance frame. A frame is identified by the presence of keys – features which code or at least give evidence for the presence of a particular frame. The performance frame can be keyed by many kinds of feature, a few examples of which are:

- Certain kinds of beginning. For example, the performer may begin with a particular fixed phrase, or by stating the title of the text, or may begin by apologizing for her or his lack of skill.
- Certain kinds of ending. For example, the performer may change posture very ostensively to indicate an ending, or may directly address the audience to ask for evaluation.
- Certain structural features of the text. For example, a high degree of patterning, as in meter, parallelism or pattern numbering in a narrative, may constitute keys of performance.
- Certain contextual features. In performance (in comparison for example to the rehearsal frame) the performer may be dressed in a particular way; or

performance might be keyed by happening in some special place or at some special time.

A text belongs to a way of speaking by virtue of having certain features. Those features must be made manifest in performance so that the audience can evaluate the performance as adhering to the rules of the way of speaking. In principle, the features which indicate the way of speaking can themselves become keys of performance. Consider for example the use of patterning of episodes in some narrative traditions, where the hero for example has groups of five parallel experiences (as the hero does in the Eskimo narrative cited in 8.1.6). This patterning might be a feature of the way of speaking. In some ways of framing the way of speaking, such as summarizing the story, the patterning might be somewhat perfunctory (perhaps all parts of each episode are not fully repeated); the patterning is present but not fully present. In contrast, full performance might involve full repetition of all the parts: this completeness of the patterning might constitute a key of performance. Thus the key of performance is a kind of accentuation of the feature of the way of speaking which is being performed.

Performance requires a way of speaking with agreed features; only then can it be evaluated. However, in practice two kinds of further complication emerge. First, while some ways of speaking may be universally recognized within a culture, and their features agreed on, other ways of speaking may be subject to disagreement or uncertainty for the members of the culture. One possible development of this would be a situation where an elite part of the audience shares knowledge of the way of speaking but the general audience does not; performance of this way of speaking is thus an act which reinforces the social divisions within its audience. The second complication is that the features of the way of speaking may emerge only in the course of the performance itself: these are called emergent features. For example there is a Malagasy (Madagascar) way of speaking called *kabary* which is associated with marriage (Keenan 1973). This is a way of speaking which is performed and which is extensively evaluated, but where there is no unified sense of what the conventions of *kabary* are; instead the conventions which define the correct performance of this way of speaking emerge differently in different contexts of performance. The *kabary* takes place in steps, each step initiated by a performer who represents the bridegroom's family, and then judged by a representative of the bridegroom's family in terms of whether it is a correct performance of *kabary*. Since members of the culture differ on what constitutes a correct performance of *kabary*, this must first be negotiated between the parties before the performance begins. Since in general no final agreement is reached, the way of speaking is therefore not fully defined before the performance begins and continues to be defined by the evaluator as the performance progresses.

9.2.2   *Other ways of framing a way of speaking*

Ways of speaking can be framed in various ways. Thus quoting is a framing of a way of speaking: I can quote from a song or I can perform the song, as two alternative ways of framing it. One of the more interesting possibilities as regards frames is that there are various other frames which are related to the performance frame. One such frame is rehearsal for a play (Bauman and Ritch 1994), which involves at some level the same way of speaking – the script is the same, and hence many of the formal features defining the way of speaking are the same. But rehearsal lacks the keys of performance. Another frame is reporting: it is possible to tell a story without performing it, by cutting out repetitions, songs, and so on. It is not uncommon for stories told to cultural outsiders to be reported rather than performed; sometimes there are cultural reasons for this. For example, a narrative in the Hopi genre called *tuuwutsi*, which includes stories about Coyote, can only be fully performed in the season of frost (i.e. the winter); however, it might be told in a truncated and summarized form, a perfunctory performance, at some other time, for example to an outsider visiting in the summer. Hymes uses the term 'performance in a perfunctory key' to describe these kinds of realization of a way of speaking in a way which does not manifest all the features of the way of speaking (Hymes 1981).

The notion of 'performance in a perfunctory key' suggests that it is possible to think of frames not as distinct from one another but as related to one another along a sliding scale so that there are degrees of performance. Gossen (1989) discusses a three-way division of ways of speaking in the Chamula society of Central America. The three divisions are *loʔil k'op* 'ordinary speech', *k'op sventa šk'išnah yoʔnton li kirsanoe* 'speech for people whose hearts are heated', and *puru k'op* 'pure speech'. 'Ordinary speech' is a way of speaking which is not performed. 'Pure speech' is a way of speaking which is fully performed, and is keyed by extensive parallelism. 'Speech for people whose hearts are heated' is considered to be mid-way between these other two ways of speaking; it is keyed by parallelism and other formal structure but to a lesser extent than 'pure speech'. Thus we can consider it to be a way of speaking which is less fully performed than pure speech; it is evaluated less stringently, for example.

The degree to which a way of speaking is performed might also vary over its extent. A story might be summarized (performed in a perfunctory key) but at a climactic moment might be fully realized with all the features of the way of speaking, and thus this climactic moment is a 'breakthrough into performance', as Hymes puts it. As an example of this, Hymes (1981: 89) describes an incident which occurred during his work with Philip Kahclamet in the 1950s. Kahclamet described how a Chinook orator spoke to the people of his village in favour of the traditional religion; Kahclamet started by describing the context, and then presented the speech in English translation, but at the very end of his presentation he 'broke through into performance', taking on the role of the orator and speaking in Chinook for the last two sentences, which ended '*K'aya t'unwit amduXa*' (= 'Don't believe in them' – *them* being the doctrines of Christianity).

9.3 Intertextuality

9.3.1 *Text and context*

Once we start to consider a text in its context, as something which is performed, we may find ourselves beginning to doubt whether we can in fact isolate a 'text', or whether this is some artifact of our approach and is not true to the material. This doubt is the basis for some influential developments in literary criticism. For example, Roland Barthes' move in *S/Z* (Barthes 1974) from structuralism to poststructuralism at the end of the 1960s was a move from a confident analysis of the text as a stable structure into an attempt to represent the text instead as a flowing, unstable object, a bundle of codes which unravels as we study it. This trend away from the text can also be seen in the work of some folklorists, for example in the writings of Dennis Tedlock on the basis of the text in performance and associated problems of how to report and transcribe such a text (see Tedlock 1978, 1983).

Barre Toelken provides an example of the embeddedness of a text into its context (Toelken 1979: 93–103). The setting is a Navajo home in Utah, visited by Toelken and two other non-Navajo anthropologists in the evening in late December in the 1970s. Toelken says that the evening as it develops is itself a development of earlier occurrences in the household, and will in turn develop into other occurrences; the outside observers interact with the household over a stretch of time, and influence the events in certain ways, but there are no sharply defined temporal boundaries. Toelken's first observation is that the children are playing and the mother is weaving; the visitors are then asked whether they are Mormons, which they are not, and subsequently offered coffee, a drink which is acceptable to Navajos but not to Mormons – hence the coffee begins to draw the visitors into the situation. While the coffee is being prepared, one of the visitors initiates a string game, encouraging the children to create representations with string; at this point a performance is beginning to emerge, since the Navajo string games are governed by cultural principles, undertaken by someone who must perform them properly, and may be evaluated. Now the father enters the performance by making strings which represent constellations, one of which is unrecognizable to the visitors and so the father takes them outside and shows them that it is the Pleiades; the father then comments obliquely on the visitors' ignorance as an illustration of the moral danger of 'getting lost' through not having a proper knowledge of the world. After a silence of ten minutes, the tape recorder is turned on and the father performs a story about *Ma'i* (Coyote); the story tells how Coyote throws his eyes too high into the air – where only birds should be able to see – and so loses them because they get caught in a tree. This story continues the general theme of health, initiated after the visitors' revelation of ignorance of the constellations. The father ends the story by looking at the visitors for the first time and saying *'now let's hear that back'*. The story is replayed, and the father discusses it and the genre of Coyote stories in general, ending by saying that the story is about not fooling about with one's body, and that the children will be warned away from doing so by hearing the story: *'You people are teachers, but I think you don't know these things.'* Then he begins another story.

Embedded into this situation is a story about Coyote, which could in principle be told independently, summarized (as it was here), translated, published in an anthology, etc. – in other words, we could extract a text from the situation. However, if the text were to be reproduced without any discussion of the situation in which it emerged – as is the case for many published 'folk stories' – we may lose the possibility of understanding, both of its own meanings and in its interconnection with other cultural practices. This is why many linguistic anthropologists have argued that we must understand verbal art by looking at it in its context.

At the same time, however, it appears that one of the consequences of performance is precisely to encourage the extraction of a text from its performance. Bauman and Briggs (1990) argue that because performance requires the explicit use of certain formal features, this explicit use brings the text into sharp relief against its context. As Jakobson pointed out, the formal features of verbal art draw attention to the form itself, to the structure, and hence to the text. Bauman and Briggs call this process 'entextualization' – the creation of a text as a distinct entity standing out from its context, a process which is achieved by performance itself. In a later article, they extend this approach to genre (Briggs and Bauman 1992). Where a speech style has known features, this is because texts in the past have had these same features: the currently performed text and these earlier texts belong to the same genre, and performance makes this explicit. In some cases, it is exactly the same text which is being recontextualized by a particular performance (e.g. in the performance of a play); in other cases it is a text which overlaps with the current text by virtue of sharing generic features. Thus performance, by drawing attention to the generic features of the text which is performed, also places that text into a context of previous other texts: thus performance leads to a situation of intertextuality. Once a text is put into a context of other texts, we can see it in two ways: both as something which has generic features and hence as part of a tradition, and as something which has unique features which differentiate it from those other texts and thus as distinct from the tradition. The closeness of the performed text to some previous text (i.e. its intertextuality) can be maximized to give an effect of 'tradition' or minimized to give an effect of 'innovation'.

9.3.2   *Oral formulae*

We have been looking at performance as a way of thinking about how texts are framed. Now we consider a very influential approach to performance which sees it as having consequences for how texts are composed. This approach is Oral-Formulaic Theory, which has its classic formulation in Albert Lord's *The Singer of Tales* (Lord 1960). Oral-Formulaic Theory developed as a theory about a particular way in which performers composed epic songs, and was based on fieldwork in Yugoslavia. The performer composed the text as he sang, with his composition to some extent determined by circumstances (e.g. audience reaction). However, while the text as a whole was new each time, it always included pieces of text which had been used before: the composer apparently drew on an inventory of re-usable textual building-blocks, to aid him in his rapid on-the-spot composition of the text. Lord draws particular attention to the fact that the text is governed by metrical rules; in principle, this increases the difficulty of composition, but Lord showed that the fragments of text which were recycled were designed to fit neatly and easily into the meter. Thus these fragments, which Lord called formulae, aided not just in composition but more specifically in metrical composition. For example, here are two lines taken from different parts of a Serbo-Croatian text in the epic decasyllable meter:

Vino pije   Kraljeviću Marko
wine is drinking Prince   Marko
'Kraljevic Marko is drinking wine'

Govorio   Kraljeviću Marko
spoke   Prince   Marko
'Kraljevic Marko spoke'

The formula in both cases is *Kraljeviću Marko*, where *Marko* is a name and *Kraljeviću* is a title meaning 'prince'. The important point for Lord is that the formula fits neatly into the metrical template for the line. Recall that the metrical template for Serbo-Croatian epic decasyllable is ten syllables with a caesura required between the first four syllables and the last six syllables (see 5.1). This formula is six syllables long, and thus can be used as the ending of a line which

can then be completed with four initial syllables. Thus the formula supplies not only re-usable text but re-usable text which already solves the problem of composing metrical lines. The use of oral formulae in composition has various possible functions. In addition to improving the possibilities of fluent and rapid composition, resulting in a smooth and even performance, oral formulae also allow the performer to adapt to the shifting dynamics of the performance situation, including the effort which the performer is prepared to devote to composing a particular section of text and the effort which the audience is prepared to devote to listening to it.

Lord's account of Serbo-Croatian performance was an account of a contemporary performance practice. What made his approach particularly radical was his proposal that these performers might be typical of composer-performers anywhere and at any time. Thus composer-performers might always use oral formulae. Lord then suggested that the argument could be reversed, such that if we could find a text of uncertain origin which contained oral formulae, we could use the presence of these formulae to argue that the text must have been composed in performance. In particular, he argued that this was true of Homer's epic poems the *Iliad* and the *Odyssey*, which can be shown to contain repeated metrical formulae and hence can be argued to have been composed in performance (rather than composed in the written form in which they have come down to us). Whallon (1969: 87) illustrates this argument in an analysis of the use of formulae in the *Iliad* and *Odyssey*, and shows that the three most frequent formulae (ranging from about eighty to about forty instances) which pair the name Odysseus with another word are:

dios Odysseus   'godlike Odysseus'
polymeetis Odysseus   'much-planning Odysseus'
polytlas dios Odysseus   'much-suffering godlike Odysseus'

The metre of the *Iliad* and the *Odyssey* is dactylic hexameter, which has the following pattern of metrical positions (see 5.2.1):

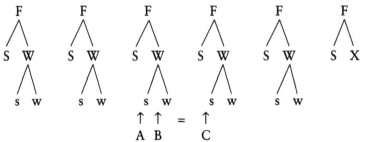

caesura in one of the places indicated with ↑

(S matches a heavy syllable, and either W matches a heavy syllable or s and w each match a light syllable: this gives two possible foot structures, ¯ ¯ and ¯ ˘ ˘.)

Each of the three formulae is metrically suited to be the last part of a line. In all three cases, the pattern of syllable lengths fits the end of the line. In the first case, the pattern fits the quantitative requirements of the last two feet:

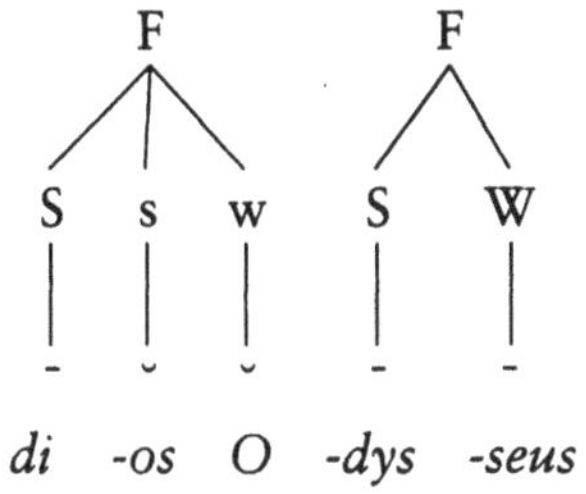

In the second case the text fits the metrical template of the end of the line, and also has a caesura falling in one of the required positions (C above):

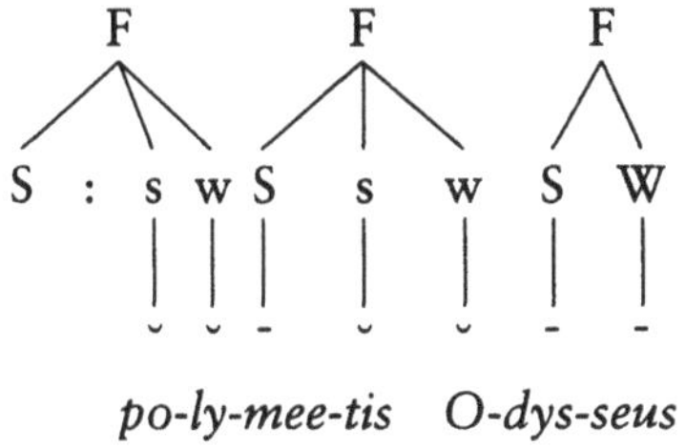

In the third case, the text fits the metrical template of the end of the line and also has a caesura falling in one of the required positions (B above):

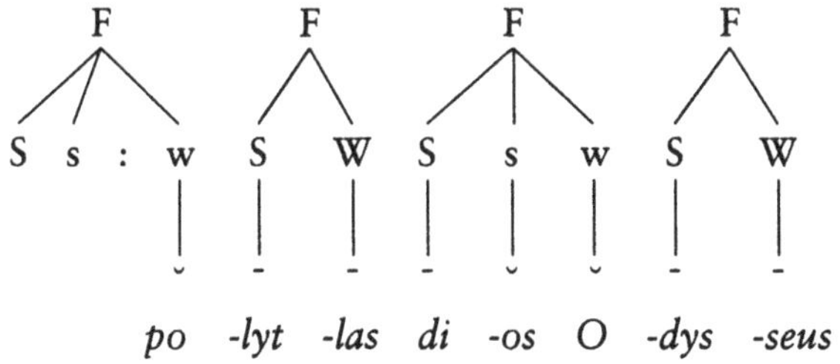

Note that the fact that these are prefabricated regular line-endings fits with the general principle that the cadence is regular.

The notion of the formula as seen in metrical poetry of this kind has been extended in various ways. First, it is extended from syllable-based traditions such as Serbian or Greek to the accent- and alliteration-based tradition of Old

English. Second, it is extended to non-metrical traditions, such that a re-usable sequence of words in any kind of text might be considered a formula. Third, it is extended to include discontinuous sequences of words, such as the parallel word-pairs of Hebrew poetry. Thus Whallon (1969) argues that the word-pairs which are realized in lexical parallelism in the Hebrew scriptures (6.1.2) constitute an equivalent to oral formulae, a resource for the construction of poetry.

We now consider the extension of the notion of oral formulae to the alliterative verse of the Old English poem *Beowulf*. *Beowulf* is governed in part by a para-metrical requirement of alliteration. Whallon (1969) lists over fifty phrases which are used to refer to the hero Beowulf. If the alliterating pattern of the line is in 'b', then he may be referred to as *bearn Ecgtheowes*; thus in this line the a-verse sets up a 'b' alliteration which is matched in the b-verse by the formula:

Beowulf mathelode bearn Ecgtheowes
'Beowulf spoke, the child of Ecgtheow'

If the alliteration is in 's', he may be referred to instead as *sunu Ecgtheowes* (the son of Ecgtheow):

slithra geslyhta sunu Ecgtheowes
'Severe onslaught, son of Ecgtheow'

Thus Beowulf's name is the basis of formulae as are Marko's name and Odysseus's name but in very different metrical traditions. (Formulae are commonly composed in this way, by combining a name with an epithet.)

One of the interesting questions about formulae is whether the grouping of the component parts has any linguistic basis. Since formulae have some role in enabling memorization, we might ask whether linguistic coherence should be a requirement. It seems in fact that it is not. Where formulae are continuous, we find that the parts are probably not a single syntactic constituent: phrases in an appositive relationship (i.e. a discursive rather than a syntactic relationship) are common, as in many formulae which consist of a name and an attribute, as in the examples involving Odysseus above. Along similar lines, Nagler (1974) has argued that formulae in Greek poetry can include syntactic fragments which are not whole constituents. Kiparsky (1976) addresses the syntactic status of formulae head-on by considering specifically formulae which are discontinuous, but then arguing that at a deeper analytical level these are in fact well-formed syntactic constituents. Thus he discusses 'flexible formulae' in Homer's poetry, such as *ookees hippoi* ('swift horses'), which is flexibly realized in various forms, including forms where another word is inserted between these two words.

The analytical side of Oral-Formulaic Theory, with its identification of repeated formulae, has been very useful in the analysis of literature and is widely used; it has particular relevance for the idea of performance as an intertextual practice, as described earlier. However, Lord's early generalizations from Serbo-Croatian practice to all oral literature are no longer widely accepted. As Finnegan (1990, 1992a) in particular has argued, there are many traditions of oral literature where the performer does not compose at the moment of performance; Somali songs and the Sanskrit *Vedas* would be examples of this, both being oral traditions where texts are preserved unchanged between performances. Thus Oral-Formulaic Theory cannot be a theory of all oral literature. Furthermore, while Lord argued that the presence of formulae proved an oral origin for a text, this claim has also been challenged, on the basis that there is no reason in principle why traditions of writing should not also make use of formulae in composition.

9.3.3 *The* kisoko *in Luganda songs*

To conclude this section on intertextuality and formulae, we consider in some detail a unit of song structure found in Luganda songs and called a *kisoko* (the singular is *kisoko*, the plural form is *bisoko*). This discussion is based on analytical work by Susan Kiguli (Kiguli 1996), Peter Cooke, and others (e.g. Katamba and Cooke 1987). The songs in question are improvised, usually around a basic theme; for example, a famous and common song is the song of *Kikwabanga and Ssematimba*, which describes a historical incident where two warriors went to war, and were so confident of success that they ordered a goat to be prepared for their return; however, they died in battle. In performance, any version of the song will contain both some pre-existing material which is typically found in the song and also some innovations. A unit of pre-existing material is a *kisoko*. To illustrate the notion, we'll consider a particular performance of this song by Albert Ssempeke, recorded by Peter Cooke; our discussion draws on Kiguli's work on this text (see e.g. Kiguli 1996). The metrical system for this song and its musical accompaniment were discussed in 4.4.2; the line is divided into two half-lines, a call by the soloist and a response by the chorus (or by the soloist, taking the chorus's part, as here). Either call or response part may be empty of text (but the music is continuous throughout). The performance begins with these lines:

CALL	RESPONSE
Lwendiva kuno ndigenda wa Kaggo When I leave here I will go to Kaggo	*Baana battu, Kikwabanga* My friends, Kikwabanga
Abaali abangi nsigadde bw'omu We were many I am left alone	*Laba Ssematimba, Kikwabanga* Look at Ssematimba Kikwabanga
	Laba Ssematimba, Kikwabanga Look at Ssematimba Kikwabanga

Abasiba	*embuzi basibira bwereere,*	*Baana battu, Kikwabanga*
Those who rear goats	they rear in vain	My friends, Kikwabanga

Abasiba	*enkoko basibira bwereere,*	*Baana battu, Kikwabanga*
Those who rear chickens	they rear in vain	My friends, Kikwabanga

Looking first at the call, the first three half-lines are traditionally found in this song and thus are *bisoko*; the fourth half-line is also a *kisoko* but a more recent innovation which is now generally found in the song. This *kisoko* is a development of the preceding *kisoko*, replacing *goats* with *chickens*. In the response, the half-line *Laba Ssematimba Kikwabanga* is a *kisoko* which is always found in the response part of this song. However, the half-line *Baana battu Kikwabanga* (literally 'children mine, Kikwabanga') is an innovation by Ssempeke, again based on a pre-existing *kisoko*. Thus all of the beginning of the song either incorporates pre-existing textual material (*bisoko*) or improvises by modifying pre-existing textual material; and some of the pre-existing textual material is itself the result of earlier material being modified, and then itself integrated into the tradition.

In this particular performance by Ssempeke, a large part of the text of the song is made either of *bisoko* or of improvisations on *bisoko* (this is not characteristic of all his performances, and may reflect the canonical status of this particular song). To illustrate further, the first line *Lwendiva kuno ndigenda wa Kaggo* ('when I leave here I will go to the Kaggo' – who was a chief who was able to provide solace and protection, particularly to musicians) is a traditional *kisoko*, picked up and modified into a more recent *kisoko* which is now part of the expected text of the song, *Lwendiva kuno ndigenda wa maama* ('when I leave here I will go to mother'). In turn, in this particular performance, Ssempeke further improvises on this *kisoko* to produce a new text, a pair of half-lines which fall in the response part of the text, with an empty call part:

CALL	RESPONSE
	Nze ndigenda wa maama silimba
I	I will go to mama certainly
	Nze ndigenda wa mange anzaala era
I	I will go to mother who bore me and

Bisoko can be taken from one song to another. For example, the half-line *Laba Ssematimba Kikwabanga* might in principle be inserted as an isolated half-line into another song on another topic, but with the same general theme (destruction, pride, etc.), as a way of invoking meanings associated with that theme. *Bisoko* also have a musical dimension: a particular text may be associated with a particular melody, and that melody by itself can constitute a kind of musical *kisoko*: just playing the melody can invoke the text, without the text being spoken.

Bisoko can thus be seen as oral formulae: pre-existing material which is metrical, and which can be inserted into the text in composition while performing. While this can be an aid to composition, however, we would misunderstood *bisoko* if we took this to be their primary function. This can be seen by considering two facts about *bisoko*. First, as Kiguli (1996) shows, *bisoko* are marked in the text first by having a greater than usual amount of alliteration, and second by being incorporated into highly parallelistic structures: thus the hearer's attention is drawn to them. Secondly, the hearers (in a traditional community, familiar with the genre) will be familiar with the *bisoko*. It seems that the *kisoko* functions to invoke traditionally known associations which are tied to the *kisoko*; thus for example the allusion to Kaggo brings with it a whole set of assumptions about the role of the king as protector, particularly in a time of crisis as described by this song. In the period during which the Buganda king was in exile (after 1966), the royal musicians who were able to continue performing were able to covertly communicate meanings relating to the king by the allusive possibilities of the *bisoko*.

9.4   Performers and audiences

9.4.1   *Joint performance*

We now consider some cases where a text is performed jointly by several people. One such situation is where a text is performed by a principal performer and a chorus. King (1981) describes one such case involving the Hausa genre of *waka* which means 'professional song' (Hausa is a Chadic language spoken in Nigeria and neighbouring countries). The song has a primary performer who is the composer-singer who performs the main text (the verses of the song), and a group who constitute the secondary performers who perform the refrain or chorus, a song constituent called an *amshi*. There is a third party: the audience. The *amshi* may remain the same throughout the text, or be varied, or change completely (resulting in several *amshi* within one performance): it is usually a couplet which uses formulae to allude to the content of the song, and thus achieves maximum expressive power in a short span. King (1981: 123) cites the following example from *Bakandamiya*, a praise-song by Narambada:

Gwarzon Shamaki na Malan toron giwa,	fearless one of Shamaki, of Malan, bull-elephant,
baban Dodo ba a kam ma da batun banza.	father of Dodo, not to be approached with triviality

This *amshi* expresses the meanings of the song as a whole: (i) authority and power, adopting the singer's analogy with the elephant, (ii) identity (the father of Dodo), and (iii) the theme of the poem, 'not to be approached with triviality'. (Notice that there is some similarity between the Hausa *amshi* and the Luganda *kisoko*.) At the beginning of the song, the primary performer will usually perform the *amshi* himself, thus expressing the basic meaning which is then collaboratively repeated by the chorus. King's particular concern in his paper is with performances where the secondary performers encroach on the main text, either joining in with the primary performer as he comes to the end of a verse and then continuing into the *amshi*, or taking over from the primary performer to perform the end of the verse themselves. King suggests that the main function of this intervention is to highlight certain parts of the text, marking them as of particular importance to the meaning of the whole. Thus earlier in this song, there is an intervention where the secondary performers take on the responsibility for singing part of the verse (King 1981: 123):

Primary performer:
Ai ga giwa tana abin da takai   Yes, see the elephant about its business

Secondary performers:
ga 'yan namu na kallon ta babu   Observe the lesser beasts who can but
   damar cewa komi   look and make no comment

The theme – that he 'may not be approached with triviality' – is emphasized by the secondary performers when they join in with the primary performer in singing this line.

Choral performance, where a number of people perform in unison, raises some interesting questions. First, in any performance where several individuals perform, they are in effect joining together to take responsibility for correct performance; this might be considered in terms of the meanings of mutuality and solidarity which thereby arise. Second, in practice much choral performance is not strictly in unison. Even where everyone is performing the same text, there may be overlaps, individual errors (or parts where individuals forget what to do), and other disruptions of unison. These may be accidental, or they may in fact be appropriate to the performance; a text may sometimes be deliberately obscured in performance, and one way of doing so is to perform it chorally but out of unison with one another (1.2.1). A third interesting issue raised by choral performance relates to the loudness of the performance (and other elements of 'bigness' such as the visual effect of a large number of performers together). It is possible that loudness – particularly loudness which alternates with the relative quietness of a single primary performer – may have a place in the emotional experience of a performance: loudness has often been one of the components of theories of the 'sublime', overwhelming emotional experiences generated by aesthetic events. Along these lines, Okpewho (1992: 72) describes his hearing of a tape-recorded choral prayer: 'The speed and force of the heavy tenor voices of the performers (all men) was quite captivating.'

A further kind of joint performance might involve two primary individuals. An everyday example of such a performance might be where two people share the narration of a story about an incident with which they are both familiar (usually which they experienced together). Wolfson (1979) discusses the structure of a story told jointly by a wife and husband. Dialogic performance is interesting partly because it illustrates the degree to which two performers are able to co-operate to build a formally well-constructed text, and Wolfson shows that the two performers of this story are consistent with each other in their use of the conversational historical present tense (CHP). As with many English stories, this text alternates between two tenses, both referring to the past – the standard morphologically marked past tense, and the conversational historical present in which the verb is morphologically unmarked (i.e. the same as for present tense) but is used to refer to a past event. Thus 'he went' would be standard past tense, and 'he goes' would be CHP if used to refer to a past event. Wolfson argues that there is no functional difference between the two tenses (i.e. she argues that CHP does not necessarily convey 'vividness' as has sometimes been argued), but instead that the difference is functional only when there is a tense-switch, from past to CHP or from CHP to past. The switch in either direction functions to signal the initiation of a different kind of event (i.e. it is a boundary marker for a new episode or micro-episode). What is interesting about the joint narration of this story is that each participant retains the previously established tense from the previous participant, with a switch occurring only when there is a new event. Thus the jointly performed narration is as consistent as a monologue in the use of this stylistic device.

9.4.2 *Poetic duels*

The above examples all involve co-operation between performers (and audience), but this is not the only possibility in joint performance; it is also possible for performers to compete (and perhaps conflict) with one another in a joint performance. Many cultures have performance-types which can be called poetic contests, where distinct performances by competing performers can be understood as together constituting an overall joint performance. This might for example be a formally arranged competition where two or more poets compete for a prize by performing texts on a particular theme, or it might be a rule-bound exchange of riddles, or of insults. Some written sole-authored texts imitate oral poetic duels, transforming a primarily oral practice into writing; examples include Chaucer's *The Canterbury Tales* or the body and soul debates in Marvell's poetry.

The poetic duel can be illustrated by Bowen's (1989) discussion of poetic duels in the Gayo culture of Indonesia. Many of the ways of speaking which are performed in Gayo society are performed as dialogue. One such way of speaking is *kekëbërën*, the telling of stories, where the principal narrator is accompanied by a secondary performer who 'ratifies' each narrative unit (without contributing storyline material). Another is *sebuku*, ritual wailing whose content is the loss of a girl in marriage, where the primary performer is a relative and the secondary performer is the girl, who responds with a few sobbed phrases. Among these dialogic ways of speaking is a group of ways of speaking classified together as *didong* or poetic duel. Bowen discusses various versions of the poetic duel within the culture and argues that there is a change in the use and form of poetic duels as part of political changes in Indonesia. The older form of the poetic duel, *didong ngerjë*, is a wedding duel which involves two virtuoso performers, each representing a social group (such as a village), and takes place at a wedding. Each performer takes the role of primary performer for around fifteen to thirty minutes, with the other taking the role of secondary performer; then they exchange roles. As the primary performer sings, he walks up and down and his gestures are shadowed and mimicked by the secondary performer, who walks close behind him. The duel is finally resolved through the exchange of riddles relating to the wedding; once a riddle is set which cannot be answered, the performance ends with a winner.

The texts which are performed have certain standard features (i.e. they key the performance of *didong ngerjë*). One such feature is the incorporation of conventionalized cultural knowledge, and allusions to the cultural past, functioning to situate the performance in a continuing culture and more generally representing the performer as a channel for the culture rather than as a creative individual in his own right (though he clearly is this too). A second feature is the extensive use of parallelism; both parallelism and the use of cultural knowledge can be illustrated with the following segment of a text:

Risik-risik risé	joking, asking
ngono-kono kinté	agreeing, proposing
berguru	preparing

The first line describes the informal steps of asking, the second describes the formal steps of asking, and the third line refers to a transition to the wedding. The first line must be followed by the second as a cultural convention; performance of these lines demonstrates the singer's cultural knowledge and thus authority. Within these lines, there is syntactic parallelism, with a reduplicated word followed by a non-reduplicated word in each line. Bowen calls this segment of text a 'head phrase', which will return in elaborated forms later in the text, as part of a larger parallelism within the text. Each performer's text thus manifests a continuity with the past and with the culture. This continuity is manifested also by the essentially co-operative nature of the contest. Both performers conform to rules governing what they do and how they interact with one another. Among the rules for content are requirements that each begins by apologizing for his inadequacies, and the loser of the riddle contest must conclude by saying 'I don't know, elder brother'. Bowen suggests that these dialogues 'present an idealized and socially salient image of social interactions'.

9.4.3 The performer and the audience

An audience may initiate a performance (by asking someone to perform), and then may respond in specific ways, which are required by the rules of the genre which is being performed and often function as encouragements to the performer to continue. In both cases (and particularly the latter) the audience itself can be seen as a subsidiary performer – and is liable to be evaluated as such by the primary performer. Thus for example Wiget (1987) describes the telling of a Hopi story by Helen Sekaquaptewa in which the audience is required to give 'back channelling behaviour' throughout the story, by saying *owi* intermittently; at the beginning of the story he describes, the storyteller chides the audience for not saying *owi* loudly enough.

Audience feedback might be a strict requirement on the overall performance. Thus Rice (1992: 285) says that Lakota narrators 'expected irregular choral responses from the audience such as *hau* and *ohan* . . . particularly after statements affirming fundamental values'. Virginia Hymes cites a particular performance where the narrator paused until the audience gave the correct feedback for that part of the story. Audience feedback thus is a crucial part of the overall performance, and can be seen as part of the text itself. The constituent structure of the text is both recognized and to some extent constituted when an audience responds at constituent boundaries, thus marking those constituent boundaries as clearly as would a particle within the narrative itself. Hymes (V. Hymes 1987: 77) suggests that in Sahaptin narratives, the response *ii—* ('yes') may be produced either at the end of what she calls a verse (a segment of text which describes a coherent eventuality or sequence of eventualities), or at the end of the first line in a new episode.

These small interventions which are performed by an audience can also be performed by a designated individual, in some cases a musician who accompanies the main performer and in some cases a member of the audience. Such a person might have the role of helping the audience in certain ways. For example, he or she might begin the clapping to indicate that a performance has come to

an end, or might help by clarifying difficult terms, asking for repetitions when
needed and so on. Another way in which such a person might help the audience
is by reining in a performer who has temporarily lost touch of the audience's
requirements (Okpewho 1992: 51–7 has some interesting examples of this).
Smith (1991: 14) gives an example of a designated co-performer in the performance of the Rajasthani epic narrative, *The Epic of Pābūjī* (India: Rajasthan). The
epic is typically performed by a husband and wife, singing the epic between
them. The story as sung is apparently relatively unstructured, with the internal
structure of the narrative to some extent obscured by the performance style (as
Smith comments, this obscurity suits the liturgical aspects of the story; see
1.2.1). However, variety enters the performance when the man interrupts the
singing to declaim an *arthāv*, an explanation of the events in the story. It is here
that a designated member of the audience called the *hūkāriyo* is expected to
respond by repeating the final word of each line of the *arthāv*; note that here
the co-performer functions to reinforce metrical boundaries. Smith further
comments: 'Sometimes the *bhopo* [primary performer] tries to trip the *hūkāriyo*
up by replacing the appropriate word with a rhyming substitute: whether the
deliberate mistake is spotted by its victim or not, much good-humoured fun
results.'

Another example of a designated co-performer is discussed by Basso (1986)
for the Kalapalo (Brazil: Mato Grosso). In addition to the narrator, there is an
individual called a *tiitsofo* (= what-sayer) who intervenes in various ways. First,
he utters monosyllabic expletives which express emotional reactions to the stories. Second, he repeats significant words, which may then be repeated again by
the narrator; thus the mutuality of understanding of the narrative is reinforced.
Third, he must ask for clarification and expansion at certain (pre-determined)
points in the narrative; the narrator may even prompt the *tiitsofo* to ask for
clarification if he omits to do so. Thus, overall, the designated co-performer
has a role in developing the meaning and structure of the narrative. In terms
of Bauman's notion of performance, Basso comments that the co-performer is
a full performer in the sense that his contributions are according to rule and are
assessed as such both by the primary performer and by the audience.

9.4.4 *Beyond the immediate culture*

Performance is a contractual relation between a performer and an audience,
based on shared knowledge of the features of a way of speaking. This situation
can be challenged in a number of ways. One challenge to performance comes
when a performer may be extracted from a community where there is shared
knowledge and instead performs to a different community which lacks this shared
knowledge. This situation arises for example in performances of 'folk culture'

to tourists or at folk festivals, or in 'world music' recordings (see for example Webb 1993; Bauman 1986). A second challenge comes when the community itself changes such that shared knowledge no longer exists. Thus for example Dixon and Koch (1996) discuss the performances of Dyirbal songs by Spider Henry, perhaps the last composer-performer of this genre in a culture where the language has been displaced by English; they suggest that his final status (and hence lack of a knowledgeable audience as well as a reinforcing culture) is responsible for his very variant performances.

We end this chapter by considering an example of cultural change which is part of Bowen's (1989) account of Gayo poetic duels, discussed earlier. The traditional form of Gayo poetic duel as outlined above is now relatively scarce, and has been replaced by another form of the poetic duel. The new form involves teams rather than individuals. It is not necessarily performed at any traditional occasion, and its contents may be determined by contemporary political concerns; in many cases, the contents of the poetic duel are sponsored, for example by the government. Performers are more likely to see themselves as individually creative artists rather than channels for the culture, and may record and sell performances commercially. Bowen argues that these changes can be understood in terms of political changes affecting the Gayo, largely as a result of intervention by the Indonesian state (within whose boundaries the Gayo live). Intervention took two basic forms. First, the state sponsored poetic duels on particular subjects, such as the promotion of the dominant political party. Second, the state arranged for the duels to be performed as entertainments, both locally and (later) at a national level. Both interventions changed the relation between performer and tradition and performer and audience, and together contributed to a separation of the poetic duel from a tightly constrained social context; whereas the traditional duel was performed at marriages and was about the marriage as a cultural event, the new duels could be performed anywhere and could be about anything. This change in turn may have affected the formal structure of poetic duels, which are now governed by rhyme rather than by traditional content-based parallelism; this frees the duel from being about the culture, and allows for the insertion of any kind of content.

9.5   Summary: performance and linguistic form

This chapter looked at the characteristics of verbal art which arise as a result of the text being performed in a context. Certain aspects of linguistic form, including those which are specialized to literature, can be seen as emerging from the demands or possibilities of performance. Thus for example the formal markedness of literary language might derive in part from its centrality to performance, both because verbal art must draw attention to itself and because it must be evaluated in terms of its adherence to rules. Aspects of the metricality of the text may relate to performance, as we saw for oral formulae; and forms of parallelism might emerge from performance situations in which there are two performers. Thus, as we saw for metrical verse in its musical context in chapter 4, a broader viewpoint which takes the performance of a text into account may lead to a more precise understanding of how the linguistic form of the text is exploited to develop its literary form.

9.6 Further reading

On classifications of speech, ways of speaking, and cultural differences in these, see Hymes (1968, 1989), Keenan and Ochs (1979), Sherzer (1990), Bauman and Sherzer (1989) and Seeger (1993). On performance, see Bauman (1984, an expansion of Bauman 1975); on performance in storytelling Bauman (1986); on entextualization and genre Bauman and Briggs (1990) and Briggs and Bauman (1992) which also have useful overviews; on degrees of performance Bauman (1993, 1996) and Hymes (1981). On joint performance see Duranti and Brenneis (1986) and on poetic duels see Erdener (1995). Toelken (1979) is an introduction to folklore which is centrally concerned with performance. Tedlock (1983) argues the case for seeing texts in performance, and Tedlock (1978) exemplifies his approach to transcription of performance. Very detailed case studies of specific Native American performances include Wiget (1987) and Evers and Molina (1987). Okpewho (1992) is an overview of performance in Africa. On Oral-Formulaic Theory see Lord (1960, 1991), Foley (1990), Whallon (1969), and Stolz and Shannon (1976) which includes Kiparsky (1976); also the journal *Oral Tradition*. Foley (1995) combines several of the approaches to performance outlined in this chapter.

9.7 Exercises

9.7.1 *'Performance art' as performance*

'Performance art' is a kind of aesthetic practice found in the twentieth century in which a person or group of people do something in obedience to a pre-existing script or plan: the transient act of doing is the aesthetic act. One of the characteristics of performance art is that each piece is in a sense its own 'way of speaking', defining its own rules according to its own script (which may not be known to any audience).

(a) *An incident with a gun*

The surrealists Jacques Vaché and André Breton used to engage in disruptive behaviour at theatrical performances, for example eating and talking loudly and so interrupting the show. Vaché was a member of the audience at the premiere of Guillaume Apollinaire's surrealist play *Les Mamelles de Tirésias* in Paris in 1917. Half-way through, he produced a gun and announced that he would kill his fellow audience members by firing into the crowd; his action caused a riot.

> *Question*: Was Vaché engaged in performance in Bauman's sense? What else might you need to know in order to decide?

(b) *John Cage: 4'33"*

This famous piece is performed by a pianist who holds his or her hands over the keyboard of the piano for four minutes and thirty-three seconds, changing posture twice to divide the piece into three movements. The audience experiences not silence but random environmental noise – coughs, movements, noise from outside the hall and so on.

> *Question*: Is the pianist engaged in performance in Bauman's sense, and can anyone else be said to be a performer in this case?

(c) *Peter Greenaway: applauding sites*

Peter Greenaway organized an 'installation' in Spain. Over a hundred days, he organized an audience in front of a hundred sites (natural, architectural etc.) and asked the audience to applaud 'as they wish'.

> *Question*: Is there a performance here and are there any performers?

(Sources: examples respectively from Kuhn and Whitehead (1992), Lander and Lexier (1990) and an interview with Greenaway in the magazine *Artifice* #3 (1995).)

9.7.2 *Molière: a joke about co-performance*

Instruction

The following dialogue is from the seventeenth-century French author Molière's play *Tartuffe*. It is in the *alexandrine* meter (see 3.6.1), and is a joke about co-performance and the *alexandrine* meter. Explain the joke.

Text

The two characters are Orgon (O) and Dorine (D).

O	*Et Tartuffe?*	And Tartuffe?
D	*Tartuffe? Il se porte à merveille*	Tartuffe? He's bearing up well.
O	*Le pauvre homme!*	The poor man!
D	*Le soir, elle eut un grand dégoût*	Last night she didn't feel like eating
O	*Et Tartuffe?*	And Tartuffe?
D	*Il soupa, lui tout seul, devant elle*	He ate, alone, in front of her.
O	*Le pauvre homme!*	The poor man!
D	*la nuit se passa tout entière*	The whole night passed.
O	*Et Tartuffe?*	And Tartuffe?
D	*Presse d'un sommeil agréable*	Overcome by an agreeable sleep.
O	*Le pauvre homme!*	The poor man!
D	*À la fin, par nos raisons gagnée*	In the end, won by our arguments
O	*Et Tartuffe?*	And Tartuffe?
D	*Il reprit courage comme il faut*	He recovered spirits, as must be.
O	*Le pauvre homme!*	The poor man!
D	*Tout deux se portent bien enfin*	Both are finally feeling better.

(Source: discussed in Halle 1992; freely translated)

9.7.3 *Hare, Hyena and the hippo hide: the performance of a Madi story*

Instructions

Note: this exercise assumes that you have read chapters 7 and 8.

(a) What evidence might suggest that this narrator keys his storytelling as a performance?
(b) The text can be divided into story (5–42) and moral (44–69). (i) Can you find any evidence that these constitute different ways of speaking in the

language: for example, are they linguistically or otherwise formally distinct? (ii) Is there any evidence that the style of the story influences the style of the moral?

(c) Analyse the developmental structure of the story.

(d) How does this narrator use pauses? (Each line in the transcription ends with a pause.) Are they randomly distributed, determined by syntactic structure, or by the need to take breath, or do they have other kinds of function in the story? (Note: there are likely to be different functions, at different parts of the story.)

(e) Identify examples of repetition or parallelism in the story, and comment on their function.

(f) Do connectives have any special function in the narration?

(g) The verb in a Madi sentence can be in second position (past tense) or final position (future, progressive, and subordinate clauses). This distinction is coded in the translation: a past tense English verb corresponds to a second position Madi verb, while an English verb with 'will', 'to' or ending in *-ing* translates a final position Madi verb. (i) Might we expect this distinction to play any role in the narrative? (ii) Look at the translations and decide whether this distinction does in fact play any role in the narrative.

(h) Retell this story in English (either orally or in writing); in Madi it is funny – try to keep it funny in English. Comment on the kinds of change which you make in adapting the story to a different narrative tradition.

Text: 'Hare and Hyena' told by Pasiquale Sebi

Madi is a language in the Central Sudanic group (Nilo-Saharan family), spoken in Southern Sudan and Northern Uganda. The narration was transcribed from tape, with a line break at each pause (of about a second or longer). There were no pauses internal to lines; internal punctuation is for ease of reading. This is a relatively free translation which represents a compromise between the need to clarify meaning and the need to express the original form. Each line of Madi is translated independently as far as possible. Constituents which are emphasized by syntactic means are translated with the English word in capital letters.

Interviewer

drìá làpwóní	Now the teacher
pàsìkwálè sébì nī sùkúrù dì ní ʔā rì	Pasiquale Sebi from this school
ká ɔ̄dà tɔ̀	he is telling a story
ɓá ní, ìlédì	to us, here it is.

Narrator

5 *mâ ɔ̄dɔ̀ bí*
My version of the story

kɔ̀tsɛ̀ kēdɛ́ bìrì.
opens up like this. [conventional beginning: see note 1 at end]

ìtó pī
Hare

à?ī
and

mòí trɔ̀.
Hyena.

10 *tà nā nà nī*
The situation at that time was

tɔ̀ɓū.
it rained all night.

èjí ōdī rà. èjí ɔ̄drì tsē àfí sì.
The rain fell. The rain halted in the morning.

ɓá rì ōkwá ótɔ́.
The people shaved the termite mounds.

drìádrɔ̄ sâ ōtsā ɔ́ɲā drí ?ī.
Now has come the time for termites.

15 *ɓá rì kóvɔ̀ vɔ̀rē ɔ́ɲā gá.*
The people are going for termites.

ìtó ēdzí ròbí ɛ́ní dī̀, dī̀ ālā létī ?ā.
Hare brought this hippo hide, this he put in the road.

drìá ɓâ zì ká ɔ́ɲā zà.
Now other people are harvesting termites.

mòí kômū ānâ ɔ́ɲā trɔ̀. kání kômū ɔ́ɲā zārē rì ?ī.
Hyena is going for his termites. He should be going to the TERMITE HARVEST.

ōnì ɛ́ní dì ēsú.
He is then finding this hide.

20 *āní drí āgɔ́ rì nī ɛ́ní gá.*
He was caught up in the hide.

ká āní ní ɛ́ní ìlɛ́dì ɲā.
He was eating that hide.

ìtó ōmū ēzà tà ìlɛ́dì pí.
Hare went and harvested those things (the termites).

mòí kófè. káɛ́ní ērà.
Hyena is running, he is remembering the hide.

kófè. ɛ́ní kóŋgù. kéràā. kélɔ̀.
He is running. The hide is smelling. He is remembering it. He is running back to it.

25 *kófè. kɛ́ràā. kɛ́lʊ̀ ɛ́ní ìlɛ́dî ʔí gá. ɔ́ɲā ɔ̄fʊ̀ ōkó.*

He is running. He is remembering it. He is running to that hide. But the termites are now finished with.

kômū mūrē ɔ́ɲā ɔ̄ŋgā túwá.

By the time he is getting there, the termites are all finished.

ìtó ēdzí ɔ́ɲā ìlɛ́dî. ìtó ēzà āgó rì ʔà ɔ́ɲā sâ trɔ̀. ìtó ēmú trɔ̀ drʊ́ pí.

Hare took his (own) termites. Hare harvested that man's (Hyena's) termites too. Hare came away from there.

mòí nī íníní ēzɛ̀ mgbē ōfè rɛ́rɛ́ ìtó drí kɔ̀rɔ̀ kɔ̀rɔ̀.

Hyena, early in the morning, immediately he ran, immediately to Hare, quickly quickly.

ōfō 'mâ ɔzî ìtógò,

He said 'My friend Mighty Hare,

30 *mâ ɔ́ɲā ɔ̄ŋgā pí. mɛ̃ sú màdí zì ɔ̄zà mâ ɔ́ɲā. mɛ̃ sú màdí nī vʊ́ lákā.*

my termites have all gone. I found that another person harvested my termites. I found that person's footprints there.

ɲēkè mání tólú. mâmū drʊ́ ídzákwí ēgárē drʊ́ màdí ná ní.

Give me an axe. I will go and chop firewood with it for that person.

má mádrí èndrʊ̀ īrōgàā rá.

I will bewitch him today.

mâ mū ītālìā.

I am going to bewitch him.

mítālìā drʊ́.'

I am bewitching him with it.'

35 *dì sì drʊ́ ìtó ōfō 'hél mòí,*

Because of this Hare says, 'Hey, Hyena,

mā īsâ màdí zì ɔ́ɲā mâ ɛ́ní rá.

Me too, someone ate my hide.

mā īsâ ɲēkè mání tólú.

Me too, give me an axe.

mâ mū mā īsâ màdí zì ídzákwí nā . . . mâ mū má íʤákwí ēgá drū. mā īsâ mémú īrōgáà.

I am going, me too, some person . . . firewood . . . (NB. the narrator makes a mistake here and corrects in the next clause) I am going to cut some firewood with it. Me too, I am going to bewitch him.

àsànì kō ɔ́ɲā mâ ɛ́ní rá.

Because he ate my hide.

40 *mítālìā ītālì.*

I am BEWITCHING him.'

dì sì drʊ́ ɔ̄dɔ̀ ɓárì drí ōkó dí pí.

And so the story between these two ends with this.

mâ ɔ̄dɔ̀ kélé kélé ʔà ìbá tsélè. mà   My story has come to the end. I inter-
pī lóí sâ kɔ̀tsē kŏ.   laced the strands so that it should not
   snap. [conventional ending: see note
   2 at end]

Interviewer

à, làpwóɲí pàsìkwálè ɔ̄dɔ̀ ɲâ tɔ̀lé   Ah, teacher Pasiquale, that story you
ìlédì ɛ́kwí ānī ká ɓá īnì àdū gá?   told, what does its meaning teach
   people?

Narrator

ɔ̄dɔ̀ ānī dì ʔī dì   This particular story

45 *ká ɓá īnì kḛ̄ ndré ɔ̀vī drɔ́ sùkúrù*   It is teaching us, like in a school

   tī drī gá.   or other situations.

   ɔ̀ ɲâ átä̀ ká ɲēzé sùkúrù gá.   Perhaps your father he is sending you
   to school.

   ɓāráŋwá zì ná́ʔā.   There is another child there.

   kófōà 'ɔ́vō ɓání   He (the child) is saying 'Let's go to get
   ourselves

50 *ìtì ḛ̄gɓàrḛ̄ kŏ sâ ɔ́vɔ̀ àríndzì ōgɓí*   tamarinds, or let's go shooting birds.'
sì.'

   drìá ɲí rīkālà àríndzī ōgɓírḛ̄ ná́ʔā.   Now you are wasting your time shooting birds there.

   ɓá tsírí ɓâ zí ḛ̄vɔ̀ díā pí. ḛ̄sú kî   Other children they came here (to
līnì rá.   school). They learned things.

   drìá ɲídrí dí́ʔā ɲâ ɓārá wɔ̄   Now as for you here, your child
   meanwhile

   ɔ̄lɔ́ àríndzī ōgɓírḛ̄ áwɔ̄.   He has been shooting birds.

55 *ɲí ḛ̄súä drìá ɓâ zí ká tìárì tū.*   Now you are finding that his companions are climbing into a plane.

   ká ɓâ zí nī bɛ́gì ādzī.   He is carrying his companions' bags.

   dì ɔ̄dɔ̀ dì ʔā ɛ́kwí ānī ʔī.   This story, this is its meaning.

   dzɔ̀   If

   ɔ̀jíɔ̄ tà nà nī nà ófō ɔ́ɓā   this is the current trend:

60	*ófō sùkúrù*	They say, school, you
	ɲīsâ ɲìzē ɲâ ɓārá sùkúrù gá.	you also, you send your child to school.
	kòmū kɔ́nà gá kŏ.	He should not go in other directions.
	kē ndré ɔ̀vīrɒ̀ vì àtā zì tó ɓārú sì rì ánī	It is like some fathers back home (Sudan)
	ēzè sì ā́ʔì à́ʔī ʔà ɓá tsírí kŏ.	in the past they didn't allow their children (to go to school).
65	*ká kî ràā ɗì ádī māmālì īdré.*	They are thinking this, that all of us are being stupid.
	kàrà māmālì kŏ.	But it isn't stupidity.
	nà ɔvīrɒ̄ vì àʔī éní.	Those who don't go to school are like the hide [ie. eaten up].
	ɔ̄, ɓá ēvɒ̀kā pí ɗì àʔī drí àʔī ɔ́ɲā.	And those who go are like the termites [ie. survive].
	ɗì ɔ̄dɒ̀ ɗì ʔā ɛ́kwí ʔī.	This is the story's meaning.

Interviewer

70	*má āndzɔ́ rá làpwóɲí.*	Thank you, teacher.

(Source: taped at Alere refugee camp in Northern Uganda in 1995. Thanks to Pasiquale Sebi, to Martin Ettore for permission to use this story, and to Mairi Blackings for translating it. See Blackings and Fabb (forthcoming) for further discussion of the language and issues of narrative style.)

Note 1. The beginning cannot be translated word-for-word. It is a fixed phrase (which is varied by different performers, but always identifiable as a beginning of a narrative), which implies that this is a pre-existing story of which this storyteller will present his version.

Note 2. The ending presents the story as though it is a rope. A rope must be woven with no loose ends or it will snap. The storyteller thus guarantees, by saying this, that the story is complete and true to the original, and hence is a reliable version of the original.

10 Communication

In this chapter we look at communication as one of the functions of language, and examine how the characteristics of communication are exploited for particular effects in verbal art. As outlined in 1.3, verbal communication involves the presentation of evidence for the informative intentions of the communicator. These informative intentions may not be explicitly formulated in the text produced (i.e. talk may be 'loose'), and this is the basis of metaphor, as I show in 10.1. Among the thoughts which the communicator intends to communicate, there may be thoughts about thoughts, attributing those thoughts to a third party and expressing an attitude towards them; I discuss this in 10.2 and 10.3.

10.1 Loose talk

In the model of communication developed by Sperber and Wilson (1986, 1995) all verbal behaviour is communicatively loose. A text, spoken or written, offers evidence for its interpretation but does not determine it: that evidence must be assessed by a communicatee to determine the informative intentions of the producer of the text.

What are the advantages for communication of the looseness of language? A first advantage is that we can communicate effectively without needing always to be explicit. If someone asks me the time I may say 'quarter past five', which may be literally untrue if it is actually 5.13. The point is that we interpret the question as a request not for the exact time but for the rough time (because it is the implications of what time it is that matter, not the actual time itself). My answer is entirely effective at a communicative level; the hearer can interpret it not in its literal meaning but as 'It is roughly quarter past five'. If language was not loose, we could not say 'it is quarter past five' and mean 'it is roughly quarter past five'. A second advantage of looseness is that it enables us to use deictic expressions rather than specifying all references. Thus we can say 'him' to refer to a person without naming that person; this looseness may require interpretive effort on the part of a hearer, but if the context is clear, then the overall effort will be less for both parties than constantly specifying all references. A third advantage of looseness is that we can communicate assumptions which are themselves not fully explicit, thoughts whose component terms are not all well defined, and so on. Sperber and Wilson cite the example of someone who opens the window in their hotel room at the seaside and sniffs ostentatiously (thus indicating communication). Such an action can successfully communicate a set of assumptions which are not fully explicit to either the communicator or the communicatee. Many literary texts are able to express profound but inexplicit meanings in exactly this way (consider for example any Romantic poem). A fourth advantage of looseness is condensation: a small text can communicate a large number of assumptions, by providing partial evidence for many different assumptions. These examples show that the looseness of language is its strength, and the source of its flexibility of meaning.

One of the important aspects of the looseness of language is that it is tied closely to matters of community and culture. Looseness in communication requires the speaker and the hearer to share a context, and for each to be confident that the other shares the context; this context is the source of the evidence which will supplement the evidence provided by the text. Where context is a major source of evidence for the interpretation of a text, one of the things which is communicated is that the communicator and communicatee share that context. Sperber and Wilson call this the effect of 'mutuality'. It appears to be a significant component of literary practice in many communities. Thus for example Maria Chona famously said in her 1936 autobiography about the songs of her own Papago culture, 'The song is very short because we understand so much' (Chona 1936, cited in Krupat 1979: 47). The practice of using very short texts as evidence for a substantial amount of interpretation can both be a powerful communicative tool (in a coherent culture) and at the same time can reinforce people's sense of their cultural togetherness.

10.1.1 *Metaphor*

Metaphor is a name for certain kinds of loose talk, characterized in particular by utterances which are literally untrue (and which must therefore be taken as evidence for meanings which are not directly encoded into them). This is the first stanza of a Hungarian wedding toast (from Transylvania), praising the bride:

Aranybárány a szép leány,
Golden lamb the pretty girl,

olyan piros, mint a márvány,
as   red   as the marble,

engedelmes, mint a bárány,
obedient   as the lamb,

nem hamis,   mint az oroszlány.
not treacherous as the lion

'The pretty girl is a golden lamb, as red as the marble, obedient as the lamb,
not treacherous like the lion' (first stanza of a text sung by József Dénes in 1953,
Hungarian text from Honko et al. 1994: 507; thanks to Judit Friedrich for help
with this text)

The first line of the text, even in its literal meaning, is loose in that we must
decide who is being described as 'the pretty girl'; the best guess, based on
various kinds of evidence, is that this is the bride. However, the first line of the
text is literally false: the girl is not a lamb. This is another aspect of the looseness
of the text, which is not fundamentally different in kind from the looseness of
reference: in both cases, we must take the text as evidence for meanings, rather
than as containing meanings. A reasonable assumption is that the girl shares
certain characteristics with a lamb, such as obedience (from line 3), softness, whiteness (in apparent contradiction to line 2), and so on. The hearer's interpretation,
the decision about which characteristics are intended, will depend on that person's
background knowledge, both of the culture and of the conventions of the poetry.
The culture-specificity of such knowledge is clear to an outsider in line 2, which
is difficult to interpret; it might perhaps mean that the girl's cheeks are red like
marble in the whiteness (like the lamb) of her skin – but as outsiders we don't
really know what was intended by the original author because we don't have
enough cultural knowledge to be able to interpret the evidence which the text
offers us. The fourth line also raises difficulties for us as outside interpreters –
and possibly for the insiders too, because it may conceal a joke. The word
oroszlány means 'lion', but it might also be heard as *orosz lány*, meaning 'Russian
girl'. Each hearer must decide whether the text offers evidence for an interpretation
of the poem whereby good native girls are compared to bad Russian girls. Here,
the audience itself might be divided between people who think that they are
justified in this interpretation and take it to have been communicated (i.e. they
'see the joke') and those who do not; the singer may or may not give additional
help to clarify whether there really is a joke here.

    The looseness of this text is a matter of the gap between what it literally says
(the logical forms which can be decoded from its words and syntax) and what
it can be taken to communicate. There is no fundamental difference between the
workings of this text and the workings of any kind of verbal behaviour, since
most kinds of verbal behaviour are loose in exactly this sense that the literal meaning of the text constitutes partial but not complete evidence for the informative intentions of the speaker or writer. We might ask how this particular text

exploits the looseness of communication to serve the functions of verbal art. First, the text is able to communicate a large set of meanings relating to the girl, many more meanings than could be communicated if each line of text encoded a single meaning; this large set includes some meanings which are clearly intended and others which are less certain. Thus the text is able to be rich in meaning by virtue of its looseness. The phenomenon whereby a text communicates a large number of possible meanings, but where many of these are only weakly evidenced by the text, is called 'weak implicature' by Sperber and Wilson. They suggest that the experience of weak implicature is one of the components of aesthetic experience. A second advantage of the looseness of the text is that because the text invokes various kinds of culture-specific knowledge in its audience, it at the same time communicates to the audience that the communicator and all the members of the audience share the cultural knowledge required to interpret it. Thus the text communicates a sense of cultural cohesion and mutuality to its audience. Notice that this text invokes meanings which include gender stereotypes, and by requiring the audience to draw upon these meanings to interpret it, it can be argued that the text also reinforces those meanings. Thus the looseness of literary texts can carry an ideological force.

10.1.2 *Convention in interpretation*

A major source of evidence for interpretations comes from context. In communication, there must be some sharing of the context between communicator and communicatee. This shared context might be physical, but it might also be cultural. A culture is, in part, a set of assumptions; where two people share the same culture then they know the same things – and can use that knowledge as evidence in interpretation. One consequence of this is the effect of mutuality, which arises when extensive use of context-based evidence proves to both speaker and hearers that they share a set of common beliefs. Convention has a place in interpretation in two senses. First, there may be conventions of interpretation, 'rules' which translate one text into another. Second, there may be conventional analogies. The metaphor of the girl being a lamb in the Hungarian poem was a conventional analogy, as is its interpretation (of docility, etc.), and hence a hearer will easily move to that interpretation.

Another example of conventional interpretations is the case of Sumbanese ritual speech (from Indonesia: Nusa Tenggara), described by Mitchell (1988). Ritual speech in this culture, as used for example in legal negotiations, involves the performance of conventional couplets consisting of parallel clauses; the couplets are in most cases believed to have remained unchanged since ancestral times. The two clauses of the couplet together metaphorically communicate a particular set of assumptions, with the communicated set being conventionally associated with the couplet. An example (from Mitchell 1988: 76) is:

Maturu-na-nya-ka na tapu   He is lying on the mat
Kadenga-na-nya-ka na api   He has his back to the fire

This means 'he is seriously ill'. Thus each clause communicates the same
assumption; the hearer will reach this interpretation by relying on conventional
knowledge. Mitchell describes other couplets as having concepts as their conventional meanings (rather than full propositions). An example (from Mitchell
1988: 81) is:

Tilu kobu moru   Eggs of the green gecko
Woya lai karara   Crocodile reddish in the current

Mitchell says: 'This couplet refers to the supernatural, and its conventional
meaning may be stated in the ordinary language phrase *na ma biha*, "that which
is supernatural".' The use of this couplet could be interpreted as a means of
communicating a determinate concept and an indeterminate set of assumptions
relating to that concept. These couplets communicate by metaphor; the assumptions communicated do not include the explicit linguistic meaning of the clauses,
but nevertheless there are cultural codes or conventions at work in guiding
which assumptions are communicated. We would be wrong, however, to think
that the meaning of these couplets is purely conventional. This is clear once we
ask speakers to explain how the metaphors work. Mitchell says that different
speakers differ in their explanations. One speaker describes the relation between
gecko eggs and the supernatural by describing how geckos lay their eggs, and
the fact that they are difficult to see but all around us – like the supernatural.
This again reinforces the point that even conventional analogies and procedures
can be used in different ways; they are simply part of the evidence for interpretation rather than determining it.

   An important characteristic of conventions for interpretation is that they are
not automatic and unconscious codes. In fact, they are best not treated as codes
at all. It is quite possible for conventions of interpretation to be themselves
very loose texts. Thus for example, according to Feld (1982), the Kaluli of New
Guinea interpret birds as people as one part of a complex interpretive system
which pervades their literary practices and culture more generally. But to say
that a bird is a person, which is a general interpretive strategy, is to produce
a metaphorical text which is not easily interpreted; like any text it provides
only part of the evidence which is required for its own interpretation. Hence
interpretive procedures are themselves the source of rich further interpretations.
Sperber (1975) has argued that this is generally true of cultural symbolism. It
has sometimes been claimed that symbols are decoded, but Sperber argues that
symbols are evidence for their own meaning but not complete evidence. In fact,
many very powerful and central cultural symbols seem to contain difficulty as

a design feature. It is perhaps no accident that religious texts in particular are often very difficult to interpret.

One of the major theorists of conventional metaphors is George Lakoff. Lakoff has gathered many sets of analogy by which metaphors can be interpreted, and has argued that these sets are found in many different human cultures. He then has a more ambitious claim to make, which is that these analogies are basic to the structure of thought itself (i.e. not simply culturally learned). Lakoff and others have argued that specific metaphors often draw upon general correspondences between conceptual domains (e.g. Lakoff and Johnson 1980; Lakoff and Turner 1989). Thus for example they might propose a general correspondence which could be stated as: PEOPLE ARE ANIMALS; this would then be realized in the metaphors in the Hungarian text as 'the pretty girl is like a lamb', 'the pretty girl is not like a lion', and so on. Lakoff's underlying claim is that thought itself is structured by these kinds of correspondence, which include for example BIRTH IS ARRIVAL, LIFE IS HEAT, DEATH IS SLEEP and so on; the precise kinds of correspondence may perhaps vary from culture to culture. These correspondences are both a way of understanding metaphors and also a tool by which metaphors can be constructed, both in poetry and in other uses of language.

10.2   Attribution and attitude

Among our thoughts are thoughts which are descriptions of the world. If the description is fully specified with all its component parts clear and is unambiguous, it is a proposition, and has a truth value (it is true or false). Some of our thoughts are propositions. If the description has the general structure of a proposition but is ambiguous or vague in some way it is a proposition schema (Sperber and Wilson 1986): this might for example be a thought which contains a term which is not fully specified, such as a pronoun or a name whose reference is not fully clear. Some of our thoughts are proposition schemas. The terms 'proposition' and 'proposition schema' invoke the truth or falsity of thoughts. It is important to have true thoughts in order to be able to act effectively in the world.

However, as far as literature is concerned, we might argue that truth and falsity as absolute characteristics of thoughts are not as important as (a) our attitudes towards thoughts, and (b) our attribution of thoughts to thinkers. Our attitudes seem to be arrayed along a scale ranging from doubt to certainty. A person attributes thoughts to herself and to other people, including – as we will see – unspecified others and fictional others. I can in principle recognize any thought which is present to me as my thought, and can both recognize and describe my attitude towards it. (This might seem a platitudinous claim, but we can see that it is not trivial by the fact that it is not true of some mental illnesses. Thus a person with schizophrenia may experience 'thought insertion' whereby he fails to recognize his thought as his own and believes it to have been inserted in his head by an outsider.)

There is clearly a relationship in principle between the truth value of thoughts and our attitudes towards thoughts. Ideally, we should believe thoughts which are true, and should disbelieve thoughts which are false. If this were the case, then all humans would draw on the same set of thoughts and we would never disagree. Clearly this is not the case. In practice, our attitudes towards thoughts are to some extent dissociated from any truth value those thoughts may have, and this has various interesting consequences for literature. First, we can have attitudes towards thoughts where those thoughts are not propositions but proposition schemas: thoughts where some of the terms are not fully specified or which are internally contradictory, or ambiguous. Second, we can in fact have very strong attitudes of certainty towards such thoughts – even though they have no truth value: many basic cultural and religious beliefs have this status. Third, we are able to cope with fictions and with various intermediate states between fact and fiction: we can entertain and have attitudes towards thoughts which have no truth value (or are simply false) because they describe fictional worlds.

Attitude and attribution have two sides. First, there is a universal psychological claim to be made about human thought: that thoughts exist in two kinds of relation to the subject – the relation of attribution (a thought is tagged as the subject's) and the relation of attitude (a subject has a certain attitude towards a thought). This is a claim about psychological structure: whatever disorder underlies thought insertion in schizophrenia will need to address these psychological relations and understand thought insertion in their terms (see C. Frith 1992). This kind of claim has some relevance to the concerns of this book, but of more relevance is the second side of attribution and attitude which is that as part of the process of communication, people attribute thoughts to themselves and others and identify attitudes towards them. In effect, as communicators we have a 'theory of thought', which happens to be true. There are two distinct claims being made here:

> One claim is that humans have a 'theory of thought' which posits the existence of thoughts and sees individuals as having attitudes towards those thoughts along a scale of strength. This claim is important for thinking about how communication works, and is the basis of the ability to understand irony.

> The other claim is that this theory is true: our mental activity really is organized into thoughts which we have attitudes towards. This claim is less important for the present book, but has some interesting implications for the more experiential aspects of our reception of literature.

This 'theory of thought' has a number of important consequences; here are four. First, we recognize ourselves as having attitudes towards thoughts, and thus can have thoughts about our thoughts: in addition to believing something I can believe that I believe it. Or I can interpret a text as evidence that the communicator believes a certain thought, which might lead me to believe it. Second, we recognize others as having attitudes towards thoughts, and as being able to communicate those attitudes. If someone I trust communicates that she has a strong commitment to a thought, then I may also develop a strong commitment to that thought. Third, a communicator can also communicate a third party's attitude towards a thought: thus an assumption can be communicated which is not an assumption of the communicator. It is possible that some cases of 'hearsay' work like this: a story is told which is considered to be true by some unspecified third party but towards which the storyteller communicates no specific attitude. And fourth, a communicator can communicate a thought, her own attitude, and someone else's attitude towards it all at the same time. Some cases of irony work like this. A speaker might indicate that someone else strongly believes a particular proposition but that she does not.

10.2.1 The communication of attribution and attitude

A text and its performance can communicate thoughts to us. These thoughts are derived as interpretations by the communicatee, using the text as partial evidence. The thoughts we derive might be (i) bare propositions, or (ii) propositions with attributions explicitly attached, or (iii) propositions with attributions and attitudes explicitly attached.

This can be illustrated with a straightforward case where a text provides evidence for a thought, for its attribution to the speaker, and for the speaker's attitude. Thus someone might say:

I know that John is at home.

This can be interpreted as communicating a thought such as 'John is at home', and it also communicates that this thought is attributed to 'I' (the speaker) and that the speaker's attitude towards it is one of 'knowledge' (i.e. somewhere between belief and certainty on the attitudinal scale). The text provides evidence for these interpretations. Note that the same interpretations are possible even where the text does not explicitly describe attribution or attitude. Thus the following utterance may have a similar range of interpretations: the thought, attributed as knowledge to the speaker:

John is at home

Our second example involves two sentences from the Madi story told by the teacher Pasiquale Sebi, cited as exercise 9.7.3. Here the speaker communicates a thought, its attribution to a third party and the third party's attitude towards it; and a thought, its attribution to himself and his attitude towards it:

ká   kî   rà-ā   dî   ádî   māmālì   ídré.   kàrà māmālì   kū.
3rd-pers. plural think-it this we-inclusive stupidity do.   But   stupidity not.

They are thinking that this is stupidity on our part. But it isn't stupidity.

Here the speaker in the first sentence communicates a thought which can be formulated as 'We are being stupid' along with an attribution of that thought to a third party (the fathers of the children) and an attitude towards that thought (the fathers believe the thought). In the second sentence the speaker communicates a thought which can be formulated as 'We are not being stupid' along with attribution of that thought (to himself) and the attitude towards that thought (he believes it). Notice that in this text the evidence for these communications varies from sentence to sentence. In the first sentence, the syntax and words of the sentence provide most of the evidence for the assignment of attribution and attitude. In the second sentence there is no explicit evidence in the text for either attribution or attitude, so we have to deduce this on the basis of other evidence, which includes (i) an assessment that in this part of the discourse any text which is not specifically attributed is assigned to the speaker as his thoughts; (ii) the intonation pattern given to the sentence (not indicated in the transcript) which is emphatic, communicating certainty; (iii) the position of the sentence in the discourse, at the end and thus gaining authority as the speaker's own thoughts by its giving closure to the anecdote; and (iv) the fact that interpreting this view as the speaker's own belief fits with our expectations of a teacher, and fits with the communicated meaning of the story as a whole.

Consider next a more complex example where questions of attribution and attitude are interconnected with problems of loose talk.

> *Peace, peace! He is not dead, he doth not sleep –*
> *He hath awakened from the dream of life –*
>
> (Shelley: 'Adonais. An Elegy on the Death of John Keats')

The sentence 'he is not dead' cannot reasonably be interpreted as communicating that the speaker believes that Keats is not dead. Instead we can interpret it as communicating that the speaker has a thought or set of thoughts which are attributed to himself and which he believes strongly; that set of thoughts are implied by the text 'he is not dead' (i.e. the text provides partial evidence for them), though they do not include the proposition 'Keats is not dead'. (Note that it is actually quite hard to fix on exactly what those thoughts might be, though it is reasonably clear what the general direction of the thoughts is.) This is an example of loose talk embedded under a strong attribution of belief. The fact that the thoughts are not communicated by a literal interpretation of the text does not prevent the speaker communicating a strong attitude of belief towards those thoughts.

It is always necessary to remember that texts do not determine their interpretations, but only provide evidence for them. Thus a text may explicitly state that a speaker believes a certain thought, but nevertheless communicates that the speaker does not believe it. The same applies to texts where the absence of explicit attribution might suggest that they should be interpreted as the speaker's beliefs: the text can only be interpreted as partial evidence for such an interpretation, not as proving it. The genre of tall stories illustrates this rather nicely: these texts are presented as though the thoughts they communicate are the speaker's own beliefs, but as the text develops this initial interpretation is proved to be wrong. Consider for example the 1996 film by the Coen brothers, *Fargo*, which begins with a written text: 'This is a true story. The events depicted in this film took place in Minnesota in 1987.' This text would appear to be interpretable as communicating the filmmaker's own belief: that these events really happened. In fact, if we interpret the genre of the film as we are encouraged to do (as the 'based on a true story' genre), we will make this interpretation, encouraged by our generic knowledge. However, as the film develops it provides evidence to the contrary: that the film should be reinterpreted as in the genre of 'tall story' and hence that the initial text should not be interpreted as communicating a belief of the speakers. (The evidence includes the fact that the narrative itself depicts people telling tall stories, but most significantly that it takes place in a town associated with Paul Bunyan and watched over by a giant statue of this hero of American tall tales.) Thus, as in all cases, the initial text provides only partial evidence for its interpretation – not just of the thought which is communicated but also of the attribution and attitudes towards the thought which are communicated. That evidence is judged in the context of other knowledge – for example our knowledge of genre and how attribution and attitude function in different genres.

This example points to a more general fact about the communication of attribution and attitude, which is that different ways of speaking function differently as regards the communication of attribution and attitude. For example, explicit statements of the speaker's belief may be characteristic of religious ways of speaking (e.g. a 'credo'). Explicit statements of attribution may be characteristic of legal ways of speaking, where it is necessary to provide as clear evidence as possible of who is responsible for saying what. Or the use of hearsay devices, whether at the level of particles or more complex descriptive attributions, can be characteristic of certain genres of storytelling, a possibility discussed shortly.

10.2.2 Representing another's thought or utterance

A speaker may attribute thoughts to herself (= the first party), or to the communicatee (= the second party), or to someone else (= a third party). Attribution to a third party has a particular importance in literature: it is extensively used in storytelling, for example, either to attribute the whole story to someone else (who is claimed to have experienced it first-hand) or to attribute thoughts to characters within the story. This section presents various issues which arise from the attribution of thoughts to second or third parties.

A text can communicate the form of another text. The communicated text might be an utterance (or written text) or a thought. A simple example of this is quotation:

I said 'this is it'.

Here, the text communicates the form of another text, the utterance *'this is it'*; it communicates the form of that other utterance by resembling it (the same words, in the same order, are embedded into the text *I said 'this is it'*). Notice that the other text is attributed – in this case to the speaker. A slightly more complex example is:

John knew that there was no hope left.

Here, the text communicates the form of another text, the thought 'there is no hope left', which is attributed to a third party (John) and where John's attitude of knowledge is also communicated. The resemblance is less than in the previous example, and here a thought is being represented, rather than an utterance. The first example is 'direct representation' in that there is a close resemblance between the text and the represented text; the second example is 'indirect representation' in that the resemblance is reduced by the replacement of certain words, particularly tense markers, pronouns and other deictic expressions such as 'was'. There is not obviously a sharp dividing line between the direct and the indirect, incidentally; all representations are inexact to some extent, and the direct representations are just more exact than the indirect representations.

A distinction is sometimes made between two kinds of indirect representation of speech or thought: 'indirect' and 'free indirect'. Free indirect thought can be illustrated with the second sentence in this text:

John looked at his watch. Now he was late.

The first sentence does not communicate any particularly significant attribution of the proposition 'John looked at his watch'; it might be attributed to the narrator if necessary, but there is no particular reason to attribute it to anyone: it is just a proposition which is part of the description of the fictional world. The second sentence communicates a thought, 'John was late', but there is some evidence to attribute this thought, or something like it, to John. The evidence comes from the word 'now' which suggests that the proposition holds true at the moment of experience for John and not at the moment of narration: in other words, this 'now' can be attributed to John, suggesting that the rest of the thought can be attributed to him as well. It is his thought. This is described as free indirect thought because there is no explicit indication that it is John's thought; the communicatee must decide that it is, on the basis of other evidence. Notice that this decision is risky: we could be wrong in attributing the thought to John, and one of the ways in which the representation of free indirect thought functions is to create some uncertainty about attribution. This can be seen clearly in the extract from Jane Austen's *Emma* in the exercise at the end of this chapter; Austen was one of the earliest users of 'free indirect' representations and arguably uses it to destabilize the reader. Another uncertainty created for the reader by free indirect representations is that they may resemble the underlying thoughts less than indirect representations: thus it may be impossible to reconstruct exactly what John's original thought was, though we can make a reasonable guess.

10.2.3 Linguistic form and the communication of attribution and attitude

The linguistic form of a text is part of the evidence for the interpretation of the text. We now consider some of the ways in which linguistic form is used to provide evidence about attribution and attitude. One means by which attribution and attitude can be communicated is by embedding a representation of the thought under a predicate of attitude. Thus in '*I think that he is leaving*' or '*I said "he is leaving"*' or '*I knew he was leaving*' the clause '*he is/was leaving*' is embedded under the predicates *think, said* or *knew* (which code attitude to varying extents) and attributed to the subject *I*. The syntax of such constructions can be very interesting (for example in some languages, the pronouns in the embedded represented thought have a special morphology to distinguish them from other pronouns).

A second means of communicating attribution and attitude is by some explicit framing text. For example a story may begin with 'This really happened to a friend of mine', a text which communicates that the thoughts expressed by the story are attributed to a third party who believes them strongly. Whether such a text also communicates that the speaker believes them strongly may depend on the genre of the story: for example, this is a common beginning to 'urban myths', a variety of tall tale which are decidedly not believed by the speaker. This illustrates a difficulty with explicit framing texts (as in fact for all indicators of attribution and attitude), which is that some generic knowledge is often required in order to interpret exactly what is being communicated by these frames. Thus for example Bauman (1986: 103) describes the situation of the Texan tall-tale teller Ed Bell when confronted with an audience unfamiliar with the cultural context of his original stories, and with the genre of tall stories more generally. When telling a tale to a class of university students he may alter the presentation so as to indicate more clearly that the tale is not true (i.e. the thoughts it represents are not attributed to him, and he has an attitude of disbelief towards them).

A third means of communicating attribution (and to some extent, attitude) is by specialized grammatical means. This can include the morphological alteration of the verb, the use of modal verbs, the use of specific words which mean 'it was said that', etc. These grammatical devices are used to communicate attribution and attitude. An example is presented by Palmer (1986: 67, citing Barnes), from the Tuyuca language. The following five sentences all communicate the thought 'he played soccer':

(1) *díiga apé-wi*
(2) *díiga apé-ti*
(3) *díiga apé-yi*
(4) *díiga apé-yigɨ*
(5) *díiga apé-hɨ̃yi*

In each case, the suffix added to the verb indicates the nature of the evidence for this thought. (1) communicates that the speaker saw the eventuality of the person playing soccer; (2) communicates that the speaker perceived the eventuality in some other way, such as hearing it; (3) communicates that the speaker has indirect evidence – such as the player's footprints on the playing field; (4) communicates that the speaker was told by a third party that the person played football; (5) communicates simply that it is a reasonable assumption, perhaps on the basis of general knowledge, but that there is no specific evidence for this eventuality. In this language, the five evidential/judgemental suffixes are considered to be ranked in terms of the strength of evidence they provide, with visual evidence considered the strongest. Suffixes differ in how they attribute the assumptions: (1–3) attribute the assumptions to the speaker while (4–5) attribute them to an unspecified third party. Palmer calls (3) and (5) judgementals (indications of how the speaker arrived at the assumption) and (1), (2) and (4) evidentials (indications that the assumption comes from a third party or is derived from specific kinds of perception). Example (4) is perhaps the most relevant to literature. This suffix -*yigi* is called a 'hearsay' (or reportative, or quotative, or evidential) item: it indicates that the thought is attributed to someone other than the speaker, and that the other person believes it. Hearsay items can be morphemes attached to other words, as here, or can be independent words. We saw examples of independent word hearsay items in 8.1.2.

10.3 Literary uses for attribution and attitude

One of the simplest consequences for verbal art of being able to represent attribution and attitude is that literary texts are therefore able to represent psychological states and linguistic behaviour. At a very basic level, the possibility of representing what someone says means that a narrator can build speech into a narrative; this possibility is in fact fundamental to many narratives, since among the actions which make up a storyline are acts of speaking (and thinking). The possibility of attributing thought to characters, and of portraying those characters' relationships with their thoughts, also means that a literary text can describe the inner mental life of characters. It has been argued that the development of free indirect representations of thought in Romantic European literature (e.g. Austen's innovations) was a response at a formal level to a contemporary reconceptualizing of the individual and a need to have a complex inventory of ways of communicating an individual character's experience. Similarly, the emergence of psychoanalysis at the beginning of the twentieth century can be correlated with the formal experiments relating to attribution and attitude made by writers such as Woolf and Joyce, which attempt to present this new concept of inner mental life.

10.3.1 *The dissociation of the speaker (including irony)*

Another of the basic opportunities allowed by the possibility of representing attitude and attribution is for the speaker to represent thoughts while dissociating herself from them: communicating that they are not attributable to her, or communicating a sceptical attitude towards them.

Thus for example hearsay particles can be used by the speaker as a way of indicating that he or she does not have full responsibility for the truth of the story, and hence that the story might not be true. Thus for the hearsay particle *giiwe* in North American Ojibwe narratives, Ghezzi (1993: 42) says: 'This type of reported speech was originally explained to me by an Ojibwe informant in

Minnesota. *Giiwe* allows the narrator to tell a story about anything or anybody, without being held responsible for the material as "truth", only what the narrator has heard rumored as true.' As another example, Gnerre (1986: 329) discusses the introduction into South American Shuar literature during the twentieth century of a hearsay item *tímiayi* ('it was said'), used at the end of narrative sections. He argues that it was introduced into myths as a result of a change in attitude towards those myths: at one time, they were told without the hearsay item and were thus uttered unembedded as truths. Gnerre interprets the introduction of the hearsay particle as indicating a shift in attitude such that the stories are no longer considered to be completely true in the same way.

'Irony' is a name for various kinds of communication where the speaker dissociates herself from the thoughts communicated. The communicated thought is attributed to a third party, who may or may not be specified, and at the same time the speaker communicates one of a particular range of attitudes of dissociation towards the set of thoughts. The dissociation might be mild disbelief or fierce disapproval. Sperber and Wilson suggest that 'irony' is the term used by English speakers to delimit this range of types of dissociation. This makes irony an emic rather than an etic category: a culturally specific notion rather than a universal. We would expect to find as universal characteristics of all languages the possibility of representing a third party's thought and the possibility of expressing attitude towards it. What will vary is whether the attitudes represented are grouped in the culture as something resembling the group of attitudes which English speakers might describe as irony. As an example of irony, consider an example of an anecdote by a West Texan narrator in which the narrative is resolved by a representation of what someone said, forming the 'punchline' final clause (from Bauman 1986: 56). A man's wife comes to collect him, only to find him staggering around drunk; the anecdote ends:

. . . Ms Brandon said, 'Why Johnny, you're drunk!'
He said, 'Yes, ma'am. You the best judge of a drunk man I ever saw.'

It is generally true of the anecdotes discussed by Bauman that the quoted speech of the final clause picks up on what the other participant has just said, and represents it again. This is true here, where Johnny's utterance communicates the thought that Ms Brandon is a good judge of a drunk man. In replying to his wife, Johnny initiates a verbal duel which he is shown by the (male) narrator as winning. First, he is able to turn his verbal opponent's words against her; given that this is a conventional practice within these anecdotes, he can thus be interpreted as correctly performing a conventional way of speaking. Second, by his exaggeration he promotes himself as an expert, someone able to judge the judge, and thus contextually superior to his wife. Third, since the narrative comes to closure with his utterance – and Ms Brandon is left speechless by the narration – the narrative therefore suggests that he is in the powerful position of having the final word and therefore winning the duel which he has initiated.

Given these various ways in which Johnny 'wins', we might now return to the thought which is communicated, that Ms Brandon is a good judge of a drunk man. Is this Johnny's own thought or attributed to a third party (such as Ms Brandon), and if it is not his own thought, what is his attitude towards it? In fact, this is a difficult question to answer, perhaps because Johnny's utterance communicates two things at the same time. On the one hand, he acknowledges his moral failing: he may not be committed to the thought that Ms Brandon is the best judge of a drunk man, but he is committed to the thought that she is an accurate judge. The exaggeration (*'the best judge . . . I ever saw'*) can thus be interpreted not as a sign of lack of commitment to the thought but as an expression of emphasis in his commitment to the thought. But the exaggeration can at the same time be interpreted in another way; since it is untrue it makes the explicit meaning of the utterance as a whole untrue and thus opens the way for it to be interpreted as his representation of a third party's utterance to which he is not committed. This reading is reinforced by the general sense in which he is presented in the narrative as winning the verbal duel. Now we might ask whether this is an example of irony. The character himself might be said to be ambiguous in his utterance between irony and non-irony. In a sense this carries over to the narrative as a whole; the narrative stands for community attitudes towards drunkenness which are themselves ambiguous, between approval and disapproval. As in many cases where there is moral ambiguity, the verbal behaviour is ambiguous between ironical and non-ironical.

10.3.2 *The reliability of third parties*

While the dissociation of the speaker and the attribution of a thought to a third party may be a means of communicating that the thought is untrue, it may also be a means of guaranteeing the truth of the thought. The Sherpa *Life of Buddha* is an example of this (Givón, cited by Palmer (1986: 85)). In Sherpa, there is a choice of two evidential morphemes which may attach to the verb; one communicates that the speaker has direct evidence to support the assumption communicated, while the other communicates that the speaker has indirect or hearsay evidence. It is the latter – the 'hearsay' morpheme – which is used in the *Life of Buddha*; this means that the truest of all stories is attributed not to the speaker but to a third party. Here it is not necessarily the case that the speaker's own commitment to an assumption is the strongest evidence for that assumption; there may be an even more reliable third party source. Thus the exact effect of a hearsay particle – whether it strengthens or weakens the evidence for the assumptions communicated – depends on the culture. As an illustration of the difficulty of deciding exactly what effect a communicative particle has, look back to the use of the hearsay phrase *séi báan* ('they say') in the Burushaski story in exercise 8.7.1; in addition to its function of indicating constituent structure, does this hearsay item strengthen the truth of the story or weaken it? Just looking at the story without knowing more about the culture, it is impossible to say.

An utterance or a thought can be attributed to the speaker herself, or to a known third party such as a character in a narrative, or to a particular person known to speaker and hearer. There is, however, no requirement that the represented utterance or thought should be attributed to a particular person at all. A common example of this is an utterance which represents conventional wisdom, such as a proverb. For example the proverb 'Rolling stones gather no moss' represents an assumption (or more plausibly a set of assumptions) which the speaker may endorse but which is not represented as originating as her own assumption; instead the assumption originates in 'the community' or 'the culture' in some sense which need not be made precise. This is another case where the de-attribution of the thought from the speaker and its re-attribution to an anonymous community serves to strengthen the validity of the thought. As we see in the next section, attribution to an unspecified third party can be used for various effects and can sometimes – as here – be a means of strengthening an assumption and sometimes a means of weakening it.

10.3.3 Attribution and the spirit world

Another use of attribution is to invoke and involve the spirit world in a performance, by attributing thoughts to spiritual third parties. Thus Powers (1986: 78) discusses songs sung in Lakota and related secret languages during the *Yuyupi* healing ceremony of the Oglala people. The first song of the ceremony is sung by the lead singers, who lead other participants in singing it. The lead singers were taught the song by the medicine man; he learned the song from spirits in a vision and the performance of the song is a re-enactment of the original vision. Powers comments that 'as is true in most sacred texts, one must first understand that the words are those of the spirits, not of the medicine man'. Here the performance involves a hierarchy of voices, each referring back to another and ending with the spirits – the reproduction of the spirits' words somehow invokes their presence.

Kuipers (1988: 111) discusses an interesting use of quotation in Weyéwa prayers (Indonesia: Nusa Tenggara). Like other kinds of ritual language in Indonesia, the prayers are organized to a large extent in parallel clauses (see 6.4). Kuipers cites a prayer by Mbulu Renda and divides it into 396 lines organized in sections averaging around 4–10 lines long. Sections quite often begin or end with phrases which describe an act of speaking; here are three examples:

ka lúmmukuni ná'ingge	So it is said by you to him (line 14)
Hínagge nátti	Thus it was said by him (line 62)
Hínna	So it is said (line 84)

In some cases, the act of speaking is itself a description of an act of speaking:

| *Lúngguba Lúnggu tákka* | It was said by me 'It is truly said by me' (lines 26–7) |
| *Lúnggu ka lúmmu* | I declare so that you will say (line 195) |

Kuipers interprets this frequency of descriptions of speaking as a means of invoking a communicative relation between the speaker and the spirits (who are the 'you' of the text). The text is thus a representation of a dialogue with the (otherwise silent) spirits which describes both sides of the dialogue: the explicit attribution of speech is a way of invoking the speakers. Notice, incidentally, that the fact that these references to speaking occur often at constituent boundaries suggests that they also have a formal function of indicating those boundaries (analogous to the use of hearsay particles in Lakota, for example: see 8.1.2).

10.4 Summary: the communicative function of language and its exploitation in literature

One of the functions of language is communication, and verbal communication is always loose. This is fundamental to the communicative potential of ordinary language, and is exploited for particular effects in literature, for example in metaphor. Among the things which language is particularly well suited to communicate are representations of speech and thought. Everyday uses of language involve the communication of third party thoughts and the speaker's attitudes towards them, and again these everyday possibilities can be exploited for particular effect in literature.

10.5 Further reading

On Relevance Theory (the basis of the account of communication in this chapter), see Sperber and Wilson (1995), which is the second edition of Sperber and

Wilson (1986); also Blakemore (1992) and the special issue of *Lingua*, vol. 87 (1992). For general overviews of theories of metaphor see Steen (1994), and the collections by Sacks (1979) and Ortony (1993). On Lakoff's influential view of metaphor see Lakoff and Johnson (1980), Lakoff and Turner (1989) and Gibbs (1994). Feld (1982) is a classic ethnopoetic study of the aesthetics of an extensive metaphorical system in Kaluli culture; for other literature-specific studies see e.g. Mindlin et al. (1987). Sperber (1975, 1985) presents an account of the embedding of 'semi-propositional' knowledge. On 'the intentional stance' whereby we attribute attitudes to other people see Dennett (1987); on breakdowns in this ability see U. Frith (1989) on schizophrenia, and C. Frith (1992) on autism. Linguistic accounts of the representation of speech and thought include Banfield (1982) and Fludernik (1993); see also the collection edited by Coulmas (1986). The more general problem of 'point of view', which is in part a matter of attribution, is discussed by Simpson (1993).

10.6   Exercises

10.6.1   *Kennings: metaphors in Icelandic poetry*

This exercise asks you to look at the use of kennings in Medieval Icelandic poetry. A kenning is a particular kind of metaphor in which two or more words stand for a single noun. Thus in this poem a kenning would be *bjǫrn flóðs*, literally 'the bear of the flood', and meaning 'the ship'.

Instructions

(a)   Translate the poem into idiomatic (everyday) English.
(b)   What is the interpretation of this text? What evidence is provided by the text for its interpretation, and what evidence must be drawn from elsewhere?
(c)   The poem can be divided into four sentences, one in each couplet. Is there any reason why particular kennings are used in particular sentences, or is the grouping and ordering random? (Note: there may be several kinds of reason.)
(d)   Each pair of lines is a sentence, usually reordered in various ways. Radical reordering of the sentence is not uncommon in this style of poetry. Can you find any pattern to the ordering of words here, or is it completely random?

Text

The poem was written in the *dróttkvætt* meter by Markús Skeggjason (d. 1107). This exercise is based on the discussion of this stanza, and the translation and glossary, in Frank (1978: 46).

> *Fjarðlinna óð fannir*
> *fast vetrliði rastar;*
> *hljóp of húna gnípur*
> *hvalranns íugtanni;*
> *bjǫrn gekk framm á fornar*
> *flóðs hafskíða slóðir;*
> *skúrǫrðigr braut skorðu*
> *skers glymfjǫtur bersi.*

Word-for-word translation

This is a word-for-word translation, with kennings and other substitutions indicated in square brackets.

fjarðlinna   *óð*   *fannir*
of the fjord-snake [= of the fish] waded through the snowdrifts

fast   *vetrliði*   *rastar*
firmly one who has passed a winter [= young bear] of the current

> *fannir fjarðlinna* (the snowdrifts of the fish) [= the billows, currents]
> *vetrliði rastar* (the young bear of the current) [= the ship]

> 'The young bear of the current waded firmly through the snowdrifts of the fjord-snake'

hljóp   *of*   *húna*   *gnípur*
jumped over of the mastheads the peaks

hvalranns   *íugtanni*
of the whale-house [= of the sea] the bear

> *gnípur hvalranns* (the peaks of the sea) [= the waves]
> *íugtanni húna* (the bear of the mastheads) [= the ship]

> 'The bear of the mastheads jumped over the peaks of the whale-house'

bjǫrn   gekk framm   áá fornar
the bear went forward on old (adjective)

flóðs   hafskíða   slóðir
of the flood of the sea-ski [= of the ship] the wake

    bjǫrn flóðs (the bear of the flood) [= the ship]

    'The bear of the flood went forward on the old wake of the sea-ski'

skúrǫrðigr   *braut*   *skorðu*
storm-rearing (adjective) broke through of the ship's support

skers   *glymfjǫtur*   *bersi*
of the rocky island the resounding fetter the bear

    glymfjǫtur skers (the resounding fetter of the rocky island) [= the sea]
    bersi skorðu (the bear of the ship's support) [= the ship]

    'The bear of the ship's support broke through the storm-rearing resounding
    fetter of the rocky island.'

10.6.2   *Speech and structure in 'Ozymandias'*

Instructions

(a)   This text can be interpreted as communicating a sequence of utterances
       (and thoughts) which are attributed to various different people. Thus the
       poem appears to begin with self-attribution, then shifts to attribution to
       a third party (the traveller), and so on. Divide the poem into sections
       according to whom the communicated utterances and thoughts are attrib-
       uted to in each part. Discuss any difficulties you have in working out the
       source of any of the thoughts, and explain why you think those difficulties
       arise (for example: are the difficulties put there deliberately?).

(b)   Now divide the poem into sections based on other criteria, such as rhyme,
       content, and so on. (This is a sonnet; you will find it helpful to bear in
       mind – or look up – the conventional divisions and rhyme schemes of
       English sonnets.) How do these divisions relate to the divisions by attribu-
       tion which you carried out in (a)?

(c)   Shelley could have ended the poem with a section in which the poet
       describes leaving the traveller. Explain why one might perhaps expect
       such an ending, and why you think Shelley did not end the poem like this.

(d)   Why is the poem called 'Ozymandias'? You might try to answer this question
       by trying out some alternative titles and seeing what the effects of this are.

Text

Ozymandias (by Percy Bysshe Shelley, 1819)

I met a traveller from an antique land
Who said: Two vast and trunkless legs of stone
Stand in the desert. Near them, on the sand,
Half sunk, a shattered visage lies, whose frown,
5   And wrinkled lip, and sneer of cold command,
Tell that its sculptor well those passions read
Which yet survive, stamped on those lifeless things,
The hand that mocked them, and the heart that fed:
And on the pedestal these words appear:
10   'My name is Ozymandias, king of kings:
Look on my works, ye Mighty, and despair!'
Nothing besides remains. Round the decay
Of that colossal wreck, boundless and bare
The lone and level sands stretch far away.

10.6.3   Austen and Burney: representations of speech and thought, and irony

One of the characteristics of 'free indirect thought' is that it enables a narrator to shift between communicating her own thoughts and communicating the thoughts of a fictional character. The shifts may be very subtle, with the subtlety of shifting used for deliberate literary effect. Jane Austen is usually cited as the originator of this practice, which was then used extensively in nineteenth-century novels; however, we can see the beginnings of it in the writing of her predecessor Fanny Burney.

Instructions

(a)   Both texts as they develop communicate a series of thoughts (some realized as actual utterances). Try to determine which thoughts are attributed to one of the fictional characters and at the same time are de-attributed from the narrator, who expresses an 'ironic' attitude towards them.
(b)   How does the text give us evidence for whom the thoughts are attributed to, and when the attribution shifts?

(c) Both Austen and Burney practise a shifting of attribution within the text.
     Based on these extracts, how does Austen's practice differ from Burney's?
     Can Burney's practice be described as an early and less worked-out
     version of Austen's practice?

Texts

Text A: from Jane Austen, *Emma*, 1816. This is the beginning of the first
chapter.

> Emma Woodhouse, handsome, clever and rich, with a comfortable home
> and happy disposition, seemed to unite some of the best blessings of
> existence; and had lived nearly twenty-one years in the world with very
> little to distress or vex her.
>   She was the youngest of the two daughters of a most affectionate,
> indulgent father, and had, in consequence of her sister's marriage, been
> mistress of his house from a very early period. Her mother had died too
> long ago for her to have more than an indistinct remembrance of her
> caresses, and her place had been supplied by an excellent woman as
> governess, who had fallen little short of a mother in affection.
>   Sixteen years had Miss Taylor been in Mr Woodhouse's family, less
> as a governess than a friend, very fond of both daughters, but particu-
> larly of Emma. Between *them* it was more the intimacy of sisters. Even
> before Miss Taylor had ceased to hold the nominal office of governess,
> the mildness of her temper had hardly allowed her to impose any restraint;
> and the shadow of authority being now long passed away, they had been
> living together as friend and friend very mutually attached, and Emma
> doing just what she liked; highly esteeming Miss Taylor's judgement, but
> directed chiefly by her own.
>   The real evils of Emma's situation were the power of having rather too
> much her own way, and a disposition to think a little too well of herself;
> these were the disadvantages which threatened alloy to her many
> enjoyments. The danger, however, was at present so unperceived, that
> they did not by any means rank as misfortunes with her.
>   Sorrow came – a gentle sorrow – but not at all in the shape of any
> disagreeable consciousness. – Miss Taylor married. It was Miss Taylor's
> loss which first brought grief. It was on the wedding day of this beloved
> friend that Emma first sat in mournful thought of any continuance.

Text B: from Fanny Burney, *Camilla: or, a Picture of Youth*, 1796. This is from near the beginning of the first chapter, with two paragraphs removed.

In the bosom of her respectable family resided Camilla. Nature, with a bounty the most profuse, had been lavish to her of attractions; Fortune, with a moderation yet kinder, had placed her between luxury and indigence. Her abode was in the parsonage house of Etherington, beautifully situated in the unequal county of Hampshire, and in the vicinity of the varied landscapes of the New Forest. Her father, the rector, was the younger son of the house of Tyrold. The living, though not considerable, enabled its incumbent to attain every rational object of his modest and circumscribed wishes; to bestow upon a deserving wife whatever her own forbearance declined not; and to educate a lovely race of one son and three daughters, with that expansive propriety which unites improvement for the future with present enjoyment.

[. . .]

Sir Hugh Tyrold was a baronet, who resided upon the hereditary estate of the family in Yorkshire. He was many years older than Mr Tyrold, who had never seen him since his marriage; religious duties, prudence, and domestic affairs having from that period detained him at his benefice; while a passion for field sports had, with equal constancy, kept his brother stationary.

The baronet began his letter with kind enquiries after the welfare of Mr Tyrold and his family, and then entered upon the state of his own affairs, briefly narrating, that he had lost his health, and not knowing what to do with himself, had resolved to change his habitation, and settle near his relations. The Cleves' estate, which he heard was just by Etherington, being then upon sale, he desired his brother to make the purchase for him out of hand; and then to prepare Mrs Tyrold, with whom he was yet unacquainted, though he took it for granted she was a woman of great learning, to receive a mere poor country squire, who knew no more of hic, haec, hoc, than the baby unborn. He begged him to provide a proper apartment for their niece Indiana Lynmere, whom he should bring with him, and another for their nephew Clermont, who was to follow at the next holidays; and not to forget Mrs Margland, Indiana's governess, she being rather the most particular in point of pleasing amongst them.

11 Literary Linguistics: Summary and Prospects

This book set out to examine the ways in which literary texts make use of language. These were some of the findings.

Some kinds of literary form are completely dependent on linguistic form: the clearest cases of this are metrical and para-metrical form. These kinds of form are the organization of linguistic form (specifically prosodic phonological form) according to a complex system which appears to be specific to meter, though it may share some aspects with musical systems. This is the most plausible case of a kind of literary form that may require specific cognitive systems, which – like the systems enabling language – may be innate. There is thus a special interest in several unanswered questions about metrical form. First, how universally is it found (beyond the familiar European and Asian traditions)? Second, what are the possible variations of kinds of metrical form – are there logically possible kinds which in practice do not exist? Third, what aspects of linguistic form does metrical form have access to (this is a question about the relation between different cognitive systems)?

For parallelism to exist, there must be some possibility of underlying similarity beneath surface difference. Many kinds of form – visual, musical, etc. – can offer this possibility, and parallelism is not restricted to verbal media. Language can also offer this possibility, because of the multiple layers of language: two different strings of words may have identical syntactic structures, and this identity at a more abstract level can be the basis of parallelism. Thus linguistic form offers material from which parallelism can be created. Perhaps the main question of linguistic interest about parallelism relates to what aspects of linguistic form it can exploit, and how deep below the surface it can go: whether for example underlying rather than surface representations can be exploited in parallelism. Questions have also re-emerged in theoretical syntax about parallelism as a fundamental principle of syntactic organization at quite an abstract level (Chomsky 1995: 125); these questions interact interestingly with questions about parallelism as an organizatory principle in verbal art.

Narrative form exists in many media, and the primary link between linguistic and narrative form in verbal narratives comes from the role of linguistic form in communicating narrative form. The organization into narrative macro-structure or into continuous sequences or into episodes are all aspects of narrative form which do not depend for their existence on language; but in order for those aspects of form to be communicated to an audience, linguistic form can be exploited in various ways. One of the questions we might ask about this is whether there are constraints on which aspects of linguistic form can be used to communicate narrative form. The study of narrative also overlaps substantially with the study of language in its discursive textual manifestations: narrative is part of our general linguistic behaviour and is not restricted to verbal art. Thus the study of narrative is part of the larger study of discourse, and a question which might be asked is whether narrative form shares certain elements of discourse form more generally: whether, for example, narratives are like conversations in certain ways.

Chapters 2–8 focused on the use of linguistic form in literary form. Chapters 9 and 10 placed less emphasis on linguistic form and more emphasis, respectively, on the contextual aspects and the communicative function of verbal behaviour. In both cases, we saw how these aspects of language are put to use in verbal art, and in both cases we saw that verbal art simply exploits already existing characteristics of language.

The hypothesis with which we began was that the use of language in literature can be studied cross-linguistically in search of generalizations. We have seen that there are in fact similarities between unconnected traditions in all aspects of their use of language. Thus for example metrical lines show certain similarities (e.g. in how they begin and end) across many metrical traditions; episodes in narratives have their boundaries indicated in similar ways in many different languages; the use of lexical parallelism to create texts is shared by widely dispersed Middle Eastern, Central American and Pacific traditions. Thus we have the basis of certain descriptive generalizations. Once we have descriptive generalizations, we can begin to formulate explanations.

Explanations for cross-linguistic and cross-literary generalizations might be of three kinds. We might explain similarities between traditions by pointing to a common ancestor, as has been attempted for the Indo-European metrical tradition. We might explain similarities along functional lines: Jakobson's formulation of the poetic function is an example of this, proposing a simultaneous explanation at a very general level for the formal phenomena of metricality, parallelism, and patterned narrative structure. And, following the lead of generative linguistics, we might explain similarities along cognitive lines: thus the many kinds of metrical text might all arise from some basic cognitive subsystem which enables humans to process metrical verse.

Future work in literary linguistics might attempt to come to more inclusive descriptive generalizations, and might explore these various kinds of explanation. Many traditions remain undescribed, and older descriptions need to be reconsidered in the light of new linguistic theories. We are likely to discover more examples of metrical verse in traditions not previously considered metrical, to reanalyse the nature of metrical traditions (so that apparently quantitative traditions might be revealed as accentual), to recognize complex narrative structure in narrative traditions which now exist only unread and in archives, and so on.

Among the tasks of explanation is a problem which has barely been touched on in this book, namely the problem of the emotional experience of verbal art. Verbal art achieves its various functions in part because it is often able to trigger profound emotional experiences in its audiences, across the whole range from pleasure to horror. Among these are experiences which blur the line between emotion and attitude, emotional experiences which are at the same time spiritual experiences: deep certainties which emerge from aesthetic experience. If we are to understand why verbal art has these effects, one part of our understanding might be able to develop from a better understanding of the form of verbal art, which in turn relates to the linguistic form from which it is built. Sperber and Wilson (1986, 1995) have argued that we can reinterpret the experience of weakly evidenced meaning, common in literary texts where meanings are obscure and indeterminate, as a type of aesthetic experience. Others, such as Dan Berlyne (1960, 1974) or Thomas Bever (1986), have argued that our experience of complexity, or the move from complexity to simplicity, might be central to aesthetic experience – and if this is true, then we must understand what 'complexity' is in a literary text, and what role is played by linguistic form.

These are open questions, a suggestion of some of the prospects just visible, and a promise of surprises to come.

References

Abondolo, D. 1996: Thoughts on Dante's *endecasillabo* and its Babitsean counterpart. In J. I. Press and F. E. Knowles (eds), *Papers from the Fourth World Congress for Soviet and East European Studies*. London: ICSEES.

Allen, W. S. 1973: *Accent and Rhythm. Prosodic Features of Latin and Greek: A Study in Theory and Reconstruction*. Cambridge: Cambridge University Press.

Andrzejewski, B. W. 1972: Poetry in Somali society. In J. B. Pride (ed.), *Sociolinguistics* (pp. 252–9). Harmondsworth: Penguin.

Andrzejewski, B. and Andrzejewski, S. (eds) 1993: *An Anthology of Somali Poetry*. Bloomington: Indiana University Press.

Anyidoho, A. 1991: Linguistic parallels in traditional Akan appellation poetry. *Research in African Literatures*, 22(1), 67–81.

Árnason, K. 1991: *The Rhythms of dróttkvætt and Other Old Icelandic Metres*. Reykjavik: Institute of Linguistics, University of Iceland.

Arnold, E. V. 1905: *Vedic Metre in its Historical Development*. Cambridge: Cambridge University Press.

Attridge, D. 1974: *Well-Weighed Syllables. Elizabethan Verse in Classical Metres*. Cambridge: Cambridge University Press.

Attridge, D. 1982: *The Rhythms of English Poetry*. Harlow: Longman.

Attridge, D. 1995: *Poetic Rhythm. An Introduction*. Cambridge: Cambridge University Press.

Austin, T. R. 1984: *Language Crafted. A Linguistic Theory of Poetic Syntax*. Bloomington: Indiana University Press.

Babalọla, S. A. 1966: *The Content and Form of Yoruba Ijala*. Oxford: Oxford University Press.

Baker, A. 1973: Parallelism: England's contribution to Biblical studies. *Catholic Biblical Quarterly*, 35, 429–40.

Bamgboṣe, A. 1970: Word play in Yoruba poetry. *International Journal of American Linguistics*, 36, 110–16.

Banfield, A. 1982: *Unspeakable Sentences. Narration and Representation in the Language of Fiction*. Boston: Routledge & Kegan Paul.

Banti, G. and Giannattasio, F. 1996: Music and metre in Somali poetry. In R. J. Hayward and I. M. Lewis (eds), *Voice and Power. The Culture of Language in North-East Africa* (pp. 83–128). London: School of Oriental and African Studies.

Barthes, R. 1964: *On Racine* (translated by Richard Howard). New York: Hill & Wang.

Barthes, R. 1974: *S/Z* (translated by Richard Howard). New York: Hill & Wang.

Basso, E. 1986: Quoted dialogues in Kalapalo narrative discourse. In J. Sherzer and G. Urban (eds), *Native South American Discourse* (pp. 119–68). Berlin: Mouton de Gruyter.

Bauman, R. 1975: Verbal art as performance. *American Anthropologist*, 77, 290–311.

Bauman, R. 1984: *Verbal Art as Performance*. Prospect Heights, IL: Waveland Press.

Bauman, R. 1986: *Story, Performance, and Event. Contextual Studies of Oral Narrative*. Cambridge: Cambridge University Press.

Bauman, R. 1993: Disclaimers of performance. In J. H. Hill and J. T. Irvine (eds), *Responsibility and Evidence in Oral Discourse* (pp. 182–96). Cambridge: Cambridge University Press.

Bauman, R. 1996: Natural histories of discourse. In M. Silverstein and G. Urban (eds), *Natural Histories of Discourse* (pp. 301–27). Chicago: University of Chicago Press.

Bauman, R. and Briggs, C. L. 1990: Poetics and performance as critical perspectives on language and social life. *Annual Review of Anthropology*, 19, 59–88.

Bauman, R. and Ritch, P. 1994: Informing performance: producing the *Coloquio* in Tierra Blanca. *Oral Tradition*, 9(2), 255–80.

Bauma, R. and Sherzer, J. 1989: *Explorations in the Ethnography of Speaking* (2nd edn). Cambridge: Cambridge University Press.

Berlyne, D. E. 1960: *Conflict, Arousal, and Curiosity*. New York: McGraw-Hill.

Berlyne, D. E. (ed.) 1974: *Studies in the New Experimental Aesthetics: Steps towards an Objective Psychology of Aesthetic Appreciation*. New York: John Wiley.

Bever, T. G. 1986: The aesthetic basis for cognitive structures. In M. Brand and R. Harnish (eds), *The Representation of Knowledge and Belief* (pp. 314–56). Tucson: University of Arizona Press.

Blackings, M. J. and Fabb, N. forthcoming: *A Grammar of Madi*. Berlin: Mouton.

Blakemore, D. 1992: *Understanding Utterances. An Introduction to Pragmatics*. Oxford: Blackwell.

Bogoras, W. 1917: *Koryak Texts*. Leiden: E. J. Brill.

Bowen, J. R. 1989: Poetic duels and political change in the Gayo highlands of Sumatra. *American Anthropologist*, 91, 25–40.

Brăiloiu, C. 1984a: The syllabic giusto. In C. Brăiloiu, *Problems of Ethnomusicology* (pp. 168–205). Cambridge: Cambridge University Press.

Brăiloiu, C. 1984b: Children's rhythms. In C. Brăiloiu, *Problems of Ethnomusicology* (pp. 206–38). Cambridge: Cambridge University Press.

Bricker, V. R. 1989: The ethnographic context of some traditional Mayan speech genres. In R. Bauman and J. Sherzer (eds), *Explorations in the Ethnography of Speaking* (pp. 368–88). Cambridge: Cambridge University Press.

Briggs, C. L. and Bauman, R. 1992: Genre, intertextuality, and social power. *Journal of Linguistic Anthropology*, 2(2), 131–72.

Briggs, K. M. 1970: *A Dictionary of British Folk Tales in the English Language*. London: Routledge.

Briggs, K. M. 1977: *British Folk Tales and Legends: A Sampler*. London: Granada.

Brody, J. 1986: Repetition as a rhetorical and conversational device in Tojolabal (Mayan). *International Journal of American Linguistics*, 52(3), 255–74.

Brower, R. H. 1972: Japanese. In W. K. Wimsatt (ed.), *Versification* (pp. 38–51). New York: Modern Language Association and New York University Press.

Bryant, K. E. 1992: Three-three-two versus four-by-four: metrical frames for the *padas* of Surdas. In R. S. McGregor (ed.), *Devotional Literature in South Asia: Current Research, 1985–1988* (pp. 209–24). Cambridge: Cambridge University Press.

Burling, R. 1966: The metrics of children's verse: a cross-linguistic study. *American Anthropologist*, 68, 1418–41.

Carmi, T. (ed.) 1981: *The Penguin Book of Hebrew Verse*. Harmondsworth: Penguin.

Carter, R. (ed.) 1982: *Language and Literature. An Introductory Reader in Stylistics.* London: Allen & Unwin.

Chadwick, H. M. and Chadwick, N. K. 1940: *The Growth of Literature*, vol. III. Cambridge: Cambridge University Press.

Chafe, W. L. (ed.) 1980: *The Pear Stories. Cognitive, Cultural and Linguistic Aspects of Narrative Production*. New Jersey: Ablex.

Chen, M. Y. 1979: Metrical structure: evidence from Chinese poetry. *Linguistic Inquiry*, 10(3), 371–420.

Chen, M. Y. 1984: Abstract symmetry in Chinese verse. *Linguistic Inquiry*, 15(1), 167–70.

Chomsky, N. 1957: *Syntactic Structures*. Berlin: Mouton.

Chomsky, N. 1995: *The Minimalist Program*. Cambridge, MA: MIT Press.

Chona, M. 1936: *The Autobiography of a Papago Woman*, ed. R. Underhill. Memoirs of the American Anthropological Association, No. 46; reprinted in 1979 as *Papago Woman*, New York: Holt, Rinehart and Winston.

Contini-Morava, E. 1987: Text cohesion and the sign: connectedness between events in Swahili narrative. In D. Odden (ed.), *Current Approaches to African Linguistics 4* (pp. 107–21). Dordrecht: Foris.

Contini-Morava, E. 1989: *Discourse Pragmatics and Semantic Categorization*. Berlin: Mouton de Gruyter.

Contini-Morava, E. 1991a: Deictic explicitness and event continuity in Swahili discourse. *Lingua*, 83, 277–318.

Contini-Morava, E. 1991b: Negation, probability and temporal boundedness: discourse functions of negative tenses in Swahili narrative. In J. Gvozdanovic and T. Jansen (eds), *The Function of Tense in Texts* (pp. 35–51). Amsterdam: North Holland.

Coulmas, F. (ed.) 1986: *Direct and Indirect Speech*. Berlin: Mouton.

Coulson, M. 1992: *Sanskrit. An Introduction to the Classical Language (= Teach Yourself Sanskrit)* (2nd edn.). London: Hodder & Stoughton.

Crystal, D. 1987: *The Cambridge Encyclopedia of Language*. Cambridge: Cambridge University Press.

Cumming, S. 1991: *Functional Change. The Case of Malay Constituent Order*. Berlin: Mouton de Gruyter.

Cumming, S. 1995: Agent position in the *Sejarah Melayu*. In P. Downing and M. Noonan (eds), *Word Order in Discourse* (pp. 51–83). Amsterdam: John Benjamins.

Cureton, R. D. 1994: Rhythm and verse study. *Language and Literature*, 3(2), 105–24.

de Moor, J. C. 1993: Syntax peculiar to Ugaritic poetry. In J. C. de Moor and W. G. E. Watson (eds), *Verse in Ancient Near Eastern Prose* (pp. 191–205). Kevelaer: Butzon und Bercker.

de Moor, J. C. and Watson, W. G. E. (eds) 1993: *Verse in Ancient Near Eastern Prose*. Kevelaer: Butzon und Bercker.

de Vale, S. C. 1984: Prologomena to a study of harp and voice sounds in Uganda: a graphic system for the notation of texture. *Selected Reports in Ethnomusicology, 5* (pp. 285–315). Los Angeles: Institute of Ethnomusicology.

Dennett, D. 1987: *The Intentional Stance.* Cambridge, MA: MIT Press.

Devine, A. M. and Stephens, L. D. 1984: *Language and Metre. Resolution, Porson's Bridge, and Their Prosodic Basis.* Chico, CA: Scholar's Press.

Dixon, R. M. W. 1980: *The Languages of Australia.* Cambridge: Cambridge University Press.

Dixon, R. M. W. 1984: Dyirbal song types: a preliminary report. In J. Kassler and J. Stubington (eds), *Problems and Solutions: Occasional Essays in Ethnomusicology presented to Alice M. Moyle* (pp. 206–27). Sydney: Hale & Ironmonger.

Dixon, R. M. W. and Koch, G. 1996: *Dyirbal Song Poetry. The Oral Literature of an Australian Rainforest People.* St Lucia: University of Queensland Press.

Downing, P. and Noonan, M. (eds) 1995: *Word Order in Discourse.* Amsterdam: John Benjamins.

Dresher, B. E. 1994: The prosodic basis of the Tiberian Hebrew system of accents. *Language,* 70(1), 1–52.

Dunn, C. W. 1972: Celtic. In W. K. Wimsatt (ed.), *Versification* (pp. 136–47). New York: Modern Language Association and New York University Press.

Durant, A. and Fabb, N. 1990: *Literary Studies in Action.* London: Routledge.

Duranti, A. and Brenneis, D. (eds) 1986: *The Audience as Co-author.* Special issue of TEXT 6(3), 239–347.

Edgerton, F. 1934: Sievers' Law and IE weak-grade vocalism. *Language,* 10, 235–65.

Edgerton, F. 1943: The Indo-European semivowels. *Language,* 19, 83–124.

Edmonson, M. S. 1971: *Lore. An Introduction to the Science of Folklore and Literature.* New York: Holt, Rinehart and Winston.

Emeneau, M. B. 1966: Style and meaning in an oral literature. *Language,* 42(2), 323–45.

Erdener, Y. 1995: *The Song Contests of Turkish Minstrels. Improvised Poetry Sung to Traditional Music.* New York: Garland.

Evers, L. and Molina, F. S. 1987: *Yaqui Deer Songs. Maso Bwikam. A Native American Poetry.* Tucson: Sun Tracks and The University of Arizona Press.

Fabb, N. 1988: Saussure and literary theory: from the perspective of linguistics. *Critical Quarterly,* 30(2), 58–72.

Fabb, N., Attridge, D., Durant, A. and MacCabe, C. (eds) 1987: *The Linguistics of Writing.* Manchester: Manchester University Press.

Feld, S. 1982: *Sound and Sentiment. Birds, Weeping, Poetics and Song in Kaluli Expression.* Philadelphia: University of Pennsylvania Press.

Finnegan, R. 1970: *Oral Literature in Africa.* Oxford: Oxford University Press.

Finnegan, R. H. 1990: What is oral literature anyway? Comments in the light of some African and other comparative material. In J. M. Foley (ed.), *Oral-Formulaic Theory. A Folklore Casebook* (pp. 243–82). New York: Garland.

Finnegan, R. 1992a: *Oral Poetry. Its Nature, Significance and Social Context.* Bloomington: Indiana University Press.

Finnegan, R. 1992b: *Oral Traditions and the Verbal Arts.* London: Routledge.

Finnegan, R. and Orbell, M. (eds) 1995: *South Pacific Oral Traditions*. Bloomington: Indiana University Press.

Fludernik, M. 1993: *The Fictions of Language and the Languages of Fiction*. London: Routledge.

Foley, J. M. (ed.) 1990: *Oral-Formulaic Theory. A Folklore Casebook*. New York: Garland.

Foley, J. M. 1995: *The Singer of Tales in Performance*. Bloomington: Indiana University Press.

Forth, G. 1988: Fashioned speech, full communication: aspects of eastern Sumbanese ritual language. In J. J. Fox (ed.), *To Speak in Pairs. Essays on the Ritual Languages of Eastern Indonesia* (pp. 129–60). Cambridge: Cambridge University Press.

Forth, G. 1996: To chat in pairs. Lexical pairing as a pervasive feature of Nage mundane speech. *Canberra Anthropology*, 19(1), 31–51.

Foster, J. L. 1975: Thought couplets in Khety's 'Hymn to the inundation'. *Journal of Near Eastern Studies*, 34(1), 1–29.

Foster, J. L. 1980: Sinuhe: the ancient Egyptian genre of narrative verse. *Journal of Near Eastern Studies*, 39(2), 89–117.

Fowler, R. 1977: *Linguistics and the Novel*. London: Routledge.

Fox, J. J. 1977: Roman Jakobson and the comparative study of parallelism. In C. H. v. Schooneveld and D. Armstrong (eds), *Roman Jakobson: Echoes of his Scholarship* (pp. 59–90). Lisse: Peter de Ridder Press.

Fox, J. J. 1982: The Rotinese chotbah as a linguistic performance. In A. Halim, L. Carrington and S. A. Wurm (eds), *Papers from the Third International Conference on Austronesian Linguistics, vol. 3: Accent on Variety* (pp. 311–8). Pacific Linguistics, C-76. Canberra: Australian National University.

Fox, J. J. (ed.) 1988: *To Speak in Pairs. Essays on the Ritual Languages of Eastern Indonesia*. Cambridge: Cambridge University Press.

Fox, J. J. 1989: Category and complement: binary ideologies and the organisation of dualism in Eastern Indonesia. In D. Maybury-Lewis and U. Almagor (eds), *The Attraction of Opposites: Thought and Society in a Dualistic Mode*. Ann Arbor: University of Michigan Press.

Fox, J. J. 1991: 'Bound to the core, held locked in all our hearts': Prayers and invocations among the Rotinese. *Canberra Anthropology*, 14(2), 30–48.

Frank, R. 1978: *Old Norse Court Poetry. The dróttkvætt Stanza* (special edition of *Islandica* XLII). Ithaca: Cornell University Press.

Frankel, H. H. 1972: Classical Chinese. In W. K. Wimsatt (ed.), *Versification* (pp. 22–37). New York: Modern Language Association and New York University Press.

Freeman, D. C. (ed.) 1970: *Linguistics and Literary Style*. New York: Holt, Rinehart and Winston.

Freeman, D. C. (ed.) 1981: *Essays in Modern Stylistics*. London: Methuen.

Frisbie, C. J. 1980: Vocables in Navajo ceremonial music. *Ethnomusicology*, 24(3), 347–92.

Frith, C. 1992: *The Cognitive Neuropsychology of Schizophrenia*. Hove: Lawrence Erlbaum Associates.

Frith, U. 1989: *Autism. Explaining the Enigma*. Oxford: Blackwell.

282 References

Fussell, P. 1979: *Poetic Meter and Poetic Form.* New York: McGraw-Hill.

Gayton, A. H. 1964: Narrative style. In D. Hymes (ed.), *Language in Culture and Society* (pp. 377–81). New York: Harper & Row.

Ghezzi, R. W. 1993: Tradition and innovation in Ojibwe storytelling. Mrs Marie Syrette's 'The Orphans and Mashos'. In A. Krupat (ed.), *New Voices in Native American Literary Criticism* (pp. 37–76). Washington: Smithsonian Institution Press.

Giamatti, A. B. 1972: Italian. In W. K. Wimsatt (ed.), *Versification* (pp. 148–64). New York: Modern Language Association and New York University Press.

Gibbs, R. W. 1994: *The Poetics of Mind. Figurative Thought, Language, and Understanding.* Cambridge: Cambridge University Press.

Gillingham, S. G. 1994: *The Poems and Psalms of the Hebrew Bible.* Oxford: Oxford University Press.

Givón, T. (ed.) 1983: *Topic Continuity in Discourse: A Quantitative Cross-Language Study.* Amsterdam: Benjamins.

Gnerre, M. 1986: The decline of dialogue: ceremonial and mythological discourse among the Shuar and Achuar of Eastern Ecuador. In J. Sherzer and G. Urban (eds), *Native South American Discourse* (pp. 307–41). Berlin: Mouton de Gruyter.

Goddard, I. 1990: Aspects of the topic structure of Fox narratives: proximate shifts and the use of overt and inflectional NPs. *International Journal of American Linguistics,* 56(3), 317–40.

Goodman, N. 1976: *Languages of Art: An Approach to the Theory of Symbols.* Indiana: Hackett.

Gossen, G. 1989: To speak with a heated heart: Chamula canons of style and good performance. In R. Bauman and J. Sherzer (eds), *Explorations in the Ethnography of Speaking* (pp. 389–413). Cambridge: Cambridge University Press.

Gray, C. T. 1992: Patterns of textual recurrence in Kiganda song. *International Review of the Aesthetics and Sociology of Music,* 23(1), 85–100.

Greenberg, J. 1960: A survey of African prosodic systems. In S. Diamond (ed.), *Culture in History. Essays in Honor of Paul Radin* (pp. 925–50). New York: Columbia University Press.

Griffen, T. D. 1981: Prosodic alliteration in cynghanedd poetry. *Bulletin of the Board of Celtic Studies,* 29, 497–503.

Grijzenhout, J. and Holtman, A. 1995: Optimality and poetic rhyme in Early Irish. In J. Don et al. (eds), *OTS Yearbook 1994* (pp. 43–62). Utrecht: OTS.

Grimes, J. E. and Glock, N. 1970: A Saramaccan narrative pattern. *Language,* 46(2), 408–25.

Hale, K. 1971: A note on a Walbiri tradition of antonymy. In D. D. Steinberg and L. A. Jakobovits (eds), *Semantics* (pp. 472–82). Cambridge: Cambridge University Press.

Hale, K. 1984: Remarks on creativity in aboriginal verse. In J. C. Kassler and J. Stubington (eds), *Problems and Solutions. Occasional Essays in Musicology presented to Alice M. Moyle* (pp. 254–62). Sydney: Hale & Iremonger.

Halle, M. 1987: A Biblical pattern poem. In N. Fabb, D. Attridge, A. Durant and C. MacCabe (eds), *The Linguistics of Writing* (pp. 252–64). Manchester: Manchester University Press.

Halle, M. 1992: On metric verse in the psalms. Unpublished manuscript.

Halle, M. and Keyser, S. J. 1971: *English Stress: Its Form, its Growth, and its Role in Verse.* New York: Harper and Row.

Halliday, M. A. K. and Hasan, R. 1976: *Cohesion in English.* London: Longman.

Hanson, K. 1991: Resolution in Modern Meters. PhD thesis, Stanford University.

Hanson, K. 1996: A theoretical perspective on the history of the modern English iambic pentameter. Unpublished manuscript.

Hanson, K. and Kiparsky, P. 1996: A parametric theory of poetic meter. *Language*, 72(2), 287–335.

Hanson, K. and Kiparsky, P. forthcoming: The nature of verse and its consequences for the mixed form.

Harold, B. B. 1995: Subject–verb word order and the function of early position. In P. Downing and M. Noonan (eds), *Word Order in Discourse* (pp. 137–61). Amsterdam: John Benjamins.

Hayes, B. 1983: A grid-based theory of English meter. *Linguistic Inquiry*, 14(3), 357–394.

Hayes, B. 1988: Metrics and phonological theory. In F. Newmeyer (ed.), *Linguistics: The Cambridge Survey*, vol. 2 (pp. 220–49). Cambridge: Cambridge University Press.

Hayes, B. 1989: The prosodic hierarchy in meter. In P. Kiparsky and G. Youmans (eds), *Phonetics and Phonology 1: Rhythm and Meter* (pp. 201–60). San Diego: Academic Press.

Hayes, B. 1995: *Metrical Stress Theory.* Chicago: University of Chicago Press.

Hayward, R. J. and Lewis, I. M. (eds) 1996: *Voice and Power. The Culture of Language in North-East Africa.* London: School of Oriental and African Studies.

Herring, S. C. and Paolillo, J. C. 1995: Focus position in SOV languages. In P. Downing and M. Noonan (eds), *Word Order in Discourse* (pp. 163–98). Amsterdam: John Benjamins.

Hobbs, J. 1990: *Literature and Cognition.* Stanford, CA: CSLI.

Hock, H. H. 1980: Archaisms, morphophonemic rules, or variable rules in the Rig-veda? *Studies in the Linguistic Sciences*, 10(1), 59–69.

Hogg, R. and McCully, C. B. 1987: *Metrical Phonology. A Coursebook.* Cambridge: Cambridge University Press.

Holtman, A. 1996: A Generative Theory of Rhyme: An Optimality Approach. PhD thesis, Utrecht University.

Honko, L., Timonen, S., Branch, M. and Bosley, K. 1994: *The Great Bear. A Thematic Anthology of Oral Poetry in the Finno-Ugric Languages.* Oxford: Oxford University Press.

Hopper, P. J. 1979: Aspect and foregrounding in discourse. In T. Givón (ed.), *Syntax and Semantics 12. Studies in Transitivity* (pp. 213–41). New York: Academic Press.

Hopper, P. J. and Thompson, S. A. 1980: Transitivity in grammar and discourse. *Language*, 56(1), 251–99.

Hymes, D. 1968: The ethnography of speaking. In J. A. Fishman (ed.), *Readings in the Sociology of Language* (pp. 99–138). The Hague: Mouton.

Hymes, D. 1981: *'In vain I tried to tell you.' Essays in Native American Ethnopoetics.* Philadelphia: University of Pennsylvania Press.

Hymes, D. 1987a: Anthologies and narrators. In B. Swann and A. Krupat (eds), *Recovering the Word. Essays on Native American Literature* (pp. 41–84). Berkeley: University of California Press.

Hymes, D. 1987b: Tonkawa poetics: John Rush Buffalo's 'Coyote and Eagle's Daughter'. In J. Sherzer and A. C. Woodbury (eds), *Native American Discourse. Poetics and Rhetoric* (pp. 17–61). Cambridge: Cambridge University Press.

Hymes, D. 1989: Ways of speaking. In R. Bauman and J. Sherzer (eds), *Explorations in the Ethnography of Speaking* (pp. 433–51). Cambridge: Cambridge University Press.

Hymes, D. 1992: Use all there is to use. In B. Swann (ed.), *On the Translation of Native American Literatures* (pp. 83–124). Washington: Smithsonian Institution Press.

Hymes, V. 1987: Warm Springs Sahaptin narrative analysis. In J. Sherzer and A. C. Woodbury (eds), *Native American Discourse. Poetics and Rhetoric* (pp. 62–102). Cambridge: Cambridge University Press.

Jackendoff, R. 1989: A comparison of rhythmic structures in music and language. In P. Kiparsky and G. Youmans (eds), *Phonetics and Phonology 1: Rhythm and Meter* (pp. 15–44). San Diego: Academic Press.

Jakobson, R. 1963: On the so-called vowel alliteration in Germanic verse. *Zeitschrift für Phonetik, Sprachwissenschaft und Kommunikationsvorschung*, XVI, 85–92.

Jakobson, R. 1966: Slavic epic verse. Studies in comparative metrics. In *Roman Jakobson Selected Writings IV. Slavic Epic Studies* (pp. 414–63). The Hague: Mouton.

Jakobson, R. 1987a: Linguistics and poetics. In K. Pomorska and S. Rudy (eds), *Roman Jakobson. Language in Literature* (pp. 62–94). Cambridge, MA: Harvard University Press.

Jakobson, R. 1987b: Grammatical parallelism and its Russian facet. In K. Pomorska and S. Rudy (eds), *Roman Jakobson. Language in Literature* (pp. 145–79). Cambridge, MA: Harvard University Press.

Johnson, J. W. 1984: Recent researches into the scansion of Somali oral poetry. In Th. Labahn (ed.), *Proceedings of the Second International Congress of Somali Studies* (pp. 313–31). Hamburg: Helmut Buske Verlag.

Johnson, J. W. 1996: Musico-moro-syllabic relationships in the scansion of Somali oral poetry. In R. J. Hayward and I. M. Lewis (eds), *Voice and Power. The Culture of Language in North-East Africa* (pp. 73–82). London: School of Oriental and African Studies.

Jouad, H. 1993: L'ordre translexical de la parole: anticipation et contrôle mnémonique du défilement sonore. *Cahiers Ferdinand de Saussure*, 47, 61–82.

Kalmár, I. 1982: Transitivity in a Czech folk tale. In P. J. Hopper and S. A. Thompson (eds), *Syntax and Semantics 15. Studies in Transitivity* (pp. 241–59). New York: Academic Press.

Katamba, F. and Cooke, P. 1987: Ssematimba ne Kikwabanga: the music and poetry of a Ganda historical song. *World of Music*, 29(2), 49–68.

Keenan, E. 1973: A sliding sense of obligatoriness: the poly-structure of Malagasy oratory. *Language in Society*, 2, 225–43.

Keenan, E. L. and Ochs, E. 1979: Becoming a competent speaker in Malagasy. In T. Shopen (ed.), *Languages and Their Speakers* (pp. 112–58). Cambridge, MA: Winthrop.

Keith, A. B. 1920: *A History of Sanskrit Literature*. London: Oxford University Press.

Kenstowicz, M. 1994: *Phonology in Generative Grammar*. Oxford: Blackwell.

Kiguli, S. 1996: Kiganda Oral Poetry: The Role of Bisoko in the Poetry of Ssempeke's Songs. M.Litt. thesis, University of Strathclyde.

King, A. 1981: Form and functions in Hausa professional songs. In U. N. Abalogu, D. G. Ashiwaju and M. R. Amadi-Tshiwala (eds), *Oral Poetry in Nigeria* (pp. 118–35). Lagos: Nigeria Magazine.

Kiparsky, P. 1970: Metrics and morphophonemics in the Kalevala. In D. C. Freeman (ed.), *Linguistics and Literary Style* (pp. 165–81). New York: Holt, Rinehart and Winston.

Kiparsky, P. 1972: Metrics and morphophonemics in the Rigveda. In M. Brame (ed.), *Contributions to Generative Phonology* (pp. 171–200). Austin: University of Texas Press.

Kiparsky, P. 1976: Oral poetry: some linguistic and typological considerations. In B. A. Stolz and R. S. Shannon (eds), *Oral Literature and the Formula* (pp. 73–125). Ann Arbor: University of Michigan Center for the Coordination of Ancient and Modern Studies.

Kiparsky, P. 1977: The rhythmic structure of English verse. *Linguistic Inquiry*, 8(2), 189–247.

Kiparsky, P. 1989: Sprung rhythm. In P. Kiparsky and G. Youmans (eds), *Phonetics and Phonology 1: Rhythm and Meter* (pp. 305–40). San Diego: Academic Press.

Kiparsky, P. and Youmans, G. (eds) 1989: *Phonetics and Phonology 1: Rhythm and Meter*. San Diego: Academic Press.

Klar, K., O'Hehir, B. and Sweetser, E. 1984: Welsh poetics in the Indo-European tradition. The case of the Book of Aneirin. *Studia Celtica*, 18, 30–51.

Knott, E. 1957: *An Introduction to Irish Syllabic Poetry of the Period 1200–1600* (2nd edn). Dublin: Dublin Institute for Advanced Studies.

Koehn, E. H. 1976: The historical tense in Apalaí narrative. *International Journal of American Linguistics*, 42(3), 243–52.

Kress, G. and Hodge, R. 1979: *Language as Ideology*. London: Routledge.

Krupat, A. 1979: *The Voice in the Margin. Native American Literature and the Canon*. Berkeley: University of California Press.

Krupat, A. (ed.) 1993: *New Voices in Native American Literary Criticism*. Washington: Smithsonian Institution Press.

Kuhn, D. and Whitehead, G. (eds) 1992: *Wireless Imagination. Sound, Radio, and the Avant-garde*. Cambridge, MA: MIT Press.

Kuipers, J. C. 1988: The pattern of prayer in Weyéwa. In J. J. Fox (ed.), *To Speak in Pairs. Essays on the Ritual Languages of Eastern Indonesia* (pp. 104–28). Cambridge: Cambridge University Press.

Kurylowicz, J. 1970: *Die sprachlichen Grundlagen der altgermanischen Metrik*. Innsbruck: Institut für vergleichende Sprachwissenschaft.

Labov, W. 1972: *Language in the Inner City. Studies in the Black English Vernacular*. Philadelphia: University of Pennsylvania Press.

Labov, W. and Waletzky, J. 1967: Narrative analysis: oral versions of personal experience. In J. Helm (ed.), *Essays on the Verbal and Visual Arts. Proceedings of the 1966 Annual Spring Meeting of the American Ethnological Society* (pp. 12–44). Seattle: University of Washington Press.

Ladefoged, P. and Maddieson, I. 1996: *The Sounds of the World's Languages*. Oxford: Blackwell.

Lakoff, G. and Johnson, M. 1980: *Metaphors We Live By*. Chicago: University of Chicago Press.

Lakoff, G. and Turner, M. 1989: *More than Cool Reason. A Field Guide to Poetic Metaphor*. Chicago: University of Chicago Press.

Lander, D. and Lexier, M. (eds) 1990: *Sound by Artists*. Ontario: Art Metropole.

Leech, G. N. 1969: *A Linguistic Guide to English Poetry*. London: Longman.

Leech, G. and Short, M. 1981: *Style in Fiction. A Linguistic Introduction to English Fictional Prose*. London: Longman.

Lodge, D. (ed.) 1988: *Modern Criticism and Theory. A Reader*. London: Longman.

Longacre, R. E. 1990: *Storyline Concerns and Word Order Typology in East and West Africa*. Los Angeles: Department of Linguistics, UCLA.

Longacre, R. E. 1995: Left shifts in strongly VSO languages. In P. Downing and M. Noonan (eds), *Word Order in Discourse* (pp. 331–54). Amsterdam: John Benjamins.

Lord, A. B. 1960: *The Singer of Tales*. Cambridge, MA: Harvard University Press.

Lord, A. B. 1991: *Epic Singers and Oral Tradition*. Ithaca: Cornell University Press.

Lorimer, D. L. R. 1935: *The Burushaski Language*, vol. 2. Oslo: H. Aschenhoug & Co.

Love, J. W. 1991: *Samoan Variations. Essays on the Nature of Traditional Oral Arts*. New York: Garland.

Macmahon, B. 1995: 'The Freudian Slip Revisited: A case of mistaken identity in *Finnegans Wake*'. *Language and Communication*. 15(4), 289–328.

Malone, J. L. 1982: Generative phonology and Turkish rhyme. *Linguistic Inquiry*, 13(3), 550–53.

Malone, J. L. 1983: Generative phonology and the metrical behaviour of u- 'and' in the Hebrew poetry of mediaeval Spain. *Journal of the American Oriental Society*, 103, 369–81.

Malone, J. L. 1987: Muted euphony and consonant matching in Irish verse. *General Linguistics*, 28, 91–101.

Malone, J. L. 1988a: On the global-phonological nature of classical Irish alliteration. *General Linguistics*, 28(2), 91–103.

Malone, J. L. 1988b: Underspecification theory and Turkish rhyme. *Phonology*, 5, 293–7.

Malone, J. L. 1991: 'Transjacence' and 'interfacing' in Chaha songs and proverbs. In A. S. Kaye (ed.), *Semitic Studies in Honor of Wolf Leslau*, vol. 2 (pp. 1004–15). Wiesbaden: Otto Harrassowitz.

Marcus, G. E. and Myers, F. R. (eds) 1995: *The Traffic in Culture. Refiguring Art and Anthroplology*. University of California Press.

McCully, C. B. and Anderson, J. J. 1996: *English Historical Metrics*. Cambridge: Cambridge University Press.

Mills, S. 1995: *Feminist Stylistics*. London: Routledge.

Mindlin, M., Geller, M. J. and Wansbrough, J. E. (eds) 1987: *Figurative Language in the Ancient Near-East*. London: School of Oriental and African Studies.

Mitchell, D. 1988: Method in the metaphor: the ritual language of Wanukaka. In J. J. Fox (ed.), *To Speak in Pairs. Essays on the Ritual Languages of Eastern Indonesia* (pp. 64–86). Cambridge: Cambridge University Press.

Monelle, R. 1992: *Linguistics and Semiotics in Music*. Chur, Switzerland: Harwood Academic Publishers.

Montgomery, M., Durant, A., Fabb, N., Furniss, T. and Mills, S. 1992: *Ways of Reading. Advanced Reading Skills for Students of English Literature*. London: Routledge.

Morris-Jones, J. 1980: *Cerdd Dafod*. Cardiff: Gwasg Prifysgol Cymru.

Moyle, R. 1987: *Tongan Music*. Auckland: Auckland University Press.

Murphy, G. 1961: *Early Irish Metrics*. Dublin: Royal Irish Academy.

Myers, H. (ed.) 1992: *Ethnomusicology. An Introduction*. New York: Norton.

Myers, H. (ed.) 1993: *Ethnomusicology. Historical and Regional Studies*. New York: Norton.

Nagler, M. N. 1974: *Spontaneity and Tradition. A Study in the Oral Art of Homer*. Berkeley: University of California Press.

Nespor, M. and Vogel, I. 1986: *Prosodic Phonology*. Dordrecht: Foris.

Newmeyer, F. 1983: *Grammatical Theory*. Chicago: University of Chicago Press.

Okpewho, I. 1992: *African Oral Literature. Backgrounds, Character, and Continuity*. Bloomington: Indiana University Press.

Ortony, A. (ed.) 1993: *Metaphor and Thought* (2nd edn). Cambridge: Cambridge University Press.

Orwin, M. 1996: A moraic model of the prosodic phonology of Somali. In R. J. Hayward and I. M. Lewis (eds), *Voice and Power. The Culture of Language in North-East Africa* (pp. 51–71). London: School of Oriental and African Studies.

Osmond-Smith, D (1985): *Playing on Words. A Guide to Luciano Berio's 'Sinfonia'*. London: Royal Musical Association.

Palmer, F. R. 1986: *Mood and Modality*. Cambridge: Cambridge University Press.

Payne, D. L. 1993: On the function of word order in Yagua narrative. *International Journal of American Linguistics*, 59(1), 1–15.

Phillips, N. 1981: *Sijobang. Sung Narrative Poetry of West Sumatra*. Cambridge: Cambridge University Press.

Pilkington, A. 1992: Poetic effects. *Lingua*, 87, 29–51.

Pomorska, K. and Rudy, S. (eds) 1987: *Roman Jakobson. Language in Literature*. Cambridge, MA: Harvard University Press.

Poppe, N. 1958: Der Parallelismus in der epischen Dichtung der Mongolen. *Ural-Altaische Jahrbücher*, 30, 195–228.

Poser, W. J. 1989: The metrical foot in Diyari. *Phonology*, 6, 117–48.

Poser, W. J. 1990: Evidence for foot structure in Japanese. *Language*, 66(1), 78–105.

Powers, W. K. 1986: *Sacred Language. The Nature of Supernatural Discourse in Lakota*. Norman: University of Oklahoma Press.

Powers, W. K. 1992: Translating the untranslatable: the place of the vocable in Lakota song. In B. Swann (ed.), *On the Translation of Native American Literatures* (pp. 293–310). Washington: Smithsonian Institution Press.

Preminger, A. and Brogan, T. V. F. (eds) 1993: *The New Princeton Encyclopedia of Poetry and Poetics*. Princeton: Princeton University Press.

Price, S. 1989: *Primitive Art in Civilized Places*. Chicago: University of Chicago Press.

Prince, A. 1989: Metrical forms. In P. Kiparsky and G. Youmans (eds), *Phonetics and Phonology 1: Rhythm and Meter* (pp. 45–80). San Diego: Academic Press.

Propp, V. 1968: *Morphology of the Folktale* (2nd edn). Austin: University of Texas Press.

Pulleyblank, D. 1990: Yoruba. In B. Comrie (ed.), *The Major Languages of South Asia, the Middle East and Africa* (pp. 265–84). London: Routledge.

Pullum, G. K. and Ladusaw, W. A. 1986: *Phonetic Symbol Guide*. Chicago: University of Chicago Press.

Rice, J. 1992: Narrative styles in *Dakota texts*. In B. Swann (ed.), *On the Translation of Native American Literatures* (pp. 276–92). Washington: Smithsonian Institution Press.

Rooley, A. (ed.) 1980: *The Penguin Book of Early Music*. Harmondsworth: Penguin.

Rowlands, E. I. 1976: *Poems of the Cywyddwyr. A Selection of Cywyddau c.1375–1525*. Oxford: Dublin Institute for Advanced Studies.

Russom, G. 1987: *Old English Meter and Linguistic Theory*. Cambridge: Cambridge University Press.

Rycroft, D. K. and Ngcobo, A. B. 1988: *The Praises of Dingana (Izibongo zikaDingana)*. Pietermaritzburg: University of Natal Press.

Sacks, S. (ed.) 1979: *On Metaphor*. Chicago: University of Chicago Press.

Said, E. 1978: *Orientalism: Western Conceptions of the Orient*. London: Routledge & Kegan Paul.

Schaefer, R. P. 1995: On the discourse function of possessor movement in Emai prose narratives. In P. Downing and M. Noonan (eds), *Word Order in Discourse* (pp. 487–516). Amsterdam: John Benjamins.

Schapera, I. 1965: *Praise-poems of Tswana Chiefs*. Oxford: Oxford University Press.

Schiffrin, D. 1981: Tense variation in narrative. *Language*, 57(1), 45–62.

Schuh, R. G. 1989: Towards a metrical analysis of Hausa verse prosody: Mutadaarik. In I. Haïk and L. Tuller (eds), *Current Approaches to African Linguistics 6* (pp. 161–75). Dordrecht: Foris.

Scollon, R. 1985: The sequencing of clauses in Chipewyan narrative. In J. Nichols and A. C. Woodbury (eds), *Grammar Inside and Outside the Clause. Some Approaches to Theory from the Field* (pp. 113–31). Cambridge: Cambridge University Press.

Sebeok, T. (ed.) 1960: *Style in Language*. Cambridge, MA: MIT Press.

Seeger, A. 1993: Systematic relationships among verbal art forms: text, time, tone and tune in a native Brazilian community. In B. C. Wade (ed.), *Text, Tone and Tune. Parameters of Music in Multicultural Perspective* (pp. 121–32). New Delhi: Oxford and IBH Publishing Co.

Sherzer, J. 1990: *Verbal Art in San Blas. Kuna Culture through its Discourse*. Cambridge: Cambridge University Press.

Sherzer, J. and Urban, G. (eds) 1986: *Native South American Discourse*. Berlin: Mouton de Gruyter.

Sherzer, J. and Woodbury, A. C. (eds) 1987: *Native American Discourse. Poetics and Rhetoric*. Cambridge: Cambridge University Press.

Shopen, T. (ed.) 1985: *Language Typology and Syntactic Description: II: Complex Constructions*. Cambridge: Cambridge University Press.

Silva-Corvalán, C. 1983: Tense and aspect in oral Spanish narrative. *Language*, 59(4), 760–80.

Simmons, D. 1958: Cultural functions of the Efik tone riddle. *Journal of American Folklore*, 71, 123–38.

Simpson, P. 1993: *Language, Ideology and Point of View*. London: Routledge.

Sloboda, J. A. 1985: *The Musical Mind: The Cognitive Psychology of Music*. Oxford: Oxford University Press.

Smith, J. D. 1979: Metre and text in Western India. *Bulletin of SOAS*, 62, 347–57.

Smith, J. D. 1991: *The Epic of Pābūjī*. Cambridge: Cambridge University Press.

Sperber, D. 1975: *Rethinking Symbolism*. Cambridge: Cambridge University Press.

Sperber, D. 1985: *On Anthropological Knowledge*. Cambridge: Cambridge University Press.

Sperber, D. 1996: *Explaining Culture. A Naturalistic Approach*. Oxford: Blackwell.

Sperber, D. and Wilson, D. 1986: *Relevance: Communication and Cognition*. Oxford: Blackwell.

Sperber, D. and Wilson, D. 1995: *Relevance: Communication and Cognition* (2nd edn). Oxford: Blackwell.

Steen, G. 1994: *Understanding Metaphor in Literature*. London: Longman.

Steriade, D. 1982: Greek Prosodies and the Nature of Syllabification. PhD thesis, MIT.

Stirling, L. 1993: *Switch-reference and Discourse Representation*. Cambridge: Cambridge University Press.

Stolz, B. A. and Shannon, R. S. (eds) 1976: *Oral Literature and the Formula*. Ann Arbor: University of Michigan Center for the Coordination of Ancient and Modern Studies.

Stout, M. and Thomson, R. 1971: Kayapó narrative. *International Journal of American Linguistics*, 37, 250–6.

Strehlow, T. G. H. 1971: *Songs of Central Australia*. Sydney: Angus and Robertson.

Suzuki, S. 1985: The role of syllable structure in Old English poetry. *Lingua*, 67, 97–119.

Suzuki, S. 1988: The Indo-European basis of Germanic alliterative verse. *Lingua*, 75, 1–24.

Swann, B. (ed.) 1983: *Smoothing the Ground. Essays on Native American Oral Literature*. Berkeley: University of California Press.

Swann, B. (ed.) 1992: *On the Translation of Native American Literatures*. Washington: Smithsonian Institution Press.

Swann, B. (ed.) 1994: *Coming to Light. Contemporary Translations of the Native Literatures of North America*. New York: Random House.

Swann, B. and Krupat, A. (eds) 1987: *Recovering the Word. Essays on Native American Literature*. Berkeley: University of California Press.

Sweetser, E. V. 1988: Line-structure and rhan-structure: the metrical units of the Gododdin corpus. In B. F. Roberts (ed.), *Early Welsh Poetry. Studies in the Book of Aneirin* (pp. 139–54). Aberystwyth: National Library of Wales.

Tarlinskaja, M. 1989: General and particular aspects of meter: literatures, epochs, poets. In P. Kiparsky and G. Youmans (eds), *Phonetics and Phonology 1: Rhythm and Meter* (pp. 121–54). San Diego: Academic Press.

Tedlock, D. (ed.) 1978: *Finding the Center. Narrative Poetry of the Zuni Indians*. Lincoln: University of Nebraska Press.

Tedlock, D. 1983: *The Spoken Word and the Work of Interpretation*. Philadelphia: University of Pennsylvania Press.

Toelken, B. 1979: *The Dynamics of Folklore*. Boston: Houghton Mifflin.

Toelken, B. 1987: Life and death in the Navajo coyote tales. In B. Swann and A. Krupat (eds), *Recovering the Word. Essays on Native American Literature* (pp. 388–401). Berkeley: University of California Press.

Toolan, M. 1988: *Narrative. A Critical Linguistic Introduction*. London: Routledge.

Toolan, M. (ed.) 1992: *Language, Text and Context. Essays in Stylistics*. London: Routledge.

Traugott, E. C. and Pratt, M. L. 1980: *Linguistics for Students of Literature*. San Diego: Harcourt Brace Jovanovich.

Urban, G. 1986: Semiotic functions of macro-parallelism in the Shokleng origin myth. In J. Sherzer and G. Urban (eds), *Native South American Discourse* (pp. 15–57). Berlin: Mouton de Gruyter.

Velázquez-Castillo, M. 1995: Noun incorporation and object placement in discourse: the case of Guaraní. In P. Downing and M. Noonan (eds), *Word Order in Discourse* (pp. 555–80). Amsterdam: John Benjamins.

Voorhoeve, C. L. 1977: Ta-poman: metaphorical use of words and poetic vocabulary in Asmat songs. In *Pacific Linguistics*, vol. C (pp. 19–38). Canberra: Australian National University.

Wade, B. C. (ed.) 1993: *Text, Tone and Tune. Parameters of Music in Multicultural Perspective*. New Delhi: Oxford and IBH Publishing Co.

Wales, K. 1989: *A Dictionary of Stylistics*. London: Longman.

Wassmann, J. 1991: *The Song to the Flying Fox. The Public and Esoteric Knowledge of the Important Men of Kandingei about Totemic Songs, Names and Knotted Cords (Middle Sepik, Papua New Guinea)* (Dennis Q. Stephenson, trans.). Boroko, PNG: National Research Institute.

Watkins, C. 1963: Indo-European metrics and archaic Irish verse. *Celtica*, 6, 194–249.

Watkins, C. 1995: *How to Kill a Dragon. Aspects of Indo-European Poetics*. Oxford: Oxford University Press.

Watson, W. J. 1959: *Bardachd Ghaidhlig. Specimens of Gaelic Poetry 1550–1900* (3rd edn). Glasgow: An Comunn Gaidhealach.

Webb, M. 1993: *Lokal Musik. Lingua Franca Song and Identity in Papua New Guinea*. Boroko, PNG: National Research Institute.

Weber, J. J. (ed.) 1996: *The Stylistics Reader. From Roman Jakobson to the Present*. London: Arnold.

West, M. L. 1982: *Greek Metre*. Oxford: Oxford University Press.

West, M. L. 1987: *Introduction to Greek Metre*. Oxford: Oxford University Press.

Whallon, W. 1969: *Formula, Character, and Context*. Cambridge, MA: Harvard University Press.

Whiteley, P. 1992: Hopitutungwni: 'Hopi names' as literature. In B. Swann (ed.), *On the Translation of Native American Literatures* (pp. 208–27). Washington: Smithsonian Institution Press.

Widdowson, H. G. 1975: *Stylistics and the Teaching of Literature*. London: Longman.

Wiget, A. 1987: Telling the tale: a performance analysis of a Hopi coyote story. In B. Swann and A. Krupat (eds), *Recovering the Word. Essays on Native American Literature* (pp. 297–336). Berkeley: University of California Press.

Williams, G. 1953: *An Introduction to Welsh Poetry. From the Beginnings to the Sixteenth Century*. London: Faber.

Williams, R. 1973: *The Country and the City*. London: Chatto & Windus.

Wilson, D. and Sperber, D. 1992: On verbal irony. *Lingua*, 87, 53–76.

Wimsatt, W. K. (ed.) 1972: *Versification. Major Language Types. Sixteen Essays*. New York: Modern Language Association and New York University Press.

Wolfson, N. 1979: The conversational historical present alternation. *Language*, 55(1), 168–82.

Woodbury, A. C. 1987: Rhetorical structure in a Central Alaskan Yupik Eskimo traditional narrative. In J. Sherzer and A. C. Woodbury (eds), *Native American Discourse. Poetics and Rhetoric* (pp. 176–239). Cambridge: Cambridge University Press.

Woodbury, A. C. 1992: Prosodic elements and prosodic structures in natural discourse. In M. Liberman and C. McLemore (eds), *Proceedings of a Workshop on Prosody in Natural Speech*. Pennsylvania: UCRS, University of Pennsylvania.

Woodbury, A. C. 1993: A defense of the proposition 'When a language dies, a culture dies'. In *Texas Linguistic Forum 33*. Austin, TX: Department of Linguistics, University of Austin.

Worth, D. S. 1977: Roman Jakobson and the study of rhyme. In C. H. v. Schooneveld and D. Armstrong (eds), *Roman Jakobson: Echoes of his Scholarship* (pp. 515–33). Lisse: Peter de Ridder Press.

Xue, P. 1989: Prosodic constituents and the tonal structure of Chinese regulated verse. *Linguistic Inquiry*, 20(4), 688–96.

Yip, M. 1984: The development of Chinese verse. A metrical analysis. In M. Aronoff & R. T. Oehrle (eds), *Language Sound Structure. Studies in Phonology Presented to Morris Halle by his Teacher and Students* (pp. 346–68). Cambridge, MA: MIT Press.

Yoder, P. P. 1972: Biblical Hebrew. In W. K. Wimsatt (ed.), *Versification* (pp. 52–65). New York: Modern Language Association and New York University Press.

Youmans, G. 1986: Iambic pentameter: statistics or generative grammar? *Language and Style*, 19, 388–404.

Zeps, V. J. 1963: The meter of the so-called trochaic Latvian folksongs. *International Journal of Slavic Linguistics and Poetics*, 7, 123–8.

Zeps, V. 1973: Latvian folk meters and styles. In S. R. Anderson and P. Kiparsky (eds), *A Festschrift for Morris Halle* (pp. 207–11). New York: Holt, Rinehart and Winston.

Zeps, V. J. 1989: Metric tendencies of the Latvian folk trochee. In V. Vikis-Freibergs (ed.), *Linguistics and Poetics of Latvian Folk Songs. Essays in Honour of the Sesquicentennial of the Birth of Kr. Barons* (pp. 247–57). Kingston and Montreal: McGill-Queens University Press.

Zwicky, A. 1976: Well, this rock and roll has got to stop. Junior's head is hard as a rock. In S. Mufwene et al. (eds), *Papers from the 12th Regional Meeting of the Chicago Linguistics Society* (pp. 676–97).

Index of Languages

General Index

abstract (in narrative) 165–6
accent 71
accentual meter 59, 61, 68, 71–7
aesthetics 8, 10, 17, 172, 237, 253, 276
Allen, W. S. 88
alliteration 28, 31, 69, 74, 116–27, 130–1, 232
  vowel alliteration 121, 125–6
anceps 61–3, 70, 79
attitude 255–67
attribution 10, 255–67
audience 15–17, 207–8, 223–5, 235–6, 239–41, 252–3, 262
Austin, T. R. 21, 147

Bamgboṣe, A. 152
Banti, G. 69–71, 98–9, 121–2
Barthes, R. 19, 227
Basso, E. 240
Bauman, R. 16, 223–4, 226, 228, 262, 264
Berlyne, D. E. 276
Bever, T. G. 276
Bowen, J. R. 238–9, 241
brevis in longo 64, 67, 89, 101
Bricker, V. R. 140–1, 144–5
bridge 27, 111–16
Briggs, C. L. 228
Brody, J. 144, 198
Bryant, K. E. 76–7

cadence 67, 91, 92, 102–3, 151
caesura 27, 50, 64, 81, 94, 111–16, 125, 149, 229–31
Carmi, T. 92, 116
Chen, M. Y. 61, 77–9, 132
chiasmus 146–7

Chomsky, N. 3, 39, 222–3, 274
Chona, M. 251
clitic group 33, 113
coda (in narrative) 166, 207, 211
coda (of syllable) 4, 30–3, 120
cognition 3–4, 21, 48, 50, 83, 95, 105–6, 122–3, 151, 256–7, 274–6
communication 6–7, 9, 10–13, 177, 182, 195, 212, 235, 250–73
complication (in narrative) 165–8, 210–11
connective 165, 187–8, 193–5, 210
Contini-Morava, E. 181–2
contraction (metrical) 62
Cooke, P. 100, 233
counting meter 56–9, 95
Cumming, S. 172, 185–6

de Saussure, F. 3
delivery instance 94
Derrida, J. 8
Devine, A. M. 113
Dixon, R. M. W. 89, 115, 241
Dresher, B. E. 35
dyadic set 153–4

Edgerton, F. 82–3
emic/etic 16–17, 49, 105, 221–2, 264
entextualization 228
episode 166, 181, 193–220
evaluation (narrative component) 165–6, 167–9, 212, 224
extrametricality 43–6, 72, 74
  phonological extrametricality 36

Feld, S. 254
fiction 174, 256
Finnegan, R. 233

9 780631 192435